The Printing Revolution in Early Modern Europe

SECOND EDITION

What difference did printing make? Although the importance of the advent of printing for the Western world has long been recognized, it was Elizabeth Eisenstein, in her monumental, two-volume work, *The Printing Press as an Agent of Change*, who provided the first full-scale treatment of the subject. This illustrated and abridged edition gives a stimulating survey of the communications revolution of the fifteenth century. After summarizing the initial changes introduced by the establishment of printing shops, it goes on to discuss how printing effected three major cultural movements: the Renaissance, the Reformation, and the rise of modern science. Specific examples show how the use of the new presses enabled churchmen, scholars, and craftsmen to move beyond the limits hand copying had imposed and thus to pose new challenges to traditional institutions.

This edition includes a new essay in which Eisenstein discusses numerous recent controversies provoked by the first edition and reaffirms the thesis that the advent of printing entailed a communications revolution. Fully illustrated and annotated, the book argues that the cumulative processes set in motion with the advent of printing are likely to persist despite the recent development of new communications technologies.

Elizabeth L. Eisenstein is the Alice Freeman Palmer Professor of History (Emerita) at the University of Michigan, Ann Arbor. She is the author of many books and articles, including *The Printing Press as an Agent of Change* (Cambridge, 1979) and *Grub Street Abroad: Aspects of the Eighteenth Century French Cosmopolitan Press* (1992). In 2002, she was awarded the American Historical Association's Award for Scholarly Distinction.

The press descending from the heavens.

THE PRINTING REVOLUTION IN EARLY MODERN EUROPE

SECOND EDITION

ELIZABETH L. EISENSTEIN

University of Michigan, Ann Arbor

CAMBRIDGE
UNIVERSITY PRESS

CAMBRIDGE UNIVERSITY PRESS
Cambridge, New York, Melbourne, Madrid, Cape Town, Singapore, São Paulo

Cambridge University Press
40 West 20th Street, New York, NY 10011-4211, USA

www.cambridge.org
Information on this title: www.cambridge.org/9780521845434

First edition published 1983
Canto edition published 1993
Second edition first published 2005

Printed in the United States of America

A catalog record for this publication is available from the British Library.

Library of Congress Cataloging in Publication Data
Eisenstein, Elizabeth L.
The printing revolution in early modern Europe / Elizabeth L. Eisenstein. – 2nd ed.
p.   cm.
Includes bibliographical references and index.
ISBN-13:   978-0-521-84543-4
ISBN-10:   0-521-84543-2
ISBN-13:   978-0-521-60774-2 (pbk.)
ISBN-10:   0-521-60774-4 (pbk.)
1. Printing – Europe – History.   2. Europe – Intellectual life.   3. Technology and
civilization.   I. Title.
Z124.E374   2005
686.2'094–dc22   2005003961

ISBN-13   978-0-521-84543-4 hardback
ISBN-10   0-521-84543-2 hardback

ISBN-13   978-0-521-60774-2 paperback
ISBN-10   0-521-60774-4 paperback

CONTENTS

List of Illustrations and Maps   *page* vii

Preface to the Second Edition   xi

Introduction   xiii

PART I   THE EMERGENCE OF PRINT CULTURE
IN THE WEST

1   An Unacknowledged Revolution   3

2   Defining the Initial Shift   13

3   Some Features of Print Culture   46

4   The Expanding Republic of Letters   102

PART II   INTERACTION WITH OTHER DEVELOPMENTS

5   The Permanent Renaissance: Mutation of a Classical
    Revival   123

6   Western Christendom Disrupted: Resetting the Stage for
    the Reformation   164

7   The Book of Nature Transformed: Printing and the Rise
    of Modern Science   209

8   Conclusion: Scripture and Nature Transformed   286

Afterword: Revisiting the Printing Revolution   313

Selected Reading   359

Index   373

ILLUSTRATIONS AND MAPS

ILLUSTRATIONS

Frontispiece	The press descending from the heavens.	*page* ii
Title Page	The foundry directed by Minerva along with the printing shop.	iii
1	Medieval scribe taking dictation.	9
2	Similarity of handwork and presswork shown in two fifteenth-century Bibles.	25
3	Visual aid keyed to text, taken from Vesalius.	30
4	A master printer in his shop.	32
5	"Seeing with a third eye": the art of memory as occult lore.	41
6	The figure of Prudence from Comenius's picture book.	43
7	Finger reckoning.	44
8	Interpreting hieroglyphs before the discovery of the Rosetta Stone.	52
9	A medieval world picture in an Elizabethan book.	55
10	"Thou shalt commit adultery," from the "wicked" Bible.	57
11	Architectural rules for the construction of the Corinthian Order.	60
12	A pattern book for sixteenth-century Spanish tailors.	62
13	An "indo-africano."	63
14	One block used to illustrate two different towns: Verona and Mantua.	67
15	One block used to illustrate two different personages: Baldus and Valla.	68

16 Two more identical portraits from the Nuremberg
    Chronicle: Compostella and Gerson.   68
17 A freshly rendered view of Venice.   69
18 A scholastic treatise produced around A.D. 1300.   74
19 A royal entry depicted for armchair travelers.   106
20 Fireworks commemorating Leicester's arrival at The
    Hague.   107
21 The lay of cases depicted in Moxon's *Mechanick
    Exercises*.   115
22 An early twelfth-century minuscule bookhand.   135
23 Roman and Gothic type styles.   138
24 An engraving of Erasmus; a woodcut portrait of Luther.   149
25 Portraits of the author and the illustrators of a
    sixteenth-century herbal.   150
26 A prize-winning engineer advertises his achievement.   153
27 An example of Lutheran propaganda.   166
28 The title page of Foxe's Book of Martyrs.   194
29 Machiavelli's name placed on the Index.   196
30 Portraits of Christopher Plantin and Benito Arias
    Montano.   200
31 The Antwerp Polyglot: frontispiece and pages of text.   203
32 A page from Commandino's edition of Euclid's *Elements*.   216
33 A Ptolemaic world map and a medieval pictogram.   222
34 An atlas publisher lists his sources.   230
35 Regiomontanus's advance book list.   237
36 A chart printer's challenge to pilots.   239
37 Tycho Brahe advertises himself: two self-portraits.   242
38 Kepler's House of Astronomy and close-up of detail.   248
39 A page from Kepler's *Rudolphine Tables*.   250
40 The three rival theories of planetary motion presented
    by Kepler.   252
41 The Tychonic scheme preferred over the Copernican by
    a Jesuit astronomer.   256
42 Works by Galileo and by Copernicus on the Index in
    1670.   264

43 Moxon promotes his book and advertises his globes on a title page. 268

44 Royal Society sponsorship of Italian science. 276

45 Books banned by Catholics were publicized in Restoration England. 282

46 Title page of Galileo's *Discorsi*. 283

47 "Beyond the pillars of Hercules." 292

Maps

1 The spread of printing in Western Europe during the age of incunabula. 17

2 The spread of printing in Western Europe during the age of incunabula. 18

Preface to the Second Edition

At the request of my publisher, I have written a review essay to serve as an "afterword" to this edition. It discusses some of the questions posed and issues raised since the publication of *The Printing Press as an Agent of Change* twenty-five years ago and provides references to recent studies in order to supplement the selected reading list, which has been retained from the first abridged edition.

Frontispiece

The frontispiece of Prosper Marchand, *Histoire de l'origine et des premiers progrès de l'imprimerie* (The Hague: Pierre Paupie, 1740). The spirit of printing is shown descending from the heavens under the aegis of Minerva and Mercury. It is given first to Germany, who then presents it to Holland, England, Italy, and France (reading from left to right). Note the diverse letters from the Latin, Greek, and Hebrew alphabets decorating the draped garments of the spirit of printing. Note also the medallion portraits of master printers. Germany holds Gutenberg and Fust (Peter Schoeffer's medallion is blank); Laurens Koster represents Holland; William Caxton, England; Aldus Manutius, Italy; and Robert Estienne, France. The choice of the last, who fled Paris for Geneva after being censured by the Sorbonne, probably reflected Marchand's experience of leaving Paris for The Hague in 1707 after his conversion to Protestantism. The composition, like the book it illustrates, suggests how publishers and printers glorified their precursors while advertising themselves.

Title Page

The foundry directed by Minerva along with the printing shop. (Engraving on first page of Prosper Marchand, *Histoire de l'origine et des premiers progrès de l'imprimerie*.) (The Hague: Pierre Paupie, 1740.) This shows how print technology was dignified by association with the Goddess of Wisdom and classical mythology. Putti are shown doing the work actually performed by mechanics and journeymen. One putto holds the motto Ars Artium Conservatrix, thereby underlining the preservative powers of print.

INTRODUCTION

I do ingenuously confess that in attempting this history of Printing
I have undertaken a task much too great for my abilities the extent
of which I did not so well perceive at first.[1]

Joseph Ames, June 7, 1749

I first became concerned with the topic of this book in the early 1960s
after reading Carl Bridenbaugh's presidential address to the American Historical Association. This address, which was entitled "The
Great Mutation," belonged to an apocalyptic genre much in vogue at
that time (and unfortunately still ubiquitous).[2] It raised alarms about
the extent to which a "run-away technology" was severing all bonds
with the past and portrayed contemporary scholars as victims of a
kind of collective amnesia. Bridenbaugh's description of the plight
confronting historians; his lament over "the loss of mankind's memory" in general and over the disappearance of the "common culture
of Bible reading" in particular seemed to be symptomatic rather than
diagnostic. It lacked the capacity to place present alarms in some
kind of perspective – a capacity which the study of history, above
all other disciplines, ought to be able to supply. It seemed unhis-
torical to equate the fate of the "common culture of Bible reading"

[1]   Joseph Ames, preface to *Typographical Antiquities or the History of Printing in England, Scotland and Ireland*, ed. Thomas Dibdin (London, 1810), I:12.
[2]   Carl Bridenbaugh, "The Great Mutation," *The American Historical Review*
LXVIII (January 1963): 315–31. Other essays on the same theme appearing at
the same time are noted in E. L. Eisenstein, "Clio and Chronos," *History and
Theory*, Beiheft 6 (1966): 36–65.

with that of all of Western civilization when the former was so much more recent – being the by-product of an invention which was only five hundred years old. Even after Gutenberg, moreover, Bible reading had remained *un*common among many highly cultivated Western Europeans and Latin Americans who adhered to the Catholic faith.

In the tradition of distinguished predecessors, such as Henry Adams and Samuel Eliot Morison, the president of the American Historical Association appeared to be projecting his own sense of a growing distance from a provincial American boyhood upon the entire course of Western civilization. As individuals grow older they *do* become worried about an unreliable memory. Collective amnesia, however, did not strike me as a proper diagnosis of the predicament which the historical profession confronted. Judging by my own experience and that of my colleagues, it was recall rather more than oblivion which presented the unprecedented threat. So many data were impinging on us from so many directions and with such speed that our capacity to provide order and coherence was being strained to the breaking point (or had it, perhaps, already snapped?). If there was a "run-away" technology which was leading to a sense of cultural crisis among historians, perhaps it had more to do with an increased rate of publication than with new audiovisual media?

While mulling over this question and wondering whether it was wise to turn out more monographs or instruct graduate students to do the same – given the indigestible abundance now confronting us and the difficulty of assimilating what we have – I ran across a copy of Marshall McLuhan's *The Gutenberg Galaxy*. In sharp contrast to the American historian's lament, the Canadian professor of English seemed to take mischievous pleasure in the loss of familiar historical perspectives. He pronounced historical modes of inquiry to be obsolete and the age of Gutenberg at an end. Here again, I felt symptoms of cultural crisis were being offered in the guise of diagnosis. McLuhan's book itself seemed to testify to the special problems posed by print culture rather than those produced by newer media. It provided additional evidence of how overload could lead to incoherence. At the same time it also stimulated my curiosity (already aroused by considering Bible printing) about the specific historical consequences of the fifteenth-century communications shift. I had long been dissatisfied with prevailing explanations for the intellectual revolutions of early modern times. Some of the changes to which McLuhan alluded suggested new ways of dealing with some long-standing problems. But McLuhan raised a number of questions about the actual effects of the advent of printing. They would have to be answered before other matters could be explored. What were some of the most important consequences of the shift from script to print? Anticipating a strenuous effort to master a large literature, I began to investigate what had been written on this obviously important subject. To my surprise, I did not find even a small literature available for consultation. No one had yet attempted to survey the consequences of the fifteenth-century communications shift.

While recognizing that it would take more than one book to remedy this situation, I also felt that a preliminary effort, however inadequate, was better than none and embarked on a decade of study – devoted primarily to becoming acquainted with the special literature (alas, all too large and rapidly growing) on early printing and the history of the book. Between 1968 and 1971 some preliminary articles were published to elicit reactions from scholars and to take advantage of informed criticism. My full-scale work, *The Printing Press as an Agent of Change*, appeared in 1979. When it was abridged and retitled for the general reader in 1983, illustrations were added but footnotes were dropped. They have been restored for this new second edition. Nevertheless, any reader seeking full identification of all citations and references should consult the bibliographical index in the unabridged version.

My treatment falls into two main parts. Part I focuses on the shift from script to print in Western Europe and tries to block out the main features of the communications revolution. Part II deals with the relationship between the communications shift and other developments conventionally associated with the transition from medieval to early modern times. (I have concentrated on cultural and intellectual movements, postponing for another book problems pertaining to political ones.) The second part thus takes up familiar developments and attempts to view them from a new angle of vision. The first part, however, covers unfamiliar territory – unfamiliar to most historians, at least (albeit not to specialists in the history of the book) and especially exotic to this historian (who had previously specialized in the study of the French Revolution and early nineteenth-century French history).

While trying to cover this unfamiliar ground, I discovered (as all neophytes do) that what seemed relatively simple on first glance became increasingly complex on examination and that new areas of ignorance opened up much faster than old ones could be closed. As one might expect from a work long in progress, first thoughts had to be replaced by second ones; even third thoughts have had to be revised. Especially when I was writing about the preservative powers of print (a theme assigned special importance and hence repeatedly sounded in the book), I could not help wondering about the wisdom of presenting views that were still in flux in so fixed and permanent a form. The reader should keep in mind the tentative, provisional character of what follows. This book should be read as an extended essay and not as a definitive text.

It also should be noted at the outset that my treatment is primarily (though not exclusively) concerned with the effects of printing on written records and on the views of already literate elites. Discussion centers on the shift from one kind of literate culture to another (rather than from an oral to a literate culture). This point needs special emphasis because it runs counter to present trends. When they do touch on the topic of communications, historians have been generally content to note that their field of study, unlike archeology or anthropology, is limited to societies which have left written records. The special form taken by these written records is considered of less consequence in defining fields than the overriding issue of whether any written records have been left. Concern with this overriding issue has been intensified recently by a double-pronged attack on older definitions of the field, emanating from African historians on the one hand and social historians dealing with Western civilization on the other. The former have had perforce to challenge

the requirement that written records be supplied. The latter object
to the way this requirement has focused attention on the behavior of
a small literate elite while encouraging neglect of the vast majority
of the people of Western Europe. New approaches are being developed – often in collaboration with Africanists and anthropologists –
to handle problems posed by the history of the "inarticulate" (as
presumably talkative albeit unlettered people are sometimes oddly
called). These new approaches are useful not only for redressing an
old elitist imbalance but also for adding many new dimensions to the
study of Western history. Work in progress on demographic and cli-
matic change, family structure, child rearing, crime and punishment,
festivals, funerals, and food riots, to mention but a few of the new
fields that are now under cultivation, will surely enrich and deepen
historical understanding.

But although the current vogue for "history from below" is helpful
for many purposes, it is not well suited for understanding the purposes of this book. When Jan Vansina, who is both an anthropologist and a historian of precolonial Africa, explores "the relationship of oral tradition to written history," he naturally skips over the
difference between written history produced by scribes and written
history after print.[3] When Western European historians explore the
effect of printing on popular culture, they naturally focus attention
on the shift from an oral folk culture to a print-made one. In both
cases, attention is deflected away from the issues that the following
chapters will explore. This is not to say that the spread of literacy
will be completely ignored. New issues posed by vernacular translation and popularization had significant repercussions within the
Commonwealth of Learning as well as outside it. Nevertheless, it
is not the spread of literacy but how printing altered *written communications within the Commonwealth of Learning* which provides the
main focus of this book. It is primarily concerned with the fate of
the *un*popular (and currently unfashionable) "high" culture of Latin-
reading professional elites.

[3] Jan Vansina, *Oral Tradition: A Study in Historical Methodology*, tr. H. M. Wright
     (London, 1973), pt. 1, sec. 2, 2 ff.

I have also found it necessary to be unfashionably parochial and stay within a few regions located in Western Europe. Thus the term "print culture" is used throughout this book in a special parochial Western sense: to refer to post-Gutenberg developments in the West while setting aside its possible relevance to pre-Gutenberg developments in Asia. Not only earlier developments in Asia, but also later ones in Eastern Europe, the Near East, and the New World, have been excluded. Occasional glimpses of possible comparative perspectives are offered, but only to bring out the significance of certain features which seem to be peculiar to Western Christendom. Because very old messages affected the uses to which the new medium was put and because the difference between transmission by hand copying and by means of print cannot be seen without mentally traversing many centuries, I have had to be much more elastic with chronological limits than with geographical ones: reaching back occasionally to the Alexandrian Museum and early Christian practices; pausing more than once over medieval bookhands and stationers' shops; looking ahead to observe the effects of accumulation and incremental change.

One final comment is in order. As the title of my large version indicates, I regard printing as *an* agent, not *the* agent, let alone *the only* agent, of change in Western Europe. It is necessary to draw these distinctions because the very idea of exploring the effects produced by any particular innovation arouses suspicion that one favors a monocausal interpretation or that one is prone to reductionism and technological determinism.

Of course, disclaimers offered in a preface should not be assigned too much weight and will carry conviction only if substantiated by the bulk of a book. Still, it seems advisable to make clear from the outset that my aim is to enrich, not impoverish, historical understanding and that I regard monovariable interpretations as antipathetic to that aim. As *an* agent of change, printing altered methods of data collection, storage and retrieval systems, and communications networks used by learned communities throughout Europe. It warrants special attention because it had special effects. In this book I am trying to describe these effects and to suggest how they may be related to other concurrent developments. The notion that these other developments could ever be *reduced* to *nothing but* a communications shift strikes me as absurd. The way they were reoriented by such a shift, however, seems worth bringing out. Insofar as I side with revisionists and express dissatisfaction with prevailing schemes, it is to make more room for a hitherto neglected dimension of historical change. When I take issue with conventional multivariable explanations (as I do on several occasions), it is not to substitute a single variable for many but to explain why many variables, long present, began to interact in new ways.

It is perfectly true that historical perspectives are difficult to preserve when claims made for a particular technological innovation are pressed too far. But this means that one must exercise discrimination and weigh the relative importance of diverse claims. To leave significant innovations out of account may also skew perspectives. I am convinced that prolonged neglect of a shift in communications has led to setting perspectives ever more askew as time goes on.

****

I am grateful to several institutions for partial support during the interval when I worked on this book. The University of Michigan at Ann Arbor and the John Simon Guggenheim Memorial Foundation helped me at the beginning. Work was completed during my term as a Fellow at the Center for Advanced Study in the Behavioral Sciences at Stanford, where support was provided by the National Endowment for the Humanities (Grant FC-20029–82) and the Andrew W. Mellon Foundation.

THE PRINTING REVOLUTION IN EARLY MODERN EUROPE

SECOND EDITION

PART I

THE EMERGENCE OF PRINT
CULTURE IN THE WEST

CHAPTER ONE

An Unacknowledged Revolution

In the late fifteenth century, the reproduction of written materials began to move from the copyist's desk to the printer's workshop. This shift, which revolutionized all forms of learning, was particularly important for historical scholarship. Ever since then historians have been indebted to Gutenberg's invention; print enters their work from start to finish, from consulting card files to reading page proofs. Because historians are usually eager to investigate major changes and this change transformed the conditions of their own craft, one would expect the shift to attract some attention from the profession as a whole. Yet any historiographical survey will show the contrary to be true. It is symbolic that Clio has retained her handwritten scroll. So little has been made of the move into the new workshops that after five hundred years, the muse of history still remains outside. "History bears witness," writes a sociologist, "to the cataclysmic effect on society of inventions of new media for the transmission of information among persons. The development of writing, and later the development of printing, are examples."[1] Insofar as flesh-and-blood historians who turn out articles and books actually bear witness to what happened in the past, the effect on society of the development of printing, far from appearing cataclysmic, is remarkably inconspicuous. Many studies of developments during the last five centuries say nothing about it at all.

[1]   N. St. John, Book review, *The American Journal of Sociology* 73 (1967): 255.

There is, to be sure, a large, ever-growing literature on the history of printing and related topics. Several works that synthesize and summarize parts of this large literature have appeared. Thus Rudolf Hirsch surveys problems associated with "printing, selling, reading," during the first century after Gutenberg. A more extensive, well-organized volume by Febvre and Martin, which skillfully covers the first three centuries of printing and was first published in a French series devoted to "the evolution of humanity," has recently been translated into English.[2] An even broader coverage, embracing "five hundred years," is provided by Steinberg's remarkably succinct semi-popular survey. All three of these books summarize data drawn from many scattered studies. But although the broader historical implications of these data are occasionally hinted at, they are never really spelled out. Like the section on printing in the *New Cambridge Modern History*, the contents of these surveys rarely enter into treatments of other aspects of the evolution of humanity.

According to Steinberg: "The history of printing is an integral part of the general history of civilization."[3] Unfortunately, the statement is not applicable to written history as it stands, although it is probably true enough of the actual course of human affairs. Far from being integrated into other works, studies dealing with the history of printing are isolated and artificially sealed off from the rest of historical literature. In theory, these studies center on a topic that impinges on many other fields. In fact, they are seldom consulted by scholars who work in any other field, perhaps because their relevance to other fields is still not clear. "The exact nature of the impact which the invention and spread of printing had on Western civilization remains subject to interpretation even today."[4] This seems to understate the case. There are few interpretations even of an inexact or approximate nature upon which scholars may draw when pursuing other inquiries.

[2] Lucien Febvre and H.-J. Martin, *The Coming of the Book – L'Apparition du Livre*, tr. David Gerard (London, 1976).

[3] S. H. Steinberg, *Five Hundred Years of Printing*, rev. ed. (Bristol, 1961), 11.

[4] Rudolf Hirsch, *Printing, Selling and Reading 1450–1550*, rev. ed. (Wiesbaden, 1974), 2.

The effects produced by printing have aroused little controversy, not because views on the topic coincide, but because almost none has been set forth in an explicit and systematic form. Indeed, those who seem to agree that momentous changes were entailed always seem to stop short of telling us just what they were.

"Neither political, constitutional, ecclesiastical, and economic events, nor sociological, philosophical, and literary movements can be fully understood," writes Steinberg, "without taking into account the influence the printing press has exerted upon them."[5] All these events and movements have been subjected to close scrutiny by generations of scholars with the aim of understanding them more fully. If the printing press exerted some influence upon them, why is this influence so often unnoted, so rarely even hinted at, let alone discussed? The question is worth posing if only to suggest that the effects produced by printing are by no means self-evident. Insofar as they may be encountered by scholars exploring different fields, they are apt to pass unrecognized at present. To track them down and set them forth – in an outline or some other form – is much easier said than done.

When authors such as Steinberg refer to the impact of printing on every field of human enterprise – political, economic, philosophical, and so forth – it is by no means clear just what they have in mind. In part at least they seem to be pointing to indirect consequences which have to be inferred and which are associated with the consumption of printed products or with changed mental habits. Such consequences are, of course, of major historical significance and impinge on most forms of human enterprise. Nevertheless, it is difficult to describe them precisely or even to determine exactly what they are. It is one thing to describe how methods of book production changed after the mid-fifteenth century or to estimate rates of increased output. It is another thing to decide how access to a greater abundance or variety of written records affected ways of learning, thinking, and perceiving among literate elites. Similarly, it is one thing to show that

---

5 Steinberg, *Five Hundred Years*, 11.

standardization was a consequence of printing. It is another to decide how laws, languages, or mental constructs were affected by more uniform texts. Even at present, despite all the data being obtained from living responsive subjects; despite all the efforts being made by public opinion analysts, pollsters, or behavioral scientists; we still know very little about how access to printed materials affects human behavior. (A glance at recent controversies on the desirability of censoring pornography shows how ignorant we are.) Historians who have to reach out beyond the grave to reconstruct past forms of consciousness are especially disadvantaged in dealing with such issues. Theories about unevenly phased changes affecting learning processes, attitudes, and expectations do not lend themselves, in any event, to simple, clear-cut formulations that can be easily tested or integrated into conventional historical narratives.

Problems posed by some of the more indirect effects produced by the shift from script to print probably can never be overcome entirely. But such problems could be confronted more squarely if other impediments did not lie in the way. Among the far-reaching effects that need to be noted are many that still affect present observations and that operate with particularly great force upon every professional scholar. Thus constant access to printed materials is a prerequisite for the practice of the historian's own craft. It is difficult to observe processes that enter so intimately into our own observations. In order to assess changes ushered in by printing, for example, we need to survey the conditions that prevailed before its advent. Yet the conditions of scribal culture can only be observed through a veil of print.

Even a cursory acquaintance with the findings of anthropologists or casual observations of preschool-age children may help to remind us of the gulf that exists between oral and literate cultures. Several studies, accordingly, have illuminated the difference between mentalities shaped by reliance on the spoken as opposed to the written word. The gulf that separates our experience from that of literate elites who relied exclusively on hand-copied texts is much more difficult to fathom. There is nothing analogous in our experience or in that of any living creature within the Western world at present. The conditions of scribal culture thus have to be artificially reconstructed by recourse to history books and reference guides. Yet for the most part, these works are more likely to conceal than to reveal the object of such a search. Scribal themes are carried forward, postprint trends are traced backward, in a manner that makes it difficult to envisage the existence of a distinctive literary culture based on hand copying. There is not even an agreed-upon term in common use which designates the system of written communications that prevailed before print.

Schoolchildren who are asked to trace early overseas voyages on identical outline maps are likely to become absentminded about the fact that there were no uniform world maps in the era when the voyages were made. A similar absentmindedness on a more sophisticated level is encouraged by increasingly refined techniques for collating manuscripts and producing authoritative editions of them. Each successive edition tells us more than was previously known about how a given manuscript was composed and copied. By the same token, each makes it more difficult to envisage how a given manuscript appeared to a scribal scholar who had only one hand-copied version to consult and no certain guidance as to its place or date of composition, its title or author. Historians are trained to discriminate between manuscript sources and printed texts; but they are not trained to think with equal care about how manuscripts appeared when this sort of discrimination was inconceivable. Similarly, the more thoroughly we are trained to master the events and dates contained in modern history books, the less likely we are to appreciate the difficulties confronting scribal scholars who had access to assorted written records but lacked uniform chronologies, maps, and all the other reference guides which are now in common use.

Efforts to reconstruct the circumstances that preceded printing thus lead to a scholarly predicament. Reconstruction requires recourse to printed materials, thereby blurring clear perception of the conditions that prevailed before these materials were available. Even when the predicament is partly resolved by sensitive scholars who manage to develop a genuine "feel" for the times after handling countless documents, efforts at reconstruction are still bound to be frustratingly incomplete.

For the very texture of scribal culture was so fluctuating, uneven, and multiform that few long-range trends can be traced. Conditions that prevailed near the bookshops of ancient Rome, in the Alexandrian Library, or in certain medieval monasteries and university towns, made it possible for literate elites to develop a relatively sophisticated "bookish" culture. Yet all library collections were subject to contraction, and all texts in manuscript were liable to get corrupted after being copied over the course of time. Outside certain transitory special centers, moreover, the texture of scribal culture was so thin that heavy reliance was placed on oral transmission even by literate elites. Insofar as dictation governed copying in scriptoria and literary compositions were "published" by being read aloud, even "book" learning was governed by reliance on the spoken word – producing a hybrid half-oral, half-literate culture that has no precise counterpart today. Just what publication meant before printing or just how messages got transmitted in the age of scribes are questions that cannot be answered in general. Findings are bound to vary enormously depending on date and place. Contradictory verdicts are especially likely to proliferate with regard to the last century before printing – an interval when paper had become available and the literate man was more likely to become his own scribe.

Specialists in the field of incunabula, who are confronted by ragged evidence, are likely to insist that a similar lack of uniformity characterizes procedures used by early printers. To generalize about early printing is undoubtedly hazardous, and one should be on guard against projecting the output of modern standard editions too far back into the past. Yet one must also be on guard against blurring a major difference between the last century of scribal culture and the first century after Gutenberg. Early print culture is sufficiently uniform to permit us to measure its diversity. We can estimate output, arrive at averages, trace trends. For example, we have rough estimates of the total output of all printed materials during the so-called age of incunabula (that is, the interval between the 1450s and 1500). Similarly, we can say that the "average" early edition ranged between two hundred and one thousand copies. There are no

Iodoci Ba. Afcenfii.ut boni iuuenes ad litterarū ſtudia feruētius iñcūbāt cohortatio:cū
ꝗdā huius opis & clariſſimi uiri Iohānis de trittenhem abbatis i ſpanhē cōmēdariūcula.

Fig. 1. Medieval scribe taking dictation, portrayed in a woodblock advertisement
for J. Badius's firm in William of Ockham, *Dialogus* (Lyons: J. Trechsel, ca. 1494).
Reproduced by kind permission of John Ehrman from Graham Pollard and Albert
Ehrman, *The Distribution of Books by Catalogue to A.D. 1800* (Cambridge: The Roxburghe Club, 1965).

comparable figures for the last fifty years of scribal culture. Indeed,
we have no figures at all. What is the "average edition" turned out
between 1400 and 1450? The question verges on nonsense. The
term "edition" comes close to being an anachronism when applied
to copies of a manuscript book.

As the difficulties of trying to estimate scribal output suggest,
quantification is not suited to the conditions of scribal culture.
The production figures which are most often cited, on the basis
of the memoirs of a Florentine manuscript bookdealer, turn out to

be entirely untrustworthy. Quattrocento Florence, in any case, is scarcely typical of other Italian centers (such as Bologna), let alone of regions beyond the Alps. But then *no* region is typical. There is no "typical" bookdealer, scribe, or even manuscript. Even if we set aside problems presented by secular book producers and markets as hopelessly complex and consider only the needs of churchmen on the eve of printing, we are still faced by a remarkable diversity of procedures. Book provisions for diverse monastic orders varied; mendicant friars had different arrangements from monks. Popes and cardinals often turned to the "multifarious activities" of the Italian *cartolai*; preachers made their own anthologies of sermons; semi-lay orders attempted to provide primers and catechisms for everyman.

The absence of an average output or a typical procedure poses a stumbling block when we try to set the stage for the advent of print. Let us take, for example, a deceptively simple summary statement which I made when first trying to describe the printing revolution. Fifteenth-century book production, I asserted, moved from scriptoria to printing shops. The assertion was criticized for leaving out of account a previous move from scriptoria to stationers' shops. In the course of the twelfth century, lay stationers began to replace monastic scribes. Books needed by university faculties and the mendicant orders were supplied by a "putting-out" system. Copyists were no longer assembled in a single room, but worked on different portions of a given text, receiving payment from the stationer for each piece (the so-called pecia system). Book production, according to my critic, had thus moved out of scriptoria three centuries *before* the advent of print.

The objection seems worth further thought. Certainly one ought to pay attention to the rise of the lay stationer in university towns and other urban centers during the twelfth and thirteenth centuries. The contrast between the free labor of monks working for remission of sins and the wage labor of lay copyists is an important one. Recent research has stressed the use of a putting-out system and has also called into question long-lived assumptions about the existence of lay scriptoria attached to stationers' shops. Thus one must be especially cautious about using the term scriptoria to apply to conditions in the later Middle Ages – more cautious than I was in my preliminary version.

Yet, on the other hand, one must also be wary about placing too much emphasis on trends launched in twelfth-century Paris, Oxford, Bologna, and other university towns where copies were multiplied rapidly to serve special institutional needs. Caution is needed when extending university regulations designed to control copyists to the actual practices of university stationers – let alone to bookdealers serving nonuniversity clientele. That relatively clear thirteenth-century patterns get smudged by the late fourteenth century must also be kept in mind. During the interval between 1350 and 1450 – the crucial century when setting our stage – conditions were unusually anarchic, and some presumably obsolete habits were revived. Monastic scriptoria, for example, were beginning to experience their "last golden age."

The existence of monastic scriptoria right down to and even beyond the days of early printing is most intriguingly demonstrated by a treatise which is often cited as a curiosity in books on early printing: Johannes Trithemius's *De laude scriptorum*. In this treatise, the Abbot of Sponheim not only exhorted his monks to copy books, but also explained why "monks should not stop copying because of the invention of printing." Among other arguments (the usefulness of keeping idle hands busy, encouraging diligence, devotion, knowledge of Scripture, and so on), Trithemius somewhat illogically compared the written word on parchment which would last one thousand years with the printed word on paper which would have a shorter life span. The possible use of paper (and scraped parchment) by copyists, or of skin for a special printed version, went unmentioned. As a Christian scholar, the abbot was clearly familiar with earlier writings which had set durable parchment against perishable papyrus. His arguments show his concern about preserving a form of manual labor which seemed especially suitable for monks. Whether he was genuinely worried about an increased use of paper – as an ardent bibliophile and in the light of ancient warnings – is an open question. But his activities show clearly that as an author he did not favor handwork over press-work. He had his *Praise of Scribes* promptly printed, as he did his weightier works. Indeed, he used one Mainz print shop so frequently that "it could almost be called the Sponheim Abbey Press."[6]

Even before 1494, when the Abbot of Sponheim made his trip from scriptorium to printing shop, the Carthusians of Saint Barbara's Charterhouse in Cologne were turning to local printers to extend their efforts, as a cloistered order bound by vows of silence, to preach "with their hands." As many accounts note, the same thing happened outside Cologne and not just among the Carthusians. A variety of reformed Benedictine orders also kept local printers busy, and in some cases monks and nuns ran monastic presses themselves. The possible significance of this intrusion of a capitalist enterprise into consecrated space is surely worth further consideration. Thus, to rule out the formula "scriptorium to printing shop" completely seems almost as unwise as to attempt to apply it in a blanket form. Even while acknowledging the significance of changes affecting twelfth-century book production, we should not equate them with the sort of "book revolution" that occurred in the fifteenth century. The latter, unlike the former, assumed a cumulative and irreversible form. The revival of monastic scriptoria during the century before Gutenberg was the last revival of its kind.

[6]   Johannes Trithemius, *In Praise of Scribes – De Laude Scriptorum*, ed. Klaus Arnold, tr. R. Behrendt (Lawrence, KS, 1974), 15, 63.

CHAPTER TWO

Defining the Initial Shift

We should note the force, effect, and consequences of inventions which are nowhere more conspicuous than in those three which were unknown to the ancients, namely, printing, gunpowder, and the compass. For these three have changed the appearance and state of the whole world.

Francis Bacon, *Novum organum*, Aphorism 129

To dwell on why Bacon's advice ought to be followed by others is probably less helpful than trying to follow it oneself. This task clearly outstrips the competence of any single individual. It calls for the pooling of many talents and the writing of many books. Collaboration is difficult to obtain as long as the relevance of the topic to different fields of study remains obscure. Before aid can be enlisted, it seems necessary to develop some tentative hypotheses relating the shift from script to print to significant historical developments.

This task, in turn, seems to call for a somewhat unconventional point of departure and for a reformulation of Bacon's advice. Instead of trying to deal with "the force, effect, and consequences" of a single postclassical invention that is coupled with others, I will be concerned with a major transformation that constituted a large cluster of changes in itself. Indecision about what is meant by the advent of printing has, I think, helped to muffle concern about its possible consequences and made them more difficult to track down. It is difficult to find what happened in a particular Mainz workshop in the 1450s. When pursing other inquiries, it seems almost prudent to bypass so problematic an event. This does not apply to the appearance of new occupational groups who employed new techniques and installed new equipment in new kinds of workshops while extending trade networks and seeking new markets to increase profits made from sales. Unknown anywhere in Europe before the mid-fifteenth century, printers' workshops would be found in every important municipal center by 1500. They added a new element to urban culture in hundreds of towns. To pass by all that, when dealing with other problems, would seem to be incautious. For this reason, among others, we will skip over the perfection of a new process for printing with movable types and will not pause over the massive literature devoted to explanations of Gutenberg's invention. We will take the term "printing" to serve simply as a convenient label, as a shorthand way of referring to a cluster of innovations (entailing the use of movable metal type, oil-based ink, wooden handpress, and so forth). Our point of departure will not be one printing shop in Mainz. Instead, we will begin where many studies end: after the first dated printed products had been issued and the inventor's immediate successors had set to work.

The advent of printing, then, is taken to mean the establishment of presses in urban centers beyond the Rhineland during an interval that begins in the 1460s and coincides, very roughly, with the era of incunabula. So few studies have been devoted to this point of departure that no conventional label has yet been attached to it. One might talk about a basic change in a mode of book production or about a communications or media revolution or perhaps, most simply and explicitly, about a shift from script to print. Whatever label is used, it should be understood to cover a large cluster of relatively simultaneous, interrelated changes, each of which needs closer study and more explicit treatment – as the following quick sketch may suggest.

First of all, the marked increase in the output of books and the drastic reduction in the number of man-hours required to turn them out deserve stronger emphasis. At present there is a tendency to think of a steady increase in book production during the first century of printing. An evolutionary model of change is applied to a situation that seems to call for a revolutionary one:

> A man born in 1453, the year of the fall of Constantinople, could
> look back from his fiftieth year on a lifetime in which about eight
> million books had been printed, more perhaps than all the scribes
> of Europe had produced since Constantine founded his city in
> A.D. 330.[1]

The actual production of "all the scribes of Europe" is inevitably
open to dispute. Even apart from the problem of trying to estimate
numbers of books that went uncatalogued and then were destroyed,
contemporary evidence must be handled with caution, for it often
yields false clues to the numbers of books involved. Since it was customary to register many texts bound within one set of covers as but
one book, the actual number of texts in a given manuscript collection
is not easily ascertained. That objects counted as one book often contained a varying combination of many provides yet another example
of the difficulty of quantifying data provided in the age of scribes.
The situation is similar when we turn to the problem of counting the
man-hours required to copy manuscript books. Old estimates based
on the number of months it took forty-five scribes working for the
Florentine manuscript book dealer, Vespasiano da Bisticci, to produce two hundred books for Cosimo de Medici's Badia library have
been rendered virtually worthless by recent research.

Thus the total number of books produced by "all the scribes of
Europe" since 330, or even since 1400, is likely to remain elusive.
Nevertheless, some comparisons are possible and they place the out-
put of printers in sharp contrast to preceding trends. "In 1483, the
Ripoli Press charged three florins per quinterno for setting up and
printing Ficino's translation of Plato's *Dialogues*. A scribe might have
charged one florin per quinterno for duplicating the same work. The
Ripoli Press produced 1,025 copies; the scribe would have turned out

---

Michael Clapham, "Printing," A *History of Technology*, vol. 3, *From the Renaissance to the Industrial Revolution*, ed. Charles Singer, E. G. Holmyard, A. R. Hall,
and Trevor Williams (Oxford, 1957), 37.

one."[2] Given this kind of comparison, it seems misguided to suggest that "the multiplication of identical copies" was merely "intensified" by the press.[3] Doubtless, hand copying could be quite efficient for the purpose of duplicating a royal edict or papal bull. Sufficient numbers of copies of a newly edited Bible were produced in the thirteenth century for some scholars to feel justified in referring to a Paris "edition" of a manuscript Bible. To turn out one single whole "edition" of any text was no mean feat in the thirteenth century, however. The one thirteenth-century scribal "edition" might be compared with the large number of Bible editions turned out in the half-century between Gutenberg and Luther. When scribal labor was employed for multiplying edicts or producing a whole "edition" of scripture, moreover, it was diverted from other tasks.

Many valued texts were barely preserved from extinction; untold numbers failed to survive. Survival often hinged on the occasional copy being made by an interested scholar who acted as his own scribe. In view of the proliferation of "unique" texts and of the accumulation of variants, it is doubtful whether one should refer to "identical copies" being "multiplied" before print. This point is especially important when considering technical literature. The difficulty of making even one "identical" copy of a significant technical work was such that the task could not be trusted to any hired hands. Men of learning had to engage in "slavish copying" of tables, diagrams, and unfamiliar terms. The output of whole editions of sets of astronomical tables did not merely "intensify" previous trends. It reversed

[2]   Albinia De la Mare, "Vespasiano da Bisticci Historian and Bookseller," (Ph.D. diss., London University, 1965), 207.
[3]   J. H. Harrington, "The Production and Distribution of Books in Western Europe to the Year 1500" (Ph.D. diss., Columbia University, 1956), 3.

Maps 1 and 2 (opposite and overleaf). The spread of printing in Western Europe during the age of incunabula. These maps, designed by Henri-Jean Martin, show the spread of printing before 1471; from 1471 to 1480; from 1481 to 1490; and from 1491 to 1500. Reprinted from L. Febvre and H.-J. Martin, L'Apparition du livre (Evolution de l'humanité series) (Paris: Albin Michel, 1958, facing p. 272), with kind permission of H.-J. Martin and Editions Albin Michel.

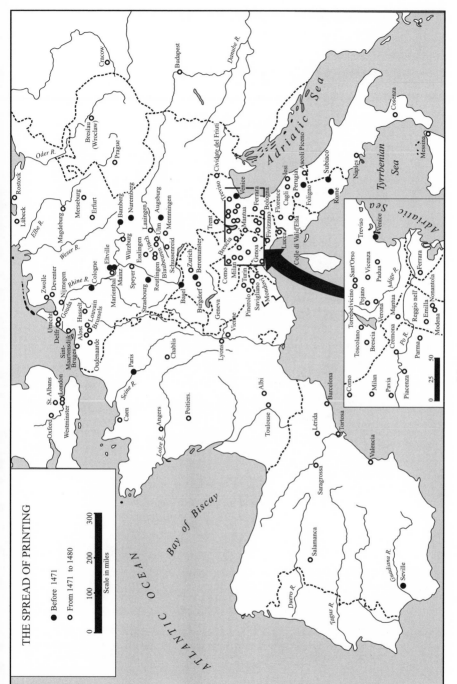

THE SPREAD OF PRINTING

● Before 1471
○ From 1471 to 1480

Scale in miles
0   100   200   300

Map 1.

Map 2.

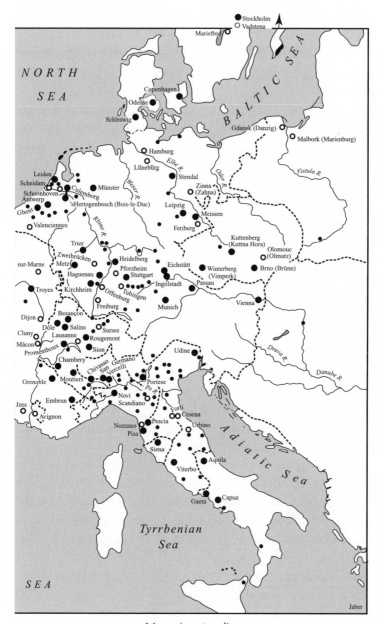

Map 2 (*continued*).

them, producing a new situation which released time for observation and research.

The previous introduction of paper into thirteenth-century Europe, it should be noted, did not have anything like a "similar" effect. Paper production served the needs of merchants, bureaucrats, preachers, and literati; it quickened the pace of correspondence and enabled more men of letters to act as their own scribes. But the same number of man-hours was still required to turn out a given text. Shops run by stationers or *cartolai* multiplied in response to an increasing demand for tablets, notebooks, prepared sheets, and other supplies. In addition to selling writing materials and school-books as well as bookbinding materials and services, some merchants helped book-hunting patrons by locating valued works. They had copies made on commission and kept some for sale in their shops. But their involvement in the book trade was more casual than one might think. "The activities of the *cartolai* were multifarious . . . Those who specialized in the sale and preparation of book materials or in bind-ings were probably concerned little, if at all, with the production or sale of manuscripts and (later) printed books, either new or secondhand."[4]

Even the retail book trade that was conducted by Vespasiano da Bisticci, the most celebrated Florentine book merchant, who served prelates and princes and "did everything possible" to attract patrons and make sales, never verged on becoming a wholesale busi-ness. Despite Vespasiano's unusually aggressive tactics in promot-ing sales and matching books with clients, he showed no signs of ever "having made much money" from all his transactions.[5] He did win notable patrons, however, and achieved considerable celebrity as "prince of publishers." His shop was praised by humanist poets along lines which were similar to those used in later tributes to Gutenberg and Aldus Manutius. His posthumous fame – achieved only in the nineteenth century after the publication of his memoirs and their

4   Albinia De la Mare, "Bartolomeo Scala's Dealings with Booksellers, Scribes and Illuminators, 1459–63," *Journal of the Warburg and Courtauld Institutes* XXXIX (1976): 241.

5   De la Mare, "Vespasiano," pp. 95–7, 226.

use by Jacob Burckhardt – is perhaps even more noteworthy. Vespasiano's *Lives of Illustrious Men* contains a reference to the beautifully bound manuscript books in the Duke of Urbino's library and snobbishly implies that a printed book would have been "ashamed" in such elegant company. This one reference by an atypical and obviously prejudiced bookdealer has ballooned into many misleading comments about the disdain of Renaissance humanists for vulgar machine-made objects. Actually, Florentine bibliophiles were sending to Rome for printed books as early as 1470. Under Guidobaldo da Montefeltro, the ducal library at Urbino acquired printed editions and (shamelessly or not) had them bound with the same magnificent covers as manuscripts. The same court also sponsored the establishment of an early press in 1482. That Vespasiano was indulging in wishful and nostalgic thinking is suggested by his own inability to find sufficient support from princely patrons to persist in his exclusive trade. His chief rival in Florence, Zanobi di Mariano, managed to stay in business until his death in 1495. "Zanobi's readiness to sell printed books – a trade which Vespasiano spurned – explains his survival as a bookseller in the tricky years of the late fifteenth century. Vespasiano dealing exclusively in manuscripts was forced out of business in 1478."[6]

One must wait for Vespasiano to close shop before one can say that a genuine wholesale book trade was launched:

> As soon as Gutenberg and Schoeffer had finished the last sheet of their monumental Bible, the financier of the firm, John Fust, set out with a dozen copies or so to see for himself how he could best reap the harvest of his patient investments. And where did he turn first of all to convert his Bibles into money? He went to the biggest university town in Europe, to Paris, where ten thousand or more students were filling the Sorbonne and the colleges. And what did he, to his bitter discomfiture, find there? A well organized and powerful guild of the booktrade, the Confrérie des Libraires, Relieurs, Enlumineurs, Ecrivains et Parcheminiers...founded in 1401...Alarmed at the appearance of an outsider with such

---

[6] De la Mare, "Bartolomeo Scala's Dealings," 241.

an unheard of treasure of books; when he was found to be selling one Bible after another, they soon shouted for the police, giving their expert opinion that such a store of valuable books could be in one man's possession through the help of the devil himself and Fust had to run for his life or his first business trip would have ended in a nasty bonfire.[7]

This story, as told by E. P. Goldschmidt, may be just as unfounded as the legend that linked the figure of Johan Fust with that of Dr. Faustus. The adverse reaction it depicts should not be taken as typical; many early references were at worst ambivalent. The ones that are most frequently cited associate printing with divine rather than diabolic powers. But then the most familiar references come either from the blurbs and prefaces composed by early printers themselves or from editors and authors who were employed in printing shops. Such men were likely to take a more favorable view than were the guildsmen who had made a livelihood from manuscript books. The Parisian *libraires* may have had good reason to be alarmed, although they were somewhat ahead of the game; the market value of hand-copied books did not drop until after Fust was dead.[8] Other members of the *confrérie* could not foresee that most bookbinders, rubricators, illuminators, and calligraphers would be kept busier than ever after early printers set up shop. Whether the new art was considered a blessing or a curse, whether it was consigned to the Devil or attributed to God, the fact remains that the initial increase in output did strike contemporary observers as sufficiently remarkable to suggest supernatural intervention. Even incredulous modern scholars may be troubled by trying to calculate the number of calves required to supply enough skins for vellum copies of Gutenberg's Bible. It should not be too difficult to obtain agreement that an abrupt rather than a gradual increase did occur in the second half of the fifteenth century.

[7] E. P. Goldschmidt, *Gothic and Renaissance Bookbindings* (Amsterdam, 1967), I:43–4.
[8] De la Mare, "Vespasiano," 113.

Scepticism is much more difficult to overcome when we turn from consideration of quantity to that of quality. If one holds a late manuscript copy of a given text next to an early printed one, one is likely to doubt that any change at all has taken place, let alone an abrupt or revolutionary one.

> Behind every book which Peter Schoeffer printed stands a published manuscript... The decision on the kind of letter to use, the selection of initials and decoration of rubrications, the determination of the length and width of the column, planning for margins... all were prescribed by the manuscript copy before him.[9]

Not only did early printers such as Schoeffer try to copy a given manuscript as faithfully as possible, but fifteenth-century scribes returned the compliment. As Curt Bühler has shown, a large number of the manuscripts made during the late fifteenth century were copied from early printed books.[10] Thus handwork and presswork continued to appear almost indistinguishable, even after the printer had begun to depart from scribal conventions and to exploit some of the new features inherent in his art.

That there were new features and they were exploited needs to be given due weight. Despite his efforts to duplicate manuscripts as faithfully as possible, the fact remains that Peter Schoeffer, printer, was following different procedures than had Peter Schoeffer, scribe. The absence of any apparent change in product was combined with a complete change in methods of production, giving rise to the paradoxical combination of seeming continuity with radical change. Thus the temporary resemblance between handwork and presswork seems to support the thesis of a very gradual evolutionary change; yet the opposite thesis may also be supported by underlining the marked difference between the two different modes of production and noting

---

[9] Hellmut Lehmann-Haupt, *Peter Schoeffer of Gernsheim and Mainz* (Rochester, NY, 1950), 37–8.

[10] Curt Bühler, *The Fifteenth-Century Book, the Scribes, the Printers, the Decorators* (Philadelphia, 1960), 16.

the new features that began to appear before the fifteenth century had come to an end.

Concern with surface appearance necessarily governed the hand-work of the scribe. He was fully preoccupied trying to shape evenly spaced uniform letters in a pleasing symmetrical design. An alto-gether different procedure was required to give directions to com-positors. To do this, one had to mark up a manuscript while scru-tinizing its contents. Every manuscript that came into the printer's hands, thus, had to be reviewed in a new way – one which encour-aged more editing, correcting, and collating than had the hand-copied text. Within a generation the results of this review were being aimed in a new direction – away from fidelity to scribal conven-tions and toward serving the convenience of the reader. The highly competitive commercial character of the new mode of book pro-duction encouraged the relatively rapid adoption of any innovation that commended a given edition to purchasers. Well before 1500, printers had begun to experiment with the use "of graduated types, running heads . . . footnotes . . . tables of contents . . . superior figures, cross references . . . and other devices available to the compositor" – all registering "the victory of the punch cutter over the scribe."[11] Title pages became increasingly common, facilitating the produc-tion of book lists and catalogues, while acting as advertisements in themselves.[12] Hand-drawn illustrations were replaced by more easily duplicated woodcuts and engravings – an innovation which even-tually helped to revolutionize technical literature by introducing "exactly repeatable pictorial statements" into all kinds of reference works.

The fact that identical images, maps, and diagrams could be viewed simultaneously by scattered readers constituted a kind of communications revolution in itself. This point has been made most forcefully by William Ivins, a former curator of prints at the Metropolitan Museum.[13] Although Ivins's special emphasis on

---

[11]   Steinberg, *Five Hundred Years*, 28.
[12]   Ibid., 145.
[13]   William M. Ivins Jr., *Prints and Visual Communication* (Cambridge, MA, 1953).

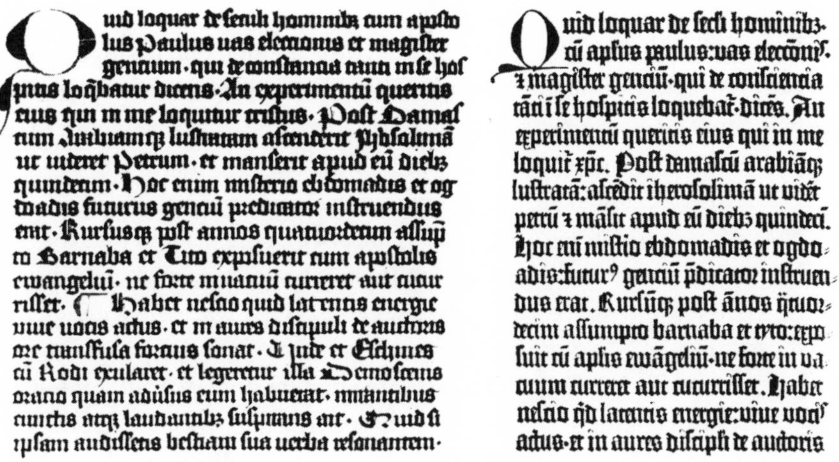

Quid loquar dr senih homnnibz cum apusto lus Paulus uas clemonis ct magister genuum · qui de constancia tanti in se hos pinis loqbatur dicens · An experimentu queritis eius qui in me loquitur cristus · Post Damaf cum Arthiam rp lustratam ascendit Ihrsolima ut wident Petrum · ct manserit apud eu dieb; quindeam · Hac enim mistorio cbdomadis ct og toadis futurus genui predicator instruendus ent · Kursus rp post annos quatuordecim assup to Barnaba ct Tito exposuerit cum apostolis ewangelui · ne forte in uacuu curreret aut curur risset · Habet nescio quid latentis energie uiue uocis actus · ct in aures discipuli de auctoris ore transfusa fortius sonat · At inte et Eschines cu Rodi exularet · ct legeretur illa Demosthenis oratio quam adusus cum habuerat · mirantibus cunctis atp laudantibz suspirans ait · G? uid si ipsam audissetis bestiam sua uerba resonantem ·

Quid loquar de secti hominibz · cu apstus paulus · uas electonis · ct magister genciu · qui de constancia tanti i se hospitis loquebat · dicens · An experimentu queritis eius qui in me loquit xpc · Post damasci arabiaq; lustrata · ascedit iherosolima ut uidit petru z masit apud eu dieb; quindeci · Hoc eni mistio ebdomadis ct ogdo adis futur' genui pdicator instruen dus erat · Kursuq; post annos quator decim assumpto barnaba ct tito expo suit cu apstis ewagdiu · ne forte in ua cuum curreret aut cucurrisset · Habet nescio qd latentis energie · uiue uocis actus · ct in aures discipli de auctoris

Fig. 2. The similarity of handwork and presswork is demonstrated by these two pages, one taken from a hand-copied Bible (the so-called Giant Bible of Mainz) and the other from a printed Bible (the celebrated Gutenberg Bible). Reproduced by kind permission of the Rare Book and Special Collections Division of the Library of Congress.

"the exactly repeatable pictorial statement" has found favor among historians of cartography,[14] his propensity for overstatement has pro- voked objections from other specialists. Repeatable images, they argue, go back to ancient seals and coins, while *exact* replication was scarcely fostered by woodblocks, which got worn and broken after repeated use. Here as elsewhere, one must be wary of underrating as well as of overestimating the advantages of the new technology. Even while noting that woodcuts did get corrupted when copied for inser- tion in diverse kinds of texts, one should also consider the corruption that occurred when hand-drawn images had to be copied into hun- dreds of books. Although pattern books and "pouncing" techniques were available to some medieval illuminators, the precise reproduc- tion of fine detail remained elusive until the advent of woodcarving

[14] See, e.g., Leo Bagrow, *History of Cartography*, rev. and ed. R. A. Skelton (Cam- bridge, MA, 1964), 89; R. A. Skelton, *Maps: A Historical Survey* (Chicago, 1972), 12; and Arthur H. Robinson, "Map Making and Map Printing," in *Five Centuries of Map Printing*, ed. David Woodward (Chicago, 1975), 1.

and engraving. Blocks and plates did make repeatable visual aids feasible for the first time. In the hands of expert craftsmen using good materials and working under supervision, even problems of wear and tear could be circumvented: worn places could be sharpened, blurred details refined, and a truly remarkable durability achieved.

It is not so much in his special emphasis on the printed image but rather in his underrating the significance of the printed text that Ivins seems to go astray. Although he mentions in passing that the history of prints as "an integrated series" begins with their use "as illustrations in books printed from movable types,"[15] his analysis elsewhere tends to detach the fate of printed pictures from that of printed books. His treatment implies that the novel effects of repeatability were confined to pictorial statements. Yet these effects were by no means confined to pictures or, for that matter, to pictures and words. Mathematical tables, for example, were also transformed. For scholars concerned with scientific change, what happened to numbers and equations is surely just as significant as what happened to either images or words. Furthermore, many of the most important pictorial statements produced during the first century of printing employed various devices – banderoles, letter-number keys, indication lines – to relate images to texts. To treat the visual aid as a discrete unit is to lose sight of the connecting links which were especially important for technical literature because they expressed the relationship between words and things.

Even though block print and letterpress may have originated as separate innovations and were initially used for diverse purposes (so that playing cards and saints' images, for example, were being stamped from blocks at the same time that hand illumination continued to decorate many early printed books), the two techniques soon became intertwined. The use of typography for texts led to that of xylography for illustration, sealing the fate of the illuminator along with that of the scribe. When considering how technical literature was affected by the shift from script to print, it seems reasonable to

[15] Ivins, *Prints and Visual Communication*, 27.

adopt George Sarton's strategy of envisaging a "double invention; typography for the text, engraving for the images."[16] The fact that letters, numbers, and pictures were *all* subject to repeatability by the end of the fifteenth century needs more emphasis. That the printed book made possible new forms of interplay between these diverse elements is perhaps even more significant than the change undergone by picture, number, or letter alone.

The preparation of copy and illustrative material for printed editions also led to a rearrangement of book-making arts and routines. Not only did new skills, such as typefounding and presswork, involve veritable occupational mutations, but the production of printed books also gathered together in one place more traditional variegated skills. In the age of scribes, book making had occurred under the diverse auspices represented by stationers and lay copyists in university towns; illuminators and miniaturists trained in special ateliers; goldsmiths and leather workers belonging to special guilds; monks and lay brothers gathered in scriptoria; royal clerks and papal secretaries working in chanceries and courts; preachers compiling books of sermons on their own; humanist poets serving as their own scribes. The advent of printing led to the creation of a new kind of shop structure; to a regrouping which entailed closer contacts among diversely skilled workers and encouraged new forms of cross-cultural interchange.

Thus it is not uncommon to find former priests among early printers or former abbots serving as editors and correctors. University professors also often served in similar capacities and thus came into closer contact with metal workers and mechanics. Other fruitful forms of collaboration brought together astronomers and engravers, physicians and painters, dissolving older divisions of intellectual labor and encouraging new ways of coordinating the work of brains, eyes, and hands. Problems of financing the publication of the large Latin volumes that were used by late medieval faculties of theology, law, and medicine also led to the formation of partnerships that

---

[16] George Sarton, *The Appreciation of Ancient and Medieval Science during the Renaissance 1450–1600*, 2nd ed. (New York, 1958), xi.

brought rich merchants and local scholars into closer contact. The new financial syndicates that were formed to provide master printers with needed labor and supplies brought together representatives of town and gown.

As the key figure around whom all arrangements revolved, the master printer himself bridged many worlds. He was responsible for obtaining money, supplies, and labor, while developing complex production schedules, coping with strikes, trying to estimate book markets, and lining up learned assistants. He had to keep on good terms with officials who provided protection and lucrative jobs, while cultivating and promoting talented authors and artists who might bring his firm profits or prestige. In those places where his enterprise prospered and he achieved a position of influence with fellow townsmen, his workshop became a veritable cultural center attracting local literati and celebrated foreigners, providing both a meeting place and message center for an expanding cosmopolitan Commonwealth of Learning.

Some manuscript bookdealers, to be sure, had served rather similar functions before the advent of printing. That Italian humanists were grateful to Vespasiano da Bisticci for many of the same services that were later rendered by Aldus Manutius has already been noted. Nevertheless, the shop structure over which Aldus presided differed markedly from that known to Vespasiano. As the prototype of the early capitalist as well as the heir to Atticus and his successors, the printer embraced an even wider repertoire of roles. Aldus's household in Venice, which contained some thirty members, has recently been described by Martin Lowry as an "almost incredible mixture of the sweat shop, the boarding house and the research institute."[17] A most interesting study might be devoted to a comparison of the occupational culture of Peter Schoeffer, printer, with that of Peter Schoeffer, scribe. Unlike the shift from stationer to publisher, the shift from scribe to printer represented a genuine occupational mutation. Although Schoeffer was the first to make the leap, many others took the same route before the century's end.

[17] Martin Lowry, *The World of Aldus Manutius: Business and Scholarship in Renaissance Venice* (Oxford, 1979), 94.

Judging by Lehmann-Haupt's fine monograph, many of Schoeffer's pioneering activities were associated with the shift from a retail trade to a wholesale industry. "For a while the trade in printed books flowed within the narrow channels of the manuscript book market. But soon the stream could no longer be contained." New distribution outlets were located; handbills, circulars, and sales catalogues were printed; and the books themselves were carried down the Rhine, across the Elbe, west to Paris, south to Switzerland. The drive to tap markets went together with efforts to hold competitors at bay by offering better products or, at least, by printing a prospectus advertising the firm's "more readable" texts, "more complete and better arranged" indexes, "more careful proof-reading" and editing. Officials serving archbishops and emperors were cultivated, not only as potential bibliophiles and potential censors, but also as potential customers who issued a steady flow of orders for the printing of ordinances, edicts, bulls, indulgences, broadsides, and tracts. By the end of the century, Schoeffer had risen to a position of eminence in the city of Mainz. He commanded a "far-flung sales organization," had become a partner in a joint mining enterprise, and had founded a printing dynasty. His supply of types went to his sons upon his death, and the Schoeffer firm continued in operation, expanding to encompass music printing, through the next generation.[18]

As the foregoing may suggest, there are many points of possible contrast between the activities of the Mainz printer and those of the Paris scribe. Competitive and commercial drives were not entirely absent among the stationers who served university faculties, the lay scribes who were hired by mendicant orders, or the semi-lay copyists who belonged to communities founded by the Brethren of the Common Life. But they were muted in comparison with the later efforts of Schoeffer and his competitors to recoup initial investments, pay off creditors, use up reams of paper, and keep pressmen employed. The manuscript bookdealer did not have to worry about idle machines or striking workmen as did the printer. It has been suggested, indeed, that the mere act of setting up a press in a monastery or in affiliation

[18] See Lehmann-Haupt, *Peter Schoeffer*, passim.

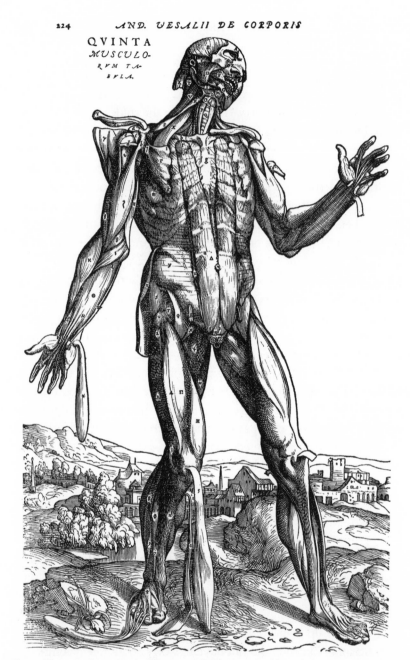

Fig. 3 (above and opposite). This example of a visual aid keyed to a text comes from Andreas Vesalius, *De humani corporis fabrica libri septem* (Basel: Johann Oporinus, 1555, pp. 224–5). Reproduced by kind permission of the Folger Shakespeare Library.

L *Os v imaginem referens, à quo primum & secundum & tertium par eorum qui id mouent musculorum re-*
secuimus.

M *Primus & secundus linguæ musculi ab osse v referente pronati.*

N *Laryngis cartilago, scutum referens, & iam narrandis musculis adhuc obtecta.*

O *Dexter duorum musculorum, qui ab osse v referente, in cartilaginem scuto similem inseruntur.*

P *Dexter duorum musculorum, qui à pectoris osse scutum imitanti laryngis cartilagini inseruntur. Ad huius*
musculi exterius latus, congeries uisitur soporariæ arteriæ, interioris uenæ iugularis, & sexti cerebri neruorum
paris.

Q *Asperæ arteriæ anterior sedes.*

R, S *Musculus ossi v referenti proprius, & à scapulæ superiori costa enatus. Singuli characteres singulos ipsius indi-*
cant uentres. Pars autem in horum medio consistens, eius musculi sedes est, tendinis substantiæ non absimilis.

T *Portio musculorum secundi paris caput mouentium.*

U *Tertius scapulam mouentium musculus, ex transuersis superiorum ceruicis uertebrarum processibus initium*
ducens.

X *Quoniam hic locus nihil aliud peculiariter, quàm septima tabula in homine ostendisset: & quia in Galeni uerba*
iurati, ipsius sententiæ, quum hæc pingerentur, plus æquo fauimus: musculum hic ex cane delineatum cernis,
quo homines prorsus destituuntur, & qui Galeno tertius thoracem mouentium habetur, sequenti tabula inte-
ger Γ notandus.

Y *Dextri lateris clauiculam hic à pectoris osse auulsimus, adhuc summo humero connexam, & sibi adhuc mu-*
Z. *sculum seruantem, qui thoracis motorum primus numerabitur, hicq̅ Z insignitur.*

a *Summus humerus, seu scapulæ elatior processus.*

b *Interior demissior ue scapulæ processus.*

c *Ligamentum brachÿ ossis ad scapulam articuli peculiarium quartum ab interiori scapulæ processu summum*
petens humerum.

d *Ligamentum teres, ab apice interioris scapulæ processus, in anteriorem sedem externi capitis humeri insertum,*
ac huius articuli, post membraneum omnibus articulis commune, primum.

e *Aliud teres ligamentum, ex eminentissima scapulæ acetabuli sede, ad externum quoq̅ humeri caput proce-*
dens, atq̅ huius articuli peculiarium ligamentorum secundum.

f *Hac sede duo ligamenta, d & e insignita, suis lateribus uniuntur, & uelut transuersum efformant ligamen-*
tum, transmittens caput externum musculi cubium flectentium anterioris, ac mox ʒ notandi.

g *Pectoris os, cui septem superiorum costarum cartilagines utrinq̅ connectuntur.*

h *Prima thoracis costa: reliquæ dein etiam, unà cum ipsarum interuallis, citra characterum opem sunt cospicuæ.*

Γ *Musculus scapulam mouentium primus. i & k huius musculi principium notant, quandam manus speciem*
i, k, l. *perinde in exortu, ac musculus ipsi succumbens, & m insignitus, in insertione repræsentans. l tendinem præsen-*
tis musculi indicat. Porro i, k & l simul, huius musculi trianguli speciem quodammodo ostendunt.

m *Musculus, qui à scapulæ basi pronatus, octo superioribus thoracis costis inseritur.*

Δ *Dexter rectorum abdominis musculorum. Ac n carneum recti abdominis musculi principium, triangulo non*
n, o. *absimile notat. o principium eiusdem musculi nerueum inscribitur, penè uniuersum efformans musculum. To-*
p, q. *to interuallo, à p ad q pertinete, recti abdominis musculi interni suis lateribus inuicem cotingunt. Tota autem*
sede supra q, aut mox supra umbilicum consistente, tanto magis musculi mutuò seiunguntur, quanto altius con-
scendunt. Cæterùm q notabit etiam obliquorum abdominis musculorum nateruosæ tenuitatis, ad transuersim

r. *abdominis musculum, hac in parte ad pectoris usq̅ sedem connexum. Porro r linea insignitur, quæ carneam re-*
cti musculi partem finit, quæq̅ ultima ipsius insertionis in homine est portio, uti in quarta tabula ad characte-
s. *rem n est cernere. Intercapedine igitur ab r ad s pertinente, se offert recti simiæ abdominis musculi tendo seu*
t. *membrana, excarnis ue musculi pars. t autem indicat carneam musculi sedem, primæ costæ & secundæ thora-*
cis insertam. estq̅ latus ille tendo & carnea hæc pars is musculus, quem Galenus quintum thorace mouentium
enumerat, in hominibus haudquaquam, ut in caudatis simÿs conibus, conspicuus. Nos autem hìc illum, Ga-
leni intelligendi gratia, delineauimus, quòd alioquin hæc pectoris sedes, sequentium duarum tabularum pe-
u, u, u. *ctoribus erat absq̅ huius musculi responsura. Postremò, u, u, u notantur inscriptiones, seu nerued delineamenta,*
transuersim recto musculo impressa, quibus obliquè ascendentis musculi neruosa exilitas pertinacissimè con-
nascitur.

x *Linea hæc portiunculam notat musculi abdominis obliquè ascendentis, qua is transuerso abdominis musculo*
inibi adeo ualide committitur, ut inter dissecandum, nisi relicto eiusmodi signo, à transuerso liberari nequeat.

y *Transuersus abdominis musculus.*

α *Obliquè ascendens abdominis musculus, ab abdomine hic reflexus.*

β Uasorum

31

PICTURE OF A PRINTING OFFICE

This cut, the work of Thymius' accurate hand
Shows all at once how printing shops are manned:
The masters' duties, the correctors' chores,
The work of readers and compositors.
To this small book then you'll apply your mind
Good reader, if you're not the vulgar kind,
So that a picture in your mind may rise
To match this picture that's before your eyes.

OFFICINÆ TYPOGRA-
PHICÆ DELINEATIO.

EN Thymii sculptoris opus,quo prodidit unâ
Singula chalcographi munera rite gregis.
Et correctorum curas,operasq́ regentum,
Quasq́; gerit lector, compositorq́; vices.
Ut vulgus fileam. tu qui legis ista, libello
Fac iteratâ animi sedulitate satis.
Sic meritz cumulans hinc fertilitatis honores,
Ceu pictura oculos, intima mentis ages.

with a religious order was a source of disturbance, bringing "a multitude of worries about money and property" into space previously reserved for meditation and good works.[19]

As self-serving publicists, early printers issued book lists, circulars, and broadsides. They put their firm's name, emblem, and shop address on the front page of their books. Indeed, their use of title pages entailed a significant reversal of scribal procedures; they put themselves first. Scribal colophons had come last. They also extended their new promotional techniques to the authors and artists whose work they published, thus contributing to new forms of personal celebrity. Reckon masters and instrument makers along with professors and preachers also profited from book advertisements that spread their fame beyond shops and lecture halls. Studies concerned with the rise of a lay intelligentsia, with the new dignity assigned to artisan crafts, or with the heightened visibility achieved by the "capitalist spirit" might well devote more attention to these early practitioners of the advertising arts.

Their control of a new publicity apparatus, moreover, placed early printers in an exceptional position with regard to other enterprises. They not only sought ever larger markets for their own products, but they also contributed to, and profited from, the expansion of other commercial enterprises. What effects did the appearance of new advertising techniques have on sixteenth-century commerce and industry? Possibly some answers to this question are known. Probably others can still be found. Many other aspects of job printing and the changes it entailed clearly need further study. The printed calendars and indulgences that were first issued from the Mainz workshops of Gutenberg and Fust, for example, warrant at least as much

[19] Wytze Hellinga, "Thomas A. Kempis – The First Printed Editions," *Quaerendo* IV (1974): 4–5.

Fig. 4 (opposite). A master printer in his shop. The Latin verse and woodblock first appeared in Jerome Hornschuch, *Orthotypographia* (Leipzig: M. Lantzenberger, 1608). The English translation comes from a facsimile edition, edited and translated by Philip Gaskell and Patricia Bradford (Cambridge University Library, 1972, p. xvi). Reproduced by kind permission of the Cambridge University Library.

attention as the more celebrated Bibles. Indeed, the mass production of indulgences illustrates rather neatly the sort of change that often goes overlooked, so that its consequences are more difficult to reckon with than perhaps they need be.

In contrast to the changes that have just been noted, those that were associated with the consumption of new printed products are more intangible, indirect, and difficult to handle. A large margin for uncertainty must be left when dealing with such changes.

On the difficult problem of estimating literacy rates before and after printing, the comments of Carlo Cipolla seem cogent:

> It is not easy to draw a general conclusion from the scattered evidence that I have quoted and from the similarly scattered evidence that I have not quoted... I could go on to conclude that at the end of the sixteenth century "there were more literate people than we generally believe"... I could equally conclude that "there were less literate people than we generally believe" for in all truth one never knows what it is that "we generally believe"... one could venture to say that at the end of the sixteenth century the rate of illiteracy for the adult population in Western Europe was below 50 percent in the towns of the relatively more advanced areas and above 50 percent in all rural areas as well as in the towns of the backward areas. This is a frightfully vague statement... but the available evidence does not permit more precision.[20]

In view of the fragmentary evidence that is available and the prolonged fluctuations that were entailed, it would seem prudent to bypass vexed problems associated with the spread of literacy until other issues have been explored with more care. That there are other issues worth exploring – apart from the expansion of the reading public or the "spread" of new ideas – is in itself a point that needs underlining (and that will be repeatedly underscored in this book). When considering the *initial* transformations wrought by print, at all events, changes undergone by groups who were already literate ought

[20]   Carlo M. Cipolla, *Literacy and Development in the West* (London, 1969), 60.

to receive priority over the undeniably fascinating problem of how rapidly such groups were enlarged.

Once attention has been focused on the already literate sectors, it becomes clear that their social composition calls for further thought. Did printing at first serve prelates and patricians as a "divine art," or should one think of it rather as the "poor man's friend"? It was described in both ways by contemporaries and probably served in both ways as well. When one recalls scribal functions performed by Roman slaves or later by monks, lay brothers, clerks, and notaries, one may conclude that literacy had never been congruent with elite social status. One may also guess that it was more compatible with sedentary occupations than with the riding and hunting favored by many squires and lords. In this light, it may be misguided to envisage the new presses as making available to low-born men products previously used only by the high born. That many rural areas remained untouched until after the coming of the railway age seems likely. Given the large peasant population in early modern Europe and the persistence of local dialects which imposed an additional language barrier between spoken and written words, it is probable that only a very small portion of the entire population was affected by the initial shift. Nevertheless, within this relatively small and largely urban population, a fairly wide social spectrum may have been involved. In fifteenth-century England, for example, mercers and scriveners engaged in a manuscript book trade were already catering to the needs of lowly bakers and merchants as well as to those of lawyers, aldermen, or knights. The proliferation of literate merchants in fourteenth-century Italian cities is no less notable than the presence of an illiterate army commander in late sixteenth-century France.

It would be a mistake, however, to assume that a distaste for reading was especially characteristic of the nobility, although it seems plausible that a distaste for Latin pedantry was shared by lay aristocrat and commoner alike. It also remains uncertain whether one ought to describe the early reading public as being "middle class." Certainly extreme caution is needed when matching genres of books with groups of readers. All too often it is taken for granted that "lowbrow" or "vulgar" works reflect "lower-class" tastes, despite contrary evidence offered by authorship and library catalogues. Before the advent of mass literacy, the most "popular" works were those which appealed to diverse groups of readers and not just to the plebes.

Divisions between Latin- and vernacular-reading publics are also much more difficult to correlate with social status than many accounts suggest. It is true that the sixteenth-century physician who used Latin was regarded as superior to the surgeon who did not, but it is also true that neither man was likely to belong to the highest estates of the realm. Insofar as the vernacular-translation movement was aimed at readers who were unlearned in Latin, it was often designed to appeal to pages as well as to apprentices; to landed gentry, cavaliers, and courtiers as well as to shopkeepers and clerks. In the Netherlands, a translation from Latin into French often pointed away from the urban laity, who knew only Lower Rhenish dialects, and toward relatively exclusive courtly circles. At the same time, a translation into "Dutch" might be aimed at preachers who needed to cite scriptural passages in sermons rather than at the laity (which is too often assumed to be the only target for "vernacular" devotional works). Tutors trying to educate young princes, instructors in court or church schools, and chaplains translating from Latin in response to royal requests had pioneered in "popularizing" techniques even before the printer set to work.

But the most vigorous impetus given to popularization before printing came from the felt need of preachers to keep their congregations awake and also to hold the attention of diverse outdoor crowds. Unlike the preacher, the printer could only guess at the nature of the audience to which his work appealed. Accordingly, one must be especially careful when taking the titles of early printed books as trustworthy guides to readership. A case in point is the frequent description of the fifteenth-century picture Bible, which was issued in both manuscript and then blockbook form, as the "poor man's" Bible. The description may well be anachronistic, based on abbreviating the full Latin title given to such books. The *Biblia pauperum praedicatorum* was aimed not at poor men but at poor preachers who had a mere smattering of Latin and found scriptural exposition easier when given picture books as guides. Sophisticated analysts have suggested the need to discriminate between actual readership as determined by library catalogues, subscription lists, and other data (with due allowance made, of course, for the fact that many book buyers are more eager to display than to read their purchases) and the more hypothetical targets envisaged by authors and publishers. All too often, titles and prefaces are taken as evidence of the actual readership although they are nothing of the kind.

> Information on the spread of reading and writing . . . must be sup-
> plemented by analysis of contents; this in turn provides circum-
> stantial evidence on the composition of the reading public: a
> cookbook . . . reprinted eight or more times in the XVth century
> was obviously read by people concerned with the preparation of
> food, the *Doctrinal des Filles* . . . a booklet on the behavior of young
> women, primarily by "filles" and "mesdames."[21]

Such "circumstantial evidence," however, is highly suspect. With-out passing judgment on the audience for early cookbooks (its char-acter seems far from obvious to me), booklets pertaining to the behavior of young ladies were probably also of interest to male tutors or confessors or guardians. The circulation of printed etiquette books had wide-ranging psychological ramifications; their capacity to heighten the anxiety of parents should not go ignored. Further-more, such works were probably also read by authors, translators, and publishers of other etiquette books. That authors and publish-ers were wide-ranging readers needs to be perpetually kept in mind. Even those sixteenth-century poets who shunned printers and cir-culated their verse in manuscript form[22] took advantage of their own access to printed materials. It has been suggested that books describing double-entry bookkeeping were read less by merchants than by the writers of accountancy books and teachers of accoun-tancy. One wonders whether there were not more playwrights and poets than shepherds who studied so-called *Shepherd's Almanacks*. Given the corruption of data transmitted over the centuries, given

---

[21] Hirsch, *Printing, Selling,* 7.
[22] J. W. Saunders, "From Manuscript to Print: A Note on the Circulation of Poetic Manuscripts in the Sixteenth Century," *Proceedings of the Leeds Philosophical and Literary Society* VI (May 1951): 507–28.

the false remedies and impossible recipes contained in medical treatises, one hopes that they were studied more by poets than by physicians. Given the exotic ingredients described, one may assume that
few apothecaries actually tried to concoct all the recipes contained
in early printed pharmacopeia, although they may have felt impelled
to stock their shelves with bizarre items just in case the new publicity might bring such items into demand. The purposes, whether
intended or actual, served by some early printed handbooks offer puzzles that permit no easy solution. What was the point of publishing
vernacular manuals outlining procedures that were already familiar
to all skilled practitioners of certain crafts? It is worth remembering,
in any event, that the gap between shoproom practice and classroom
theory was just becoming visible during the first century of printing
and that many so-called practical handbooks and manuals contained
impractical, even injurious, advice.

While conjectures about social and psychological transformations
can be postponed, certain points should be noted here. One must distinguish, as Altick suggests, between literacy and habitual book reading. By no means all who mastered the written word have, down to
the present, become members of a book-reading public.[23] Learning
to read is different, moreover, from learning *by reading*. Reliance on
apprenticeship training, oral communication, and special mnemonic
devices had gone together with mastering letters in the age of scribes.
After the advent of printing, however, the transmission of written
information became much more efficient. It was not only the craftsman outside universities who profited from the new opportunities
to teach himself. Of equal importance was the chance extended to
bright undergraduates to reach beyond their teachers' grasp. Gifted
students no longer needed to sit at the feet of a given master in order
to learn a language or academic skill. Instead, they could swiftly
achieve mastery on their own, even by sneaking books past their
tutors – as did the young would-be astronomer, Tycho Brahe. "Why
should old men be preferred to their juniors now that it is possible for

[23]   Richard Altick, *The English Common Reader: A Social History of the Mass Reading Public 1800–1900* (Chicago, 1963), 31.

the young by diligent study to acquire the same knowledge?" asked the author of a fifteenth-century outline of history.[24]

As learning by reading took on new importance, the role played by mnemonic aids was diminished. Rhyme and cadence were no longer required to preserve certain formulas and recipes. The nature of the collective memory was transformed.

> In Victor Hugo's *Notre Dame de Paris* a scholar, deep in medi-tation in his study...gazes at the first printed book which has come to disturb his collection of manuscripts. Then...he gazes at the vast cathedral, silhouetted against the starry sky..."Ceci tuera cela," he says. The printed book will destroy the building. The parable which Hugo develops out of the comparison of the building, crowded with images, with the arrival in his library of a printed book might be applied to the effect on the invisible cathedrals of memory of the past of the spread of printing. The printed book will make such huge built-up memories, crowded with images, unnecessary. It will do away with habits of immemo-rial antiquity whereby a "thing" is immediately invested with an image and stored in the places of memory.[25]

To the familiar romantic theme of the Gothic cathedral as an "encyclopedia in stone," Frances Yates has added a fascinating sequel by her study of the long-lost arts of memory. Not only did printing eliminate many functions previously performed by stone figures over portals and stained glass in windows, but it also affected less-tangible images by eliminating the need for placing figures and objects in imaginary niches located in memory theaters. By making it possi-ble to dispense with the use of images for mnemonic purposes, print-ing reinforced iconoclastic tendencies already present among many Christians. Successive editions of Calvin's *Institutes* elaborated on the need to observe the Second Commandment. The favorite text of the defenders of images was the dictum of Gregory the Great that

[24] Jacobo Filippo Foresti, "Supplementum Chronicarum" (Venice, 1483), cited by Martin Lowry, *The World of Aldus Manutius*, 31.
[25] Frances Yates, *The Art of Memory* (London, 1966), 131.

statues served as "the books of the illiterate."[26] Although Calvin's
scornful dismissal of this dictum made no mention of printing, the
new medium did underlie the Calvinist assumption that the illiterate should not be given graven images but should be taught to read.
In this light it may seem plausible to suggest that printing fostered a
movement "from image culture to word culture," a movement which
was more compatible with Protestant bibliolatry and pamphleteering
than with the baroque statues and paintings sponsored by the post-
Tridentine Catholic church.

Yet the cultural metamorphosis produced by printing was really
much more complicated than any single formula can possibly
express. For one thing, engraved images became more, rather than
less, abundant after the establishment of print shops throughout
Western Europe. For another thing, Protestant propaganda exploited
printed image no less than printed word – as numerous caricatures
and cartoons may suggest. Even religious imagery was defended by
some Protestants, and on the very grounds of its compatibility with
print culture. Luther himself commented on the inconsistency of
iconoclasts who tore pictures off walls while handling the illustrations in Bibles reverently. Pictures "do no more harm on walls than
in books," he commented and then, somewhat sarcastically, stopped
short of pursuing this line of thought: "I must cease lest I give occasion to the image breakers never to read the Bible or to burn it."[27]

If we accept the idea of a movement from image to word, furthermore, we will be somewhat at a loss to account for the work of
Northern artists, such as Dürer or Cranach or Holbein, who were
affiliated with Protestantism and yet owed much to print. As Dürer's
career may suggest, the new arts of printing and engraving, far from
reducing the importance of images, increased opportunities for image
makers and helped to launch art history down its present path. Even

---

[26] Myron P. Gilmore, "Italian Reactions to Erasmian Humanism," *Itinerarium
Italicum*, ed. H. Oberman (Leiden, 1975), 87–8.

[27] Martin Luther, "Against the Heavenly Prophets in the Matter of Images and
Sacraments" (1525), *Luther's Works* XL, ed. C. Bergendorff and H. T. Lehmann
(Philadelphia, 1958), 99–100.

A R S   M E M O R I Æ.

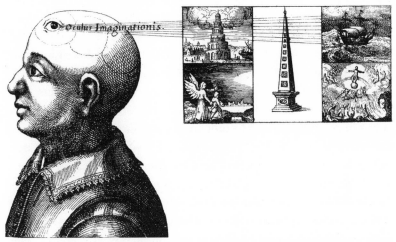

Fig. 5. Seeing with a "third eye" in the seventeenth century. After their original functions were outmoded, ancient memory arts acquired an occult significance and received a new lease on life in printed form. From Robert Fludd, *Utriusque cosmi maioris*... (Oppenheim: Johan-Theodor de Bry, typis Hieronymi Galleri, 1621, II, 47). Reproduced by kind permission of the Folger Shakespeare Library.

the imaginary figures and memory theaters described by Frances Yates did not vanish when their mnemonic functions were outmoded, but received a "strange new lease on life." They provided the content for magnificent emblem books and for elaborate baroque illustrations to Rosicrucian and occult works in the seventeenth century. They also helped to inspire an entirely new genre of printed literature – the didactic picture book for children. Leipzig boys in Leibniz's day "were brought up on Comenius' picture book and Luther's Catechism."[28] In this form, the ancient memory images reentered the imagination of Protestant children, ultimately supplying Jung and his followers with evidence that suggested the hypothesis of a collective unconscious. Surely the new vogue for image-packed emblem books was no

[28] Yates, *Art of Memory*, 134, 377.

less a product of sixteenth-century print culture than was the image-less "Ramist" textbook.

Furthermore, in certain fields of learning, such as architecture, geometry, or geography, and many of the life sciences as well, print culture was not merely incompatible with the formula offered above; it actually increased the functions performed by images while reducing those performed by words. Many fundamental texts of Ptolemy, Vitruvius, Galen, and other ancients had lost their illustrations in the course of being copied for centuries and regained them only after script was replaced by print. To think in terms of a movement going from image to word points technical literature in the wrong direction. It was not the "printed word" but the "printed image" which acted as a "savior for Western science" in George Sarton's view. Within the Commonwealth of Learning it became increasingly fashionable to adopt the ancient Chinese maxim that a single picture was more valuable than many words.[29] In early Tudor England, Thomas Elyot expressed a preference for "figures and charts" over "hearing the rules of a science"[30] which seems worth further thought. Although images were indispensable for prodding memory, a heavy reliance on verbal instruction had also been characteristic of communications in the age of scribes. To be sure, academic lectures were sometimes supplemented by drawing pictures on walls; verbal instructions to apprentices were accompanied by demonstrations; the use of blocks and boards, fingers and knuckles were common in teaching reckoning; and gestures usually went with the recitation of key mnemonics. Nevertheless, when seeking rapid duplication of a given set of instructions, words simply had to take precedence over other forms of communication. How else save by using words could one dictate a text to assembled scribes? After the advent of printing, visual aids multiplied; signs and symbols were codified; different kinds of iconographic and nonphonetic communication were rapidly developed. The fact that printed picture books were newly designed

[29] Sarton, *Appreciation of Ancient and Medieval Science*, 91, 95.
[30] See citation from the "Boke Called the Gouvernour" (1531) in Foster Watson, *The Beginning of the Teaching of Modern Subjects in England* (London, 1909), 136.

C X.

Prudence.   *Prudentia.*

Prudence, 1.	*Prudentia,* 1.
looketh upon all things	omnia circumſpectat,
as a Serpent, 2.	ut *Serpens,* 2.
and doeth,	nihilq; agit,
ſpeaketh, or thinketh	loquitur, & cogitat
nothing in vain.	in caſſum.
She looks backward, 3	*Reſpicit,* 3.
as into a looking-glaſs, 4	tanquam in *Speculum,* 4.
to things paſt ;	ad *Præterita* ;
and ſeeth before her, 5.	& *Proſpicit,* 5.
as with a Perſpective-	
glaſs, 7.	tanquam *Teleſcopio,* 7.
things to come,	*Futura*
or the end ; 6.	ſeu *Finem :* 6.
and ſo ſhe perceiveth	atq; ita perſpicit

what

Fig. 6. An ancient mnemonic image transposed for didactic purposes into an illus-
tration for the first children's picture book. The figure of Prudence from Johann
Amos Comenius, *Orbis sensualium pictus* (1658); translated into English by Charles
Hoole (London, 1685). Reproduced by kind permission of the Folger Shakespeare
Library.

by educational reformers for the purpose of instructing children and
that drawing was considered an increasingly useful accomplishment
by pedagogues also points to the need to think beyond the simple
formula "image to word."

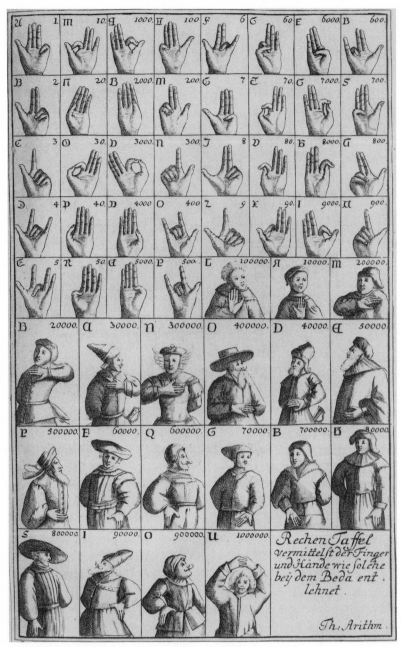

Fig. 7. Although the use of fingers and gestures for reckoning was superseded by the use of printed arithmetic books, charts, and tables, these ancient arts were codified and given a long lease on life in printed form. This engraving from Jacob Leupold, *Theatrum arithmetica-geometricum*... (Leipzig: C. Zunkel, 1727), is reproduced by kind permission of the Department of Special Collections, Stanford University Libraries.

As these comments may suggest, efforts to summarize changes wrought by printing in any one statement or neat formula are likely to lead us astray. Even while acknowledging that there was an increased reliance on rule books and less on rules of thumb or that learning by reading gained at the expense of hearing or doing, one must also consider how printing encouraged new objections to bookish knowledge based on "slavish" copying and how it enabled many observers to check freshly recorded data against received rules. Similarly, one must be cautious about assuming that the spoken word was gradually silenced as printed words multiplied or that the faculty of hearing was increasingly neglected in favor of that of sight. Surely the history of Western music after Gutenberg argues against the latter suggestion. As for the many questions raised by the assertion that print silenced the spoken word, a few are noted elsewhere in this book; all must be passed over here.

The purpose of this preliminary discussion has been simply to demonstrate that the shift from script to print entailed a large ensemble of changes, each of which needs more investigation and all of which are too complicated to be encapsulated in any single formula. But to say that there is no simple way of summarizing the complex ensemble is not the same thing as saying that nothing had changed. To the contrary!

CHAPTER THREE

Some Features of Print Culture

Granted that some sort of communications revolution did occur during the late fifteenth century, how did this affect other historical developments? Most conventional surveys stop short after a few remarks about the wider dissemination of humanist tomes or Protestant tracts. Several helpful suggestions – about the effects of standardization on scholarship and science, for example – are offered in works devoted to the era of the Renaissance or to the history of science. By and large, the effects of the new process are vaguely implied rather than explicitly defined and are also drastically minimized. One example may illustrate this point. During the first centuries of printing, old texts were duplicated more rapidly than new ones. On this basis most authorities conclude that "printing did not speed up the adoption of new theories."[1] But where did these new theories come from? Must we invoke some spirit of the times? Or is it possible that an increase in the output of old texts contributed to the formulation of new theories? Maybe other features that distinguished the new mode of book production from the old one also contributed to such theories. We need to take stock of these features before we can relate the advent of printing to other historical developments.

Without attempting to draw up a complete inventory, I have singled out some of the features which appear in the special literature on early printing and held them in mind while passing in review selected historical developments. Conjectures based on this approach may be sampled here under headings that indicate my main lines of inquiry.

[1] Febvre and Martin, *Coming of the Book*, 420–1.

46

A Closer Look at Wide Dissemination:
Increased Output and Altered Intake

Most references to wide dissemination are too fleeting to make clear the specific effects of an increased supply of texts directed at different markets. Just as the "spread" of literacy tends to take priority over changes experienced by already literate sectors, so too the "spread" of Lutheran views or the failure of Copernican theories to "spread" as rapidly as Ptolemaic ones seems to outweigh all other issues. Too often the printer is assigned the sole function of serving as a press agent. His effectiveness is judged by circulation figures alone. Even while more copies of one given text were being "spread, dispersed, or scattered" by the issue of a printed edition, different texts, which had been previously dispersed and scattered, were also being brought closer together for individual readers. In some regions, printers produced more scholarly texts than they could sell and flooded local markets. In all regions, a given purchaser could buy more books at lower cost and bring them into his study or library. In this way, the printer who duplicated a seemingly antiquated backlist was still providing the clerk with a richer, more varied literary diet than had been provided by the scribe. "A serious student could now endeavor to cover a larger body of material by private reading than a student or even a mature scholar needed to master or could hope to master before printing made books cheap and plentiful."[2] To consult different books it was no longer so essential to be a wandering scholar. Successive generations of sedentary scholars were less apt to be engrossed by a single text and expend their energies in elaborating on it. The era of the glossator and commentator came to an end, and a new "era of intense cross referencing between one book and another"[3] began.

That something rather like a knowledge explosion was experienced in the sixteenth century has often been suggested, in

[2] Craig Thompson, ed., *The Colloquies of Erasmus* (Chicago, 1965), 458.
[3] Denys Hay, "Literature: The Printed Book," *The New Cambridge Modern History*, vol. 2, *The Reformation 1520–1559*, ed. G. R. Elton (Cambridge, 1958), 366.

connection with the Northern Renaissance if not with the advent of printing. Few studies of the literature of the era fail to cite relevant passages from Marlowe or Rabelais indicating how it felt to become intoxicated by reading and how bookish knowledge was regarded as if it were a magic elixir conferring new powers with every swallow. Yet when dealing with any major intellectual change in the sixteenth century, the ferment engendered by access to more books is likely to be ignored. In a recent perceptive account of the sense of intellectual crisis reflected in Montaigne's writing, for example, we are told about the shattering impact of the Reformation and wars of religion and "the extension of mental horizons" produced by geographical discoveries and humanist recoveries.[4] It would be foolish to assert that the most newsworthy events of the age made no impression on so sensitive an observer as Montaigne. But it also seems misguided to overlook the event that impinged most directly on his favorite observation post. That he could see more books by spending a few months in his tower study than earlier scholars had seen after a lifetime of travel also needs to be taken into account. In explaining why Montaigne perceived greater "conflict and diversity" in the works he consulted than had medieval commentators in an earlier age, something should be said about the increased number of texts he had at hand.

More abundantly stocked bookshelves obviously increased opportunities to consult and compare different texts. Merely by making more scrambled data available, by increasing the output of Aristotelian, Alexandrian, and Arabic texts, printers encouraged efforts to unscramble these data. Some medieval coastal maps had long been more accurate than many ancient ones, but few eyes had seen either. Much as maps from different regions and epochs were brought into contact in the course of preparing editions of atlases, so too were technical texts brought together in certain physicians' and astronomers' libraries. Contradictions became more visible, divergent traditions more difficult to reconcile. The transmission

---

4   P. M. Rattansi, "The Social Interpretation of Science in the Seventeenth Century," *Science and Society 1600–1900*, ed. Peter Mathias (Cambridge, 1972), 7.

of received opinion could not proceed smoothly once Arabists were set against Galenists or Aristotelians against Ptolemaists. Not only was confidence in old theories weakened, but an enriched reading matter also encouraged the development of new intellectual combinations and permutations. Combinatory intellectual activity, as Arthur Koestler has suggested, inspires many creative acts. Once old texts came together within the same study, diverse systems of ideas and special disciplines could be combined. Increased output directed at relatively stable markets, in short, created conditions that favored new combinations of old ideas at first and then, later, the creation of entirely new systems of thought.

It should be noted that cross-cultural interchange was experienced first of all by the new occupational groups responsible for the output of printed editions. Even before a given reference work had come off the press, fruitful encounters between typefounders, correctors, translators, copy editors, illustrators or print dealers, indexers, and others engaged in editorial work had already occurred. Early printers themselves were the very first to read the products that came off their own presses. They also kept an anxious eye on their competitors' output. The effects of access to more books (and, indeed, of all the varied features associated with typography) were thus first and most forcefully experienced within printers' workshops, by the new book producers themselves. Whereas other libraries were nourished by the output of master printers such as the Estiennes or Christopher Plantin, the valuable collections they themselves built up contained many by-products of their own daily shopwork.

That a remarkable amount of innovative work in both scholarly and scientific fields was done outside academic centers in the early modern era is often noted. The new attraction exerted by printers' workshops upon men of learning and letters may help to explain this development. The same point holds good for discussion of the new interchanges between artists and scholars or practitioners and theorists which proved so fruitful in early modern science. Printing encouraged forms of combinatory activity which were social as well as intellectual. It changed relationships between men of learning as well as between systems of ideas.

Cross-cultural interchange stimulated mental activities in contradictory ways. The first century of printing was marked above all
by intellectual ferment and by a "somewhat wide-angled, unfocused,
scholarship."[5] Certain confusing cross currents may be explained by
noting that new links between disciplines were being forged before
old ones had been severed. In the age of scribes, for instance, magical
arts were closely associated with mechanical crafts and mathematical
wizardry. When "technology went to press," so too did a vast backlog of occult lore, and few readers could discriminate between the
two. Historians who are still puzzled by the high prestige enjoyed by
alchemy, astrology, "magia and cabala," and other occult arts within
the Commonwealth of Learning during early modern times might
find it helpful to consider how records derived from ancient Near
Eastern cultures had been transmitted in the age of scribes. Some
of these records had dwindled into tantalizing fragments pertaining
to systems of reckoning, medicine, agriculture, mythic cults, and so
forth. Others had evaporated into unfathomable glyphs. Certain cos-
mic cycles and life cycles are experienced by all men, and so common
elements could be detected in the fragments and glyphs. It seemed
plausible to assume that all came from one source and to take seriously hints in some patristic works about an Ur text set down by
the inventor of writing, which contained all the secrets of Creation
as told to Adam before the Fall. It also seemed plausible that the
teachings contained in this Ur text, after being carefully preserved
by ancient sages and seers, had become corrupted and confused in the
course of barbarian invasions. A large collection of writings containing ancient lore was received from Macedonia by Cosimo de Medici,
translated from Greek by Ficino in 1463, and printed in fifteen editions before 1500. It took the form of dialogues with the Egyptian god
Thoth, whose Greek name was Hermes Trismegistus. The writings
retrieved in the fifteenth century seemed to come from the same corpus of texts as other fragmentary dialogues known to earlier scholars
and also attributed to Hermes Trismegistus. The hermetic corpus ran

5   E. Harris Harbison, *The Christian Scholar in the Age of the Reformation* (New York,
    1956), 54.

through many editions until 1614, when a treatise by Isaac Casaubon showed it had been compiled in the post-Christian era. On this basis we are told that Renaissance scholars made a "radical error in dating." No doubt they had. A neo-Platonic, post-Christian compilation had been mistaken for a work which preceded and influenced Plato. Yet to assign definite dates to scribal compilations, which were probably derived from earlier sources, may be an error as well.[6]

The transformation of occult and esoteric scribal lore after the advent of printing also needs more study. Some arcane writings (in Greek, Hebrew, or Syriac, for example) became less mysterious. Others became more so. Thus hieroglyphs were set in type more than three centuries before their decipherment. These sacred carved letters were loaded with significant meaning by readers who could not read them. They were also used simply as ornamental motifs by architects and engravers. Given baroque decoration on one hand and complicated interpretations by scholars, Rosicrucians, or Freemasons on the other, the duplication of Egyptian picture writing throughout the Age of Reason presents modern scholars with puzzles that can never be solved. So we must not think only about new forms of enlightenment when considering the effects of printing on scholarship. New forms of mystification were encouraged as well.

In this light it seems necessary to qualify the assertion that the first half-century of printing gave "a great impetus to wide dissemination of accurate knowledge of the sources of Western thought, both classical and Christian."[7] The duplication of the hermetic writings, the sibylline prophecies, the hieroglyphics of "Horapollo," and many other seemingly authoritative, actually fraudulent esoteric writings worked in the opposite direction, spreading inaccurate knowledge even while paving the way for later purification of Christian sources. Here, as elsewhere, we need to distinguish between initial and delayed effects. An enrichment of scholarly libraries came rapidly; the sorting out of their contents took more time. Compared

---

[6] Frances Yates, *Giordano Bruno and the Hermetic Tradition* (London, 1964), passim.
[7] Myron P. Gilmore, *The World of Humanism 1453–1517* (New York, 1952), 190.

Specimen Lectionis Idealis, in primo latere Obelisci exhibitum.

Hemphta Numen ſupre- | mum .& Archetypon
inſluit virtutem | & munera ſua

in ſiderei Mundi ani- | mã,id eſt ſolare Nume ſi bi ſubditu

　　vnde vitalis motus in | Mundo Hylæo, ſiue Elementari ,
omniumque rerum abun- | dãtia, & ſpecierũ varietas prouenit.
　　ex vbertate Cra- | teris Oſiriaci, in quem mira
　　quadam ſympathia | tractus continuò inſluit

　　duplici in ſibi ſub | dita dõminio potens .

　　Vigilantiſſimus | Chenoſiris
　　ſacrorum canalium | cuſtos , ideſt Natu ræ humidæ
　　in qua vita rerum | omnium conſiſtit .

　　Ophionius | Agathodæmon
　　ad cuius fa- | uorem obtinendum

　　vitamque pro- | pagandam
　　Sacra hæc ei | Tabula conſecranda eſt ;
cuius beneficio cæleſte | Heptapyrgon ideſt arx planetarum
　　diuini Oſiridis | Agathodæmonis humidi

aſſiſtentia ab om- | nibus aduerſis conſeruatur .

　　Præterea in ſacri- | ficijs & cerimonijs in hunc
　　finem eiuſdem | ſtatua circumfetenda eſt ;

Epariſterium Naturæ | ſiue fons Hecatinus, ſiue vetigineus
id eſt Naturæ efflu- | uium inter ſacrificia aperiendum.

Quo allectus Poly- | morphus Dæmon, vberem 　(do
　　varietatem | rerũ cõcedet in quadripartito Mũ-

Typhonis technæ | vitæ inſidiatrices , elidentur

Vnde vita rerum | innoxia conſeruabitur

ad quod plurimum | quoq;conducét hæc, quæ ſequútur

　　pentacula , ſiue | periammata , ob myſticas

　　rationes , quibus | conſtructa ſunt .

　　ſunt enim viiæ | bonorum omnium

acquirendorum potentes | illecebræ .

with the large output of unscholarly vernacular materials, the number of trilingual dictionaries and Greek or even Latin editions seems so small that one wonders whether the term "wide dissemination" ought to be applied to the latter case at all.

Dissemination, as defined in the dictionary, seems especially appropriate to the duplication of primers, ABC books, catechisms, calendars, and devotional literature. Increased output of such materials, however, was not necessarily conducive either to the advancement of scholarship or to cross-cultural exchange. Catechisms, religious tracts, and Bibles would fill some bookshelves to the exclusion of all other reading matter. The new wide-angled, unfocused scholarship went together with a new single-minded, narrowly focused piety. At the same time, practical guidebooks and manuals also became more abundant, making it easier to lay plans for getting ahead in this world – possibly diverting attention from uncertain futures in the next one. Sixteenth-century map publishers thus began to exclude "Paradise" from this world as being of too uncertain a location. Eventually Cardinal Baronius would be cited by Galileo as distinguishing between "how to go to heaven" – a problem for the Holy Spirit – and "how the heavens go" – a matter of practical demonstration and mathematical reasoning.[8] It would be a mistake to press this last point too far, however, for many of the so-called practical guides contained nonsensical and mystifying material, making them highly impractical. Moreover, until Newton's *Principia*, the output of conflicting theories and astronomical tables offered very uncertain guidance on "how the heavens go." Manuals on devotional exercises and

---

[8] Galileo Galilei, "Letter to the Grand Duchess Christina" (1615), printed in *Discoveries and Opinions of Galileo*, tr. and ed. Stillman Drake (New York, 1957), 186.

Fig. 8 (opposite). The duplication of Egyptian picture writing contributed more to mystification than to enlightenment. Hieroglyphs, set in type long before being deciphered, were assigned divergent meanings by learned men such as the Jesuit whose work appears. From Athanasius Kircher, *Obelisci aegyptiaci*... (Rome: Ex typographia Varesij, 1666, p. 78). Reproduced by kind permission of the Folger Shakespeare Library.

guidebooks on spiritual questions provided clear-cut advice. Readers who were helped by access to road maps, phrase books, conversion tables, and other aids were also likely to place confidence in guides to the soul's journey after death. Tracts expounding the Book of Revelation entailed a heavy reliance on mathematical reasoning. The fixing of precise dates for the Creation or for the Second Coming occupied the very same talents that developed new astronomical tables and map-projection techniques.

It is doubtful, at all events, whether "the effect of the new invention on scholarship"[9] was more significant than its effect on vernacular Bible reading at the beginning of the sixteenth century. What does need emphasis is that many dissimilar effects, all of great consequence, came relatively simultaneously. If this could be spelled out more clearly, seemingly contradictory developments might be confronted with more equanimity. The intensification of both religiosity and secularism could be better understood. Some debates about periodization also could be bypassed. Printing made more visible long-lived and much used texts which are usually passed over and sometimes (mistakenly) deemed obsolete when new trends are being traced. Many medieval world pictures were duplicated more rapidly during the first century of printing than they had been during the so-called Middle Ages. They did not merely survive among conservative Elizabethans "who were loth to upset the old order."[10] They became more available to poets and playwrights of the sixteenth century than they had been to minstrels and mummers of the thirteenth century. Given the use of new media, such as woodcuts and metal engravings, to depict medieval cosmologies, we cannot think simply of mere survival but must consider a more complex process whereby long-lived schemes were presented in new visual forms.

In view of such considerations, I cannot agree with Sarton's comment: "It is hardly necessary to indicate what the art of printing meant for the diffusion of culture but one should not lay too much

[9] Gilmore, *World of Humanism*, 189.
[10] E. M. W. Tillyard, *The Elizabethan World Picture* (New York, 1942), 8.

Fig. 9. Medieval world pictures became more available in the sixteenth century than they had been in the Middle Ages, thanks to the use of blocks and plates which presented long-lived schemes in new visual form. A medieval king representing Atlas is holding an Aristotelian cosmos in this engraving taken from William Cunningham, *The Cosmographical Glasse* (London: John Day, 1559, folio 50). Reproduced by kind permission of the Folger Shakespeare Library.

stress on diffusion and should speak more of standardization."[11] How printing changed patterns of cultural diffusion deserves much more study than it has yet received. Moreover, individual access to diverse texts is a different matter from bringing many minds to bear on a single text. The former issue is apt to be neglected by too exclusive an emphasis on "standardization."

Considering Some Effects Produced by Standardization

Although it has to be considered in conjunction with many other issues, standardization certainly does deserve closer study. One must be careful not to skew historical perspectives by ignoring the vast difference between early printing methods and those of more recent times. But it is equally important not to go too far in the other direction and overestimate the capacity of scribal procedures to achieve the same results as did the early presses. Certainly early printing methods made it impossible to issue the kinds of "standard" editions with which modern scholars are familiar. Press variants multiplied rapidly and countless errata had to be issued. The fact remains that Erasmus or Bellarmine could issue errata; Jerome or Alcuin could not. The very act of publishing errata demonstrated a new capacity to locate textual errors with precision and to transmit this information simultaneously to scattered readers. It thus illustrates rather neatly some of the effects of standardization. However late medieval copyists were supervised – and controls were much more lax than many accounts suggest – scribes were incapable of committing the sort of "standardized" error that was produced by a compositor who dropped the word "not" from the Seventh Commandment and thus created the "wicked" Bible of 1631. If a single compositor's error could be circulated in a great many copies, so too could a single scholar's emendation.

---

[11] George Sarton, "The Quest for Truth: Scientific Progress during the Renaissance," *The Renaissance: Six Essays* (New York, 1962), 66.

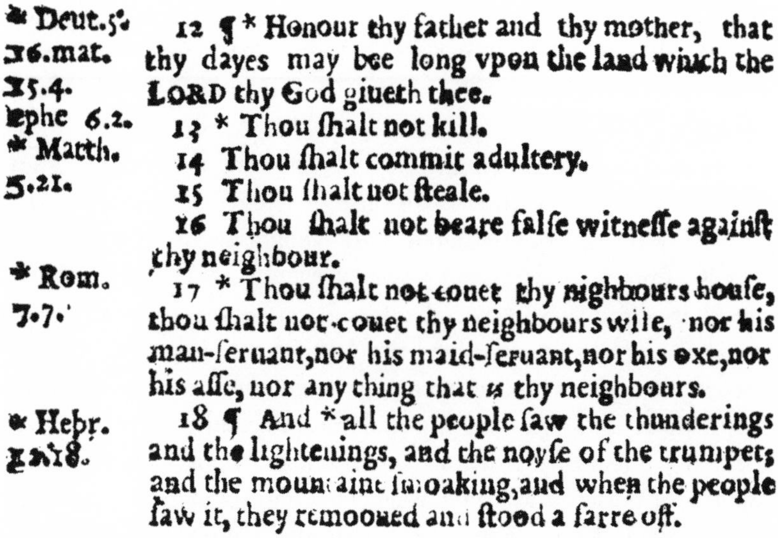

Deut.5.
16.mat.
25.4.
ephe 6.2.
Matth.
5.21.

12 ¶ * Honour thy father and thy mother, that thy dayes may bee long vpon the land which the LORD thy God giueth thee.
13 * Thou shalt not kill.
14 Thou shalt commit adultery.
15 Thou shalt not steale.
16 Thou shalt not beare false witnesse against thy neighbour.

Rom.
7.7.

17 * Thou shalt not couet thy neighbours house, thou shalt not couet thy neighbours wife, nor his man-seruant,nor his maid-seruant,nor his oxe,nor his asse, nor any thing that is thy neighbours.

Hebr.
12.18.

18 ¶ And * all the people saw the thunderings and the lightenings, and the noyse of the trumpet; and the mountaine smoaking,and when the people saw it, they remooued and stood a farre off.

Fig. 10. An enlarged passage from the so-called "wicked" Bible, printed by R. Barker in 1631, showing the commandment "thou shalt commit adultery." Reproduced by kind permission of the Rare Books Division, New York Public Library.

The need to qualify the thesis of standardization is perhaps less urgent than the need to pursue its ramifications. Sarton's remark, "Printing made it possible for the first time to publish hundreds of copies that were alike and yet might be scattered everywhere,"[12] is too important to get lost in quibbling over the fact that early printed copies were not all precisely alike. They were sufficiently uniform for scholars in different regions to correspond with each other about the same citation and for the same emendations and errors to be spotted by many eyes.

In suggesting that the implications of standardization may be underestimated, I am thinking not only about textual emendations and errors, but also about calendars, dictionaries, ephemerides, and other reference guides; about maps, charts, diagrams, and other visual aids. The capacity to produce uniform spatiotemporal images is often assigned to the invention of writing without adequate allowance being made for the difficulty of multiplying identical images by hand.

[12] Ibid., 66.

The same point applies to systems of notation, whether musical or mathematical. Indeed, it is likely that exact repeatability transformed the disciplines of the *quadrivium* rather more than those of the *trivium*.

Too many important variations were played on the theme of standardization for all of them to be listed here. This theme entered into every operation associated with typography, from the replica casting of precisely measured pieces of type to the making of woodcuts that were exactly the right dimension for meeting the surface of the types.[13] It also involved the "subliminal" impact upon scattered readers of repeated encounters with identical type styles, printers' devices, and title page ornamentation. Calligraphy itself was affected. Sixteenth-century specimen books stripped diverse scribal "hands" of personal idiosyncrasies. They did for handwriting what style books did for typography itself; what pattern books did for dressmaking, furniture, architectural motifs, or ground plans. Writing manuals, like pattern sheets and model books, were not unknown in the age of scribes. But like the manuscript grammar books and primers used by different teachers in different regions, they were variegated rather than uniform.

It seems likely that the very concept of a "style" underwent transformation when the work of hand and "stylus" was replaced by more standardized impressions made by pieces of type. Distinctions between bookhand and typeface are such that by placing a given manuscript against a printed text one can see much more clearly the idiosyncratic features of the individual hand of the scribe.[14] When set against a printed replica, a given sketch or drawing offers an even more dramatic contrast. It appears much fresher and more "original" than when it is set against a hand-drawn copy. Thus distinctions between the fresh and original as against the repeatable and copied were likely to have become sharper after the advent of printing. The

---

[13] Steinberg, *Five Hundred Years*, 25; E. P. Goldschmidt, *The Printed Book of the Renaissance: Three Lectures on Type, Illustration, Ornament* (Cambridge, 1950), 38.

[14] Bühler, *The Fifteenth-Century Book*, 37.

process of standardization also brought out more clearly all deviations from classical canons reflected in diverse buildings, statues, paintings, and *objets d'art*. "Gothic" initially meant not yet classic; "barocco," deviation from the classic norm. Ultimately the entire course of Western art history would be traced in terms of fixed classical canons and various deviations therefrom: "That procession of styles and periods known to every beginner – Classic, Romanesque, Gothic, Renaissance, Mannerist, Baroque, Rococo, Neo-Classical, Romantic – represent only a series of masks for two categories, the classical and the nonclassical."[15]

With the disappearance of variegated bookhands, styles of lettering became more sharply polarized into two distinct groups of type fonts: "Gothic" and "Roman." A similar polarization affected architectural designs. A heightened consciousness of the three orders set down by Vitruvius accompanied the output of architectural prints and engravings along with new treatises and old texts. Heightened awareness of distant regional boundaries was also encouraged by the output of more uniform maps containing more uniform boundaries and place names. Similar developments affected local customs, laws, languages, and costumes. A given book of dress patterns published in Seville in the 1520s made "Spanish" fashions visible throughout the far-flung Habsburg Empire. New guidance was provided to tailors and dressmakers, and at the same time, the diversity of local attire became all the more striking to the inhabitants of Brussels or Lima.

A fuller recognition of diversity was indeed a concomitant of standardization. Sixteenth-century publications not only spread identical fashions but also encouraged the collection of diverse ones. Books illustrating diverse costumes, worn throughout the world, were studied by artists and engravers and duplicated in so many contexts that stereotypes of regional dress styles were developed. They acquired a paper life for all eternity and may be recognized even now on dolls, in operas, or at costume balls.

[15] E. H. Gombrich, *Norm and Form: Studies in the Art of the Renaissance* (London, 1966), 83–4.

Moduli. 2. Parte. 14.

Moduli. 5. et Parte. 10.

XXII

SCRITTIONE DE LL

XII.

SE il piedestallo di quest' ordine Corintio fosse la terza parte della colonna, sarebbe moduli sei e duoi terzi, ma si puo comportare di moduli sette per piu sueltezza, conforme molto, e conveniente a simil ordine, & anco perche il netto del piedestallo senza la cimasa e bassamento riesca di duoi quadri, come si puo ve- dere per li suoi numeri il resto cioe la base, è la cimisa, & il bassamento, per essere notato minutamente, e anco la imposta dell' arco, non accade altra scrittura.
A Torro overo bastone superiore, B Toro overo bastone inferiore.

Indien het Pedestael van dese Corintische Orden is het derdepart van de colomne / soo sal het houden ses Modulos ende ⅔ / maer men mach het wel maken van 7 Modulos, om te meer stijvicheyt / die dese Orden seer ghevoeghlijck is ende wel past: Oock mede op dat het pedestael / sonder het Cimatium ende basement / even op twee vierkanten uptkomt / gelijck men sien mach aen de getallen. De reste / te weten het basis 't cimatium ende basement / de wijl sy op 't nauste zijn aengeteeckent / als mede d imposta oft opstellingh van de boge / soo en hoeven wy daer niet meer van te schrijven.
A De Torus oft stock van boven / B De Torus oft stock van beneden.

SI le Piedestal de ceste ordonnance Corinthienne est le tiers de la colomne, il tiendra six mo- dules & ⅔, mais on le pourra bien faire de sept Modules pour plus grande solidité, fort con- forme & convenable a ceste ordonnance : & aussi, afin que le Piedestal, sans la cimace & base- ment, revienne a deux quarrez, comme l'on pourra voir par les nombres. Le reste, c'est a savoir la base, la cimace & basement, puis qu'ils sont notez par menu, comme aussi l'imposition de l'arc, il n'est ja besoing d'en escrire d'avantage.
A Le Tore ou baston d'enhaut, B Le Tore ou baston d'embas.

Me sal das Pedestal von diser Corintischen orden das dritteheil ist von die Colomne / so sol es halten 6 Moduln vnd ⅔ / aber man mag es wol machen von 7 Moduln / wegen mehrer stercke / welche diesen orden gar fuglich ist / vnd auch / auff dass es Pedestal / ohn das Cimatium / vnd basement / gerad auff zwey viereckten auß kompt / gleich man an die zalh sehen mag. De rest / nemblich das Cimatium vnd Basement / die weil sie auffs genawste sein angezeichnet / wie auch die imposta oder auffstellung von denen boge / so ist nicht nötig davon mehr zu schreiben.
A Der Torus oder stock von oben / B Der Torus oder stock von vnten.

IF the Pedestal of this Corinthian Order bee the third part of the Columne, it shall containe six modulos en and two thirds, but you may make it of 7 modulos, for the greater solidi- ty, which is verry conformable and befitting this Order : as also, that the Pedestal, without the Cimaet and basement commeth out even in 2 fouresquares even as you may see by the Num- bers. The rest, to witt the base, the Cimate and basement the while they are noted least, as also the Impost er setting up of the Bow or Arch, so that wee neede not write more thereof.
A The Torus or piece on high, B The Torus or piece belou.

Fig. 11 (opposite and above). A heightened consciousness of the ancient archi- tectural orders described by Vitruvius accompanied the output of prints and printed texts. Detailed rules for the Corinthian Order (above) are set forth in Italian, Dutch, French, German, and English, accompanying the engraving on the opposite page. From Giacomo Barozzio Vignola, *Regola de cinque ordini d'architettura* (Amsterdam: Jan. Janz., 1642, pp. 54–5). Reproduced by kind permission of the Folger Shake- speare Library.

61

Fig. 12. Books for dressmakers and tailors published in sixteenth-century Seville made "Spanish" fashions visible through the far-flung Habsburg Empire. The pattern shown above comes from Diego de Freyle, *Geometria y traca para el oficio de los sastres* (Seville: Fernando Diaz, 1588, folio 17 verso). Reproduced by kind permission of the Folger Shakespeare Library.

Concepts pertaining to uniformity and to diversity – to the typical and to the unique – are interdependent. They represent two sides of the same coin. In this regard one might consider the emergence of a new sense of individualism as a by-product of the new forms of standardization. The more standardized the type, indeed, the more compelling the sense of an idiosyncratic personal self. It was just this sense that was captured in the *Essays* of Montaigne. As a volatile creature, concerned with trivial events, the author of the *Essays* contrasted in almost every way with the ideal types conveyed by other books. The latter presented princes, courtiers, councillors, merchants, schoolmasters, husbandmen, and the like in terms which made readers ever more aware, not merely of their shortcomings in their assigned roles, but also of the existence of a solitary singular self, characterized by all the peculiar traits that were unshared by others – traits which had no redeeming social or exemplary functions and hence were deemed to be of no literary worth. By presenting himself, in all modesty, as an atypical individual and by portraying with loving care every one of his peculiarities, Montaigne brought this private self out of hiding, so to speak. He displayed it for public inspection in a deliberate way for the first time.

Traditional rhetorical conventions had allowed for the difference in tone between addressing a large assemblage in a public arena, where strong lungs and broad strokes were required, and pleading a case in a courtroom, which called for careful attention to detail

Fig. 13. Diversity accompanied standardization. Books illustrating diverse costumes were also issued in the sixteenth century. This picture of an "indo-africano" comes from Cesare Vecellio, *Degli habiti antichi et moderni di diverse parti del mondo* (Venice: Damian Zenaro, 1590, pp. 495–6). Reproduced by kind permission of the Folger Shakespeare Library.

and a more soft-spoken, closely argued, intimate approach. But no precedent existed for addressing a large crowd of people who were not gathered together in one place but were scattered in separate dwellings and who, as solitary individuals with divergent interests, were more receptive to intimate interchanges than to broad-gauged rhetorical effects. The informal essay which was devised by Montaigne was a most ingenious method of coping with this new situation. He thus established a new basis for achieving intimate contact with unknown readers who might admire portraits of worthy men from a distance but felt more at home when presented with an admittedly unworthy self. Above all, he provided a welcome assurance that the isolating sense of singularity which was felt by the solitary reader had been experienced by another human being and was, indeed, capable of being widely shared.

Even while an author such as Montaigne was developing a new informal and idiosyncratic genre of literature and laying bare all the quirks and peculiarities that define the individual "me, myself" as against the type, other genres of literature were defining ideal types and delineating appropriate roles for priest and merchant, nobleman and lady, well-bred boy and girl.

Here as elsewhere the "exactly repeatable pictorial statement" helped to reinforce the effects of issuing standard editions. Repeated encounters with identical images of couples representing three social groups – noble, burgher, peasant – wearing distinctive costumes and set against distinctive regional landscapes probably encouraged a sharpened sense of social divisions as well as regional ones. At the same time the circulation of royal portraits and engravings of royal entries made it possible for a reigning dynast to impress a personal presence in a new way upon the consciousness of all subjects. The difference between the older repeatable image which was stamped on coins and the newer by-product of print is suggested by one of the more celebrated episodes of the French Revolution. The individual features of emperors and kings were not sufficiently detailed when stamped on coins for their faces to be recognized when they traveled incognito. But a portrait engraved on paper money enabled an alert Frenchman to recognize and halt Louis XVI at Varennes.

It should be noted that a new alertness to both the individual and the typical was likely to come first to those who were responsible for compiling and editing the new costume manuals, style books, commemorations of royal entries, and regional guides. Just as the act of publishing errata sharpened attention to error within the printer's workshop, so too did the preparation of copy pertaining to architectural motifs, regional boundaries, place names, details of dress, and local customs. It seems likely that a new awareness of place and period and more concern about assigning the proper trappings to each were fostered by the very act of putting together illustrated guidebooks and costume manuals. To be sure, the use – in the Nuremberg Chronicle, for example – of the same woodcut to designate several different cities (such as Mainz and Bologna and Lyons) or of the same portrait head to designate different historic personages may seem to argue against such a thesis. Early printers often frugally used a few prints for many diverse purposes. An Ulm edition of 1483 "has one cut which is used thirty-seven times and altogether nineteen blocks do duty for one hundred and thirty-four illustrations."[16] Yet the 1480s also saw an artist-engraver commissioned to produce fresh renderings of cities and plants encountered on a pilgrimage to the Holy Land. Erhard Reuwich's illustrations of cities for Breydenbach's *Peregrinatio in Terram Sanctam* (1486) and of plants for Schoeffer's vernacular herbal *Gart der Gesundheit* (1485) did point the way to an increasingly precise and detailed recording of observations in visual form. The careless reuse of a few blocks for many purposes also needs to be distinguished from the deliberate reuse of a "typical" town or portrait head to serve as pointers or guide marks helping readers find their way about a text. Whatever the purpose served by the cuts of towns and heads in a work such as the Nuremberg Chronicle, previous remarks about individuation and standardization also seem cogent. The more standardized the image of typical town, head, or plant, the more clearly the idiosyncratic features of separate towns, heads, or plants could be perceived by observant draftsmen. Painters and carvers had been rendering natural forms on manuscript margins, church vestments, or stone fonts during previous centuries. But their

[16] David Bland, *A History of Book Illustration*, 2nd ed. (Berkeley, 1969), 106.

talents were used for new ends by technical publication programs initiated by master printers and learned editors from the days of Peter Schoeffer on.

Here as elsewhere, we need to recall that early printers were responsible not only for publishing innovative reference guides but also for compiling some of them. To those of us who think in terms of later divisions of labor, the repertoire of roles undertaken by early printers seems so large as to be almost inconceivable. A master printer himself might serve not only as publisher and bookseller, but also as indexer-abridger-translator-lexicographer-chronicler. Many printers, to be sure, simply replicated whatever was handed them in a slapdash way. But there were those who took pride in their craft and who hired learned assistants. Such masters were in the unusual position of being able to profit from passing on to others systems they devised for themselves. They not only practiced self-help but preached it as well. In the later Middle Ages, practical manuals had been written to guide inquisitors, confessors, priests, and pilgrims – and lay merchants as well. Although large *summae* now attract scholarly attention, medieval scribes also turned out compact *summulae*, comprehensive guidebooks designed to offer practical advice on diverse matters – ranging from composing a sermon to dying in one's bed.[17] Here, as in many other ways, the printer seems to have taken over where the clerical scribe left off. But in so doing, he greatly amplified and augmented older themes. There is simply no equivalent in scribal culture for the "avalanche" of "how-to" books which poured off the new presses, explaining by "easy steps" just how to master diverse skills, ranging from playing a musical instrument to keeping accounts.

[17] Edward M. Peters, "Editing Inquisitors' Manuals in the 16th Century...," *The Library Chronicle* (University of Pennsylvania) XL (Winter 1974): 95–107.

———→

Fig. 14 (opposite). The use of one block to illustrate several towns is shown on the opposite page by the way Verona (above) and Mantua (below) are presented in the Nuremberg Chronicle. From Hartmann Schedel, *Liber chronicorum* (Nuremberg: Anton Koberger, 12 July 1493, folios 68 and 84). Reproduced by kind permission of the Folger Shakespeare Library.

Verona

Mantua

Fig. 15. Identical portrait heads of Baldus and Lorenzo Valla also decorate the Nuremberg Chronicle. The reuse of a given woodcut may have been aimed at pointing the reader to a given topic (such as a town or personage) rather than at conveying a particular profile. From Hartmann Schedel, *Liber chronicorum* (Nuremberg: Anton Koberger, 12 July 1493, folios 236 and 246). Reproduced by kind permission of the Folger Shakespeare Library.

Fig. 16. Identical portrait heads of Compostella and Jean Gerson also from the Nuremberg Chronicle. From Hartmann Schedel, *Liber chronicorum* (Nuremberg: Anton Koberger, 12 July 1493, folios 213 and 240). Reproduced by kind permission of the Folger Shakespeare Library.

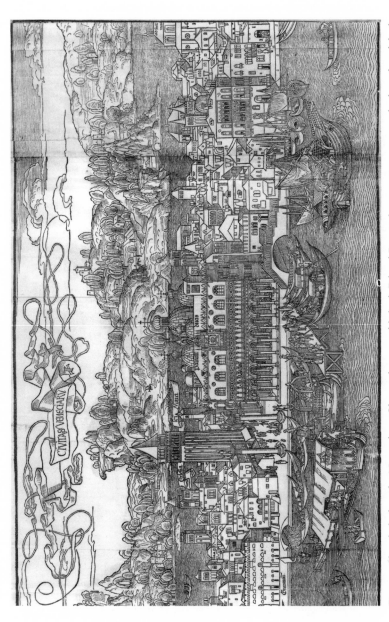

Fig. 17. Shortly before the Nuremberg Chronicle was published, Erhard Reuwich, an artist-engraver, had produced fresh renderings of cities and plants encountered on a trip to the Holy Land. His picture of Venice contains recognizable architectural features (along with a conventional out-of-place landscape in the background). From Erhard Reuwich's illustration of Venice in Bernhard von Breydenbach, *Peregrinatio in Terram Sanctam* (Mainz: Erhard Reuwich [types of Peter Schoeffer], 1486). Reproduced by kind permission of the Department of Special Collections, Stanford University Libraries.

Many early capitalist industries required efficient planning, methodical attention to detail, and rational calculation. The decisions made by early printers, however, directly affected both tool making and symbol making. Their products reshaped powers to manipulate objects, to perceive and think about varied phenomena. Scholars concerned with "modernization" or "rationalization" might profitably think more about the new kind of brainwork fostered by the silent scanning of maps, tables, charts, diagrams, dictionaries, and grammars. They also need to look more closely at the routines pursued by those who compiled and produced such reference guides. These routines were conducive to a new *esprit de système*. In his preface to his pioneering atlas which contained supplementary texts and indexes, Abraham Ortelius likened his *Theatrum* to a "well furnished shoppe" which was so arranged that readers could easily find whatever instruments they might want to obtain.[18] "It's much easier to find things when they are each disposed in place and not scattered haphazardly," remarked another sixteenth-century publisher.[19] He was justifying the way he had reorganized a text he had edited. He might equally well have been complaining to a clerk who had mislaid some account papers pertaining to the large commercial enterprise he ran.

Some Effects Produced by Reorganizing Texts and Reference Guides: Rationalizing, Codifying, and Cataloguing Data

Editorial decisions made by early printers with regard to layout and presentation probably helped to reorganize the thinking of readers. McLuhan's suggestion that scanning lines of print affected

---

[18] Abraham Ortelius, "Message to the Reader," *Theatre of the Whole World* (London, 1606), facsimile ed. (Antwerp, 1968).

[19] Cited by Natalie Z. Davis, "Publisher Guillaume Rouillé, Businessman and Humanist," *Editing Sixteenth Century Texts*, ed. R. J. Schoeck (Toronto, 1966), 100.

thought processes is at first glance somewhat mystifying. But further reflection suggests that the thoughts of readers are guided by the way the contents of books are arranged and presented. Basic changes in book format might well lead to changes in thought patterns.

For example, printed reference works encouraged a repeated recourse to alphabetical order. Ever since the sixteenth century, memorizing a fixed sequence of discrete letters represented by meaningless symbols and sounds has been the gateway to book learning for all children in the West. This was so little the case before printing that a Genoese compiler of a thirteenth-century encyclopedia could write that "'amo' comes before 'bibo' because 'a' is the first letter of the former and 'b' is the first letter of the latter and 'a' comes before 'b'... by the grace of God working in me, I have devised this order."[20]

Other ways of ordering data were no less likely to be used in scribal reference works. As for scribal library catalogues, the full use of alphabet systems by the fabled custodians of the Alexandrian Library had vanished with the institution itself. "When it comes to cataloguing, a poem is a far cry from a card index," note Reynolds and Wilson, in connection with some verses attributed to Alcuin describing the eighth-century library at York.[21] The rhymed book list was incomplete because metrical exigencies required the exclusion of various works. Medieval library catalogues, to be sure, were not usually in verse, but they were, nevertheless, far from being ordered along the lines of modern card indexes – or, for that matter, along any kind of uniform lines. They reflected the multiform character of scribal culture and were, for the most part, idiosyncratically arranged, designed to help a given custodian find his way to the books which reposed in cupboards or chests or were chained on desks in a special chamber.

[20] Cited in Lloyd W. Daly, *Contributions to a History of Alphabetization in Antiquity and the Middle Ages* (Brussels, 1967), 91.
[21] L. D. Reynolds and N. G. Wilson, *Scribes and Scholars* (Oxford, 1968), 76.

The increasing use of full alphabetical order, both for book cat-alogues and for indexes, has been attributed to the introduction of paper, which made it less costly to prepare the necessary card files. Doubtless, cheaper writing materials made indexing and catalogu-ing less costly, but they did little to overcome a natural resistance to repeatedly copying out long lists by hand. There were occasional efforts to make one index valid for several copies, but they were invariably thwarted by scribal errors of diverse kinds. For the most part, the owner of a medieval compendium, preparing an index for his own use, felt no obligation to employ anybody else's system but rather followed whatever method he chose. Similarly, a custodian keeping track of a library collection had no incentive to arrange his records in accordance with those of other librarians – and no incen-tive, either, to make the arrangement of volumes follow any clear order at all. (On the basis of encounters with some living guardians of rare books, one suspects that the more unfathomable the arrange-ment of a given inventory the better some medieval custodians were pleased.) After the advent of printing, however, shelf lists were sup-plemented by sales catalogues aimed at readers outside library walls, while any index compiled for one text could be duplicated hundreds of times. Thus the competitive commercial character of the printed book trade when coupled with typographical standardization made more systematic cataloguing and indexing seem not only feasible but highly desirable as well. To tap markets and attract potential pur-chasers while keeping competitors at bay called for booksellers' lists that presented titles in a clear and coherent arrangement and for edi-tions that could be described as "well indexed" as well as "new and improved."

Peter Schoeffer's prospectus, which claimed that his firm offered "more complete and better arranged" indexes as well as "more read-able" texts than those of his competitors, should not be taken at face value. The early printer, like the modern press agent, often promised more than he could deliver. Nevertheless, the pressure of competi-tion did spur efforts to look for ways of improving familiar products and worked against the inherent resistance to change which had hitherto characterized the copying of valued texts. A rationalization of format helped to systematize scholarship in diverse fields. Robert Estienne's five Paris book catalogues issued between 1542 and 1547 reflect a rapid advance along many fronts. Divided along trilingual lines, with each section arranged in a uniform progression, beginning with alphabets in Hebrew, Greek, and Latin, and going on to grammars, dictionaries, and texts, these catalogues have justly been described as "a miracle of lucid arrangement."[22] The same skills were used by Estienne for his pioneering work in lexicography and his succession of biblical editions.[23] Much as Estienne's successive improved editions of the Bible produced in sixteenth-century Paris might be compared with the one so-called edition turned out by scribes in thirteenth-century Paris, so, too, his many contributions to lexicography might be compared with that single unique bilingual lexicon produced by thirteenth-century schoolmen under the direction of Robert Grosseteste.

Such comparisons are useful, not only because they show what the new power of the press could achieve, but also because they suggest that attempts at lexicography had been made before print. Efforts at codifying and systematizing which predated the new presses had long been made by preachers and teachers who had compiled concordances for the use of other churchmen or arranged scriptural passages, sermon topics, and commentaries for themselves. A poem is not only "a far cry from a card index"; it is also fairly distant from many scholastic treatises on medical and legal as well as theological subjects. Such treatises were surrounded by glosses and bristled with abbreviations and marginal notations. Some contained diagrams which showed the branches of learning, schematized abstract concepts, or connected human organs with heavenly bodies. Others were furnished with small tabs made of parchment or paper to permit easy reference. One must be wary, in other words, of overstating the novelties introduced by printing or of overlooking how

---

[22] Graham Pollard and Albert Ehrman, *The Distribution of Books by Catalogue from the Invention of Printing to A.D. 1800* (Cambridge, 1965), 53.

[23] DeWitt T. Starnes, *Robert Estienne's Influence on Lexicography* (Austin, TX, 1963), 86–7.

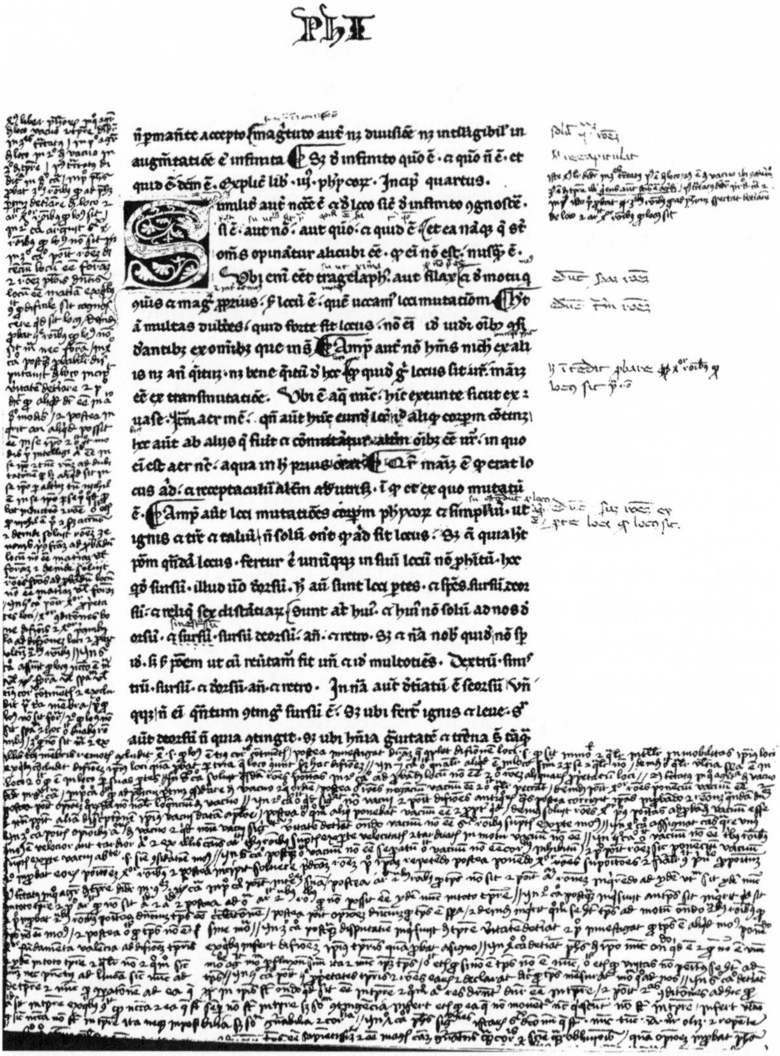

Fig. 18. This example of a medieval treatise, surrounded by a gloss and bristling with abbreviations, is taken from a manuscript copy on vellum of Aristotle, *Physica* (ca. 1300, leaf 22 recto). Reproduced by kind permission of the Folger Shakespeare Library.

previous developments helped to channel the uses to which the new tool was put. Such devices as diagrams and brackets, along with the habit of cross referencing between one passage and another, were not uncommon among medieval compilers and commentators, even though such practices took idiosyncratic and variegated forms. Just as the uniform use of alphabetic order for all reference words did not result from the invention of printing alone but required an alphabetic written language as a base, so, too, much of the cataloguing, cross referencing, and indexing that marked sixteenth-century scholarship should be regarded not only as by-products of typographic culture but also as reflecting new opportunities among clergymen and clerks to realize old goals:

> At his most characteristic, medieval man...was an organizer, a codifier, a builder of systems. He wanted a place for everything and everything in the right place. Distinction, definition, tabulation were his delight... There was nothing medieval people did better or liked better than sorting out and tidying up. Of all our modern inventions, I suspect that they would most have admired the card index.[24]

As this citation from C. S. Lewis suggests, one need not think only of "well furnished shops" when considering the urge to rationalize Western institutions. A desire to have "everything in its right place" was shared by the medieval schoolman and the early capitalist alike. The printing shop performed a significant, albeit neglected, function by bringing together intellectual and commercial activities which reinforced each other and thus created an especially powerful, almost irresistible drive.

On the other hand, one must guard against the temptation to make too much of occasional medieval anticipations of trends that could not be really launched until after printing. The schoolmen might have admired our card index, but their sense of order was not based upon its use. A unique bilingual lexicon cannot do the same

---

[24] C. S. Lewis. *The Discarded Image: An Introduction to Medieval and Renaissance Literature* (Cambridge, 1974), 10.

work as hundreds of trilingual reference guides. There is simply no counterpart in medieval houses of study or monastic libraries for the printed polyglot Bibles of the sixteenth and seventeenth centuries or for the reference apparatus which accompanied them.

Between 1500 and 1800 more than seventy lexicons devoted solely to Hebrew would be issued. In the second half of the sixteenth century, Christopher Plantin set out to produce a slightly revised edition of the Complutensian Polyglot Bible of 1517–1522. He ended by publishing a monumental new work containing five volumes of text and three of reference materials which included grammars and dictionaries for the Greek, Hebrew, Aramaic, and Syriac languages. Further expansion came with the Paris polyglot edition of 1645, and the climax came in mid-seventeenth-century England. The London "polyglotte" of 1657 was announced by a prospectus which boasted of its superiority to all prior editions (in terms which were later echoed by Bishop Sprat in his praise of the Royal Society). Its contents suggest how much territory had been conquered after two centuries of printing. It presented texts in "Hebrew, Samaritan, Septuagint Greek, Chaldee, Syriac, Arabic, Ethiopian, Persian and Vulgate Latin," thus adding to the stock of type fonts used by Western scholars for oriental studies. Its elaborate appendixes showed how Bible printing spurred the modern knowledge industry. They comprised

> a vast apparatus including a table of ancient chronology prepared by Louis Cappel, descriptions and maps of the Holy Land and of Jerusalem; plans of the temple; treatises on Hebrew coins, on weights and measures, on the origin of language and of the alphabet, on the Hebrew idiom; an historical account of the chief editions and principal versions of the Scriptures; a table of variant readings, with an essay on the integrity and authority of the original texts and other matter.[25]

---

[25] Preserved Smith, *A History of Modern Culture*, vol. 1, *The Great Renewal*, rev. ed. (New York, 1930), retitled *Origins of Modern Culture 1543–1687* (New York, 1962), 251.

The output of tables, catalogues, gazetteers, and other reference works satisfied practical as well as religious impulses. Whereas Robert Estienne's work on lexicography came as a fallout from his biblical editions, one of Christopher Plantin's lexicographic contributions came simply from his position as an immigrant businessman. After settling in Antwerp and establishing ties with Leiden, Plantin decided to learn Dutch. Never one for wasted effort, he "placed in piles and in alphabetical order" each word that he learned. Thus was launched a collaborative venture which resulted in the *Thesaurus theutonicae linguae* of 1573 – the "first Dutch dictionary worth its name."[26]

Placing words (and letters) in piles according to alphabetical order was indeed a ubiquitous routine in the printer's workshop. The preparation of each index was in itself an exercise in textual analysis – one which was applied to many works that had never been indexed before. Indexing and other procedures entailed in copyediting pointed scholarly activities in a somewhat different direction than had the preparation of orations, dialogues, and other occasional commemorative pieces which had preoccupied earlier humanists. Objections posed by the latter to the barbarous language and bookhands used by the schoolmen were supplemented by new objections to the barbarous arrangement of medieval compendia with their great mass of elaborate digressions and seemingly unrelated details. The earliest printed editions were faithful replicas of these "barbarous" scribal compendia, to be sure; but the very act of duplication was a necessary preliminary to later rearrangement. A disorder previously concealed by oral presentation and piecemeal copying became more visible to copy editors and indexers and more offensive to publishers who valued systematic routines. Classical criteria of unity, internal consistency, and harmony were extended beyond orations, poems, and paintings to encompass the rearrangement of

[26] Leon Vöet, *The Golden Compasses: A History and Evaluation of the Printing and Publishing Activities of the Officina Plantiniana at Antwerp* (Amsterdam, 1969), I:132.

large compilations and of entire fields of study which were not within the early humanist domain.

> Clarity and logic of organization, the disposition of matter on the printed page became . . . a preoccupation of editors, almost an end in itself. It is a phenomenon familiar to a student of encyclopedic books of the late sixteenth century, relating to the increased fascination with the technical possibilities of typesetting and the great influence exerted by the methodology of Peter Ramus . . . The Ramist doctrine that every subject could be treated topically, that the best kind of exposition was that which proceeded by analysis was enthusiastically adopted by publishers and editors.[27]

As Neal Gilbert suggests, the term "methodus," which had been banned as barbarous by early humanists, came into its own a full century before Descartes – appearing "with almost unbelievable frequency in the titles of sixteenth-century treatises."[28] The Ramist doctrine probably owed much of its popularity to the fact that printing made of textbook writing a new and profitable genre. The mere preparation of differently graded textbooks for teaching varied disciplines encouraged a reassessment of inherited procedures and a rearrangement of approaches to diverse fields. But the new emphasis placed on system and method was not exclusively pedagogical or confined to textbook writing. It was also applied to texts that the early humanists held in disdain; that is, to texts used for graduate studies by the faculties of theology, law, and medicine.

The medieval teacher of the *Corpus Juris* was "not concerned to show how each component was related to the logic of the whole,"[29] partly because very few teachers on law faculties had a chance to see the *Corpus Juris* as a whole. The accidental separation of portions of the manuscript of the *Digest* had given rise to two separate "ordinary"

[27] Gerald Strauss, "A Sixteenth-Century Encyclopedia: Sebastian Münster's *Cosmography* and its Edition," *From the Renaissance to the Counter-Reformation*, ed. C. H. Carter (New York, 1965), 152.

[28] Neal Gilbert, *Renaissance Concepts of Method* (New York, 1960), 66.

[29] Julian Franklin, *Jean Bodin and the Sixteenth Century Revolution in the Methodology of Law and History* (New York, 1963), 27–8.

and "extraordinary" lecture series even before successive layers of commentary were deposited by the glossators and post-glossators.[30] The subdivision of portions into "puncta" to be read aloud within time limits set by academic calendars also led to fragmentation and to throwing sequences into further disarray. To gain access to the most important manuscript source for the *Digest* required a pilgrimage to Pisa, where the Florentine Codex was closely guarded and could be examined, if at all, only for a short time.[31] For a full century after the advent of printing, this problem of access continued to plague those who tried to clean "the Augean stables of law" by cutting through the thicket of commentaries and reconstructing the corpus in its ancient form. The legal scholars were barred (quite literally in the case of Budé, who saw the manuscript only through a grate) by the guardians of the precious Codex who allowed visitors only fleeting glimpses of the relic.[32] Its publication in 1553 was thus an event of some significance – one which enabled a new generation, led by Jacques Cujas, to complete what earlier scholars, such as Budé, Alciato, and Amerbach, had begun. Cujas's corrections ranged from "the simplest textual errors" to "anachronistic substitutions." He also undertook "the job of indexing the citations." By the end of the century the whole compilation had been made available in an emended and indexed form.[33] Stripped of the encrustation of glosses, the ancient compilation was rendered ever more stylistically coherent and internally consistent. By the same token, it came to seem less and less relevant to contemporary jurisprudence. Very much as was the case with Ciceronian Latin, when complete restoration had been successfully applied to the letter of the ancient code, its living spirit vanished for good.

A body of living law was also affected by copyediting, indexing, and emendation. Even while ancient compilations such as the

[30] H. Rashdall, *The Universities of Europe in the Middle Ages*, ed. F. M. Powicke and A. B. Emden (Oxford, 1936), I:205.

[31] Ibid., 255.

[32] Donald R. Kelley, *Foundations of Modern Historical Scholarship* (New York, 1970), 67, 113.

[33] Ibid., 114.

Corpus Juris seemed less relevant to current practice, a sharper cutting edge was given to some statutes and *ordonnances* which were in
effect. In Tudor England, royal proclamations, once printed, were no
longer merely fixed to walls and doors and other public places, but
were also collected into a convenient octavo volume and furnished
with a table of contents for easy reference. Beginning with Caxton's
little-known contemporary, W. de Machlinia, in the 1480s, English
law printing attracted an increasing number of enterprising Londoners such as Pynson, Redman, Berthelet, and Thomas More's versatile
brother-in-law, John Rastell:

> Keenly aware of one another's output, each made efforts to keep
> their own wares up to date and attractive to the legal public.
> It was probably to counter the complete abridgement of the
> Statutes . . . published by Redman in 1528, that Pynson reissued
> his 1521 edition . . . with a new title page and four folios of "newe
> addicions" . . . Rastell could not let these actions go unchallenged
> and replied with his *Magnum Abbreviamentum* listing the statutes
> down to 1523 abridged in . . . Latin, Anglo-French and English.[34]

Publications of abridgments and lists of statutes issued by John
Rastell and his son offer a good illustration of how a rationalized
book format might affect vital organs of the body politic. The systematic arrangement of titles, the tables which followed strict alphabetical order, the indexes and cross references to accurately numbered paragraphs all show how new tools available to printers helped
to bring more order and method into a significant body of public
law.[35] Until the end of the fifteenth century, it was not always easy
to decide just "what a statute really was," and confusion had long
been compounded concerning diverse "great" charters. In "Englishing and printing" the *Great Boke of Statutes 1530–1533*, John
Rastell took care to provide an introductory "Tabula": a forty-six-
page "chronological register by chapters of the statutes 1327 to
1523." He was not merely providing a table of contents; he was also

---

[34]   H. S. Bennett, *English Books and Readers 1475–1557* (Cambridge, 1952), 77.
[35]   John Cowley, "The Abridgement of Statutes," *The Library*, 4th ser. XII (September 1931): 128.

offering a systematic review of parliamentary history – the first many readers had ever seen.[36]

This sort of spectacular innovation, while deserving close study, should not divert attention from much less conspicuous, more ubiquitous changes. Increasing familiarity with regularly numbered pages, punctuation marks, section breaks, running heads, indexes, and so forth helped to reorder the thought of *all* readers, whatever their profession or craft. The use of arabic numbers for pagination suggests how the most inconspicuous innovation could have weighty consequences – in this case, a more accurate indexing, annotation, and cross referencing resulted. Most studies of printing have, quite rightly, singled out the regular provision of title pages as the most significant new feature associated with the printed book format. How the title page contributed to the cataloguing of books and the bibliographer's craft scarcely needs to be spelled out. How it contributed to new habits of placing and dating, in general, does, I think, call for further thought.

THE NEW PROCESS OF DATA COLLECTION: FROM THE CORRUPTED COPY TO THE IMPROVED EDITION

When turning out successive editions of a given reference work or set of maps, printers did not only compete with rivals and improve on their predecessors. They were also able to improve on themselves. The succession of Latin Bibles turned out by Robert Estienne and the succession of atlases turned out by Ortelius suggest how the immemorial drift of scribal culture had been not merely arrested but actually reversed.

In making this point, one is likely to run up against objections posed by scholars who have good reason to be sceptical about all claims made on behalf of early printers. Prefaces and blurbs which repeatedly boast of improvement are belied by actual evidence of uncritical copying and – even worse – of ignorant emendation.

---

[36] H. J. Graham, "'Our Tong Maternall Marvellously Amendyd and Augmentyd': The First Englishing and Printing of the Medieval Statutes at Large, 1530–1533," *U. C. L. A. Law Bulletin* XIII (November 1965): 58–98.

Comparisons of scribal reference works with early printed versions often show that an age-old process of corruption was aggravated and accelerated after print. In the field of Bible illustration, for example, inferior-quality blocks used repeatedly led to unintelligible lettering; misinterpretations of blurred captions by ignorant crafts-men produced mystifying juxtapositions; all errors were compounded by pirated editions issued over the course of decades.[37]

Early printed botany books underwent much the same kind of degradations as did early printed Bibles. A sequence of printed herbals beginning in the 1480s and going to 1526 reveals a "steady increase in the amount of distortion," with the final product – an English herbal of 1526 – providing a "remarkably sad example of what happens to visual information as it passed from copyist to copy-ist."[38] But in the very course of accelerating a process of corruption, which had gone on in a much slower and more irregular fashion under the aegis of scribes, the new medium made this process more visible to learned men and offered a way of overcoming it for the first time. In the hands of ignorant printers driving to make quick profits, data tended to get garbled at an ever more rapid pace. But under the guidance of technically proficient masters, the new technology also provided a way of transcending the limits which scribal procedures had imposed upon technically proficient masters in the past. Under proper supervision, fresh observations could at long last be dup-licated without being blurred or blotted out over the course of time.

Some sixteenth-century editors and publishers simply duplicated old compendia. But others created vast networks of correspondents and solicited criticism of each edition, sometimes publicly promising to mention the names of readers who sent in new information or who spotted the errors which would be weeded out:

> By the simple expedient of being honest with his readers and invit-ing criticism and suggestions, Ortelius made his *Theatrum* a sort of cooperative enterprise on an international basis. He received

---

[37] James Strachan, *Early Bible Illustrations: A Short Study* (Cambridge, 1957), passim.

[38] Ivins, *Prints and Visual Communications*, 40.

helpful suggestions from far and wide and cartographers stumbled over themselves to send him their latest maps of regions not covered in the *Theatrum*.

The *Theatrum* was . . . speedily reprinted several times . . . Suggestions for corrections and revisions kept Ortelius and his engravers busy altering plates for new editions . . . Within three years he had acquired so many new maps that he issued a supplement of 17 maps which were afterwards incorporated in the *Theatrum*. When Ortelius died in 1598 at least 28 editions of the atlas had been published in Latin, Dutch, German, French and Spanish . . . The last edition was published by the House of Plantin in 1612.[39]

Not every edition, to be sure, eliminated all the errors that were spotted; good intentions stated in prefaces failed to be honored in actual manufacture. Even so, the requests of publishers often encouraged readers to launch their own research projects and field trips, which resulted in additional publication programs. Thus a knowledge explosion was set off. The fallout from Ortelius's editions, for example, encompassed treatises on topography and local history ranging from Muscovy to Wales.

The solicitor or recipient of new data was not always a printer or publisher. Often it was the author or editor of a given series of editions who heard from readers about errors or additions to be incorporated in a later edition. As Mattioli's commentaries on Dioscorides, first published in 1554, ran through one edition after another, they were periodically revised and corrected on the basis of specimens and information received from correspondents. Exotic plants were thus introduced to Europeans (so that the horse chestnut, lilac, and tulip came from Turkey into botanical gardens in Europe via Mattioli's edition of 1581). The proliferation of foreign reports pertaining to fruits and seeds also led to more complete and precise descriptions of domestic plants.

By the middle of the sixteenth century, botanists were vying with each other to obtain novelties from India, from the New

[39] Lloyd A. Brown, *The Story of Maps* (Boston, 1959), 163–4.

World, from frozen countries, marshes, and deserts – from any-where and everywhere. The plants and animals of distant exotic countries were either radically new or sufficiently different from those already known to cause perplexities and to invite further investigation... There emerged a new kind of scientist, the trav-eling naturalist... The greedy adventurers of early days were now replaced by men in search of knowledge...

The discoveries made in foreign lands excited the natural-ists who were obliged to stay at home, such as physicians, pro-fessors and keepers of botanical gardens and greenhouses, and forced them to describe more accurately and completely the fau-nas and floras of their own countries... So much new knowledge was amassed that it tended to create confusion and there was an increasing need for new surveys.[40]

The new surveys led, in turn, to further interchanges, which set off new investigations and the accumulation of more data, mak-ing necessary more refined classification, and so on – *ad infinitum*. The sequence of improved editions and ever-expanding reference works was a sequence without limits – unlike the great library collec-tions amassed by Alexandrian rulers and Renaissance princes. The destruction of the Alexandrian Library in the distant past and the destruction of the great collection amassed by Matthias Corvinus in the recent past were noted by Conrad Gesner in the dedication of the first edition of his massive bibliography, the *Bibliotheca universalis* (1545), which listed some ten thousand titles of Latin, Greek, and Hebrew works.[41] The natural sciences and the library sciences which Gesner helped to found were capable of unlimited expansion. They entailed an open-ended, indefinitely continuous process. The term "feedback" is ugly and much overused, yet it does help to define the difference between data collection before and after the communi-cations shift. After printing, large-scale data collection did become

---

[40] George Sarton, *Six Wings: Men of Science in the Renaissance* (Bloomington, IN, 1957), 137.

[41] Hans Fischer, "Conrad Gesner (1516–1565) as Bibliographer and Encyclope-dist," *The Library*, 5th ser. XXI (December 1966): 271.

subject to new forms of feedback which had not been possible in the age of scribes.

Here as elsewhere, there are advantages to delineating the new features of print culture instead of merely noting in passing that, of course, printing was a prerequisite for early modern scholarship and science, before going on to cover other things. If the effects of printing received more attention one might be less inclined to attribute unusual moral virtues to sixteenth-century scholars or to set "greedy adventurers" against disinterested naturalists. If authors, editors, and publishers adopted "the simple expedient of being honest" by citing contributors, it was not because they were unusually noble but because this simple expedient had become more satisfying to mixed motives after printing than had been the case before. When Ortelius listed contributors to his atlas, he was pointing toward the "modern idea of scientific cooperation." But that is no reason to draw invidious comparisons between "honest" and cooperative craftsmen who sought to benefit others and vain, devious, self-serving schoolmen or literati who worked only for themselves.[42] No occupational group had a monopoly on a given virtue or vice. Socially useful techniques could be publicized after the sixteenth century, not because cooperative artisans became influential but because of the advent of print. Indeed, artisan-authors were no less "greedy," no less attracted by the lure of new intellectual property rights, than were literati and schoolmen.

It is noteworthy that high-minded passages justifying the writing of books by "humble" craftsmen often went together with appeals to the reader to visit the author's workshop where "marvelous things can be seen" and with the inclusion of addresses where instruments were on sale. When an artisan-author told his readers they could get his address from his publisher and come for a free demonstration to his shop, he was probably hoping to attract potential purchasers of his wares. The important point is that selfishness and altruism could be served at the same time.

[42] Edgar Zilsel, "The Genesis of the Concept of Scientific Progress," *Journal of the History of Ideas* VI (1945): 344–5.

This point is just as applicable to the "brain children" of professors as to those of instrument makers – if, indeed, the two figures can be kept apart. A certain ambivalence concerning new forms of publicity characterized academicians no less than artisans at first. Both groups contained authors who expressed their desire to disclose information for disinterested virtuous motives even while seeking fame and engaging in priority disputes. Similarly, a collaborative approach to data collection and honest acknowledgment of sources and contributions were by no means confined to the natural sciences. Bibliography no less than zoology became collaborative and subject to incremental change. Indeed, the so-called father of these two disciplines was the same man.

Insofar as the change from a sequence of corrupted copies to a sequence of improved editions encompassed all scholarly and scientific fields, it might be expected to have a fairly widespread effect upon the entire Commonwealth of Learning. It needs to be taken into consideration, I think, when dealing with massive intellectual movements such as the growing orchestration of themes associated with limitless progress and the muting of older "decay-of-nature" themes. "The Power which Printing gives us of continually improving and correcting our Works in successive Editions," wrote David Hume to his publisher, "appears to me the chief advantage of that art."[43] What was true of a single author's work applied with even greater force to large collaborative reference works. A series of new and augmented editions made the future seem to hold more promise of enlightenment than the past.

"Until half a century after Copernicus's death," Thomas Kuhn wrote, "no potentially revolutionary changes occurred in the data available to astronomers."[44] Yet Copernicus's life (1473–1543) spanned the very decades when a great many changes, now barely visible to modern eyes, were transforming "the data available" to all

---

[43] Cited in J. A. Cochrane, *Dr. Johnson's Printer: The Life of William Strahan* (London, 1964), p. 19, n.2.

[44] Thomas S. Kuhn, *The Copernican Revolution: Planetary Astronomy in the Development of Western Thought* (Cambridge, MA, 1957), 131.

book readers. A closer study of these changes could help to explain why systems of charting the planets, mapping the earth, synchronizing chronologies, codifying laws, and compiling bibliographies were all revolutionized before the end of the sixteenth century. In each instance, one notes, Hellenistic achievements were first reduplicated and then, in a remarkably short time, surpassed. In each instance, the new schemes, once published, remained available for correction, development, and refinement. Successive generations could build on the work left by sixteenth-century polymaths instead of trying to retrieve scattered fragments of it. The varied intellectual "revolutions" of early modern times owed much to the features that have already been outlined. But the great tomes, charts, and maps that are now seen as "milestones" might have proved insubstantial had not the preservative powers of print also been called into play. Typographical fixity is a basic prerequisite for the rapid advancement of learning. It helps to explain much else that seems to distinguish the history of the past five centuries from that of all prior eras – as I hope the following remarks will suggest.

Considering the Preservative Powers of Print: Fixity and Cumulative Change

Of all the new features introduced by the duplicative powers of print, preservation is possibly the most important. To appreciate its importance, we need to recall the conditions that prevailed before texts could be set in type. No manuscript, however useful as a reference guide, could be preserved for long without undergoing corruption by copyists, and even this sort of "preservation" rested precariously on the shifting demands of local elites and a fluctuating incidence of trained scribal labor. Insofar as records were seen and used, they were vulnerable to wear and tear. Stored documents were vulnerable to moisture and vermin, theft and fire. However they might be collected or guarded within some great message center, their ultimate dispersal and loss were inevitable. To be transmitted by writing from one generation to the next, information had to be conveyed by drifting texts and vanishing manuscripts.

This aspect of scribal culture is not often appreciated by modern scholars. It is completely concealed by recent anthropological stud-ies which focus on the contrasts between oral and written records exhibited during the last few hundred years. Thus anthropologists are likely to assign to handwriting the capacity to produce "permanently recorded versions of the past."[45] Yet a single manuscript record, even on parchment, was fairly impermanent unless it was stored away and not used. More than one record required copying, which led to tex-tual drift. Durable records called for durable materials. Stone inscrip-tions endured; papyrus records crumbled. These tangible differences gave rise to the rule: "Much is preserved when little is written; little is preserved when much is written."[46] After the advent of printing, however, the durability of writing material became less significant; preservation could be achieved by using abundant supplies of paper rather than scarce and costly skin. Quantity counted for more than quality. Even while time-tested rules were being duplicated, they were being made obsolete. One is reminded of the way modern schol-ars smile at the notion of an abbot instructing his monks to copy printed books so that texts would not perish. Yet modern scholars are just as prone as fifteenth-century monks to be deceived by appear-ances, and appearances have become increasingly deceptive.

By and large, printing required the use of paper – a less durable material than parchment or vellum to begin with, and one that has become ever more perishable as the centuries have passed and rag content has diminished. Whereas the scraping and reuse of skin does not obliterate letters completely, the scraping or reconversion of dis-carded printed matter leaves no palimpsests behind. When written messages are duplicated in such great abundance that they can be consigned to trash bins or converted into pulp, they are not apt to prompt thoughts about prolonged preservation. Manuscripts guarded in treasure rooms, wills locked in vaults, diplomas framed behind

---

[45]   Jack Goody and Ian Watt, "The Consequences of Literacy," *Comparative Studies in Society and History* V (1963): 345.

[46]   Harold Innis, *Empire and Communications* (Oxford, 1950), 10.

glass do appear to be less perishable than road maps, kitchen calendars, or daily newspapers. Moreover, we are repeatedly reminded of the remarkable survival value of ancient documents which have been buried under lava or stored in jars for thousands of years. A process of retrieval that was launched after printing has led to the uncovering of so many long-lost records that we are likely to underestimate the perishability of manuscripts which were not buried but were used. The development of new techniques for restoration and duplication, which bring lost writings to light, also encourages absentmindedness about losses which were incurred before the new techniques were employed.

Earlier scholars were less absentminded. Thomas Jefferson, for one, was keenly aware of the preservative powers of print. He wrote to George Wythe:

> Very early in the course of my researches into the laws of Virginia, I observed that many of them were already lost, and many more on the point of being lost, as existing only in single copies in the hands of careful or curious individuals, on whose deaths they would probably be used for waste paper. I set myself therefore to work to collect all which were then existing ... in searching after these remains, I spared neither time, trouble, nor expense ... But ... the question is What means will be the most effectual for preserving these remains from future loss? All the care I can take of them, will not preserve them from the worm, from the natural decay of the paper, from the accident of fire, or those of removal when it is necessary for any public purpose ... Our experience has proved to us that a single copy, or a few, deposited in MS in the public offices cannot be relied on for any great length of time. The ravages of fire and of ferocious enemies have had but too much part in producing the very loss we now deplore. How many of the precious works of antiquity were lost while they existed only in manuscript? Has there ever been one lost since the art of printing has rendered it practicable to multiply and disperse copies? This leads us then to the only means of preserving those remains

of our laws now under consideration, that is, a multiplication of printed copies.[47]

This revealing letter is described by Julian Boyd as leading directly to the publication of Hening's *Statutes of Virginia*. According to Boyd, it reflects the same views Jefferson expressed much earlier "to the author of Hazard's *Historical Collections*: 'the lost cannot be recovered; but let us save what remains: not by vaults and locks which fence them from the public eye and use, in consigning them to the waste of time but by such a multiplication of copies, as shall place them beyond the reach of accident.'"[48]

It seems in character for Jefferson to stress the democratizing aspect of the preservative powers of print which secured precious documents not by putting them under lock and key but by removing them from chests and vaults and duplicating them for all to see. The notion that valuable data could be preserved best by being made public, rather than by being kept secret, ran counter to tradition, led to clashes with new censors, and was central both to early modern science and to Enlightenment thought. In deploring the loss of the "precious works of antiquity" while "they existed only in manuscript" Jefferson also sounded an older humanist theme which linked the rebirth of ancient learning to the new art of printing. Problems associated with this linkage will be discussed in the next chapter. Here let me merely note that a classical revival, which was already under way when the first printers moved into Italy, persisted despite Ottoman advances in Eastern Europe, the French invasions of Italy, the despoiling of English monasteries, and all the horrors of the religious wars. Once Greek type fonts had been cut, neither the disruption of civil order in Italy, the conquest of Greek lands by Islam, nor even the translation into Latin of all major Greek texts saw knowledge of Greek wither again in the West. But the implications of typographical fixity are scarcely exhausted by thinking about

---

[47] Julian Boyd, "These Precious Moments of…Our History," *The American Archivist* XXII, 2 (1959): 175–6.
[48] Ibid., 175–6.

the permanent retrieval of Greek letters. Nor are they exhausted by reckoning the number of other ancient languages that have been retrieved and secured after being lost – not just to Western Europe but to the entire world – for thousands of years. They involve the whole modern "knowledge industry" itself, with its ever-expanding bibliographies, its relentless pressure on bookshelf space and library facilities.

They also involve issues that are less academic and more geopolitical. The linguistic map of Europe was "fixed" by the same process and at the same time as Greek letters were. The importance of the fixing of literary vernaculars is often stressed. The strategic role played by printing is, however, often overlooked. How strategic it was is suggested by the following paraphrased summary of Steinberg's account:

> Printing "preserved and codified, sometimes even created" certain vernaculars. Its absence during the sixteenth century among small linguistic groups "demonstrably led" to the disappearance or exclusion of their vernaculars from the realm of literature. Its presence among similar groups in the same century ensured the possibility of intermittent revivals or continued expansion. Having fortified language walls between one group and another, printers homogenized what was within them, breaking down minor differences, standardizing idioms for millions of writers and readers, assigning a new peripheral role to provincial dialects. The preservation of a given literary language often depended on whether or not a few vernacular primers, catechisms or Bibles happened to get printed (under foreign as well as domestic auspices) in the sixteenth century. When this was the case, the subsequent expansion of a separate "national" literary culture ensued. When this did not happen, a prerequisite for budding "national" consciousness disappeared; a spoken provincial dialect was left instead.[49]

Studies of dynastic consolidation and of nationalism might well devote more space to the advent of printing. Typography arrested

---

[49] Steinberg, *Five Hundred Years*, 120–6.

linguistic drift, enriched as well as standardized vernaculars, and paved the way for the more deliberate purification and codification of all major European languages. Randomly patterned sixteenth-century type casting largely determined the subsequent elaboration of national mythologies on the part of certain separate groups within multilingual dynastic states. The duplication of vernacular primers and translations contributed in other ways to nationalism. A "mother's tongue" learned "naturally" at home would be reinforced by inculcation of a homogenized print-made language mastered while still young, when learning to read. During the most impressionable years of childhood, the eye would see a more standardized version of what the ear had heard. Particularly after grammar schools gave primary instruction in reading by using vernacular instead of Latin readers, linguistic "roots" and rootedness in one's homeland would be entangled.

Printing contributed in other ways to the permanent fragmentation of Latin Christendom. Erastian policies long pursued by diverse rulers could, for example, be more fully implemented. The duplication of documents pertaining to ritual, liturgy, or canon law, handled under clerical auspices in the age of the scribe, was undertaken by enterprising laymen, subject to dynastic authority, in the age of the printer. Local firms, lying outside the pope's control, were granted lucrative privileges by Habsburg, Valois, and Tudor kings to serve the needs of national clergies. An Antwerp printer joined forces with a king of Spain to supply all Spanish priests with some 15,000 copies of a sixteenth-century breviary – its text having been slightly altered from the version authorized by post-Tridentine Rome. Philip II thus demonstrated royal control over the clergy of his realm, and Christopher Plantin thus evaded payments to the privileged Italian printer who had won a lucrative monopoly on the newly authorized Roman version.[50] The other varied ways in which printers, by pursuing their own interests, contributed to loosening or severing links

---

[50] Robert M. Kingdon, "Patronage, Piety and Printing in Sixteenth-Century Europe," *A Festschrift for Frederick Artz*, ed. D. Pinkney and T. Ropp (Durham, NC, 1964), 32–3.

with Rome, to nationalist sentiment, and to dynastic consolidation cannot be explored here. But they surely call for further study.

Many other consequences of typographical fixity also need to be explored. As Chapter 6 suggests, sixteenth-century religious divisions within Latin Christendom proved to be peculiarly permanent. When a heresy was condemned or a schismatic king excommunicated, such actions left a more indelible imprint than had been the case in earlier centuries. Similarly, as edicts became more visible, they also became more irrevocable. Magna Carta, for example, was ostensibly "published" (that is, proclaimed) twice a year in every shire. By 1237 there was already confusion as to which "charter" was involved.[51] In 1533, however, Englishmen glancing over the "Tabula" of the *Great Boke* could see how often it had been repeatedly confirmed in successive royal statutes.[52] In France also the "mechanism by which the will of the sovereign" was incorporated into the "published" body of law by "registration" was probably altered by typographical fixity.[53] It was no longer possible to take for granted that one was following "immemorial custom" when granting an immunity or signing a decree. Much as M. Jourdain learned that he was speaking prose, monarchs learned from political theorists that they were "making" laws. But members of parliaments and assemblies also learned from jurists and printers about ancient rights wrongfully usurped. Struggles over the right to establish precedents became more intense as each precedent became more permanent and hence more difficult to break.

Fixity also made possible more explicit recognition of individual innovation and encouraged the staking of claims to inventions, discoveries, and creations. It is no accident, I think, that printing is the first "invention" which became entangled in a priority struggle and rival national claims. Arguments over Gutenberg versus Coster or

---

[51] J. C. Holt, *Magna Carta* (Cambridge, 1965), 288–90.
[52] Graham, "Our Tong Maternall," 93.
[53] Franklin Ford, *Robe and Sword: The Regrouping of the French Aristocracy after Louis XIV* (Cambridge, 1953), 80.

Jenson set the pattern for later "Columbus Day" type disputes. One might compare the anonymity of the inventor of spectacles with later disputes over Galileo's right to claim priority in the case of the telescope. How much credit should be assigned to map publishers and printers for the naming of the New World itself? The way names were fixed to human organs and to the craters of the moon is also indicative of the way individual immortality could be achieved by means of print.

By 1500, legal fictions were already being devised to accommodate the patenting of inventions and assignment of literary properties. Once the rights of an inventor could be legally fixed and the problem of preserving unwritten recipes intact was no longer posed, profits could be achieved by open publicity provided new restraints were not imposed. Individual initiative was released from reliance on guild protection, but at the same time new powers were lodged in the hands of a bureaucratic officialdom. Competition over the right to publish a given text also introduced controversy over new issues involving monopoly and piracy. Printing forced legal definition of what belonged in the public domain. A literary "common" became subject to "enclosure movements," and possessive individualism began to characterize the attitude of writers to their work. The "terms plagiarism and copyright did not exist for the minstrel. It was only after printing that they began to hold significance for the author."[54]

Personal celebrity is related to printed publicity at present. The same point may be applied to the past – in a manner that is especially relevant to debates over the difference between medieval and Renaissance individualism. Cheaper writing materials encouraged the separate recording of private lives and correspondence. Not paper mills but printing presses, however, made it possible to preserve personal ephemera intact. The "drive for fame" itself may have been affected by print-made immortality. The urge to scribble was manifested in Juvenal's day as it was in Petrarch's. The wish to see

---

[54]   Michael B. Kline, "Rabelais and the Age of Printing," *Etudes Rabelaisennes* IV; *Travaux d'Humanisme et Renaissance* LX (Geneva, 1963): 54.

one's work in print (fixed forever with one's name in card files and anthologies) is different from the desire to pen lines that could never be fixed in a permanent form, might be lost forever, altered by copy-ing, or – if truly memorable – be carried by oral transmission and assigned ultimately to "anon." Until it became possible to distinguish between composing a poem and reciting one, or writing a book and copying one; until books could be classified by something other than incipits; the modern game of books and authors could not be played.

The thirteenth-century Franciscan, Saint Bonaventura, said that there were four ways of making books:

> A man might write the works of others, adding and changing nothing, in which case he is simply called a "scribe" (*scriptor*). Another writes the work of others with additions which are not his own; and he is called a "compiler" (*compilator*). Another writes both others' work and his own, but with others' work in principal place, adding his own for purposes of explanation; and he is called a "commentator" (*commentator*) ... Another writes both his own work and others' but with his own work in principal place adding others' for purposes of confirmation; and such a man should be called an "author" (*auctor*).[55]

This passage is remarkable, not only for its omission of completely original composition from the otherwise symmetrical scheme, but also for the unitary conception of writing which it implies. A writer is a man who "makes books" with a pen just as a cobbler is a man who makes shoes on a last.

Many problems about assigning proper credit to scribal "authors" may result from misguided efforts to apply print-made concepts where they do not pertain. The so-called forged book of Hermes is only one of many illustrations of this point. Who *wrote* Socrates' lines, Aristotle's works, Sappho's poems, any portion of the Scriptures? "God was not the author" of the written text of Scripture, writes a reviewer of a recent book, *Biblical Inspiration.* "But who was?

[55] John Burrow, "The Medieval Compendium," *Times Literary Supplement* (21 May 1976): 615.

That is the new and radical question which has since been raised by scholarship, disclosing to us centuries of development and complex multiplicity of authorship in the biblical documents as we now read them. Isaiah did not 'write' *Isaiah*."[56]

The new forms of authorship and literary property rights undermined older concepts of collective authority in a manner that encompassed not only biblical composition but also texts relating to philosophy, science, and law. Veneration for the wisdom of the ages was probably modified as ancient sages were retrospectively cast in the role of individual authors – prone to human error and possibly plagiarists as well. Treatment of battles of books between "ancients and moderns" might profit from more discussion of such issues. Since early printers were primarily responsible for forcing definition of literary property rights, for shaping new concepts of authorship, for exploiting bestsellers and trying to tap new markets, their role in this celebrated quarrel should not be overlooked. By the early sixteenth century, for example, staffs of translators were employed to turn out vernacular versions of the more popular works by ancient Romans and contemporary Latin-writing humanists. The tremendous impetus given by printers to the vernacular-translation movements in diverse countries needs to be taken into account when discussing debates between Latinists and the advocates of new vulgar tongues.

It is also worth considering that different meanings may have been assigned terms such as ancient and modern, discovery and recovery, invention and imitation before important departures from precedent could be permanently recorded. "Throughout the patristic and medieval periods, the quest for truth is thought of as the *recovery* of what is embedded in tradition . . . rather than the *discovery* of what is new."[57] Most scholars concur with this view. It must have been difficult to distinguish discovering something new from recovering it in the age of scribes. To "find a new art" was easily confused with

---

[56] "The Author and His Ghosts," *Times Literary Supplement* (22 September 1972): 1121.

[57] Harbison, *Christian Scholar*, 5.

retrieving a lost one, for superior techniques and systems of knowledge *were* frequently discovered by being recovered. Probably Moses, Zoroaster, or Thoth had not "invented" all the arts that were to be found. But many were retrieved from ancient giants whose works reentered the West by circuitous routes bearing few traces of their origins, even while testifying to remarkable technical expertise. Some pagan seers were believed to have been granted foreknowledge of the Incarnation. Possibly they had also been granted a special secret key to all knowledge by the same divine dispensation. Veneration for the wisdom of the ancients was not incompatible with the advancement of learning, nor was imitation incompatible with inspiration. Efforts to think and do as the ancients did might well reflect the hope of experiencing a sudden illumination or of coming closer to the original source of a pure, clear, and certain knowledge that a long Gothic night had obscured.

When unprecedented innovations did occur, moreover, there was no sure way of recognizing them before the advent of printing. Who could ascertain precisely what was known – either to prior generations within a given region or to contemporary inhabitants of far-off lands? "Steady advance," Sarton says, "implies exact determination of every previous step." In his view, printing made this determination "incomparably easier."[58] He may have understated the case. *Exact* determination must have been impossible before printing. Progressive refinement of certain arts and skills could and did occur. But no sophisticated technique could be securely established, permanently recorded, and stored for subsequent retrieval. Before trying to account for an "idea" of progress, we might look more closely at the new dynamic process entailed in a continuous accumulation of fixed records. Permanence introduced a new form of progressive change. The preservation of the old, in brief, was a prerequisite for a tradition of the new.

The advancement of learning had taken the form of a search for lost wisdom in the age of scribes. This search was rapidly propelled after printing. Ancient maps, charts, and texts once arranged and

[58] Sarton, "The Quest for Truth," 66.

dated, however, turned out to be dated in more ways than one. Map publishers turned out genuinely new and improved editions of atlases and star maps which showed that modern navigators and star gazers knew more things about the heavens and earth than did ancient sages. "The simple sailors of today," wrote Jacques Cartier in his *Brief Narration* of 1545, "have learned the opposite of the philosophers by true experience."[59] New, improved editions of ancient texts also began to accumulate, uncovering more schools of ancient philosophy than had been dreamed of before. Scattered attacks on one authority by those who favored another provided ammunition for a wholesale assault on all received opinion.

Incompatible portions of inherited traditions could be sloughed off, partly because the task of preservation had become less urgent. Copying, memorizing, and transmitting absorbed fewer energies. Useful reference books were no longer blotted out or blurred with the passage of time. Cadence and rhyme, images and symbols ceased to fulfill their traditional function of preserving the collective memory. Once technical information could be conveyed directly by unambiguous numbers, diagrams, and maps, the esthetic experience became increasingly autonomous. Although books on the memory arts multiplied after printing, the need to rely on these arts decreased. Scribal systems, elaborated in print, ultimately petrified and are only now being reassembled, like fossil remains, by modern research. The special formulas that had preserved recipes and techniques among closed circles of initiates also disappeared. Residues of mnemonic devices were transmuted into mysterious images, rites, and incantations.

Nevertheless, scribal veneration for ancient learning lingered on long after the conditions that had fostered it had gone. Among Rosicrucians and Freemasons, for example, the belief persisted that the "new philosophy" was in fact very old. Descartes and Newton had merely retrieved the same magical key to nature's secrets that had once been known to ancient pyramid builders but was later withheld from the laity or deliberately obscured by a deceitful priesthood. In

---

[59] Cited by Hiram Haydn, *The Counter Renaissance* (New York, 1950), 208.

fact, the Index came only after printing, and the preservation of pagan learning owed much to monks and friars. Some enlightened freethinkers, however, assigned Counter-Reformation institutions to the Gothic Dark Ages and turned Zoroaster into a Copernican. Similarly, once imitation was detached from inspiration, copying from composing, the classical revival became increasingly arid and academic. The search for primary sources, which had once meant drinking from pure wellsprings, came to be associated with dry-as-dust pedantry. But the reputation of ancient seers, bards, and prophets was not, by the same token, diminished. Claims to have inherited their magic mantle were put forth by new romanticists who reoriented the meaning of the term "original," sought inspiration by dabbling in the occult, and tried to resurrect scribal arts in the age of print. Even the "decay-of-nature" theme, once intimately associated with the erosion and corruption of scribal writings, would be reworked and reoriented by gloomy modern prophets who envisaged a "run-away technology" and felt regress, not progress, characterized their age.

Amplification and Reinforcement: The Persistence of Stereotypes and of Sociolinguistic Divisions

Many other themes embedded in scribal writings, detached from the living cultures that had shaped them, were propelled as "typologies" on printed pages. Over the course of time, archetypes were converted into stereotypes, the language of giants, as Merton puts it, into the clichés of dwarfs. Both "stereotype" and "cliché" are terms deriving from typographical processes developed three and a half centuries after Gutenberg. They point, however, to certain other features of typographical culture in general that deserve closer consideration. During the past five centuries, broadcasting new messages has also entailed amplifying and reinforcing old ones. I am referring to effects produced by an ever more frequent repetition of identical chapters and verses, anecdotes and aphorisms, drawn from very limited scribal sources. Quite apart from the constant republication of classical, biblical, or early vernacular works, there has been an unwitting collaboration between countless authors of new books or articles. For five hundred years, authors have jointly transmitted certain old messages with augmented frequency even while separately reporting on new events or spinning out new ideas. Thus if they happen to contain only one passing reference to the heroic stand at Thermopylae, a hundred reports on different military campaigns will impress Herodotus's description on the mind of the reader who scans such reports with a hundredfold impact. Every dissimilar report of other campaigns will be received only once. As printed materials proliferate, this effect becomes more pronounced. The more wide ranging the reader at present, the more frequent will be the encounter with the identical version and the deeper the impression it will leave. Since writers are particularly prone to wide-ranging reading, a multiplying "feedback" effect results. When it comes to coining familiar quotations, describing familiar episodes, originating symbols or stereotypes, the ancients (that is, those who went to press first) will generally outstrip the moderns. How many times has Tacitus's description of freedom-loving Teutons been repeated since a single manuscript of *Germania* was discovered in a fifteenth-century monastery? And in how many varying contexts – Anglo-Saxon, Frankish, as well as German – has this particular description appeared?

The frequency with which all messages were transmitted was primarily channeled by the fixing of literary linguistic frontiers. A particular kind of reinforcement was involved in relearning mother tongues when learning to read. It went together with the progressive amplification of diversely oriented national "memories." Not all the same portions of an inherited Latin culture were translated into different vernaculars at the same time. More important, entirely dissimilar dynastic, municipal, and ecclesiastical chronicles, along with other local lore, both oral and scribal, were also set in type and more permanently fixed. The meshing of provincial medieval *res gestae* with diverse classical and scriptural sources had, by the early seventeenth century, embedded distinctively different stereotypes within each separate vernacular literature. At the same time, to be sure, a more cosmopolitan *Respublica Litterarum* was also expanding.

Messages in Latin (and, later, in French) were broadcast across linguistic frontiers to an international audience. An even more effective means of transcending language barriers was being developed by contributors to technical literature. Mathematical and pictorial statements conveyed identical messages to virtuosi and scientific correspondents in all lands without need for translation. Although Latin learned journals, a lively French-language press, and scientific transactions did reach a sizable portion of the reading public by the eighteenth century, the diverse cosmopolitan literary cultures did not have the powers of amplification that the separate vernaculars had. Messages received in foreign languages from abroad only intermittently and occasionally reinforced the shared references that were learned in familiar tongues at home.

On the other hand, the fixing of religious frontiers that cut across linguistic ones in the sixteenth century had a powerful effect on the frequency with which certain messages were transmitted. Passages drawn from vernacular translations of the Bible, for example, would be much more thinly and weakly distributed throughout the literary cultures of Catholic regions than of Protestant ones. The abandonment of church Latin in Protestant regions made it possible to mesh ecclesiastical and dynastic traditions more closely within Protestant realms than in Catholic ones – a point worth noting when considering how church–state conflicts were resolved in different lands. Finally, the unevenly phased social penetration of literacy, the somewhat more random patterning of book-reading habits, the uneven distribution of costly new books and cheap reprints of old ones among different social sectors also affected the frequency with which diverse messages were received within each linguistic group.

CHAPTER FOUR

THE EXPANDING REPUBLIC OF LETTERS

THE RISE OF THE READING PUBLIC

Given the religious, linguistic, and socioeconomic diversity of European readers, it is difficult to imagine just what figure Marshall McLuhan had in mind when he wrote about the "making of typographical man."[1] By making us more alert to the possibility that the advent of printing had social and psychological consequences, McLuhan performed, in my view at least, a valuable service. But he also glossed over multiple interactions that occurred under widely varying circumstances. Granted that the replacement of discourse by silent scanning, of face-to-face contacts by more impersonal interactions, probably did have important consequences; it follows that we need to think less metaphorically and abstractly, more historically and concretely, about the sorts of effects that were entailed and how different groups were affected. Even at first glance both issues appear to be very complex.

We will not pause for long over one complication that has recently attracted attention: namely, Paul Saenger's demonstration that habits of silent reading developed during the Middle Ages.[2] It is now clear that McLuhan and the scholars upon whom he relied overstated the oral character of medieval interchanges and mistakenly assigned to printing responsibility for introducing habits of silent

[1] Marshall McLuhan, *The Gutenberg Galaxy: The Making of Typographical Man* (Toronto, 1962).
[2] Paul Saenger, "Silent Reading: Its Impact on Late Medieval Script and Society," *Viator* 13 (1982).

scanning which had already developed among some literate groups in the age of scribes. But although printing did not introduce silent reading, it did encourage an increasing recourse to "silent instructors, which nowadays carry farther than do public lectures" (in the words of a sixteenth-century professor of medicine). To show that the habit predated Gutenberg does not diminish the significance of its becoming increasingly more pervasive and ever more elaborately institutionalized after the shift from script to print.

Even while insisting on this point, we shall need to be cautious about assuming, as did McLuhan and other authorities, that the spread of habits of silent scanning invariably diminished recourse to the spoken word. Although the textbook industry flourished, classroom lectures never died. Printed sermons and orations did not remove preachers from their pulpits or speakers from their podiums. To the contrary, priests and orators both benefited from the way their personal charisma could be augmented and amplified by the printed word.

The increased recourse to silent publication undoubtedly altered the character of some spoken words. Exchanges between members of parliament, for example, were probably affected by the printing of parliamentary debates. The printing of poems, plays, and songs altered the way "lines" were recited, composed, and sung. On the one hand, some "dying speeches" were fabricated for printing and never did get delivered; on the other, printed publicity enabled evangelists and demagogues to practice traditional arts outdoors before an expanded hearing public. A literary culture created by typography was conveyed to the ear, not the eye, by repertory companies and poetry readings. No simple formula will cover the changes these new activities reflect.

The same is true of how different groups were affected. Most rural villagers, for example, probably belonged to an exclusively hearing public at least until the nineteenth century. Yet what they heard had, in many instances, been transformed by printing two centuries earlier. For the storyteller was replaced by the exceptional literate villager who read out loud from a stack of cheap books and ballad sheets turned out anonymously for distribution by peddlers. A fairly sleazy

"popular" culture, based on the mass production of antiquated vernacular medieval romances, was thus produced well before the steam
press and mass literacy movements of the nineteenth century. Yet the
bulk of this output was consumed by a hearing public, separated by
a psychological gulf from their contemporaries who belonged to a
reading one.

The disjunction between the new mode of production and older
modes of consumption is only one of many complications that need
further study. Members of the same reading public, who confronted
the same innovation in the same region at the same time, were
nonetheless affected by it in markedly different ways. Trends pointing both to modernism and to fundamentalism, for example, were
launched by Bible printing – as later discussion suggests. Pornography as well as piety assumed new forms. Book reading did not
stop short with guides to godly living or practical manuals and texts,
any more than printers stopped short at producing them. The same
silence, solitude, and contemplative attitudes associated formerly
with spiritual devotion also accompanied the perusal of scandal
sheets, "lewd Ballads," "merry bookes of Italie," and other "corrupted
tales in Inke and Paper."[3] Not a desire to withdraw from a worldly
society or the city of man, but a gregarious curiosity about them,
could be satisfied by silent perusal of journals, gazettes, or newsletters. Complaints about the "sullen silence" of newspaper readers in
seventeenth-century coffeehouses point to the intrusive effects of
printed materials on some forms of sociability.

As communion with the Sunday paper has replaced churchgo-
ing, there is a tendency to forget that sermons had at one time
been coupled with news about local and foreign affairs, real estate
transactions, and other mundane matters. After printing, however, news gathering and circulation were handled more efficiently
under lay auspices. As contemporaries observed, there were resem-
blances between coffeehouse and conventicle. But the pipe-smoking
habitués of the former gave otherworldly concerns low priority. Such

---

[3]   Cited by Louise B. Wright, *Middle Class Culture in Elizabethan England* (Chapel
Hill, NC, 1935), 232–3.

considerations might be noted when thinking about the "seculariza-tion" or "desacralization" of Western Christendom. For in all regions (to go beyond the eighteenth century for a moment) the pulpit was ultimately displaced by the periodical press, and the dictum "noth-ing sacred" came to characterize the journalist's career. Pitted against "the furious itch of novelty" and the "general thirst after news"[4] efforts by Catholic moralists and Protestant evangelicals, even Sun-day schools and other Sabbatarian measures,[5] proved of little avail. The monthly gazette was succeeded by the weekly and finally by the daily paper. More and more provincial newspapers were founded. By the last century, gossiping churchgoers could often learn about local affairs by scanning columns of newsprint in silence at home.

   The displacement of pulpit by press is significant not only in con-nection with secularization but also because it points to an explana-tion for the weakening of local community ties. To hear an address delivered, people have to come together; to read a printed report encourages individuals to draw apart. "What the orators of Rome and Athens were in the midst of a people *assembled*," said Malesherbes in an address of 1775, "men of letters are in the midst of a *dispersed* people."[6] His observation suggests how the shift in communications may have changed the sense of what it meant to participate in pub-lic affairs. The wide distribution of identical bits of information pro-vided an impersonal link between people who were unknown to each other.

   By its very nature, a reading public was not only more dispersed; it was also more atomistic and individualistic than a hearing one. To catch the contrast, Walter Ong suggests that we imagine a speaker addressing an audience equipped with texts and stopping at one point with the request that a textual passage be read silently. When the readers look up again, the fragmented audience has to be

4   Citations from the "British Mercury" of 1712 and Addison in Preserved Smith, *A History of Modern Culture*, vol. 2, *The Enlightenment 1687–1776* (New York, 1934), 284.
5   See Altick, *English Common Reader*, 128.
6   Cited by Arthur Wilson, *Diderot: The Testing Years, 1713–1759* (Oxford, 1957), 162 (italics mine).

Fig. 19. A royal entry depicted for armchair travelers. From *La Joyeuse & Magnifique Entrée de Monseigneur Francoys, fils de France... en sa tres-renomée ville d'Anvers* (Antwerp: Christopher Plantin, 1582, Plate 5). Reproduced by kind permission of the Folger Shakespeare Library.

reassembled into a collectivity. Insofar as a traditional sense of community entailed frequent gathering together to receive a given message, this sense was probably weakened by the duplication of identical messages which brought the solitary reader to the fore. To be sure, bookshops, coffeehouses, and reading rooms provided new kinds of communal gathering places. Yet subscription lists and corresponding societies represented relatively impersonal group formations, while the reception of printed messages in any place still required temporary isolation – just as it does in a library now. The notion that society may be regarded as a bundle of discrete units or that the individual is prior to the social group seems to be more compatible with a reading public than with a hearing one. The nature of man as a political

Fig. 20. This picture of the fireworks which celebrated the Earl of Leicester's arrival at The Hague in 1586 shows how prints enabled stay-at-homes to envisage "public" festivals. From Jacob Savery, *Delineatio pompae triumphalis qua Robertus Dudlaeus comes Leicestrensis Hagae Comitis fuit exceptus* (The Hague, 1586, Plate II). Reproduced by kind permission of the Folger Shakespeare Library.

animal was less likely to conform to classical models after tribunes of the people were transmuted from orators in public squares to editors of news sheets and gazettes.

Even while communal solidarity was diminished, vicarious participation in more distant events was also enhanced; and even while local ties were loosened, links to larger collective units were being forged. Printed materials encouraged silent adherence to causes whose advocates could not be found in any one parish and who addressed an invisible public from afar. New forms of group identity began to compete with an older, more localized nexus of loyalties. Urban populations were not only pulled apart, they were also linked in new ways by the more impersonal channels of communication. The exchange of goods and services, real estate transactions, the provision of charity were all eventually affected. Personal attendance was increasingly supplemented by vicarious participation in civic functions and municipal affairs. Cheap versions of the magnificent prints which commemorated civic ceremonies, such as royal entries, enabled some stay-at-homes to experience "public" festivals.

The features of individual rulers and of members of their entourage came into sharper focus for scattered subjects in a given realm. The circulation of prints and engravings made it possible for a reigning dynast to impress a personal presence on mass consciousness in a new way. The effect of duplicating images and portraits of rulers – which were eventually framed and hung in peasant hovels throughout Catholic Europe, along with saints and icons – has yet to be assessed by political scientists. The mass following of a single leader and the nationwide extension of his or her charismatic appeal, at all events, are possible by-products of the new communications systems which ought to be further explored. Joseph Klaits's study of Louis XIV's propaganda efforts describes how early modern rulers deliberately set out to exploit the new presses:

> Princes who had employed the cumbersome methods of manuscript to communicate with their subjects switched quickly to print to announce declarations of war, publish battle accounts, promulgate treaties or argue disputed points in pamphlet form. Theirs was an effort . . . "to win the psychological war which prepared and accompanied the military operations" of rulers. . . . The English crown under Henry VIII and Thomas Cromwell made systematic use of both Parliament and press to win public support for the Reformation. . . .
>
> In France the regency of Louis XIII saw the last meeting of the Estates General before 1789; it also saw the founding of the first royally sponsored newspaper in Europe. The replacement of the volatile assembly by the controlled weekly *Gazette* is a concurrence symptomatic of the importance Cardinal Richelieu attached to print in his state-building objectives.[7]

As these references to Richelieu and Thomas Cromwell suggest, even while making room for the heightened visibility of individual rulers, we also need to note how the powers of officials and bureaucrats were extended once government regulations became subject to the duplicative powers of print. The expansion of leviathan states, as might be expected, provoked countermeasures from parliaments and

---

[7]   Joseph Klaits, *Printed Propaganda under Louis XIV* (Princeton, NJ, 1976), 6–7.

assemblies. Traditional tensions between court and country, crown and estates, were exacerbated by propaganda wars. A greater uniformity began to characterize provincial demands, with the circulation of model petitions and lists of grievances.

Recently some historians have begun to abandon, as fruitless, older debates about the "rise" of a new class to political power in early modern times. They seek to focus attention instead on the reeducation and regroupment of older governing elites – and have, thereby, precipitated new debates.[8] Both lines of inquiry might be reconciled and fruitfully pursued if the consequences of printing received more attention.

THE RISE OF A NEW CLASS OF "MEN OF LETTERS"

In addition to the regroupment of old elites and enhanced political consciousness among literate commoners, social historians might also take into consideration the formation of new groups engaged in the production and distribution of printed materials. For all the attention devoted to "alienated intellectuals" in Tudor and Stuart England or to the "desertion of intellectuals" in Bourbon France, very little has been written about the rise of intellectuals as a distinctive social class.[9] The distance which separated the most eminent culture heroes, such as Erasmus and Voltaire, from the unknown Grub Street hack remains to be assessed. The early modern Grub Street itself awaits its historian. A series of fascinating studies by Robert Darnton has illuminated the "low-life of literature" in eighteenth-century France and the strategic role played by frustrated literary careerists in translating Enlightenment doctrines into radical political action. Glimpses of a distinctive subculture associated with literary hackwork are offered in scattered studies devoted

---

[8] See, e.g., J. H. Hexter, *Reappraisals in History* (Evanston, IL, 1961), chap. 4; Lawrence Stone, *The Crisis of Aristocracy 1558–1641* (Oxford, 1965), 673; Ford, *Robe and Sword*, passim.

[9] Mark Curtis, "The Alienated Intellectuals of Early Stuart England," *Past and Present* 23 (November 1962): 25–41. Also, Crane Brinton, *The Anatomy of Revolution* (New York, 1938).

to early sixteenth-century Venice and Elizabethan London, but the full picture, which would provide a needed perspective on French eighteenth-century developments, has not yet been sketched. The same point applies to the development of a profitable clandestine book trade and black markets for forbidden books. Again, glimpses of this phenomenon can be obtained from studies of assorted topics – ranging from the smuggling of vernacular Bibles in the early sixteenth century to Galileo's evasion of the officials who placed him under house arrest. But the full dimensions of the topic remain, like those of a gigantic iceberg, submerged. Only the tip is visible – largely defined by debates on the significance of inflammatory literature in prerevolutionary France. Beginning with the remarkably versatile occupational groups associated with the early printed book trade and ending, perhaps, with the staffs of the journals who took over the government of France in 1848, the story of the rise of a "fourth estate" also remains to be told. Largely because the growing power of the press as an independent force in early modern Europe is concealed, men of letters tend to be regarded as spokesmen for the interests of all classes save their own. The values which were common to members of the Commonwealth of Learning and the institutions which were peculiar to the Republic of Letters still remain undefined. It is clear enough that "News from the Republic of Letters," as edited by Pierre Bayle, came from Rotterdam. Rotterdam also provided "the only patron Bayle needed": namely, Reiner Leers, his publisher. Leers "in turn relied on the relative freedom enjoyed by Dutch printers and on the existence of a sufficiently large international reading public" for support.[10] It is also clear that the language of the inhabitants of the literary Republic had shifted in the course of the seventeenth century from Latin to French. Its central city in the eighteenth century was neither Paris nor Rotterdam, however. According to most authorities, it was Amsterdam,[11] which had earlier provided Europeans with their first newspapers and which continued until the eve of the French Revolution to serve newspaper readers in France.

[10] K. H. D. Haley, *The Dutch in the Seventeenth Century* (London, 1972), 173.
[11] Febvre and Martin, *Coming of the Book*, 298.

But a margin for uncertainty has to be left when one pinpoints the headquarters or designates the frontiers of this "Republic" on real maps. It remained, from the beginning, a somewhat elusive, often deliberately mysterious, domain. Its inhabitants rarely used their proper names – preferring more elegant Latinate or Greek versions, when not deliberately concealing their identity behind vernacular pseudonyms or complete anonymity. Even the colophons of the printers they relied on often reflected a desire not to attract potential customers to bookshops (as was the usual purpose of early colophons), but to distract officials and avoid fines or arrest. Products issued from "Utopia" and "Cosmopolis" helped to publicize these novel terms but also added to the sense of unreality and impracticality associated with the circulation of ideas. Yet those who took advantage of the new careers opened to the talents of skillful writers were not disembodied spirits who must be materialized to be believed. They were, rather, complex flesh-and-blood human beings. (Some forty-odd volumes were required to cover the lives of the more celebrated inhabitants of the "Republic of Letters" by the mid-eighteenth century.[12]) Moreover, real foundries, workshops, and offices were built to serve the needs of this presumably fictitious realm; real profits were made by tapping the talents which gravitated to it.

A mixture of shrewd practicality with a seemingly idealistic preference for places such as "Cosmopolis" and "Utopia" (not to mention Eleuthera and Philadelphia) was exhibited by many early leaders of the expanding printing industries. Paradoxically enough, the same presses which fanned the flames of religious controversy also created a new vested interest in ecumenical concord and toleration; the same wholesale industry which fixed religious, dynastic, and linguistic frontiers more permanently also operated most profitably by tapping cosmopolitan markets. Paradoxically also, the same firms made significant contributions to Christian learning by receiving infidel Jews and Arabs, schismatic Greeks, and a vast variety of

---

[12] Jean Pierre Niceron, *Mémoires pour Servir à L'Histoire des hommes illustres dans la République des Lettres*, 43 vols. (Paris, 1729–1745).

dissident foreigners into their shops and homes. Circles associated with the firms of Daniel Bomberg or Aldus Manutius in Venice; with the Amerbachs or Oporinus in Basel; with Plantin in Antwerp or the Wechels in Frankfurt point to the formation of polyglot households in scattered urban centers upon the continent. During the sixteenth century, such printing shops represented miniature "international houses." They provided wandering scholars with a meeting place, message center, sanctuary, and cultural center all in one. The new industry encouraged not only the formation of syndicates and far-flung trade networks, similar to those extended by merchants engaged in the cloth trade or in other large-scale enterprises during early modern times. It also encouraged the formation of an ethos which was specifically associated with the Commonwealth of Learning – ecumenical and tolerant without being secular, genuinely pious yet opposed to fanaticism, often combining outward conformity to diverse established churches with inner fidelity to heterodox creeds.

The many tensions created for authors by the expansion of literary markets after printing have been illuminated by several recent studies.[13] Despite these studies, however, there is a tendency when discussing the commercialization of *belles lettres* or the disappearance of patronage to take too much at face value the images purveyed by literary artists. The advent of an "industrial" society is too often made responsible for conditions that were shaped by the momentum of an ongoing revolution in communications. From the first, authorship was closely linked to the new technology. As Febvre and Martin suggest, it is a "neologism" to use the term "man of letters" before the advent of printing.[14] The romantic figure of the aristocratic or patrician patron has tended to obscure the more plebeian and prosaic early capitalist entrepreneur who hired scholars, translators, editors,

---

[13] Apart from Altick's *English Common Reader*, see Louis Dudek, *Literature and the Press* (Toronto, 1960); Robert Escarpit, *Sociologie de la Littérature* (Paris, 1958); César Graña, *Bohemian Versus Bourgeois* (New York, 1964); Raymond Williams, *Culture and Society 1780–1950* (New York, 1960); Lewis A. Coser, *Men of Ideas: A Sociologist's View* (New York, 1965); Thomas Molnar, *The Decline of Intellectuals* (New York, 1961).

[14] Febvre and Martin, *Coming of the Book*, 18.

and compilers when not serving in these capacities himself. Partly because copyists had, after all, never paid those whose works they copied, partly because new books were a small portion of the early book trade, and partly because divisions of literary labor remained blurred, the author retained a quasi-amateur status until the eighteenth century. During this interval, printers served as patrons for authors, acted as their own authors, and sought patronage, privileges, and favors from official quarters as well. This was the era when men of letters and learning were likely to be familiar with print technology and commercial trade routes in a manner that later observers overlook.

The intelligentsia are thus singled out by Karl Mannheim as peculiarly lacking "direct access to any vital and functioning segment of society":

> The secluded study and dependence on printed matter afford only a derivative view of the social process. No wonder this stratum remained long unaware of the social character of change . . . The proletariat had already perfected its own world view when these latecomers appeared on the scene.[15]

For Mannheim, "the rise of the intelligentsia marks the last phase of the growth of social consciousness." In my view, however, he has put first things last. Most inhabitants of the sixteenth-century Republic of Letters spent considerable time in printers' workshops. They were thus in direct contact with a "vital and functioning segment of society." Authors who "composed" their work with a composing stick in hand were not uncommon in the age of Erasmus – nor in that of Benjamin Franklin. Indeed, the simplicity of the early press made it possible for American men of letters to act as their own printers – much as Italian humanists had acted as their own scribes.

> A literate person – man or woman by the way – with a copy of Moxon's *Mechanick Exercises* (1683) in hand could teach himself or herself the trade, from beginning to end. Simplicity of operation

---

[15] Karl Mannheim, *Essays on the Sociology of Culture*, ed. and tr. E. Manheim (Oxford, 1956), pt. 2, sec. 2, p. 101.

was not a factor of prime importance in London . . . But it was cru-
cially important in the provinces and colonies, where printing-
houses were small and pressmen few. There, if necessary, one man
who knew his business could mix his own ink, compose his folio
halfsheet page at type cases, operate the press himself, dry the
pages and even take the papers in his own hands to the neigh-
boring taverns and coffee houses for sale and distribution if he did
not have a printer's devil and could not find a boy who would do
it for him for a penny. The process was a natural school for the
autodidact and the way was open for the development of authors
who could complete the process by actually composing their work,
in both senses of the word, with the composing stick. Two who
did so were those autodidact printers Mark Twain and Benjamin
Franklin.[16]

Benjamin Franklin's experience with printing might be expected
to intrigue a sociologist of knowledge, such as Mannheim, who is
concerned with the way social activities enter into world views. But,
as many discussions of Max Weber's thesis suggest, sociologists are
strangely oblivious to Benjamin Franklin's particular occupation. In
Mannheim's coverage of intellectual associations during the early
modern era, we are told about universities, chancelleries, courts,
salons, and academies; but of the printing shop, which provided
jobs, food, lodging, and all manner of interchanges, nothing is said.
Because of its presence in numerous urban centers the "historical and
social consciousness" of men of letters in early modern Europe was
well in advance of that of other groups. Even in the early nineteenth
century, a professional man of letters such as Sir Walter Scott could
write: "I love to have the press thumping, clattering and banging in
my ear. It creates the necessity which always makes me work best."[17]
The "secluded study" which now provides a setting for many sociologists of knowledge should not be projected too far back into the

---

[16] Calhoun Winton, "Richard Steele, Journalist and Journalism," *Newsletters
to Newspapers: Eighteenth Century Journalism*, ed. D. Bond and R. McLeod
(Morgantown, VA, 1977), 22–3.

[17] Cited by Coser, *Men of Ideas*, 55.

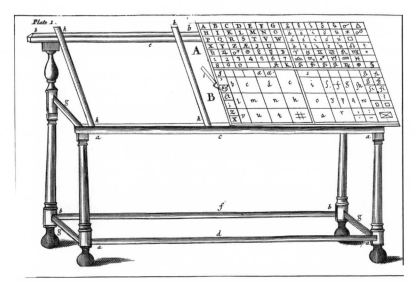

Fig. 21. With a copy of Moxon in hand, one could teach oneself the trade of printing. The lay of cases and their partitions diagrammed and keyed to the text, from Joseph Moxon, *Mechanick Exercises . . . Applied to the Art of Printing* (London: for Joseph Moxon, 1683, Vol. II, Plate I). Reproduced by kind permission of the Folger Shakespeare Library.

past. Between the sixteenth and eighteenth centuries, at all events, intellectuals, mechanics, and capitalists were not out of touch.

But even during this interval, a somewhat more indirect and more ambivalent relationship to the new technology was experienced by poets, playwrights, fabulists, satirists, and romancers who were linked both to *la cour et la ville* and poised somewhat uncertainly between royal patronage and publishers' stipends. Ambivalence over whether they were serving the muses or mechanic printers, engaged in a "divine art" or a "mercenary métier," was already manifested in French literary circles during the seventeenth century.[18] Often treated with contempt by aristocrats, these "scribblers" belonged to a highly volatile, unstable status group. No traditional institutions or systems pertaining to rank, priority, and degree took their existence

[18] See citation from Boileau and discussion by John Lough in *An Introduction to Seventeenth Century France* (London, 1960), 177.

into account. They wavered between the lofty position of arbiters of taste and inspired "immortals" and the lowly role of supplying, for favor or payment, commodities sold for profit on the open market. Tension between these two extreme and entirely contradictory roles thus existed before the advent of new paper mills, steam presses, and a mass fiction-reading public. It simply became more acute as the literary marketplace expanded and new groups of readers were tapped.

The competent business or professional man, who had been the natural ally of the early printer, was the natural enemy of the professional fiction writer or lionized poet. A hardworking man who relied on facts and figures, any man who worked hard for a living, could not afford to spend much time reading novels or poetry. Adolescent bookworms, young apprentices and clerks, and a wide spectrum of feminine readers were more apt to have hearts that could be touched and imaginations that could be held in thrall. A vested interest in idleness, in promoting the value of pleasure seeking and leisure, in cultivating consumption of the "finer" things of life, was built into the trade of all novelists and poets (and of other artists as well). Claims to superior historical dignity and spiritual value were uneasily reconciled with turning out bestselling works that sold like drugs on the market – and were similarly advertised in the daily press. The complaint of being misunderstood by heartless, unimaginative philistines had, as Graña noted, a paradoxical aspect,[19] for it implied merely that a work was not selling well.

Anxiety about getting attention and holding it was also built into the trade of the new professional author. Not only did his work have to hold its own against energetic competition from rivals. Once space had been secured for serial publication or favorable notice from literary journalists had been won, the distracting effect of headline-grabbing politicians, advertising space buyers, and news-making reporters had to be countered. His pecuniary rewards and prestige depended on printed publicity – like those of any business

[19] Graña, Bohemian, 56.

firm. But an inversion of values here again occurred. A reputation was gained not by respectability but by a *succès de scandale*; *épater le bourgeois* was also a profitable venture. Business or professional men might be offended, but few of them would be attracted to fiction in any case. A feminine and youthful audience was more likely to be captivated than deterred by vicarious participation in this particular sport.[20] The courting of scandal was by no means confined to the assault on ostensibly respectable family men. "The reader refused to be caught save by a book baited with a small corpse in the first stage of putrefaction...Men are not as unlike fishes as most people seem to think."[21] May not this search for ever more thrilling or shocking effects account for the syndrome described by Mario Praz as the "romantic agony"?

Although many authors expressed disgust at the vulgar sensationalism of others, none could afford to abandon the hope of creating a sensation himself. Alone with his quill pen, altogether remote from workshops and foundries, equally remote from the fickle readers upon whom his fame and fortune hinged, the professional author did not simply mirror the alienation of others from an industrial or urbanized society. He was himself an alienated man who worked hard to promote leisure, fought for a commercial success that he despised, set wives against husbands, fathers against sons, and celebrated youth even in his old age. Even if new factories, mines, and slag heaps had never appeared, given the momentum of the ongoing communications revolution, he would probably still have felt nostalgia for scribal culture, worried about cultural anarchy and the vulgarization of taste, seen the public in the guise of a many-headed beast, and assailed the "cash nexus" as well as the heartless businessman.

During the nineteenth century, among many of the most sensitive artists and most gifted image makers, the effort to reconcile

---

[20] Philip Collins, "The Fiction Market," *Times Literary Supplement* (20 April 1977): 537.

[21] Théophile Gautier, Preface to "Mademoiselle de Maupin" (1835), tr. F. de Sumichrast in *Paths to the Present*, ed. E. Weber (New York, 1960), 82.

a commercial métier with the role of immortal was abandoned altogether. Earning daily bread was divorced from turning out a *succès d'estime*. Increasingly, the most strikingly "original" and arresting images were shaped within secluded ivory towers for small groups of connoisseurs. Keeping faith with the muses was rewarded, often posthumously, by a place in the last chapter of a literary anthology. But the preservative powers of print also made this loftier ambition ever more difficult for each new generation to achieve. The more strident the voice of one generation, the more deafening the static interference became for the next. Among the variety of reactions that ensued two might be singled out: on the one hand, a museum culture, preserved in anthologies and taught in the schoolroom, was savagely assaulted; on the other, modern cultural "anarchy" and the society that sustained it were nostalgically repudiated. Nihilistic images pertaining to a "dustbin of the past" and a "wasteland of the present" were, in turn, dutifully recorded and expounded. Several last chapters of current anthologies now contain such images. (They serve, one might note, to introduce the present generation of students to the society in which they are coming of age.) Thus the same process that had, earlier, introduced eponymous authorship and harnessed the drive for fame to print-made immortality led to an overpopulation of Parnassus. An ever more strenuous effort was required to handle an increasing "burden of the past." How the later phases of the ongoing revolution contributed to cultural pessimism and the multiple variations played upon this theme cannot, however, be explored here.

This brief excursion beyond the early modern era has been offered merely to suggest that particular perturbations, emanating from a permanent, cumulative print-made culture, need to be taken into account when trying to reconstruct the experience of literate elites during the last few centuries. They also need to be taken into consideration when attempting to understand the sense of cultural crisis which has become ever more acute in recent years. This last point needs special emphasis in view of the possible distracting effect of new electronic media. Whatever damage has been done to youthful reading habits, old literary themes continue to be amplified by script writers and song writers over air waves even now. Moreover, there is no sign that our libraries and museums without walls have begun to contract or that the burden of the past is diminishing for the literati of today. Thus, although I believe that scribal culture did come to an end, I am not persuaded that one can say the same about print culture. The effects of printing seem to have been exerted always unevenly, yet always continuously and cumulatively from the late fifteenth century on. I can find no point at which they ceased to be exerted or even began to diminish. I find much to suggest that they have persisted, with ever-augmented force, right down to the present. Recent obituaries on the Age of Gutenberg show that others disagree.[22] As yet, however, so few historians have been heard from that final verdicts seem unacceptable and, in more ways than one, premature.

It would also be premature at this point to make any final remarks. This introductory section was intended to open up a field for future study and not to provide a basis upon which conclusions may be drawn. Let me simply recapitulate. A new method for duplicating handwriting – an *ars artificialiter scribendi* – was developed and first utilized five centuries ago. "It brought about the most radical transformation in the conditions of intellectual life in the history of western civilization ... its effects were sooner or later felt in every department of human life."[23] At present we must reckon with effects "felt in every department of human life" without knowing which came sooner, which later, and, indeed, without any clear notions as to what these effects were. Explicit theories, in short, are now overdue. To make a start at providing them, a preliminary sketch has been offered. It was designed to block out the topic as a whole, to indicate some of its neglected ramifications, and to suggest its possible bearing on many different forms of historical change.

[22] The obsolescence of print technology and its supersession by electronic media has been repeatedly asserted by McLuhan, not only in *The Gutenberg Galaxy* but also in *Understanding Media*. See also George Steiner's "Retreat from the Word," *Kenyon Review* (Spring 1961): 187–216.
[23] Gilmore, *World of Humanism*, 186.

In Part II of this work selected developments receive closer attention. Possible relationships and connections are explored with the
aim of providing a basis for some tentative conclusions concerning the effects of the communications shift upon three movements
which seem strategic in the shaping of the modern mind.

PART II

INTERACTION WITH OTHER
DEVELOPMENTS

The Permanent Renaissance

MUTATION OF A CLASSICAL REVIVAL

> We all know... that down to the fifteenth century all European
> books were pen written and that ever since that time most of
> them have been printed. We know likewise that in that same fif-
> teenth century Western culture laid off its medieval characteristics
> and became distinctively modern. But we are quite unable to con-
> ceive realistically any connection between these technological and
> cultural changes except that they happened in the same period.[1]

This statement, which was made by Pierce Butler in 1940, describes a
situation which seems current even now. Although the relationship
between technology and culture in general has been the subject of a
growing literature, the more specific relationship between the advent
of printing and fifteenth-century cultural change has not yet been
explored. This is partly because the very act of drawing connections
is not as easy a task as one might think. Butler goes on to refer to an
"intimate connection" which becomes apparent "the moment our
thought penetrates through bare facts," but I must confess I cannot
imagine just what connection he had in mind. Although the shift
from pen-written book to printed one may be taken as a known fact,
it is not the kind of fact that can be said to "speak for itself." As
previous chapters suggest, a complex ensemble of many interrelated
changes was involved.

When one turns to the other side of the equation, matters are no
less complicated and even more obscure. Do we really "all know" in

---

[1] Pierce Butler, *The Origin of Printing in Europe* (Chicago, 1940), 9.

which century Western culture became "distinctively modern"? Historians are more likely to claim knowledge of the large literature of controversy which has grown around this very point. In the absence of any consensus, and given prolonged inconclusive debate, one may be tempted simply to dismiss the question as a semantic trap. There is a difference, however, between historical theory and practice. In theory, periodization problems may never get solved, but in practice, definite lines have to be drawn. In most course catalogues and scholarly journals, the lines which are drawn seem to support Butler's view. Judging by academic divisions of labor, reflected in courses and articles, the fifteenth century does seem to be taken as an interval where the expertise of medievalists ends and that of specialists in early modern Europe begins.

But here, again, matters are not as simple as an outsider might think. The same division which seems only natural when one considers the policies of journals such as *Speculum* or the *Journal of Modern History* will seem arbitrary and even misguided when one considers *Studies in the Renaissance*. From the viewpoint of most Renaissance scholars, the advent of printing comes too late to be taken as a point of departure for the transition to modern times. From their viewpoint, this transition begins with the generations of Giotto and Petrarch and with a classical revival that was already under way by the early quattrocento – well before Gutenberg had set to work. Before making much headway in drawing the connections to which Butler alludes, one must first deal with the argument that his technological and cultural changes do not really coincide and that the major cultural metamorphosis had occurred under the auspices of scribes.

That the "rinascita" came to Italy before printing was developed in Mainz may be taken as firmly established. But although the question of chronology is easily settled, the problem of periodization remains. It is one thing to show that the Petrarchan revival was flourishing in Italy in the age of hand-copied books. It is another to show why Petrarch and his successors should be taken as agents of epochal change. This latter point is far from being firmly established. Jacob Burckhardt asserted that the Italians of Petrarch's day were the "first born sons of modern Europe." But for every argument supporting

Burckhardt's thesis, a counterargument has been found. In the absence of any consensus concerning the specific agents of epochal change, many historians have tended to fall back on the notion of a transitional age – an elastic period encompassing some three hundred years during which Western Europe is seen to have experienced the cultural equivalent of a chemical change of phase.[2] Unlike the chemical change of a liquid into a solid or into a gas, however, the precise nature of the cultural transition is never defined. We are told that "something rather decisive" or "of crucial importance" or "immeasurably different" happened.[3] Something "important and revolutionary occurred . . . and we might as well go on calling that something the Renaissance"[4] – a review thus sums up a recent book on the familiar theme. The nature of the "something" is elusive, however; uncertainty persists as to how to track it down. To the question posed by Huizinga in 1920 – "What actually was the cultural transformation we call the Renaissance? What did it consist of, what was its effect?"[5] – no clear answer has been found.

Accordingly, other scholars object that the question is based on a false premise. They see certain decisive changes occurring in the twelfth century or before; others, in the seventeenth century or after; but none of major consequence in the intervening period. By prolonging the Middle Ages for some purposes, by advancing the advent of modern times for others, they close the conjectured gap and eliminate the need for a transitional era to bridge it. These conflicting views are swathed in semantic confusion since the term

[2] Wallace K. Ferguson, "The Interpretation of the Renaissance: Suggestions for a Synthesis," *The Renaissance: Medieval or Modern?* ed. K. H. Dannenfeldt (New York, 1959).

[3] Erwin Panofsky, *Renaissance and Renascences in Western Art* (Uppsala, 1960), 4; Wallace K. Ferguson, *The Renaissance in Historical Thought: Five Centuries of Interpretation* (Cambridge, MA, 1948), 393; Giorgio de Santillana, *The Age of Adventure* (New York, 1956), 12.

[4] Frank J. Warnke, "Mazzeo on the Renaissance," *Journal of the History of Ideas* XXVIII (April–June 167): 288.

[5] Johan Huizinga, "The Problem of the Renaissance" (1920), in *Men and Ideas: Essays by Johan Huizinga*, tr. J. S. Holmes and H. van Marle (New York, 1966), 278.

"Renaissance" is used by both schools to designate a specific classical revival and esthetic style. Confusion arising over the extension
of the label to encompass a transitional epoch provokes additional
dispute. The basic issue is whether the period, however labeled, contains a major historical transformation and hence should be set apart
or whether it is a spurious construct and should be discarded. One
objectionable feature of this debate is the way it encourages both
sides alike to pass over in silence an actual transformation in order
to argue about a hypothetical one that cannot be clearly defined.

To solve the problem of the Renaissance, Huizinga suggests, we
should begin by contrasting the Middle Ages with the Renaissance
and the Renaissance with modern culture.[6] Similarly, Ferguson calls
for a "systematic analysis both of the essential differences between
medieval and modern civilization and of what was peculiar to the
transitional age itself."[7] It would be more sparing of scholarly energies, I think, to begin by answering directly and tersely the question:
"What was peculiar to the transitional age itself?" Among new things
reserved to this age, we might say, echoing a sixteenth-century
chronicler, "printing deserves to be put first."[8] By adopting this tac-
tic we can bypass debates about equivocal labels and constructs. We
can direct attention to something that really did happen, that was
obviously of crucial importance, that occurred in the second half of
the fifteenth century and at no other time in the history of the West.

Verbal labels such as "medieval" and "modern" cannot be oper-
ationally defined. The specific phenomena they are meant to designate can be shuffled around so easily that useful comparisons are
almost impossible to achieve. But to analyze the differences between
hand-copied texts and printed ones requires examining tangible
objects and the activities of definite groups. Varying interpretations
must, perforce, be grounded on examining the same empirical data.
Not only did it entail a specific cluster of changes (unlike the notion

---

[6]   Ibid., 278.
[7]   Ferguson, *Renaissance in Historical Thought*, 391.
[8]   Louis le Roy, excerpt from "De La Vicissitude ou Variété des Chose en l'Univers"
       (1575), tr. J. B. Ross, *The Portable Renaissance Reader* (New York, 1969), 98.

of a "transitional age"), but the shift from script to print also involved a Europe-wide transformation which occurred in a relatively short span of time. In a few decades, printers' workshops were established in urban centers throughout Europe. By 1500, various effects produced by the output of printed materials were already being registered. Compared with the three centuries that stretch from 1250 to 1550 or 1300 to 1600, the age of incunabula is short indeed. Nor is it necessary to move from one region to another in order to locate a major shift. One must leave Paris and its environs with its Gothic cathedrals and faculties of theology, cross over the Alps, and journey into Italy to find an early Renaissance. When one considers what was happening elsewhere on the Continent between 1350 and 1450, one may wonder if an encounter with peculiar local conditions has not been mistaken for the advent of a new age. But one may move freely across all sorts of European frontiers – from Mount Etna to regions north of Stockholm, from Atlantic coasts to the mountains of eastern Montenegro – during the last half of the fifteenth century and one will find that the same sorts of new workshops in major urban centers are producing books in almost all the languages of Western Europe.[9] New trades such as that of compositor or typefounder are being created; traditional skills developed by metal workers, merchants, and scholars are being directed toward new ends. New occupational groups are, in all regions, being mobilized by lay entrepreneurs driving to tap new markets, extend new trade networks, and get their products on display at annual book fairs. By 1500, one may say with some assurance that the age of scribes had ended and the age of printers had begun.

Why then is there so much controversy about where to end one era and begin another; so much debate about a hypothetical transition instead of an actual occurrence; and, above all, such an abundance of false starts? To put the question less rhetorically: Why has it become common practice to lump together developments that

[9] Curt Bühler, *Fifteenth Century Books and the Twentieth Century: An Address and a Catalogue of an Exhibition at the Grolier Club*, April–June 1952 (New York, 1952), 21–2.

occurred during the last century or so of scribal culture with those that occurred during the first century or so of typographical culture, thereby creating a troublesome transitional era even while conceal-ing a genuine revolutionary transformation? One might argue that the impact of the new mode of book production was bound to be muf-fled or delayed since it could have no effect on unlettered folk and hence initially affected only a very small literate elite. Fortunately, we can dismiss this sort of argument without having to worry about inadequate data on fifteenth-century literacy rates. For scholars who deal with the problem of the Renaissance – who point to the survival of a "medieval world picture" beyond the sixteenth century or who take Petrarch's inversion of pagan darkness and Christian light as their point of departure for a new cultural epoch – are looking only at literate elites.

To bring the problem into a sharper focus: the advent of printing, we are told, was the most important event "in the *cultural* history of mankind"; it "brought about the most radical transformation in the conditions of *intellectual* life in the history of Western civiliza-tion."[10] Yet intellectual and cultural historians, in particular, have been unable to find room for it in their periodization schemes. To account for this paradox it seems necessary to look more closely at the paradoxical nature of the radical transformation itself. Instead of coupling the advent of printing with other innovations or regarding it as an example of some other development, we must single it out as an event which was *sui generis* and to which conventional mod-els of historical change cannot be applied. Although printing trans-formed the conditions under which texts were produced, distributed, and consumed, it did so not by discarding the products of scribal cul-ture, but by reproducing them in greater quantities than ever before. Even while the conditions of scribal culture were being outmoded, texts reflecting those conditions were becoming more abundant, and different spirits from different times were being simultaneously released.

[10] Douglas McMurtrie, *The Book* (Oxford, 1943), 136; Gilmore, *World of Human-ism*, 186 (italics mine).

Later scholars, looking back on the first century of printing, will necessarily see few signs of the advent of a new culture unless they know in advance what to look for. The most significant changes ushered in by typography cannot be detected by scanning booksellers' catalogues in search of new titles. This very activity inhibits recognition that a frequent use of title pages was new (and booksellers' catalogues were too) during the first century of printing.

As previous discussion of dissemination may suggest, printers initially contributed to "the advancement of disciplines" less by marketing so-called new works than by providing individual readers with access to *more* works. The sheer increase in the quantity of copies in circulation was actually of immense significance. Augmented book production altered patterns of consumption; increased output changed the nature of individual intake. The literary diet of a given sixteenth-century reader was qualitatively different from that of his fourteenth-century counterpart. His staple diet had been enriched, and intellectual ferment had been encouraged, whether he consulted living authors or dead ones, "new" books or "old" ones. But a twentieth-century observer, intent on tracing trends or shifts in styles of thought and expression, is poorly situated to see this. With regard to the social history of art, we are informed by one authority: "In the fifteenth century . . . it is true, a number of things come to fruition but as good as nothing absolutely new begins."[11] Another account dealing with developments in astronomy finds that "no mutational elements of significance appear to have been introduced in the fifteenth century."[12]

Elsewhere I have suggested that a mutational element of significance was introduced into the study of astronomy during the fifteenth century when Regiomontanus set up his Nuremberg press. Here, I want to suggest that printing produced a mutation of the

[11] Arnold Hauser, *The Social History of Art*, vol. 2, *Renaissance, Mannerism, Baroque*, tr. S. Godman (New York, 1957), 3.

[12] Dana B. Durand, "Tradition and Innovation in 15th Century Italy: 'Il Primato dell'Italia' in the Field of Science," *Toward Modern Science*, vol. 2, ed. R. Palter (New York, 1961), 35.

classical revival itself. This entails adopting a somewhat different strategy from that employed in the citation at the head of this chapter. The relationship between a given technological and a given cultural change will be approached, not by taking them to coincide, as Butler does, but by acknowledging that they came at different times and by investigating how they affected each other. Let us then set aside, for the moment, the problem of locating a transition from medieval to modern times and take as a starting point the Italian cultural revival which antedated printing. Given a cultural revival already under way, we may then ask: How was it affected by the shift from script to print?

In attempting to answer this question, the first consideration that comes to mind is a distinction drawn by the celebrated art historian, Erwin Panofsky: "To put it briefly, the two medieval renascences were limited and transitory; the Renaissance was total and permanent."[13] Given a classical revival that was still under way when new preservative powers were brought into play, one might expect that this revival would acquire peculiar characteristics. Since it was initiated under one set of circumstances and perpetuated under different ones, it would probably begin by resembling previous revivals and yet take an increasingly divergent course. Among other differences that would become apparent with the passage of time, one would expect this revival to be more permanent than previous ones.

As Panofsky's formulation suggests, the issue of permanence does figure prominently in current debates. However, typographical fixity does not. Instead of being attributed to the new technology, or even recognized as a new cultural trait that needs to be accounted for, permanence currently serves as a debating point. As an inherent virtue somehow exuded by Renaissance culture, it is invoked to shore up the thesis that the Italian Renaissance introduced epochal change. No explanation is offered as to why medieval classical revivals were more transitory than that which occurred in quattrocento Italy. The fact that the latter did prove more permanent and hence lent itself to continuous systematic development is taken to justify setting it apart

[13] Panofsky, *Renaissance and Renascences*, 106.

from prior revivals and inaugurating a new epoch with its advent. In this way, objections posed to Burckhardt's thesis can be countered and a seemingly interminable debate prolonged.

By now it is evident that many of the criteria employed to distinguish the Italian Renaissance from prior revivals may, with equal validity, also be employed to distinguish these prior revivals from each other. The Italian Renaissance had certain peculiar features which deserve to be singled out as novel and significant. But so too did the Carolingian revival and that of the twelfth century. Why, then, attribute a special epoch-making role to the quattrocento revival? It seems to be difficult to justify this attribution without straining the evidence by reading back into quattrocento cultural products anticipations of later developments. In the nineteenth century, early humanist texts were made to point to the secular and modernist heresies that were being listed in the Syllabus of Errors. At present, Renaissance humanists look less like nineteenth-century freethinkers than they once did. But they look more like twentieth-century historians instead. As "the ancestors of modern philologists and historians,"[14] they resemble contemporary professional scholars too closely, in my view, for their true likeness to be caught.

In the Middle Ages there was in relation to the Antique a cyclical succession of assimilative and non-assimilative stages. Since the Renaissance the Antique has been constantly with us, whether we like it or not. It lives in our mathematics and natural sciences . . . it is firmly entrenched behind the thin but thus far unbroken walls of history, philology and archeology.

The formation and, ultimately, formalization of these three disciplines – foreign to the Middle Ages in spite of all the Carolingian and twelfth century "humanists" – evince a fundamental difference between the medieval and modern attitude toward . . . antiquity . . . In the Italian Renaissance the classical past began to be looked at from a fixed distance, quite comparable to the "distance between the eye and the object" in that most

[14] Paul Kristeller, *Renaissance Thought: The Classic, Scholastic and Humanist Strains* (New York, 1961), 98.

characteristic invention of this very Renaissance, focused perspective . . . this distance prohibited direct contact . . . but permitted a total and rationalized view.[15]

It is undeniable that there is a fundamental difference between medieval and modern views of antiquity. Medieval scholars did not see the classical past from a fixed distance as we do now. They did not regard it as a container of objects to be placed in glass cases and investigated by specialists in diverse scholarly fields. Nor were they familiar with the historical disciplines as they are practiced today. Agreement on these points, however, still leaves open to dispute the views of Renaissance humanists and the correct interpretation of their attitude toward the past. Given their celebration of a revival based on classical models and their passion for recovering, collecting, and examining antique works; given also their more novel belief that a dark interval of barbarism separated them from antiquity, were they the harbingers of a distinctively modern historical consciousness? Did their sense of temporal distance come close to resembling our own? Panofsky, of course, answers affirmatively, and many other distinguished authorities agree with him. Passages drawn from a variety of Renaissance texts – ranging from Petrarch to Erasmus – are cited to support him.[16] It is taken almost for granted at present that a capacity to view the past from a fixed distance may be singled out as a distinguishing feature of Renaissance thought – one that links the Italian revival with later developments and separates it from prior ones.

Despite the formidable support it commands, I think this interpretation is open to dispute. That a "total rationalized" view of any past civilization could be developed before the output of uniform reference guides and gazetteers seems implausible to me. How could the entire classical past be viewed "from a fixed distance" until a permanent temporal location had been found for antique objects, place

---

[15] Panofsky, *Renaissance and Renascences*, 108.
[16] Gilmore, *World of Humanism*, 236, and Harbison, *Christian Scholar*, 93, provide relevant citations accompanied by apposite interpretations.

names, personages, and events? The capacity to see the past in this way could not be obtained by new optical effects devised by Renaissance artists. It required a rearrangement of documents and artifacts rather than a rearrangement of pictorial space.

It took at least a century of printing before the multiform maps and tangled chronologies inherited from scribal records were sorted out, data reworked, and more uniform systems for arranging materials developed. Before then, there was no fixed spatiotemporal reference frame which men of learning shared. This is not to deny that a growing sensitivity to anachronism was manifested by quattrocento scholars. There was discrimination between Gothic and antique styles, medieval and Ciceronian Latin, republican and imperial institutions, the Rome of ancient Caesars and of medieval popes. But it occurred within an amorphous spatiotemporal context that was still fundamentally different from the modern one. Within this context some portions of the past might appear to be very close at hand, even while others might be placed at a great distance. Since we are told that an Attic stele from the fifth century B.C. could not be distinguished by sixteenth-century connoisseurs from a piece of sculpture by Michelangelo,[17] it would appear that some portions of the Greco-Roman past must have seemed very close at hand even after the quattrocento had ended.

Panofsky regards it as characteristic of the medieval mind that it viewed classical antiquity as "too strongly present" and at the same time as "too far removed" to be "conceived as an historical phenomenon... Linguists looked upon Cicero and Donatus as their forefathers... mathematicians traced their ancestry back to Euclid" even while there was awareness of "an unsurmountable gap" between pagan and Christian eras. "These two tendencies were as yet not balanced so as to permit a feeling of historical distance... No medieval man could see the civilization of antiquity as a phenomenon complete in itself... belonging to the past... detached from the contemporary world."[18] His discussion seems equally pertinent to the mind

[17] Panofsky, *Renaissance and Renascences*, 41.
[18] Erwin Panofsky, *Studies in Iconology* (New York, 1939), 27.

of the quattrocento humanists and indeed to that of many cinquecento scholars.

In this regard, the mentality of those artists and literati who collected ancient art works and copied ancient inscriptions during the
quattrocento needs to be distinguished from that of modern curators
and scholars who are still engaged in similar activities. The latter are
alert to the difference between ancient Roman styles of lettering and
those of Carolingian scribes. They are unlikely to confuse the work
of an ancient artist with that of a cinquecento one. The contrary was
true of Renaissance scholars and connoisseurs.

Not only were the works of contemporary artists confused with
ancient ones and pagan forms still employed for Christian subjects, but some medieval bookhands (notably Carolingian minuscule) were also mistakenly attributed to antiquity.[19] When they
handled manuscript books copied by eleventh- and twelfth-century
scribes, quattrocento literati thought they were looking at texts that
came right out of the bookshops of ancient Rome. When they sat
down and wrote out their own books in a similar bookhand, they
must have also experienced a sense of closeness to ancient authors
that is quite unlike our own. We might compare the experience of a
humanist who was engaged in copying one of Livy's books, and thus,
in a sense, was engaged in "writing" one of Livy's books, with our
experience in taking down a bound volume in the Loeb series from
some library shelf.

Doubtless, the very activity of copying and commenting on books
by ancient authors such as Livy did help to sharpen awareness of
the difference between ancient and contemporary Latin grammar
as well as between ancient styles of thought and expression and
those reflected in the medieval Latin texts which were used in the
schools. A sophisticated approach to philology as a key to dating
documents was manifested by some Renaissance scribal scholars,
most notably by Lorenzo Valla. But the heavy reliance on memory training and speech arts, combined with the absence of uniform

---

[19] Kristeller, *Renaissance Thought*, 21.

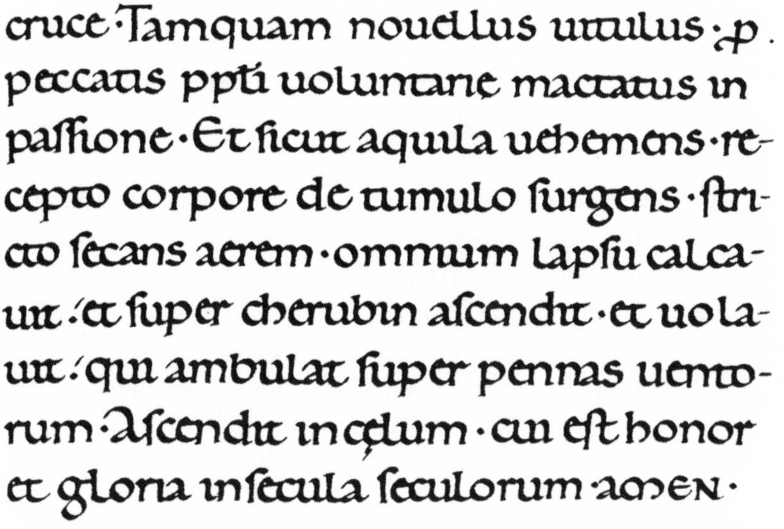

cruce·Tamquam nouellus uitulus·p.
peccatis ppti uoluntarie mactatus in
paffione·Et ficut aquila uehemens·re-
cepto corpore de tumulo furgens·ftri-
cto fecans aerem·omnium lapfu calca-
uit·et fuper cherubin afcendit·et uola-
uit·qui ambulat fuper pennas uento-
rum·Afcendit in cęlum·cui eft honor
et gloria infecula feculorum amen·

(cruce · Tamquam novellus vitulus · p*ro* | peccatis pop*u*li voluntarię mactatus
in | passione · Et sicut aquila vehemens · re cepto corpore de tumulo surgens ·
stri|cto secans aerem · omnium lapsu calca vit ! et super cherubin ascendit ·
et vola vit ! qui ambulat super pennas vento rum · Ascendit in cęlum · cui
est honor | et gloria in secula seculorum · amen ·)

Fig. 22. Carolingian minuscule was mistakenly attributed to the ancient Romans by
Renaissance humanists. This example of an early twelfth-century minuscule book-
hand comes from Edward Maunde Thompson, *An Introduction to Greek and Latin
Paleography* (Oxford: Clarendon Press, 1912, facsimile 181).

conventions for dating and placing, worked against any reinforcement of this embryonic consciousness. Given ubiquitous training in
the *ars memorandi*, classical images were more likely to be placed in
niches in "memory theaters" than to be assigned a permanent location in a fixed past.

I would argue then, that "a total rationalized view" of antiquity
began to appear only after the first century of printing rather than
in Petrarch's lifetime and that the preservative powers of print were
a prerequisite for this new view. It is not "since the Renaissance,"
but since the advent of printing and engraving, that "the antique
has been continuously with us." Furthermore, it seems likely that

the same changes which affected the classical revival in Italy also affected medieval survivals on both sides of the Alps. The so-called historical revolution of the sixteenth century owed perhaps as much to the "systematization and codification of existing customary law" as it did to the systematic investigation of the legal heritage from Rome.[20] Views of the medieval past were altered in much the same manner as the classical past, so that it, too, came to be observed from "a fixed distance." Even Gothic art was eventually entrenched behind the same museum walls as classical art. During the interval when Gothic was synonymous with "barbaric," there were some bar-barian folkways that evoked admiration (as numerous citations from Tacitus's *Germania* suggest). From the fifteenth century on, praise for feudal institutions and pride in vernacular literatures were scarcely less common in learned circles than the cult of antiquity. "We were having a little Renaissance of our own; or a Gothic revival if you please."[21] Maitland's comment seems to apply, beyond developments in Tudor and Stuart England, to the contemporaneous continental scene as well. It was, finally, in opposition to a full-blown Gothic revival that the nineteenth-century concept of a "Renaissance" was shaped.

Such considerations are worth keeping in mind when we look at the way Panofsky tries to illustrate his thesis:

Our own script and letter press derive from the Italian Renais-sance types patterned in deliberate opposition to the Gothic upon Carolingian and twelfth century models which in turn had been evolved on a classical basis. Gothic script one might say symbolizes the transitoriness of the medieval renascences; our modern letter press, whether Roman or Italic, testifies to the enduring quality of the Italian Renaissance. Thereafter the classical element in our civilization could be opposed (though it should not be forgotten

[20] Franklin, *Jean Bodin*, 36–8, discusses this development in sixteenth-century France.
[21] Cited by J. G. A. Pocock, *The Ancient Constitution and the Feudal Law* (Cambridge, 1957), p. 15, n. 4. Much of Pocock's study is relevant to the above discussion.

that opposition is only another form of dependence) but it could not entirely disappear again.[22]

The end of this passage seems to apply with equal force to the "Gothic" element in our civilization. That so-called Gothic type forms competed on equal terms with "antiqua" in most regions during the first century of printing; that they outlasted the Renaissance in Dutch, Scandinavian, and German regions; that they continued to impress their mark on German texts through the nineteenth century and beyond – all this also seems to have been left out of account. Modern letter forms testify to a complicated cluster of changes which came in the wake of printing. These changes cannot be understood by thinking about the "enduring quality of the Italian Renaissance" or the "transitoriness" of medieval revivals, but only by examining the effects of typography on fifteenth-century bookhands. By the seventeenth century, the patterning of type styles reflected the fixing of new religious frontiers and markedly departed from Renaissance conventions. "The twentieth century reader," writes Panofsky, "finds Carolingian script easier to decipher than Gothic and this ironic fact tells the whole story."[23] What is ironic is that this is by no means the whole story and that it comes from a twentieth-century reader who probably learned to read his native language as a schoolboy from texts set in a "Gothic" type.

The contrast of "Gothic script," taken as a symbol of transience, with "our modern letter press," taken to signify the enduring Renaissance, suggests how confusion is compounded when Renaissance humanism is credited with functions performed by the new technology. Insofar as bookhands are involved, Gothic is a singularly inappropriate symbol for the sort of revival that sponsored Carolingian minuscule, while the type form that was popularized by Lutheran Bible printers never was medieval and has not proved to be transitory. A twentieth-century American singling out today's copy of *The New York Times* or *The Washington Post* from newsstand piles has no

---

[22] Panofsky, *Renaissance and Renascences*, 108.
[23] Ibid., 107.

Alimenta ſanis cor⸗
poribus agricultu⸗
ra: Sanitatem autem
ægris Medicina pro-
mittit. Corn. Celſ.

Runde Antiqua.

Æſtimatione noĉturnæ
quietis, dimidio quiſque
ſpatio vitæ ſuæ vivit. Plin.

Cölniſche Antiqua.

Vita quid eſt hominis? Spes
& formido futuri;
Mœſticiæ multum, læti-
tiæq; parum.

Tertia Antiqua.

Damnum turpi lucro longe
præferendum eſt: illud enim ſemel dolet; hoc ſemper. Chilon.

Mittel Antiqua.

Vt Spicæ, quæ inclinatæ ad terram
vergunt, plenæ ſunt; & quæ ſurſum at-
tolluntur, inanes: ita qui de ſeipſis
modeſte ſentiunt & loquuntur, vere ſa-
pientes & boni; qui magnifice, rudes
& improbi.

Cicero Antiqua.

O quàm compoſitum reddit omnem
corporis ſtatum diſciplina! Cervicem ſub-
mittit; ponit ſupercilia; componit vultum;
ligat oculos: Cachinnationes cohibet; mo-
deratur lingvam; frenat gulam; ſçdat iram;
format inceſſum. Bernh.

Antiqua auff 32. zeilen.

In converſatione cedendum majori; minori
cum modeſtia perſvadendum; æquali aſſentien-
dum; & hac via nunquam ad contentionem
pervenietur. Epiĉtet.

Corpus Antiqua.

Ego ita comperi, omnia regna, civitates, nationes,
uſque eò proſperum imperium habuiſſe, dum apud
eos vera conſilia valuerunt. Saluſt.

Concordanz Antiqua.

Nulla remedia, quæ vulneribus adhibentur, tam faciunt
dolorem, quàm quæ ſunt ſalutaria. Cicero.

Chriſtus iſt des
Geſetzes ende/wer
an den gleubet/der
iſt gerecht. Rom. 10.

Tewerdanck.

So halten wir es nu/
daß der Menſch gerecht
werde / ohn des Geſetzes
werck / allein durch den
Glauben. Rom. 3.

Bibel ⸗ oder Textſchrifft.

Alle die gottſelig leben
wollen in Chriſto Jeſu/
müſſen verfolgung leiden.
2. Tim. 3.

Grobe Fractur Bapſts.

Wer ſein Leben verleuret/
vmb meinen vnd des Euan⸗
gelij willen / der wirds behal⸗
ten. Marc. 8.

Tertia Fractur.

Das iſt gewießlich war/ſterben
wir mit / ſo werden wir mit leben/
Dulden wir / ſo werden wir mit
herrſchen. 2. Tim. 2.

Mittel Fractur Bapſts.

Dem Gerechten muſs das Liecht
immer wieder auffgehen/ vnd frew⸗
de den frommen hertzen. Pſal. 97.

Poſtillſchrifft.

Wer gedültig iſt/ der iſt weiſe/
wer aber vngedültig iſt/ der offen⸗
baret ſeine Thorheit. Prov. 14.

Mittel Fractur.

Das kein auge geſehen / vnd kein Ohr
gehöret hat/vnd in keines Menſchen hertz

Fig. 23. These examples of antiqua or Roman type styles (left) and of Gothic or Fractur type styles (right) come from a facsimile edition of Jerome Hornschuch, *Orthotypographia* (Leipzig: M. Lanzenberger, 1608). Reproduced by kind permission of the Cambridge University Library.

trouble deciphering Gothic letters. The Renaissance type form left a permanent imprint not because it drew on one style of lettering rather than another but because it was impressed by type and not by a human hand.

Until the advent of printing, classical revivals were necessarily limited in scope and transitory in effect; a sustained and permanent recovery of all portions of the antique heritage remained out of reach. This was true even after the introduction of paper. Cheaper writing material encouraged the recording of more sermons, orations, adages, and poems. It contributed greatly to more voluminous correspondence and to the keeping of more diaries, memoirs, copybooks, and notebooks. The shift from parchment to paper thus had a significant impact upon the activities of merchants and literati. Nevertheless, as already noted, paper could do nothing to lighten the labors or increase the output of the professional copyist. As long as texts could be duplicated only by hand, perpetuation of the classical heritage rested precariously on the shifting requirements of local elites. Texts imported into one region depleted supplies in others; the enrichment of certain fields of study by an infusion of ancient learning impoverished other fields of study by diverting scribal labor. For a full century after the coronation of Petrarch, the revival of learning in Italy was subject to the same limitations as had been previous revivals. If we accept the distinction between several limited and transient renascences on the one hand and a permanent Renaissance of unprecedented range and scope on the other, then we must wait for a century and a half after Petrarch before we can say that a genuinely new pattern was established.

The fate of Greek studies after the fall of Constantinople offers a dramatic example of how printing transformed traditional patterns of cultural change.

One of the strangely persistent myths of history is that the humanist study of Greek works began with the arrival in Italy in 1453 of learned refugees from Constantinople who are supposed to have fled the city in all haste, laden with rare manuscripts. Aside from the essential improbability of their doing any such thing, and the well-established fact that the opening years of the fifteenth century had seen intense activity... there is the testimony of the humanists themselves that the fall of Constantinople represented a tragedy to them. Characteristic is the cry of the humanist Cardinal, Aeneas Sylvius Piccolomini... who wrote despairingly to Pope Nicholas in July, 1453: "How many names of mighty men will perish! It is a second death to Homer and to Plato. The fount of the Muses is dried up forever more."[24]

The "strangely persistent" myth points to a remarkable reversal of previous trends. To the best of my knowledge, it represents the very first time that the dispersal of major manuscript centers ever got associated with a revival of learning rather than with the onset of a dark age. The humanist cardinal was expressing expectations that were based on all the lessons of history which were available in his day and which showed how learning was eclipsed when great cities fell. We now tend to take for granted that the study of Greek would continue to flourish after the main Greek manuscript centers had fallen into alien hands and hence fail to appreciate how remarkable it was to find that Homer and Plato had not been buried anew but had, on the contrary, been disinterred forever more.

The flourishing of Hellenic studies in the West, despite the disruption of peaceful contacts with the Greek learned world, provides only one of many indications that typography endowed scholarship with new powers. Hebrew and Arabic studies also gained a new lease on life. Medieval Bible studies had depended on Christian contacts with Jews as well as with Greeks. Until after the fifteenth century, Western Christendom had been unable to sustain "an unbroken tradition of skill in semitic languages."[25] A Venetian printing firm run by Daniel Bomberg, an emigré from Antwerp, laid new foundations for Western semitic scholarship, spurring studies in Hebrew and Arabic much as Aldus Manutius had spurred the study of Greek. Other languages, hitherto completely foreign among Europeans, became available to

---

[24] Marie Boas, *The Scientific Renaissance* (New York, 1962), 24.
[25] Beryl Smalley, *The Study of the Bible in the Middle Ages* (South Bend, IN, 1964), 44.

Western scholars for the first time. Polyglot Bibles were turned out by presses located in Alcalà, Antwerp, Paris, and London between 1517 and 1657.[26] Each of the four editions surpassed its predecessors in the number of languages used; no less than nine (including Persian and Ethiopic) had to be mastered by the compositors and correctors of the London edition of 1657. Once fonts had been cut and multilingual dictionaries and grammars had been issued, durable foundations for the development of new erudite disciplines had been laid.

The recovery of ancient languages followed the same pattern as the recovery of ancient texts. A process which had hitherto been intermittent became subject to continuous, incremental change. Once a finding could be permanently secured by being registered in print, the way was paved for an unending series of discoveries and for the systematic development of investigatory techniques. Probes into the past were steadily extended; texts and languages lost, not merely to the West, but to all men everywhere for thousands of years, were retrieved from the dead, reconstructed, and deciphered. Compared with the refined techniques employed at present, sixteenth-century methods appear crude and clumsy. Yet however sophisticated present findings have become, we still have to call upon a fifteenth-century invention to secure them. Even at present, a given scholarly discovery, whatever its nature (whether it entails using a shovel or crane, a code book, a tweezer, or carbon 14), has to be registered in print – announced in a learned journal and eventually spelled out in full – before it can be acknowledged as a contribution or put to further use.

Archeology, writes Roberto Weiss, "was a creation of the Renaissance. Reverence for the antique has . . . nearly always existed. But one would search the classical world or the Middle Ages in vain for a systematic study of antiquity."[27] Systematic study, however, was still in the future during the century which followed Petrarch.

---

[26] D. B. Updike, *Printing Types: Their History Forms and Use: A Study in Survivals* (Cambridge, MA, 1937), II:98.

[27] Roberto Weiss, *The Renaissance Discovery of Classical Antiquity* (Oxford, 1969), 203.

As Weiss himself points out, during the first half of the quattro-cento, classical studies were still in an unsystematic state. System-atization came only after the humanist impulse could be combined with new features supplied by print culture. Furthermore, the sys-tematic development of the investigation of antiquity had medieval as well as Renaissance antecedents. Curiosity about ancient artifacts and languages was perpetually stimulated by the need to copy and emend both the writings of church fathers and the sacred Scriptures themselves.

In this light, it seems misleading to stop short with the human-ist movement in Italy when trying to account for the so-called rise of classical scholarship and the development of auxiliary disciplines. Humanism may have encouraged the pursuit of classical studies for their own sake, sharpened sensitivity to anachronism, and quickened curiosity about all aspects of antiquity, but it could not supply the new element of continuity that is implied by the use of the term "rise." Findings relating to lost texts and dead languages began to accumulate in an unprecedented fashion, not because of some dis-tinctive ethos shaped in quattrocento Italy, but because a new tech-nology had been placed at the disposal of a far-flung community of scholars.

A wide variety of other developments that are usually associated with the culture of the Italian Renaissance and that seem to point toward modern times lend themselves to a similar interpretation. We might look, for example, at Burckhardt's introduction to his section on "the development of the individual":

> In the Middle Ages both sides of human consciousness . . . lay dreaming or half awake beneath a common veil. The veil was woven of faith, illusion, and childish prepossession, through which the world and history were seen clad in strange hues. Man was conscious of himself only as a member of a race, people, party, fam-ily, or corporation – only through some general category. In Italy this veil first melted into air; an objective treatment of the state and of all the things of this world became possible . . . at the same time . . . man became a spiritual individual and recognized himself

as such . . . It will not be difficult to show that this result was owing above all to the political circumstances of Italy.[28]

Certain portions of this passage seem to me to be invalid – especially the assertion about medieval man lacking consciousness of self. It is probably misguided to assign group consciousness to one era and individual consciousness to another. The sense of belonging to a "general category" *and* of being a "spiritual individual" seems to have coexisted in Western Christendom in the days of Saint Augustine and in those of Saint Bernard. If, indeed, there was a change in human consciousness during the early modern era, it probably entailed the sense *both* of group identity and of an individual one. Other portions of the passage also need to be reformulated. As they stand, they are so ambiguous that one cannot be certain just what Burckhardt means by "this result."

Nevertheless, I would not join those who argue that the passage contains no substantive issues or that there was no real shift in human consciousness that needs to be explained. Unlike certain critics, moreover, I do not doubt that political circumstances in Italy helped to shape a distinctive ethos which contained much that was new and proved historically significant. At the same time, I think much more is owed to the advent of printing and much less to local circumstances in Italy than is suggested by the passage or by later interpretations of it. Given a shift in human consciousness and a concurrent revolution in communications, it seems far-fetched to attribute the shift to political conditions in Italy.

Of the two sides of human consciousness discussed by Burckhardt, the so-called objective aspect need not detain us for long, since changing views of "the world and history" have entered into previous discussion. Let me note in passing, however, that the problem might be handled more satisfactorily if it were posed somewhat differently. Whether or not the medieval mentality was peculiarly child-like or credulous is, in my view, an unedifying question. I would

---

[28] Jacob Burckhardt, *The Civilization of the Renaissance in Italy*, tr. S. G. C. Middlemore, ed. B. Nelson and C. Trinkaus (New York, 1958), I:143.

prefer instead to stress the common acceptance on the part of otherwise hardheaded, intelligent, and literate adults (belonging to ancient, medieval, and/or Renaissance elite groups) of what has been described elsewhere as "fantastic history and imaginary geography."[29] An inability to discriminate between Paradise and Atlantis on the one hand, Cathay and Jerusalem on the other, between unicorns and rhinoceroses, the fabulous and the factual, does seem to separate earlier mentalities from our own in a way that arouses curiosity and requires explanation. How may we account for this strangely colored vision? Surely it is not adequately explained by Burckhardt's vague poetic allusions to medieval dreams and veils which melted into air under the impact of political circumstances in Italy. As previous comments suggest, I think more adequate explanations can be found by considering the conditions of scribal culture and how they changed after print. After reviewing the controversy over the location of Paradise, which contemporaries were placing in such dissimilar places as Syria and the Arctic Pole, Abraham Ortelius, the sixteenth-century map publisher, decided to exclude it as a problem for geographers: "By Paradise I do think the blessed life to be understood."[30] When considering how veils were lifted, the programs of atlas publishers and globe makers should not be ignored. The absence of uniform maps delineating political boundaries seems to me to be more relevant to blurred political consciousness during prior eras than has yet been noted in most historical studies. For Ortelius, as for Herodotus, geography was the "eye of history." Printing altered what could be seen by this metaphorical eye. An atlas such as the *Theatrum* did enable men to envisage past worlds and the present one more clearly. This was because methods of data collection rather than political circumstances in Italy had been changed.

Without dwelling longer on this point, let me turn now to Burckhardt's treatment of the "subjective" side of human consciousness. Even at first glance it is evident that the theme of growing self-awareness is handled unevenly. The author begins on shaky grounds

---

[29] H. J. Chaytor, *From Script to Print* (Cambridge, 1945), 26.
[30] Ortelius, "Message to the Reader," ij.

and ends on firmer ones when he moves from the age of scribes to that of printers. His opening passages, describing how "at the close of the thirteenth century, Italy began to swarm with individuality," seem vulnerable to criticism from many quarters.[31] The section closes, however, with a much more straightforward account of a new career, one which pointed the way to the future and was based on exploiting the new power of the press:

> Aretino affords the first great instance of the abuse of publicity... The polemical writings which a hundred years earlier Poggio and his opponents interchanged are just as infamous in their tone and purpose but they were not composed for the press... Aretino made all his profit out of a complete publicity and in a certain sense may be considered the father of modern journalism. His letters and miscellaneous articles were printed periodically after they had already been circulated among a tolerably extensive public.[32]

The title "father of modern journalism" may be somewhat too dignified for one of the founders of the gutter press. Although Aretino was not the first blackguard to pursue a literary career, he was the first to take advantage of the new publicity system. His activities, like those pursued by his Grub Street successors, do at least suggest that new powers were placed at the disposal of men of letters after the advent of printing.

That these powers could be used by literati in their own behalf needs to be kept in mind when considering Renaissance individualism. As Pierre Mesnard has noted, the Republic of Letters during the sixteenth century resembled a newly liberated state where every citizen felt he had an irresistible vocation for serving as prime minister.[33] Many of the devices which are still being used by press agents were

---

[31] Burckhardt, *Civilization of the Renaissance*, I:143.
[32] Ibid., 170–1.
[33] Pierre Mesnard, "Le Commerce Epistolaire comme Expression Sociale de l'Individualisme Humaniste," *Individu et Société de la Renaissance: Colloque International – 1965* (Brussels, 1967), 26.

first tried out during the age of Erasmus. In the course of exploiting new publicity techniques, few authors failed to give high priority to publicizing themselves. The art of puffery, the writing of blurbs, and other familiar promotional devices were also exploited by early printers who worked aggressively to obtain public recognition for the authors and artists whose products they hoped to sell.

In general, the new powers of the press seem to be so pertinent to the heightened recognition accorded individual achievement that it is disconcerting to find them unmentioned in most treatments of the latter topic. The testimony of prophets and preachers may be cited to suggest that public curiosity about private lives, like the desire for worldly fame and glory – like avarice, lechery, or vanity, for that matter – had venerable antecedents. But printing made it possible to supplement tales of saints and saintly kings by biographies and autobiographies of more ordinary people pursuing heterogeneous careers. It also encouraged publishers to advertise authors and authors to advertise themselves. Scribal culture could not sustain the patenting of inventions or the copyrighting of literary compositions. It worked against the concept of intellectual property rights. It did not lend itself to preserving traces of personal idiosyncrasies, to the public airing of private thoughts, or to any of the forms of silent publicity that have shaped consciousness of self during the past five centuries.

In accounting for the emergence of uniquely distinguished, personally celebrated artists out of the ranks of more anonymous artisans, the preservative powers of print deserve more attention. This is not to deny that individual artists were already being singled out for praise as eminent citizens (especially in Florence) well before the advent of printing. Nor is it to overlook the evidence of heightened self-esteem and self-consciousness which was provided by several scribal treatises written by Florentine artists about themselves and their craft. It is merely to say that the cult of personality was repeatedly undermined by the conditions of scribal culture and was powerfully reinforced after the advent of printing. The personal histories of even the most celebrated masters could not be recorded until writing materials became relatively abundant. And until records could be duplicated, they were not likely to be preserved intact for very long. When fifteenth-century manuscripts found their way into print, ephemeral materials were secured along with formal work. Treatises, orations, intimate correspondence, anecdotes, and drawings all were collected by Vasari for his celebrated *Lives*.

Vasari's work is often heralded as the first book devoted specifically to art history.[34] The novelty of his theory of cultural cycles also is often stressed. But there are other, less familiar, aspects of his enterprise which deserve more attention because they show how the art of biography profited from changes wrought by print. The sheer number of separate individuals, all engaged in a similar endeavor, covered by the second edition of his multivolume work is, in itself, noteworthy. To match artworks with biographical records for 250 separate cases represented an unprecedented feat. In addition to the expansion in scale, there was a new effort at research in depth. Vasari's was the first systematic investigation, based on interviews, correspondence, and field trips, of the procedures used and the objects produced by generations of European artists. The *Lives* also reflects the new opportunity offered by print to extend the scope of a given work from one edition to another. The second edition of 1568 was a vastly expanded version of the first one in 1550. It broke out of the limits imposed by Florentine civic loyalties and introduced no less than seventy-five new biographical sketches. Among other notable innovations, woodcut portraits were designed to go with each biographical sketch. Significantly enough, despite the special effort made to match faces with names, purely conjectural portraits had to be supplied for artists who lived before the fifteenth century.

Before the fifteenth century, even artists' self-portraits were deprived of individuality. The conditions of scribal culture thus held narcissism in check. A given master might decide to place his own features on a figure in a fresco or on a carving over a door; but in the absence of written records, he would still lose his identity in the

---

34 See Richard Krautheimer, "The Beginnings of Art Historical Writing in Italy" (1929), *Studies in Early Christian, Medieval, and Renaissance Art* (New York, 1969), 268; E. H. Gombrich, "Art and Scholarship," *Meditations on a Hobby Horse* (London, 1963), 106–19; and Anthony Blunt, *Artistic Theory in Italy 1450–1600* (Oxford, 1966), 98.

eyes of posterity and become another faceless artisan who performed some collective task. The same point also applies to those occasional author portraits which survived from antiquity. In the course of continuous copying, the face of one author got transferred to another's text, and distinctive features were blurred or erased. After the passage of centuries, the figure at the desk or the robed scholar holding a book became simply an impersonal symbol of the author at large. As noted earlier, these impersonal images did not disappear when print replaced script. On the contrary, they were subject to a greater degree of standardization and multiplied by woodcuts and engravings. Just as the same city profile might be labeled with different place names in an early printed chronicle, so, too, an identical human profile served to illustrate diverse individuals performing the same occupational role. Careless handling of corrupted woodcuts also led to further comedies of errors and mistaken identities. At the same time, however, the drive for fame moved into high gear; the self-portrait acquired a new permanence, a heightened appreciation of individuality accompanied increased standardization, and there was a new deliberate promotion by publishers and print dealers of those authors and artists whose works they hoped to sell. Along with title pages and booksellers' catalogues, came portrait heads of authors and artists. More and more, distinct physiognomies became permanently attached to distinct names. Sixteenth-century portraits of Erasmus, Luther, Loyola, and others were multiplied with sufficient frequency to be duplicated in innumerable history books and to remain recognizable even now.

When historical figures can be given distinct faces, they also acquire a more distinctive personality. The characteristic individuality of Renaissance masterpieces in comparison with earlier ones is probably related to the new possibility of preserving by duplication the faces, names, birthplaces, and personal histories of the makers of objects of art. The hands of medieval illuminators or stone carvers were in fact no less distinctive – as investigations by art historians show. But the personalities of the masters (who are usually known only by their initials or by the books, altarpieces, and tympana they produced) are as unfamiliar to us as those of cabinetmakers

Fig. 24. Portraits of Erasmus and Luther were multiplied so frequently as to remain recognizable even now. On the left is an engraving of Erasmus from Jean Jacques Boissard, *Icones quinquaginta virorum illustrium* (Frankfurt: M. Becker, 1597–99, Vol. I, p. 220). On the right is a woodblock portrait of Luther, variously attributed to Hans Baldung-Grien and Lucas Cranach, from Martin Luther, *De captivitate babylonica* (Basel: Adam Petri, 1520, verso of title page). Reproduced by kind permission of the Folger Shakespeare Library.

or glaziers. Even those masters whose names are known because they lacked the modesty often attributed to "humble" medieval craftsmen and took pains to carve their names on permanent materials – even such men seem to lack individuality because there are no other written records to accompany the proud inscriptions they left behind.

Every hand-copied book, it is sometimes said, "was a personal achievement." Actually, a great many hand-produced books were farmed out piecemeal to be copied and worked over by several hands. But even where a single hand runs from incipit to colophon and a full signature is given at the end, there is almost no trace of personality left by the presumably "personal achievement." Paradoxically, we must wait for impersonal type to replace handwriting and a standardized colophon to replace the individual signature, before singular experiences can be preserved for posterity and distinctive personalities can be permanently separated from the group or collective type.

LEONHARTVS FVCHSIVS
AETATIS SVAE ANNO XLI.

Fig. 25 (above and opposite). Only the hands of medieval illuminators are known, whereas the faces of some early modern illustrators are preserved. In addition to a portrait of the herbal's author, Fuchs, portraits of its artist-illustrators and its engraver are provided in this edition of Leonhart Fuchs, *De historia stirpium* (Basel: Isingrin, 1542). Reproduced by kind permission of the Department of Special Collections, Stanford University Libraries.

Much as the new medium was used to publicize the names and faces of authors and artists, so, too, it was exploited by the designers of siege engines, canal locks, and other large-scale public works. The new woodblocks, engravings, broadsheets, and medallions made more visible and also glamorized a variety of "ingenious" devices. Major "public works," once published, became tourist attractions which vied with old pilgrimage sites and Roman ruins.[35] In the hands of skillful artists, the somewhat prosaic functions of levers, pulleys, gears, and screws were dramatized; engineering feats were illustrated in the same heroic vein as epic poems. At least some of these sixteenth-century engineering epics may be described as promotional ventures undertaken by ambitious technicians in search of patrons and commissions. As the winner of a competition to move an obelisk for Sixtus V, Fontana was not crowned with laurel wreaths, but he did manage to publicize his successful achievement with a lavishly illustrated folio, which was followed by a flurry of pamphlets.[36] Other elaborate picture books, devoted to presenting "theaters of machines," also served as advertising for their authors.

"The Renaissance bridged the gap which had separated the scholar and thinker from the practitioner."[37] Of course, the "Renaissance" is too much of an abstraction to have done this. Like others who discuss the issue, Panofsky really means that the gap was bridged *during* the Renaissance and, like others also, he has certain specific factors in mind. Whereas others focus on certain socioeconomic factors, he stresses the versatility displayed by quattrocento artists: the "demolition of barriers between manual and intellectual labor was first achieved by the artists (who tend to be neglected by Zilsel and Strong)."[38] Actually, many diverse groups – medical and musical as well as architectural – sought to combine handwork with brainwork

---

[35] Alexander G. Keller, "Mathematic Technologies and the Growth of the Idea of Technical Progress in the Sixteenth Century," *Science, Medicine and Society in the Renaissance*, ed. Alan Debus (New York, 1974), 22.

[36] Ibid., 22.

[37] Erwin Panofsky, "Artist, Scientist, Genius: Notes on the 'Renaissance-Dämmerung'," *The Renaissance: Six Essays* (New York, 1962), 135–6.

[38] Ibid., p. 136, n. 13.

Fig. 26. The winner of a competition to move an obelisk for Pope Sixtus V advertised his achievement by issuing a folio with his own portrait on the title page. Taken
from Domenico Fontana, *Del modo tenuto nel trasportare l'obelisco Vaticano* (Rome,
1589). Reproduced by kind permission of the Folger Shakespeare Library.

at different times. In my view, the permanent achievement of this combination, however, could not come until after printing. When it did come, it resulted in occupational mutations which affected anatomy no less than art.

In seeking to explain new interactions between theory and practice, schoolman and artisan, few authorities even mention the advent of printing. Yet here was an invention which made books more accessible to artisans and practical manuals more accessible to scholars, which encouraged artists and engineers to publish theoretical treatises and rewarded schoolmasters for translating technical texts. Before the Renaissance, says Panofsky,

> the absence of interaction between manual and intellectual methods . . . had prevented the admirable inventions of medieval engineers and craftsmen from being noted by what were then called the natural philosophers and . . . conversely had prevented the equally admirable deductions of logicians and mathematicians from being tested by experiment.[39]

The printing press was one invention that did not escape the attention of natural philosophers. Although it came from Vulcan's workshop and was capable of provoking snobbish disdain, it served grammarians and philosophers no less than artisans and engineers. It was also associated with Minerva, goddess of wisdom, as the frontispiece to this book graphically demonstrates. Tributes to the first press established in Paris show that literati as well as churchmen greeted the new technology as a "divine art."

The new mode of book production not only brought the work of philosophers to the attention of craftsmen and vice versa. It also brought bookworms and mechanics together in person as collaborators within the same workshops. In the figure of the master printer, it produced a "new man" who was adept in handling machines and marketing products even while editing texts, founding learned societies, promoting artists and authors, advancing new forms of data collection, and contributing to erudite disciplines. The sheer variety

[39] Ibid., 137.

of activities, both intellectual and practical, sponsored by the more celebrated firms of the sixteenth century is breathtaking. Greek and Latin classics, law books, herbals, Bible translations, anatomy texts, arithmetic books, beautifully illustrated volumes of verse – all these, issued from a single shop, pointed to fertile encounters of diverse kinds. Contemporary tributes to master printers and their products must be taken in a sceptical spirit – just as one takes the overblown claims made by blurb writers and publicists today. But hyperbole does not seem misplaced when applied to the number and variety of interchanges fostered by the master printers of Venice, Lyons, Basel, Paris, Frankfurt, Antwerp, and other major centers of the sixteenth-century trade.

It is, indeed, surprising that the figure of the master printer does not loom larger in Panofsky's treatment of "groups and friendships conducive to cross-fertilization."[40] In the printer's hands the work of editing, translating, and textual analysis was transferred from cloistered precincts to bustling commercial establishments where robed scholars and merchants worked alongside craftsmen and mechanics. The master printer's activities combined forms of labor which had been divided before and would be divided again, on a different basis, later. His products introduced new interactions between theory and practice, abstract brainwork and sensory experience, systematic logic and careful observation.

The new interactions which were encouraged, both within the printer's workshop and by the circulation of his products, would probably not have proved so fruitful had it not been for typographical fixity. The preservative powers of print made it possible to dispense with the "barriers" of which Panofsky speaks. "The Renaissance was a period of decompartmentalization: a period which broke down the barriers that had kept things in order – but also apart – during the Middle Ages."[41] As he notes, these barriers had previously divided different forms of knowledge into separate compartments and had conveyed them by separate "transmission belts." Whereas he regards

[40] Ibid., 138.
[41] Ibid., 128.

the "irresistible urge to compartmentalize" as an "idiosyncrasy of the high medieval mind,"[42] I am inclined to think, instead, of discontinuities which were inherent in the conditions of scribal culture. Keeping channels of transmission apart probably helped to prevent the dilution or corruption of information as it was passed from one generation to another.

Many forms of knowledge had to be esoteric during the age of scribes if they were to survive at all. Quite apart from issues associated with religious orthodoxy, closed systems, secretive attitudes, and even mental barriers served important social functions. Despite drifting texts, migrating manuscripts, and the dispersal or destruction of record collections, much could be learned by trial and error over the course of centuries. But advanced techniques could not be passed on without being guarded against contamination and hedged in by secrecy. To be preserved intact, techniques had to be entrusted to a select group of initiates who were instructed not only in special skills but also in the "mysteries" associated with them. Special symbols, rituals, and incantations performed the necessary function of organizing data, laying out schedules, and preserving techniques in easily memorized forms.

Curiously enough, doctrines cultivated by cloistered monks and veiled nuns were less hedged in by secrecy than trades and mysteries known to lay clerks and craftsmen. The church with its armies of apostles and missionaries, its oral and visual propaganda, its pervasive exoteric symbols and rituals, seems to have represented a remarkable exception to prevailing rules. Despite reliance on scribes, it succeeded in transmitting Christian doctrine even while proclaiming it openly and eschewing the sort of secrecy that had characterized pagan priesthoods and mystery cults. But the church, which controlled most centers of book production and the recruitment and training of copyists, was probably the only institution that was capable of instructing its priests while openly proclaiming the Truth to the laity. Heroic efforts were required to ensure that the special meaning associated with Christian symbols, ritual, and liturgy

---

[42] Panofsky, *Renaissance and Renascences*, 106.

would not be lost or diluted over the course of centuries, but would become increasingly available to a partly Latinized, largely barbarian population. Energies mobilized for this evangelical task tended to exhaust the capacities of scribal culture to transmit other messages without restricting access to select minorities who perpetuated divergent closed systems of knowledge by using separate channels of transmission.

The process of cross-fertilization that occurred when these compartmentalized systems entered the public domain was by no means a neat or elegant one. Retrospective studies of the interlocking of the relatively rigorous trades and disciplines practiced by artists, anatomists, mechanics, astronomers, and the like are misleading in this regard. According to Frances Yates, mechanics and machines were "regarded in the Hermetic tradition as a branch of magic."[43] During the age of scribes, the tendency to associate magical arts with mechanical crafts was not, however, confined to those who followed the doctrines of Hermes Trismegistus. As long as trade skills had been passed down by closed circles of initiates, unwritten recipes of all sorts seemed equally mysterious to the uninitiated. Even when instructions were written down and preserved in lodgebooks, they might still appear as "mysteries" to people on the outside. The mason's apron might serve just as well as the eye of Horus to indicate secrets veiled from the public at large. Secret formulas used by the alchemist could not be distinguished from those used by apothecaries, goldsmiths, glaziers, or luthiers. All had belonged to the same "underworld of learning"[44] and emerged into view at more or less the same time.

Thus when "technology went to press" so too did a vast backlog of occult practices and formulas, and few readers were able to discriminate between the two. For at least a century and a half confusion persisted. Publications dealing with unseen natural forces wandered all over the map and into the spirit world as well. What later came to

43 Yates, *Art of Memory*, 340.
44 R. R. Bolgar, *The Classical Heritage and Its Beneficiaries: From the Carolingian Age to the End of the Renaissance* (New York, 1964), 180.

be described as a "natural history of nonsense" was greatly enriched. The same publicity system that enabled instrument makers to advertise their wares and contribute to public knowledge also encouraged an output of more sensational claims. Discoveries of philosophers' stones, the keys to all knowledge, the cures to all ills were proclaimed by self-taught and self-professed miracle workers who often proved to be more adept at press agentry than at any of the older arts. At the same time, medieval secretive attitudes persisted among many artisans, even after the decline of craft guilds. More than two centuries after Gutenberg, Joseph Moxon was still complaining: "Letter cutting is a handy-work hitherto so conceal'd among artificers of it that I cannot learn anyone hath taught it any other."[45]

Fear of new censors as well as ambivalence about new publicity also provoked widely varying reactions among professional and academic elites. Deliberate resort to "Aesopian language," the use of veiled allusions and cryptic comment, were, if anything, more common after printing than had been the case before. Ancient esoteric injunctions to withhold the highest truths from the public were amplified and reinforced at first. Whereas some natural philosophers followed Francis Bacon in urging the opening of closed shops and a freer trade in ideas, others, like Sir Walter Raleigh, reacted against new publicity by praising ancient sages for withholding or disguising certain truths. Copernicus and Newton were as reluctant as Vesalius or Galileo were eager to break into print. "The conception of scientific collaboration as a meeting of illuminati jealously guarding their precious and mysterious discoveries"[46] was by no means decisively defeated in Francis Bacon's day. Nevertheless, the basis for this conception had been drastically transformed almost as soon as the first booksellers' catalogues appeared.

Views which were shaped by the need to preserve data from corruption were incongruous with mass-produced objects sold on

---

[45] Cited by Clapham, "Printing," 385.
[46] Paolo Rossi, *Francis Bacon: From Magic to Science*, tr. S. Rabinovich (Chicago, 1968), 27.

the open market. Insistence on concealment, as Bishop Sprat later noted, came oddly from authors who were turning out bestsellers and "ever printing their greatest mysteries." "We ask you," wrote Paracelsus, "to handle and preserve this divine mystery with the utmost secrecy."[47] The request, which seems appropriate when addressed to a select group of initiates, becomes absurd when disseminated, via commercial promotion, to the public at large. Similarly, to hear someone talk of protecting pearls from swine when he is trying to sell gems to all comers is to provoke scepticism both about his intentions and about the real worth of the products he purveys. The sorcerer who exploited fear of the unknown eventually became the charlatan who exploited mere ignorance – at least in the eyes of "enlightened" professional and academic elites. The study of "magia and cabala" was gradually detached from scholarly research. By now, the detachment is so complete that it is difficult for us to imagine how the study of dusty records and dead languages could have ever caused such a stir.

Modern historians who work in the field of Renaissance studies find it necessary to remind their readers that a "sense of revivification... accompanied the effort to interpret the original sources."[48] It is difficult for us to recapture this sense because the meaning of the term "original source" (or, for that matter, "primary source") has long since been emptied of its inspirational associations. When deciphering an ancient inscription, a modern philologist or archeologist is more apt to anticipate finding a merchant's bill of lading or even a grocery list than a clue to the secrets God entrusted to Adam. Awesome powers *are* still associated with decoding the Book of Nature, to be sure, but the key is not sought by studying Linear B or the Dead Sea Scrolls.

"How... could a critical theory like that of close imitation secure a strong hold on intelligent people or how could there have been such extravagant and servile worship of men who had lived many

---

[47] Ibid., 29.
[48] Gilmore, *World of Humanism*, 199.

ages before?"[49] asked a scholar who was trying to explain the defense of the "Ancients" after the battle of books had commenced. His inadequate answer is that the classical "decay-of-nature" theme simply lingered. I think it more likely that this theme was transformed after it had been detached from the conditions of scribal culture. Although it was propelled by print, it lost its relevance to the living experience of literate elites and became ever more artificial and conventional.

Before printing, no artifice was required to sustain the belief that loss and corruption came with the passage of time. As long as ancient learning had to be transmitted by hand-copied texts, it was more likely to be blurred or blotted out than to be augmented and improved over the course of centuries. The assumption that "the ancientest must needs be the right, as nearer the Fountain the purer the streams and the errors sprang up as the ages succeeded"[50] conformed so completely with the experience of learned men throughout the age of scribes that it was simply taken for granted. Only after that age came to an end would the superior position of the ancients require a defense.

Because the "mere restoration of ancient wisdom" has by now been completely drained of its inspirational content, we are likely to overlook its many contributions to cognitive advance in an earlier age. We are also likely to misinterpret the effect of attributing superior feats in all fields to the ancients. Far from hindering innovation, belief in prior superlative performance encouraged emulators to reach beyond their normal grasp. The notion that supreme mastery of a given art had been obtained under divine dispensation in an earlier golden age linked imitation to inspiration. Much as a new form of music drama, the opera, was created as a way of resurrecting Greek drama, so too new ocean routes were developed while searching for

---

[49] Richard Foster Jones, *Ancients and Moderns: A Study of the Rise of the Scientific Movement in 17th Century England*, 2nd ed. (Berkeley, 1965), 45.

[50] R. E. Burns, book review, *American Historical Review* CXXIV (October 1968): 181.

fountains of youth and cities of gold. Even the "invention" of central perspective may have been sparked by efforts to reconstruct lost illustrations to an ancient Alexandrian text. Only after ancient texts had been more permanently fixed to printed pages would the study of "dead" letters or the search for primary sources seem incompatible with the release of creative energies or the claim to be specially inspired:

> The whole idea of the Italian "rinascita" is inseparably connected with the notion of the preceding era as an age of obscurity. The people living in that "renascence" thought of it as a time of revolution. They wanted to break away from the medieval past and all its traditions and they were convinced that they had effected such a break.[51]

Significantly enough, most of the terms used in this citation, insofar as they *were* current during the quattrocento, have shifted their meaning since then. The wish "to break away from the medieval past and all its traditions" no longer conveys a desire to master Latin grammar, read the church fathers, or restore texts and images to their original state. Revolution (as many studies note) also means something quite different to us from what it did to Machiavelli and Copernicus. The idea of a "rinascita" was similarly affected. When Petrarch hoped that his descendants might walk back into the "pure radiance" of the past, his outlook was oriented in an opposite direction from that of Condorcet. Insofar as the Enlightenment may be regarded as an heir of the Renaissance, the notion of a movement away from darkness toward radiance has been preserved. But when the direction of the movement was reversed (so that it pointed toward a clear light of reason that grew ever brighter and away from the pristine sources of ancient wisdom), its implications were transformed as well. The advancement of disciplines was detached from the recovery of ancient learning. Inspiration was set against imitation, moderns

---

[51] Theodor E. Mommsen, "Petrarch's Conception of the 'Dark Ages'," *Speculum* XVII (April 1942): 241.

against ancients; and the early humanists, themselves, increasingly appeared in a Janus-like guise, looking hopefully in two opposite directions at once.

This is not to deny that the early Italian humanists made much of the "notion of belonging to a new time." My point is, rather, that this notion was fundamentally reoriented after it had been introduced, so that an imaginative leap is required for modern scholars to get at its original context.

To return to a remark cited at the beginning of this chapter: I agree that "something important and revolutionary occurred" between the fourteenth and sixteenth centuries, but I disagree with the suggestion that "we might as well go on calling that something the Renaissance."[52] Instead, I propose that we distinguish between two of the disparate developments now covered by this troublesome label. It makes sense to employ the term "Renaissance" when referring to a two-phased cultural movement which was initiated by Italian literati and artists in the age of scribes and expanded to encompass many regions and fields of study in the age of print. But needless confusion is engendered when the same term is also used to cover the ensemble of changes which were ushered in by print.

Not only is a major communications revolution obscured by this practice, but so, too, is the reorientation of the cultural movement. It becomes difficult to guard against prematurely endowing the Petrarchan revival with the attributes of print culture. Our modern sense of antiquity "as a totality cut off from the present" gets confusingly coupled with the quattrocento sense of antiquity on the verge of being reborn. A paradoxical hybrid construct is created: the notion of a "permanent Renaissance." A rebirth which is permanent is a contradiction in terms. Living things are perishable; only dead ones can be embalmed and indefinitely preserved. The idea of permanent postmortem, which (alas) may be compatible with modern academic history, is at odds with the sense of quickening manifested in the cultural movement called the Renaissance.

---

[52] Warnke, "Mazzeo on the Renaissance," 288.

By prolonging a process of retrieval while draining it of its inspirational significance, the preservative powers of print seem to have had a negative and largely deadening effect. From the viewpoint of romantic critics of modern culture, at all events, the academic historian appears to be a bloodless, desiccated creature in comparison with the Renaissance Man. Yet it must be remembered that early humanists, from Petrarch to Valla, owe their still vital reputation as culture heroes to the prosaic print-made knowledge industry. They would not now be heralded as founding fathers of historical scholarship if it were not for the new forms of continuity and incremental change which came after their work was done. Earlier scholars had been less fortunate.

It also should be noted that the full flowering of high Renaissance culture in cinquecento Italy owed much to early printers – especially to those in Venice, where not only Greek and Hebrew publishing but vernacular translations, new compositions in the "lingua volgare," the arts of woodcut and engraving, and the first Grub Street subculture also thrived. In this light, emphasis on the devitalizing and negative effects of the new medium needs to be balanced by considering its stimulating effect on inventive and imaginative faculties and its contributions to a heightened sense of individuality and personality – a sense which continues to distinguish Western civilization from other civilizations even now.

One more observation is in order before moving on to the next chapter. It would be a mistake to assume (as media analysts sometimes do) that the advent of printing affected all vital movements in the same way. The regional location of the movement, the specific content of the textual tradition, and above all the "accident" of timing have to be taken into account. Under the aegis of the early presses, a classical revival in Italy was reoriented. Under the same auspices, German Protestantism was born.

CHAPTER SIX

WESTERN CHRISTENDOM DISRUPTED

RESETTING THE STAGE FOR
THE REFORMATION

Between 1517 and 1520, Luther's thirty publications probably sold well over 300,000 copies . . . Altogether in relation to the spread of religious ideas it seems difficult to exaggerate the significance of the Press, without which a revolution of this magnitude could scarcely have been consummated. Unlike the Wycliffite and Waldensian heresies, Lutheranism was from the first the child of the printed book, and through this vehicle Luther was able to make exact, standardized and ineradicable impressions on the mind of Europe. For the first time in human history a great reading public judged the validity of revolutionary ideas through a mass-medium which used the vernacular language together with the arts of the journalist and the cartoonist.[1]

As the opening citation from A. G. Dickens suggests, the impact of print, which is often overlooked in discussions of the Renaissance, is less likely to go unnoted in Reformation studies. In this latter field, historians confront a movement that was shaped at the very outset (and in large part ushered in) by the new powers of the press. "The Reformation was the first religious movement," it has been said, "which had the aid of the printing press."[2] Even before Luther, however, Western Christendom had already called on printers to help with the crusade against the Turks. Church officials had already hailed the new technology as a gift from God – as a providential

---

[1] Arthur Geoffrey Dickens, *Reformation and Society in Sixteenth Century Europe* (New York, 1968), 51.
[2] Louise Holborn, "Printing and the Growth of a Protestant Movement in Germany from 1517–1524," *Church History* XI (June 1942): 1.

invention which proved Western superiority over ignorant infidel forces.[3]

Although the anti-Turkish crusade was thus the "first religious movement" to make use of print, Protestantism surely was the first fully to exploit its potential as a mass medium. It was also the first movement of any kind, religious or secular, to use the new presses for overt propaganda and agitation against an established institution. By pamphleteering directed at arousing popular support and aimed at readers who were unversed in Latin, the reformers unwittingly pioneered as revolutionaries and rabble-rousers. They also left "ineradicable impressions" in the form of broadsides and caricatures. Designed to catch the attention and arouse the passions of sixteenth-century readers, their antipapist cartoons still have a strong impact when encountered in history books today. By its very nature, then, the exploitation of the new medium by Protestants is highly visible to modern scholars.

Moreover, the reformers were aware that the printing press was useful to their cause and they acknowledged its importance in their writings. The theme of printing as proof of spiritual and cultural superiority, first sounded by Rome in its crusade against "illiterate" Turks, was taken over by German humanists trying to counter Italian claims. Gutenberg had already joined Arminius as a native culture hero before he gained added stature for providing Lutheran preachers and princes and knights with their most effective weapon in their gallant struggle against popes.[4] Luther himself described printing as "God's highest and extremest act of grace, whereby the business of the Gospel is driven forward."[5] From Luther on, the sense of a special blessing conferred on the German nation was associated with Gutenberg's invention, which emancipated the Germans from

---

[3] Geoffroy Atkinson, *Les Nouveaux Horizons de la Renaissance Française* (Paris, 1935), 57.

[4] Lewis Spitz, *The Religious Renaissance of the German Humanists* (Cambridge, MA, 1963), 84–5.

[5] Luther's remarks cited by M. H. Black, "The Printed Bible," *Cambridge History of the Bible*, vol. 3, *The West from the Reformation to the Present Day*, ed. S. L. Greenslade (Cambridge, 1963), 432.

Das Wolffgesang.

Eyn ander hertz/ein ander kleid/Tragē falsche wölff in ō heyd
Do mit sy den gēsen lupffen/Den pflūm ab dē kröpffen rupfen
Magstu hie by gar wol verston/Wo du lisest die Büchlin schon

Fig. 27. Lutheran propagandists pioneered with caricatures and cartoons aimed at a mass audience. The example of antipapist propaganda shown here is a title page woodcut from a pamphlet usually attributed to Joachim von Watt, *Das Wolffgesang* (Basel: Adam Petri, 1520). It attacks Thomas Murner, one of Luther's opponents, and the Catholic clergy. The pope flanked by cardinals and bishops, all with wolves' heads, catch geese in a net they are holding. A monk with the head of a cat plays a musical accompaniment to "the song of the wolf." This is the earliest known caricature of Murner, who from 1520 on was depicted with a cat's head. Reproduced by kind permission of the Folger Shakespeare Library.

166

bondage to Rome and brought the light of true religion to a God-fearing people. The mid-century German historian, Johann Sleidan, developed this theme in *An Address to the Estates of the Empire* of 1542, a polemic which was republished more than once.

> As if to offer proof that God has chosen us to accomplish a special mission, there was invented in our land a marvelous new and subtle art, the art of printing. This opened German eyes even as it is now bringing enlightenment to other countries. Each man became eager for knowledge, not without feeling a sense of amazement at his former blindness.[6]

Variations on the German theme were played in Elizabethan England in a manner that has continued to resonate down to the present day. By associating printing with the providential mission of a prospering expansive realm, English Protestants pointed the way to later trends – to revolutionary messianism in the Old World and "manifest destiny" in the New. "The art of Printing will so spread knowledge, that the common people, knowing their own rights and liberties will not be governed by way of oppression and so, little by little, all kingdoms will be like to Macaria."[7] Protestant divines diverged from Enlightened *philosophes* on many issues. But both viewed printing as a providential device which ended forever a priestly monopoly of learning, overcame ignorance and superstition, pushed back the evil forces commanded by Italian popes, and, in general, brought Western Europe out of the Dark Ages. "The Lord began to work for His Church not with sword and target to subdue His exalted adversary, but with printing, writing and reading," wrote John Foxe in his best-selling Book of Martyrs. "How many presses there be in the world, so many block-houses there be against the high castle of St. Angelo, so that either the pope

---

6   Cited by Gerald Strauss, "The Course of German History: The Lutheran Interpretation," *Renaissance: Studies in Honor of Hans Baron*, ed. A. Molho and J. Tedeschi (Dekalb, IL, 1971), 684.
7   Gabriel Plattes, "A Description of the Famous Kingdome of Macaria," in Charles Webster, *Samuel Hartlib and the Advancement of Learning* (Cambridge, 1970), 89.

must abolish knowledge and printing or printing must at length root him out."[8]

Printing and Protestantism seem to go together naturally, as printing and the Renaissance do not, partly because vestiges of early historical schemes are carried over into present accounts. The new presses were not developed until after Petrarch's death and had no bearing on early concepts of a "rinascita"; they were in full operation before Luther was born and did enter into his views of a religious reformation. In the latter case, moreover, they affected events as well as ideas and actually presided over the initial act of revolt.

When Luther proposed debate over his Ninety-five Theses his action was not in and of itself revolutionary. It was entirely conventional for professors of theology to hold disputations over an issue such as indulgences, and "church doors were the customary place for medieval publicity."[9] But these particular theses did not stay tacked to the church door (if indeed they were ever really placed there). To a sixteenth-century Lutheran chronicler, "it almost appeared as if the angels themselves had been their messengers and brought them before the eyes of all the people."[10] Luther himself expressed puzzlement when addressing Pope Leo X six months after the initial event:

> It is a mystery to me how my theses, more so than my other writings, indeed, those of other professors were spread to so many places. They were meant exclusively for our academic circle here . . . They were written in such a language that the common people could hardly understand them. They . . . use academic categories.[11]

According to a modern scholar, it is still "one of the mysteries of Reformation history how this proposal for academic disputation,

---

[8] Cited from Foxe's Book of Martyrs in William Haller, *The Elect Nation: The Meaning and Relevance of Foxe's Book of Martyrs* (New York, 1963), 110.

[9] G. R. Elton, *Reformation Europe 1517–1559* (New York, 1966), 15.

[10] Fredrich Myconius, Selections from *Historia Reformationis, The Reformation*, ed. and tr. Hans Hillerbrand (New York, 1964), 47.

[11] Letter from Martin Luther, 30 May 1518, in *The Reformation*, ed. Hillerbrand, 54.

written in Latin, could have kindled such enthusiastic support and thereby have such far-reaching impact."[12]

Precisely when were Luther's theses first printed outside Wittenberg? Just who was responsible for their being translated into German at first and then into other vernaculars? How did it happen that, soon after being printed in a handful of towns, such as Nuremberg, Leipzig, and Basel, copies were multiplied in such quantities and distributed so widely that the theses won top billing throughout central Europe – competing for space with news of the Turkish threat in print shop, bookstall, and country fair? These questions cannot be answered in detail here. I have posed them simply to direct attention to the important intermediate stages between the academic proposal and the popular acclaim. The mystery, in other words, is primarily the result of skipping over the process whereby a message ostensibly directed at a few could be made accessible to the many. If we want to dispel it, we should, instead of jumping directly from church door to public clamor, move more cautiously, a step at a time, looking at the activities of the printers, translators, and distributors who acted as agents of the change. Probably we ought to pause with particular care over the interval in December 1517 when three separate editions were printed almost simultaneously by printers located in three separate towns.

It is possible that Luther helped his friends on this occasion. His surprise at the interest he aroused may have entailed self-deception. One of his letters, written in March 1518, reveals his anxious ambivalence over the question of publicity. Although he "had no wish nor plan to publicize these Theses," he wrote, he was willing to have his friends do the job for him and left it to them to decide whether the theses were to be "suppressed or spread outside." Given this choice, did he doubt how his friends would choose? "It is out of the question," writes Heinrich Grimm, "for Luther not to have known of the publication of his theses or for them to have been published against his will."[13] Although Wittenberg was not yet a major

---

[12] *The Reformation*, ed. Hillerbrand, 32.
[13] Heinrich Grimm, "Luther's 'Ablassthesen' . . . ," *Gutenberg Jahrbuch* (1968): 144.

printing center, Brother Martin was well acquainted with the new powers of the press. He had already acquired experience editing texts in Latin and German for printers. He had already demonstrated sensitivity to diverse German book markets and discovered that vernacular works appealed to a diversified clientele.

A letter from Beatus Rhenanus to Zwingli in 1519 suggests how the tactics employed by the small Latin-reading audience, whom Luther addressed, might produce distant repercussions in a short time. "He will sell more of Luther's tracts if he has no other to offer," Zwingli was told by Beatus in a letter recommending a book peddler. The peddler should go from town to town, village to village, house to house, offering nothing but Luther's writings for sale. "This will virtually force the people to buy them, which would not be the case if there were a wide selection."[14] The linking of concern about salvation with shrewd business tactics and a so-called hard sell seems to have been no less pronounced in the early sixteenth century than among Bible salesmen today. Deliberate exploitation of the new medium helps to explain the paradox, which is noted in many Reformation studies, that a return to early Christian church traditions somehow served to usher in modern times.

"Rarely has one invention had more decisive influence than that of printing on the Reformation." Luther "had invited a public disputation and nobody had come to dispute." Then "by a stroke of magic he found himself addressing the whole world."[15] Here is an example of revolutionary causation where normally useful distinctions between precondition and precipitant are difficult to maintain. For there seems to be general agreement that Luther's act in 1517 did precipitate the Protestant Revolt. October 31 "continues to be celebrated in Lutheran countries as the anniversary of the Reformation and justly so. The controversy over indulgences brought together the man and the occasion: it signalled the end of the medieval Church."[16] To understand how Luther's theses served as such a

---

[14] Beatus Rhenanus to Zwingli, 2 June 1519, in *The Reformation*, ed. Hillerbrand, 125.

[15] Gordon Rupp, *Luther's Progress to the Diet of Worms*, 1521 (Chicago, 1951), 54.

[16] Elton, *Reformation Europe*, 15.

signal, we cannot afford to stand at the door of the Castle Church in Wittenberg looking for something tacked there. If we stay at the Wittenberg church with Luther, we will miss seeing the historical significance of the event. As Maurice Gravier pointed out, it was largely because traditional forms of theological disputation had been transformed by entirely new publicity techniques that the act of the German monk had such a far-reaching effect.[17]

> The theses...were said to be known throughout Germany in a fortnight and throughout Europe in a month...Printing was recognized as a new power and publicity came into its own. In doing for Luther what the copyists had done for Wycliffe, the printing presses transformed the field of communications and fathered an international revolt. It was a revolution.[18]

The advent of printing was an important precondition for the Protestant Reformation taken as a whole; for without it one could not implement a "priesthood of all believers." At the same time, however, the new medium also acted as a precipitant. It provided "the stroke of magic" by which an obscure theologian in Wittenberg managed to shake Saint Peter's throne.

In this respect, the contrast drawn by several authorities between the fate of Luther, who had the new vehicle at his disposal, and that of earlier heretics, who did not, is worth further consideration. Just how did the advent of printing actually affect the heresies that were current during the later Middle Ages? In seeking to answer this question we ought to keep typographical fixity in mind. Thus medieval heresies can be distinguished from the Protestant Revolt in much the same manner as medieval revivals from the Italian Renaissance. In both instances, localized transitory effects were superseded by widespread permanent ones. In both, lines were traced back as well as forward so that culture heroes and heresiarchs gained increased stature as founding fathers of movements that expanded continuously over the course of time. Partly because

---

[17] Maurice Gravier, *Luther et L'Opinion Publique* (Paris, 1942), 19.
[18] Margaret Aston, *The Fifteenth Century: The Prospect of Europe* (London, 1968), 76.

religious dissent was implemented by print, it could leave a much more indelible and far-reaching impression than dissent had ever left before.

For example, there had been many schisms within the Western church. Popes had often been at odds with emperors and kings, with church councils, and with rival claimants to the throne. But no episode that occurred from Canossa to Constance – not even a contest between three rival popes – shattered the unity of the church as decisively or permanently as did the contested divorce case of a sixteenth-century English king. "The first . . . campaign ever mounted by any government in any state in Europe" to exploit fully the propaganda potential of the press was that conducted by Thomas Cromwell to back up the actions of Henry VIII.[19] The English minister proved to be as skillful as Luther's German friends in mobilizing propagandists and attracting a large public by vernacular translations. The output of polemical tracts to sway opinion in favor of an antipapist royal action had occurred before printing, as the campaigns mounted by the councillors of Philip the Fair may suggest. But scribal campaigns had had a shorter wave resonance and produced more transitory effects. When implemented by print, divisions once traced were etched ever more deeply and could not be easily erased.

Sixteenth-century heresy and schism shattered Christendom so completely that even after religious warfare had ended, ecumenical movements led by men of good will could not put all the pieces together again. Not only were there too many splinter groups, separatists, and independent sects who regarded a central church government as incompatible with true faith; but the main lines of cleavage had been extended across continents and carried overseas along with Bibles and breviaries. Within a few generations, the gap between Protestant and Catholic had widened sufficiently to give rise to contrasting literary cultures and lifestyles. Long after Christian theology had ceased to provoke wars, Americans as well as Europeans were

---

[19] Geoffrey R. Elton, *Policy and Police: The Enforcement of the Reformation in the Age of Thomas Cromwell* (Cambridge, 1972), 206.

separated from each other by invisible barriers that are still with us today.

****

The lasting establishment of antipapist churches and the continuous propagation of heterodox faiths were of enormous consequence to Western civilization. But the impact of print on Western Christendom was by no means confined to the implementation of protest or the perpetuation of heterodoxy. Orthodox beliefs and institutions were also affected in ways that should be taken into account.

> The invention of the printing press made it possible, for the first time in Christian history, to insist upon uniformity in worship. Hitherto the liturgical texts could be produced only in manuscript, and local variations were inevitably admitted and indeed tolerated. But now printed editions were produced with uniform texts and rubrics. Since the Latin language was retained as the medium of worship in all western countries of the Roman obedience, the same texts could be recited and the same ceremonies performed, in the same way, throughout the Catholic world. At the same time all spontaneous growth and change and adaptation of the liturgy was prevented, and the worship of the Roman Catholic Church fossilized.[20]

This picture of complete uniformity, needless to say, oversimplifies the "spotted actuality," for kings were just as eager as popes to take advantage of printing and used it to keep churchmen in line. Some Catholic rulers ensured uniformity within their realms while refusing precise agreement with forms sent out from Rome. Nevertheless, in comparison with earlier times, one may say that Catholic liturgy *was* standardized and fixed for the first time in a more or less permanent mold – at least one that held good for roughly four hundred years.

Nor was liturgy the only field in which printing enabled orthodox churchmen to implement long-existing goals. Indeed, church

---

[20] J. Daniélou, A. H. Contratin, and John Kent, *Historical Theology* (London, 1969), 233.

traditions were already being affected by the advent of printing well before Martin Luther had come of age. When fixed in a new format and presented in a new way, orthodox views were inevitably transformed. The doctrines of Thomas Aquinas, for example, acquired a new lease on life after appearing in print. Thomism became the subject of a deliberate revival and then won official approval at the Council of Trent. Acceptance of Aristotle's cosmology had caused some difficulty among faculties of theology in the thirteenth century. Rejection of the same cosmology would cause even more trouble after the scholastic synthesis had been fixed in a more permanent mold.

Mysticism, like scholasticism, was also transformed. Meditative forms of mental prayer became subject to rule books issued in uniform editions. Attempts to inspire lay devotion, previously characteristic of a localized movement, such as the Northern *devotio moderna*, became much more widespread. In Southern Europe, friars began to address the lay public through printing as well as preaching, and devotional works were turned out in large editions aimed less at monks than at worldly men.

The role of the confessor and the sacrament of confession became more problematic than had been the case when there were fewer books to intervene between sinner and priest. The output of manuals directed at priests, classifying categories of sins and listing penalties and pardons, made visible the complexities and contradictions in orthodox doctrines, posing problems that seemed insoluble without advanced training in casuistry. The contrast between the simplicity of Christ's own teachings and the complex rigmarole of officially approved doctrines became sharper and more dismaying to those who felt a genuine religious vocation.

Sermon literature also underwent significant changes. Pedantic handbooks for preachers set forth rigid rules governing pulpit oratory. The new rule books, it has been suggested, ultimately killed off flexible medieval Latin speech. On the other hand, lively sermons designed to keep congregations awake proved especially well suited to the new mass medium. Gifted preachers, such as Savonarola or Geiler von Keysersberg, were able to send their messages from beyond the grave, as editions of their collected sermons continued to be published long after their deaths.

Ultimately, gifted boys who might have become preachers simply became publicists instead. "The preaching of sermons is speaking to a few of mankind," wrote Daniel Defoe, "printing books is talking to the whole world."[21] As an English journalist, a dissenter, and a pioneering novelist, Defoe presents many contrasts with the Christian humanists of the early sixteenth century. Yet Erasmus sounded a similar theme. When he was attempting to win the favor of a lay patron, he compared those who preached obscure sermons and were heard in one or two churches with his own books which were "read in every country in the world."[22]

In thus celebrating the carrying power of their publications, both Defoe and Erasmus were actually ringing variations on an old scribal theme.

> Praise for the apostolate of the pen . . . is met with at every period and . . . had been developed perhaps for the first time by Cassiodorus. Alcuin took it up in a poem which was inscribed over the entrance to the scriptorium at Fulda. Peter the Venerable was thinking of it when he spoke of the solitary . . . cloistered life: "He cannot take up the plow? Then let him take up the pen . . . He will preach without opening his mouth; without breaking silence he will make the Lord's teaching resound in the ears of the nations; and without leaving his cloister he will journey far over land and sea."[23]

Thus monastic scriptoria supplied the topos which lay publicists adapted to new ends. Once harnessed to the press, the "apostolate of the pen" – like Erasmus himself – left the monastery for the world. By the nineteenth century, "glad tidings" would be almost drowned

---

[21] Cited from "The Storm" (1704) in Ian Watt, *The Rise of the Novel*, rev. ed. (Berkeley, 1967), 103.

[22] Cited by Harbison, *Christian Scholar*, 80.

[23] Jean Leclercq, *The Love of Learning and the Desire for God*, tr. C. Misrahi (New York, 1962), 128.

out by the flood of news from other quarters. Yet even then Christian missionaries continued to set up printing presses in remote parts of the world to turn out Gospels and Psalters as had been done in Mainz four hundred years earlier.

The notion of an "apostolate of the pen" points to the high value assigned to the written word as a means of accomplishing the church's mission on earth. It helps to explain the enthusiastic welcome given to the press by the fifteenth-century Roman church. In hailing printing as God's highest act of grace, Luther was elaborating on a theme which found favor not only among other monks but also among prelates and popes. The very phrase "divine art" was attributed to a cardinal (Nicholas of Cusa) by a churchman who was later made bishop (Gianandrea de' Bussi, Bishop of Aleria). Even the censorship edicts issued by archbishops and popes from the 1480s down through 1515 hail the invention as divinely inspired and elaborate on its advantages before going on to note the need to curtail its abuses. Not only did the church legitimate the art of printing, it provided a most important market for the infant industry. The poor priest needed books even more urgently than did the prosperous layman. For fifty years before the Protestant Revolt, churchmen in most regions welcomed an invention which served both.

There is considerable irony about the enthusiastic reception accorded to printing by the church. Heralded on all sides as a "peaceful art," Gutenberg's invention probably contributed more to destroying Christian concord and inflaming religious warfare than any of the so-called arts of war ever did. Much of the religious turbulence of the early modern era may be traced to the fact that the writings of church fathers and the Scriptures themselves could not continue to be transmitted in traditional ways. As a sacred heritage, Christianity could be protected against most forms of change. As a heritage that was transmitted by texts and that involved the "spreading of glad tidings," Christianity was peculiarly vulnerable to the revolutionary effects of typography.

Processing texts in new workshops was, to be sure, a peaceful activity undertaken by pacific urban craftsmen and merchants. Nevertheless, it brought into focus many troublesome issues which had been more easily glossed over before. Oral testimony, for example, could be distinguished much more clearly from written testimony when poets no longer composed their works in the course of chanting or reciting them and when giving dictation or reading out loud became detached from the publication of a given work. Accordingly, questions were more likely to arise about the transmission of the teaching that came from the lips of Christ or from the dictation of the Holy Spirit to the Apostles. Was all of the Christian heritage set down in written form and contained solely in Scripture? Was not some of it also preserved "in the unwritten traditions which the Apostles received from Christ's lips or which, under the inspiration of the Holy Spirit, were by them, as it were, passed down to us from hand to hand"?[24] Was it meant to be made directly available to all men in accordance with the mission to spread glad tidings? Or was it rather to be expounded to the laity only after passing through the hands of priests, as had become customary over the course of centuries? But how could the traditional mediating role of the priesthood be maintained without a struggle when lay grammarians and philologists had been summoned by scholar-printers to help with the task of editing old texts? The priest might claim the sacred office of mediating between God and man, but when it came to scriptural exegesis many editors and publishers felt that Greek and Hebrew scholars were better equipped for the task.

It was, then, printing, not Protestantism, which outmoded the medieval Vulgate and introduced a new drive to tap mass markets. Regardless of what happened in Wittenberg or Zurich, regardless of other issues raised by Luther, Zwingli, or Calvin, sooner or later the church would have had to come to terms with the effect on the Bible of copyediting and trilingual scholarship on the one hand and expanding book markets on the other. Whether or not the Lutheran heresy spread, whether or not clerical abuses were reformed, the forces released by print, which pointed to more democratic and

---

[24] Draft of the "Decree on the Acceptance of the Holy Scriptures and the Apostolic Traditions," 22 March 1545, in Herbert Jedin, *A History of the Council of Trent*, tr. E. Graf (Edinburgh, 1961), II:74.

national forms of worship, would have had to be contained or permitted to run their course.

The argument that Catholic policies no less than Protestant ones reflected adaptation to "modernizing" forces in the sixteenth century needs to be qualified by considering the divergence over forces associated with printing. Some authorities have argued that Gutenberg's invention "cut both ways" by helping Loyola as well as Luther and by spurring a Catholic revival even while spreading Lutheran tracts. It is true that the Catholic Reformation of the sixteenth century used printing for proselytizing and that Catholic firms made profits by serving the Roman church. They produced breviaries and devotional works for priests on far-flung missions, schoolbooks for seminaries run by new orders, devotional literature for pious laymen, and tracts which could later be used by the seventeenth-century Office of the Propaganda. Furthermore, in England, after the Anglicans gained the upper hand, Catholic printers proved as skillful as their Puritan counterparts in handling problems posed by the surreptitious printing and the clandestine marketing of books.

If one confines the scope of inquiry to the mere spreading of books and tracts, then one may be inclined to argue that the new medium was exploited in much the same way by Catholics and Protestants alike. But, as I argue throughout this book, new functions performed by printing went beyond dissemination. Catholic policies framed at Trent were aimed at holding these new functions in check. By withholding authorization of new editions of the Bible, by stressing lay obedience and imposing restrictions on lay reading, by developing new machinery such as the Index and Imprimatur to channel the flow of literature along narrowly prescribed lines, the post-Tridentine papacy proved to be anything but accommodating. It assumed an unyielding posture that grew ever more rigid over the course of time. Decisions made at Trent were merely the first in a series of rear-guard actions designed to contain the new forces Gutenberg's invention had released. The long war between the Roman church and the printing press continued for the next four centuries and has not completely ended. The *Syllabus of Errors* in the mid-nineteenth century showed how little room was left for maneuver after four hundred years. Even after Vatican II, a complete cessation of hostilities between popes and printer's devils is still not clearly in sight.

Among decisions made at Trent, the insistence on upholding the medieval Latin version of the Bible is worth singling out. Here Catholic policy was designed to withstand two different threats, emanating from Greek and Hebrew studies on the one hand and from vernacular translations on the other. For Bible printing subjected the authority of the medieval clergy to a two-pronged attack. It was threatened by lay erudition on the part of a scholarly elite and by lay Bible reading among the public at large. On the elite level, laymen became more erudite than churchmen; grammar and philology challenged the reign of theology; Greek and Hebrew studies forced their way into the schools. On the popular level, ordinary men and women began to know their Scripture as well as most parish priests; markets for vernacular catechisms and prayer books expanded; church Latin no longer served as a sacred language veiling sacred mysteries. Distrusted as an inferior translation by humanist scholars, Jerome's version was also discarded as too esoteric by evangelical reformers.

These two levels were not entirely discrete, of course. A conscientious translator required access to scholarly editions and some command of trilingual skills. A Tyndale or a Luther necessarily took advantage of the output of scholar-printers, while scholar and translator could easily be combined in one person – as was the case with Lefèvre d'Etaples. Moreover, the two-pronged attack was mounted from one and the same location – that is, from the newly established printer's workshop. The new impetus given scholarship by compilers of lexicons and reference guides went together with a new interest in tapping mass markets and promoting bestsellers. Robert Estienne, the Paris printer, working on his successive editions to the distress of Sorbonne theologians, provides one illustration of the disruptive effects of sixteenth-century Bible printing. Richard Grafton, the London printer, pestering Thomas Cromwell to order the placing of the Matthew Bible in every parish church and abbey, provides another.

Although they were coupled in various ways, there are nonetheless good reasons for considering the two prongs of the attack separately. There is no need to dwell on the distinctions that are inherent in my reference to two *levels* – that is, distinctions based on social stratification and market definition. The fact that scholarly editions circulated among a select readership and vernacular translation was aimed at a mass audience, in other words, seems too obvious to call for extended discussion. There are other distinctions, however, which seem less obvious and need more attention. For example, the approaches of scholars and evangelists to the sacred Word did not always converge and were sometimes at odds. Jerome and Augustine had themselves disagreed over Bible translation, and in the sixteenth century old arguments flared anew. Luther attacked Erasmus for being more of a grammarian than a theologian. From a different standpoint, Thomas More attacked Lutheran translators such as Tyndale and objected to placing vernacular Scriptures instead of Latin grammars in schoolboy hands. More stood with Erasmus and against obscurantists in working to introduce Greek studies into English universities. But the two friends parted company over the question of lay evangelism.

Moreover, Renaissance princes tended to share More's position. As patrons of learning they sponsored scholarly editions but exhibited more caution about vernacular translation. The latter issue was much more politically explosive and complicated delicate negotiations over church affairs. Catholic kings might act as did Philip II by sponsoring polyglot Bibles and by providing local clergy with special breviaries and missals. But they stopped short of substituting vernaculars for church Latin or displacing the Vulgate. The tortuous policy of Henry VIII illustrates rather well the half-Catholic, half-Protestant position of the schismatic Tudor king. He began by persecuting Tyndale and other Lutheran translators; then encouraged Cromwell to turn loose his coterie of publicists and printers against the pope; then accused his minister of having false books translated into the mother tongue. In 1543 the government seemed to grant with one hand what it withdrew with the other:

An Act of 1543 prohibited the use of Tyndale or any other annotated Bible in English and forbade unlicensed persons to read or expound the Bible to others in any church or open assembly . . . Yet in 1543 Convocation ordered that the Bible should be read through in English, chapter by chapter every Sunday and Holy Day after *Te Deum* and *Magnificat*.[25]

There was no logical contradiction, but the two acts worked at cross purposes, nevertheless. Prohibiting the use of annotated English Bibles, forbidding unlicensed persons to read or expound Scripture, and placing Bible reading out of bounds for "women, artificers, apprentices, journeymen, yeomen, husbandmen and laborers"[26] were not logically incompatible with ordering the clergy to read from an English Bible in church. But if one wanted to keep English Bibles from lay readers, it was probably unwise to tantalize congregations by letting them hear a chapter each week. Appetites are usually whetted by being told about forbidden fruit. The actions of 1543 probably worked together to increase the market for English Bibles. After Henry's death, of course, the prohibitions were abandoned and a less ambivalent royal policy was pursued. Despite a sharp setback under Mary Tudor and intermittent reactions against Puritan zealots, the Englishing of the Bible moved ahead under royal auspices, reaching a triumphant conclusion under James I. With the Authorized Version, the English joined other Protestant nations to become a "people of the Book."

Once a vernacular version was officially authorized, the Bible was "nationalized," so to speak, in a way that divided Protestant churches and reinforced extant linguistic frontiers. "Translation of the Bible into the vernacular languages," wrote Hans Kohn, "lent them a new dignity and frequently became the starting point for the development of national languages and literatures. The literature was made accessible to the people at the very time that the invention of printing made the production of books easier and cheaper."[27]

[25] S. L. Greenslade, "English Versions of the Bible A.D. 1525–1611," *Cambridge History of the Bible*, vol. 3, *The West from the Reformation to the Present Day* (Cambridge, 1963), p. 153, n. 1.

[26] Categories of those forbidden to read by the Act of 1543 are taken from Bennett, *English Books and Readers*, 27.

[27] Hans Kohn, *Nationalism: Its Meaning and History* (New York, 1955), 14.

Of course, I think it more than a mere coincidence that these developments occurred "at the very time" costs were lowered by printing. Nevertheless, Kohn's suggestion that the vernaculars were dignified by their association with the sacred book contains a valuable insight. And so does his observation that "Latin was dethroned at the very moment when . . . it had started to become the universal language for a growing class of educated men."[28] Thus Kohn shows why it is necessary to keep the two prongs of the attack on the Vulgate separate; for vernacular translations, by reinforcing linguistic barriers, ran counter to the cosmopolitan fellowship encouraged by biblical scholarship.

Although the authority of Jerome's version was undermined by Greek and Hebrew studies, the sense of belonging to the same Commonwealth of Learning remained strong among Christian scholars in all lands. A network of correspondence and the actual wanderings of scholars thus helped to preserve ties between Catholic Louvain and Protestant Leiden during the religious wars. Publication of polyglot Bibles pulled together scholars of diverse faiths from different realms. Collaboration with heterodox enclaves of Jews and Greeks encouraged an ecumenical and tolerant spirit, particularly among scholar-printers, who often provided room and board in exchange for foreign aid and were, thus, forced to be quite literally "at home" with travelers from strange lands. Work on polyglot lexicons also encouraged scholars to look beyond the horizons of Western Christendom toward exotic cultures and distant realms. Vernacular Bible translation, while it owed much to trilingual studies, had precisely the opposite effect. It led to the typical Protestant amalgam of biblical fundamentalism and insular patriotism.

Sixteenth-century vernacular-translation movements also had anti-intellectual implications which worked at cross purposes with the aims of classical scholars. Of course, this was not true of the erudite group which produced the Geneva Bible in the 1550s or of the

---

[28] Hans Kohn, *The Idea of Nationalism: A Study in Its Origins and Background* (New York, 1944), 143.

learned committee which labored over the King James translation. There were many publicists, however, who championed the cause of Englishing the Bible by roundly condemning erudition and pedantry. Protestant objections to veiling Gospel truths were adopted by such popularizers and used for more secular ends. For example, they argued that the liberal arts and sciences should not be "hidden in Greke or Latin," but made familiar to the "vulgare people." In "blunt and rude English," they set out "to please ten thousand laymen" instead of "ten able clerks."[29] They sought to close the gap not so much between priest and laity as between academic or professional elites and "common" readers who were variously described as "unskilfull," "unlettered," and "unacquainted with the latine tounge."[30] In this way, they linked the lay evangelism of Protestants with the cause of so-called popularizers who campaigned against academic monopolies and professional elites. Scholastic theologians, Aristotelian professors, and Galenic physicians were attacked in much the same way by diverse opponents of Latin learning. Nicholas Culpeper, an aggressive and prolific medical editor and translator during the Commonwealth, made his debut with an unauthorized translation of the office guide to London apothecaries – the *Pharmacopeia Londinensus* – and accused the College of Physicians of being papists because they resisted using vernaculars in medicine.[31]

The assault on old professional elites did not always stop short of political elites. Indeed, the two motifs were combined during the English revolution. The Englishing of lawbooks had been defended on patriotic grounds under the early Tudors by the versatile law printer and publicist, John Rastell.[32] The same theme was turned against both the legal profession and the Stuart monarchy by rebellious subjects such as John Lilburne. The latter held that the law of

---

[29] Thomas Norton, "The Ordinall of Alchemy" (ca. 1477), cited by R. F. Jones, *The Triumph of the English Language* (Oxford, 1953), p. 5, n. 8.

[30] Altick, *English Common Reader*, 18.

[31] Charles Webster, *The Great Instauration: Science Medicine and Reform 1626–1660* (London, 1975), 268.

[32] A. W. Reed, *Early Tudor Drama* (London, 1962), 204.

the land should not be hidden in Latin and old French, but should be in English so that "every Free-man may reade it as well as the lawyers."[33] In their insistence on converting knowledge which had been esoteric, "rare, and difficult," into a form where it was "relevant and useful for all," and in their confidence in the intelligence of the reading public at large, the prefaces of the translators seem to have anticipated much of the propaganda of the Enlightenment. In their expressed desire to bring learning within reach of artisans, they reflected a drive toward new markets that was powered by the new presses. "Learning cannot be too common and the commoner the better . . . Why but the vulgar should not know all," said Florio, whose translations and dictionaries put the dictum into practice.[34] The common reader could be reached only by using a mother tongue, however. Unlike later Enlightened *philosophes*, the translators played insistently on chauvinistic themes – reworking and democratizing the defense of the "volgare" which had been sponsored by princes and despots during the Renaissance.

The same combination of democratic and patriotic themes accompanied Protestant Bible translation. Indeed, the drive to bring the Bible within reach of everyman had paradoxical aspects which help to illustrate the contradictory effects of the printing revolution as a whole. Everyman spoke in many tongues, and the Christian Scriptures had to be nationalized to be placed within his reach. "What is the precise meaning of the word universal in the assertion that *Pilgrim's Progress* is 'universally known and loved'?" asks a reviewer.[35] The question is worth posing, for it draws attention to an important process which is often overlooked. The desire to spread glad tidings, when implemented by print, contributed to the fragmentation of Christendom. In the form of the Lutheran Bible or the

---

[33] "England's Birth-Right Justified" (1645), cited by Pauline Gregg, *Free-born John: A Biography of John Lilburne* (London, 1961), 128.

[34] For citations, see J. G. Ebel, "Translation and Cultural Nationalism in the Reign of Elizabeth," *Journal of the History of Ideas* XXX (October-December 1969): 295–8.

[35] "A Garland for Gutenberg," *Times Literary Supplement* (22 June 1967): 561.

King James Version, the sacred book of Western civilization became more insular as it grew more popular. It is no accident that nationalism and mass literacy have developed together. The two processes have been linked ever since Europeans ceased to speak the same language when citing their Scriptures or saying their prayers.

In questioning the familiar equation of Protestantism with nationalism, J. H. Hexter points out that the claims of the Calvinists "were *not* national . . . they were quite as universal, quite as catholic and in that dubious sense quite as medieval as the claims of the Papacy."[36] The case of Calvinism, to be sure, is somewhat exceptional because the language spoken by the inhabitants of the small Swiss canton which served as the Protestant Rome happened to coincide with that of the most populous and powerful seventeenth-century realm. Whereas Calvin himself could not read Luther's German works, the Prussian Hohenzollerns could and did read Calvin in French. Partly because of the influence it had long exerted as the medieval *lingua franca*, partly because of the new radiation of Genevan culture in the age of Calvin, but mainly because of the successful statecraft of the Bourbons, French *did* displace Latin as the international language for most purposes. Nevertheless, Calvin's native tongue never achieved the cosmopolitan status which medieval Latin had achieved in religious affairs.

As a common sacred language, medieval Latin continued to unite Catholic Europe and "Latin" America as well. Protestant churches were forever divided by early modern linguistic frontiers, and here the Presbytery was caught up in the same contradictions as all other Protestant churches. Its claims were universal, as Hexter says, but there was no way of making the Bible more "universally" accessible without casting the Scriptures into a more national mold. Thus the Genevan Bible which circulated among English and Scotch Puritans was written in a language that was foreign to the so-called Protestant Rome. A fund of lore based on Shakespeare, Blackstone, and the King James Version is often described by nostalgic Americans as

---

[36] Hexter, *Reappraisals in History*, 33.

providing "a common culture" which the twentieth century has lost. This reading matter did reach across the ocean, it is true, and linked backwoods lawyers in the New World with Victorian empire builders in the Old. It stopped at the water's edge, nonetheless. Across the Channel, on the Continent among cultivated Europeans, this culture was not common at all. Outside Catholic Europe, then, a scriptural faith penetrated deeply into all social strata and provided the foundation for some sort of "common culture." But although a Bible Belt left permanent marks across many lands, the "old-time religion" was abruptly arrested at new linguistic frontiers.

Possibly the most fundamental divergence between Catholic and Protestant cultures can be found closest to home. The absence or presence of family prayers and family Bibles is a matter of some consequence to all social historians. "Masters in their houses ought to be as preachers to their families that from the highest to the lowest they may obey the will of God,"[37] ran a marginal note in the Geneva Bible. Unlike nobles who had family chaplains, ordinary householders of moderate means had relied on the parish church for spiritual guidance. Now they were told it was their duty to conduct family services and catechize children and apprentices. They thus achieved a position in Protestant households that Catholic family men entirely lacked.

> The head of the household was required to see that his subordinates attended services and that children and servants were sent to be catechized. He was expected to conduct daily worship at home ... The master was both king and priest to his household.[38]

In this field, as elsewhere, the printer was quick to encourage self-help: "To help guide him, the father could rely on the numerous pocket-size manuals that came off the printing presses, such as A

---

[37] See Christopher Hill, *Society and Puritanism in Pre-Revolutionary England* (New York, 1967), chap. 13, title and epigraph.

[38] Keith Thomas, "Women and Civil War Sects," *Crisis in Europe 1560–1660*, ed. Trevor Aston (London, 1965), 333.

Werke for Householders (1530)"[39] or "Godly private prayers for house-holders to meditate upon and say in their families (1576)."[40]

> Through prayer and meditation, models for which they could find in scores of books, the draper, the butcher...soon learned to approach God without ecclesiastical assistance...The London citizen learned to hold worship in his own household...the private citizen had become articulate in the presence of the Deity.[41]

Puritan tradesmen who had learned to talk to God in the presence of their apprentices, wives, and children were already on their way to self-government. However low they were ranked among parishioners in church, they could find at home satisfying acknowledgment of their own dignity and worth.

Catholic tradesmen and businessmen were deprived of the chance to conduct religious services at home. A Catholic cardinal during Mary Tudor's reign warned Londoners against reading Scripture for themselves. "You should nott be your owne masters," said Reginald Pole in his address to the citizens of London.[42] That "household religion was a seed-bed of subversion" was taken for granted by the Counter-Reformation church. It discouraged "domestic Bible reading" and created no effective substitute to ensure religious observances within the family circle.[43]

Perhaps the French businessman was more likely to aspire to noble status and to spend his money not by reinvesting in business but by purchasing land and offices, partly because the stigma of being in trade had never been counterbalanced by the chance to play king and priest in his home. Certainly the more forbidding aspects of

---

[39] Kenneth Charlton, *Education in Renaissance England* (London, 1965), 201.

[40] Cited by Wright, *Middle Class Culture*, 245.

[41] Ibid., 239–41.

[42] Reginald Pole's "Speech to the Citizens of London on behalf of Religious Houses," is cited by J. W. Blench, *Preaching in England in the Late Fifteenth and Sixteenth Centuries: A Study of English Sermons 1450–c. 1600* (Oxford, 1964), 50–1.

[43] John Bossy, "The Counter Reformation and the People of Catholic Europe," *Past and Present* 47 (May 1970): 68–9.

Calvinist doctrine – such as its insistence on human depravity and its tendency to encourage repression, anxiety, and guilt – ought to be balanced against the opportunities it offered for the achievement of a new sense of self-mastery and self-worth.

The transformation of the Protestant home into a church and of the Protestant householder into a priest, in any event, seems to bear out Weber's suggestion that

> the Reformation meant not the elimination of the Church's con-trol over everyday life, but rather the substitution of a new form of control for the previous one. It meant the repudiation of a control that was very lax . . . in favor of a regulation of the whole of con-duct which, penetrating to all departments of private and public life, was infinitely burdensome and earnestly enforced.[44]

By thinking about Bible reading in particular rather than the Ref-ormation in general, one could become more specific about the dif-ference between new and old controls. Instead of merely contrasting laxity with strictness, one might compare the effects of listening to a Gospel passage read from the pulpit with reading the same passage at home for oneself. In the first instance, the Word comes from a priest who is at a distance and on high; in the second it seems to come from a silent voice that is within.

This comparison, to be sure, needs to be handled with caution and should not be pressed too far. Informal gatherings assembled for Gospel readings were probably more significant in the birth of Protestant communities than solitary Bible reading.[45] The latter, moreover, had earlier been practiced by some medieval monks. The contrast between churchgoer and solitary reader moreover should not be taken as pointing to mutually exclusive forms of behavior. During the sixteenth century, most Protestants listened to preach-ers in church *and* read the Gospels at home. Nevertheless, I think that the "deep penetration of new controls" to all departments of life becomes more explicable when we note that printed books are

---

[44] Max Weber, *The Protestant Ethic and the Spirit of Capitalism*, tr. Talcott Parsons (London, 1948), 36.

[45] Henri Hauser, *Etudes sur la Réforme Française* (Paris, 1909), 86–7.

more portable than pulpits and more numerous than priests, and the messages they contain are more easily internalized.

A variety of social and psychological consequences resulted from the new possibility of substituting Bible reading for participation in traditional ceremonies – such as that of the mass. The slogan: *sola scriptura*, as Bernd Moeller says, was equivocal. It could be used in an inclusive sense to mean "not without Scripture" or assigned the meaning that Luther gave it: "with Scripture alone."[46] When taken in this latter sense, Bible reading might take precedence over all other experiences to a degree and with an intensity that was unprecedented in earlier times. The rich and varied communal religious experiences of the Middle Ages provided a basis for the "common culture" of Western man that differed from the new reliance on Bible reading. Open books, in some instances, led to closed minds.

Within Protestant Europe, then, the impact of printing points in two quite opposite directions – toward tolerant "Erasmian" trends and ultimately higher criticism and modernism, and toward more rigid dogmatism, culminating in literal fundamentalism and Bible Belts.

Vernacular Bible translation took advantage of humanist scholarship only in order to undermine it by fostering patriotic and populist tendencies. It has to be distinguished from scholarly attacks on the Vulgate because it was connected with so many nonscholarly, antiintellectual trends. Moreover, it coincided, as scholarly editions and "profitless polyglots" did not, with the profit-making drives of early printers. Not all printers were scholars, nor were all of them pious, but unless they were assured of steady patronage, they had to make profits to stay in business.

After the duplication of indulgences and the promotion of relics were taken over by printers, traditional church practices became more obviously tainted with commercialism. But the same spirit of "double-entry bookkeeping" which appeared to infect the Renaissance popes also pervaded the movement which

---

[46] Bernd Moeller, *Imperial Cities and the Reformation: Three Essays*, tr. H. E. Midelfort and M. U. Edwards (Philadelphia, 1972), 29.

spearheaded the antipapal cause. Indeed, however much they attacked "mechanical devotions," Protestants relied much more than did papists on the services of "mechanick printers." Insofar as their doctrine stressed an encounter with the Word and substituted reading Scripture for participating in the mass, it bypassed the mediation of priests and the authority of the pope only to become more dependent on the efficacy of Bible printers and Bible salesmen.

Even while describing the art of printing as God's highest act of grace, Luther also castigated printers who garbled passages of the Gospel and marketed hasty reprints for quick profit. In a preface to his Bible of 1541 he said of them, "They look only to their greed."[47] Nevertheless, by insisting on Bible reading as a way of experiencing the Presence and achieving true faith, Luther also linked spiritual aspirations to an expanding capitalistic enterprise. Printers and booksellers had to be enlisted in order to bypass priests and place the Gospels directly into lay hands. Protestant doctrines harnessed a traditional religion to a new technology with the result that Western Christianity embarked on a course never taken by any world religion before and soon developed peculiar features which gave it the appearance, in comparison with other faiths, of having undergone some sort of historical mutation.

****

Given the convergence of interests among printers and Protestants, given the way new presses implemented older religious goals, it seems pointless to argue whether material or spiritual, socioeconomic or religious, "factors" were more important in transforming Western Christianity. It is by no means pointless, however, to insist that printing be assigned a prominent position when enumerating "factors" or analyzing causes. To leave the interests and outlook of printers out of the amalgam (as most accounts do) is to lose one chance of explaining how Protestant–Catholic divisions related to other concurrent developments that were transforming European

---

[47] Cited by Black, "Printed Bible," 432.

society. Not all changes ushered in by print were compatible with the cause of religious reform; many were irrelevant to that cause, some antipathetical to it. Pastors and printers were often at odds in regions governed by Lutherans and Calvinists. Nevertheless, Protestants and printers had more in common than Catholics and printers did. Religious divisions were of critical importance to the future development of European society partly because of the way they interacted with other new forces released by print. If Protestants seem to be more closely affiliated with certain "modernizing" trends than do Catholics, it is largely because reformers did less to check these new forces and more to reinforce them at the start.

In Protestant regions, for example, regular orders were dissolved and the printer was encouraged to perform the apostolic mission of spreading glad tidings in different tongues. Within frontiers held by the Counter-Reformation church, contrary measures were taken. New orders, such as the Jesuits or the Congregation of the Propaganda, were created; teaching and preaching from other quarters were checked by Index and Imprimatur. Thereafter, the fortunes of printers waned in regions where prospects had previously seemed bright and waxed in smaller, less populous states where the reformed religion took root.

Before lines were drawn in the sixteenth century, men in Catholic regions appear to have been just as eager to read the Bible in their own tongues as were men in what subsequently became Protestant regions. Similarly, Catholic printers combined humanist scholarship with piety and profit seeking. They were just as enterprising and industrious as Protestant printers. They also served the most populous, powerful, and culturally influential realms of sixteenth-century Europe: Portugal and Spain (with their far-flung empires), Austria, France, southern German principalities, and Italian city-states. But they were less successful in expanding their markets and in extending and diversifying their operations during the sixteenth and seventeenth centuries. "The Lutheran Reformation had spent its impetus by the middle of the sixteenth century; but Protestantism, and consequently the Protestant book trade, maintained its ascendancy over the intellectual life of Germany well into the beginning of the nineteenth century. This, incidentally, meant the shift from the south to central and north Germany."[48] Steinberg's description of developments in Germany is relevant to what happened through-out Europe as a whole after 1517. Throughout the Continent, the movement of printers toward Protestant centers and the tendency for markets to expand and diversify more rapidly under Protestant than Catholic rule seems marked enough to be correlated with other developments.

Needless to say, the fortunes of printing industries resembled those of other early capitalist enterprises in being affected by many dif-ferent variables and concurrent changes. The expansion of Venice and Lyons as major early printing centers may be explained by examining late medieval trade patterns rather than religious affairs. On the other hand, one must take religion into account to under-stand why Wittenberg and Genevan firms began to thrive. The first export industry to be established in Geneva was placed there by religious refugees from France: "The French installed Geneva's first export industry, publishing... When Calvin died in 1564 the only exportable product which his Geneva produced – the printed book – was a religious as well as an economic enterprise."[49] The influx of religious refugees into Calvin's Geneva in the 1550s "radically" altered the professional structure of the city. The number of print-ers and booksellers jumped from somewhere between three and six to some three hundred or more.[50] As was the case with Basel after the Sorbonne condemnations of the 1520s, Geneva gained in the 1550s at French expense. "Wealthy religious refugees surreptitiously transferred capital out of France."[51] Major printing firms went. The movement of workers between Lyons and Geneva, which had until then involved a two-way traffic, "suddenly became one way and the

[48] Steinberg, *Five Hundred Years*, 194.
[49] E. William Monter, *Calvin's Geneva* (New York, 1967), 21.
[50] Ibid., pp. 5, 166.
[51] The most thorough study is H. J. Bremme, *Buchdrucker und Buchhandler zur Zeit der Glaubenskämpfe: Studien zur Genfer Druckgeschichte, 1565–1580* (Geneva, 1969). See review by R. M. Kingdon, *American Historical Review* LXXV (June 1970): 1481.

proportions were reversed."[52] Some French printers, such as Robert Estienne, moved to Geneva from Paris, but the main flight of labor and capital came from Lyons. By the time that Jean II de Tournes moved from Lyons to Geneva in 1585, the firms that remained in the once-great French printing center were engaged mainly in repackaging books printed in Geneva, adding title pages that disguised their Calvinist origins, before shipping them off to Catholic Italy and Spain. The reasons Lyons printers became dependent on Geneva firms by the end of the century were many and complex. Labor costs, paper supplies, and many other factors played important roles. But so too did religious affiliations and curbs on vernacular Psalters, Bibles, and bestsellers of varied kinds.

Like the printers of Lyons and Antwerp, those of Venice were caught up in a process of decline that had many diverse causes, including the vast movement from Mediterranean to oceanic trade. But there, also, the free-wheeling operations of the early sixteenth century were curbed by the Counter-Reformation church. When considering the phenomenon which preoccupied Max Weber – the prevalence of Protestants among "higher technically and commercially trained personnel"[53] – the fact that so many printers and paper makers "voted with their feet" for Protestant regions deserves further thought.

So too does the question of varying incentives toward literacy extended by the diverse creeds. Here the contrast registered on the title page illustration of Foxe's *Actes and Monuments* – showing devout Protestants with books on their laps and Catholics with prayer beads in their hands – is worth further thought. In the course of the sixteenth century, vernacular Bibles that had been turned out on a somewhat haphazard basis in diverse regions were withheld from Catholics and made compulsory for Protestants. An incentive to learn to read was thus eliminated among lay Catholics and officially

---

[52] Paul F. Geisendorf, "Lyons and Geneva in the Sixteenth Century: The Fairs and Printing," *French Humanism 1470–1600*, ed. W. Gundersheimer (New York, 1969), 150.

[53] Weber, *Protestant Ethic*, 35.

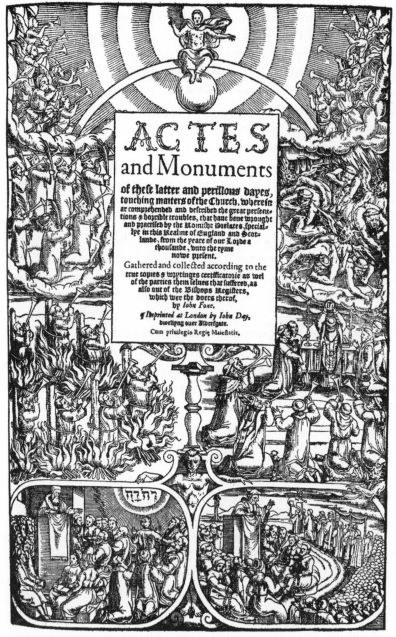

Fig. 28. The full title page of Foxe's Book of Martyrs contrasts the fate of Protestants (on the left), who are burned on earth but triumph forever in heaven, with the fate of Catholics (on the right), who celebrate the triumph of their sacrament of the mass on earth but suffer eternal torment in hell thereafter.

Fig. 28. (*cont.*) The two bottom panels of Foxe's title page are enlarged to show the Protestants holding books and kneeling before the sacred Word; the Catholics holding beads and following, in sheeplike formation, a priestly procession. From John Foxe, *Actes and Monuments...Touching...Great Persecutions...*(London: John Day, 1563). Reproduced by kind permission of the Folger Shakespeare Library.

Fig. 29. The Index provided free publicity for titles listed thereon and guided Protestant printers toward authors, such as Machiavelli, who could be advertised as forbidden fruit. Machiavelli's name has been added to this copy of the *Index librorum prohibitorum* (Rome, 1559). Reproduced by kind permission of the Rare Book and Special Collections Division, Library of Congress.

enjoined upon Protestants. Book markets were likely to expand at different rates thereafter. Bible printing, once authorized, often became a special privilege, so that its decline in Catholic centers had a direct impact on a relatively small group of printers. The entire industry, however, suffered a glancing blow from the suppression of the large potential market represented by a Catholic lay Bible-reading public. Furthermore, vernacular Bibles were by no means the only bestsellers that were barred to Catholic readers after the Council of Trent. Erasmus had made a fortune for his printers before Luther outstripped him. Both, along with many other popular authors, were placed on the Index. Being listed as forbidden served as a form of publicity and may have spurred sales. It was, however, more hazardous for Catholic printers than for Protestant ones to profit thereby.

Given the existence of profit-seeking printers outside the reach of Rome, Catholic censorship boomeranged in ways that could not be foreseen. The Index provided free publicity for titles listed thereon. Lists of passages to be expurgated directed readers to "book, chapter, and line" where anti-Roman passages could be found, thus relieving Protestant propagandists of the need to make their own search for anti-Catholic citations drawn from eminent authors and respected works. "Early copies of all the original Indexes found their way as soon as they were produced to Leiden, Amsterdam and Utrecht and were promptly utilized by the enterprising Dutch publisher as guides."[54] Indeed, there was much to be gained and little to be lost for the Protestant printer who developed his list of forthcoming books with an eye on the latest issue of the Index. Decisions made by Catholic censors thus inadvertently deflected Protestant publication policies in the direction of foreign heterodox, libertine, and innovative trends. This deflecting action is worth pausing over. It suggests why printers have to be treated as independent agents when trying to correlate Catholic–Protestant divisions with other developments. It was the profit-seeking printer and not the Protestant divine who

---

[54] G. H. Putnam, *The Censorship of the Church of Rome and Its Influence upon the Production and Distribution of Literature* (New York, 1906), I:40.

published Aretino, Bruno, Sarpi, Machiavelli, Rabelais, and all the other authors who were on Catholic lists. When the intervening agent is left out of account, it becomes difficult to explain why such a secular, freethinking, and hedonist literary culture should have flourished in regions where pious Protestants were in control.

After all, militant Calvinists were just as willing as Dominican inquisitors to resort to coercion and the stake. When the cause of toleration was first defended in early modern Europe, it was championed from printing shops located outside the Calvinists' control.

> Official Basle loyally backed the action taken against Servetus in Geneva; yet nobody could fail to notice that it also listened sympathetically to Castellio's pleas for toleration . . . There was no point in joining the witch hunt of the Genevans . . . Ambiguity seemed less dangerous than controversy. The printing industry must have welcomed this calculated indecision . . . It was on the side of Castellio and tolerance.[55]

From the days of Castellio to those of Voltaire, the printing industry was the principal natural ally of libertarian, heterodox, and ecumenical philosophers. Eager to expand markets and diversify production, the enterprising publisher was the natural enemy of narrow minds. If he preferred the Protestant Rome to the Catholic one, it was not necessarily because he was committed to Calvinism. Geneva was also preferred by uncommitted printers because it could be more easily disregarded since it was powerless to control the book trade beyond the confines of a single small town.

Uncommitted printers were not only prepared to run with Protestant "hares" and hunt with Catholic "hounds" during the religious wars. Their interests differed also from those of nation-building statesmen who raised armies and waged dynastic wars. Their business flourished better in loosely federated realms than in strongly consolidated ones, in small principalities rather than in large and expanding ones. The politics of censorship made them the natural opponents

---

[55] P. G. Bietenholz, *Basle and France in the Sixteenth Century: The Basle Humanists and Printers in Their Contacts with Francophone Culture* (Toronto, 1971), 132.

not only of church officials but also of lay bureaucrats, regulations, and red tape. As independent agents, they supplied organs of publicity and covert support to a "third force" that was not affiliated with any one church or one state. This third force was, however, obviously affiliated with the interests of early modern capitalists. Even the heterodox creeds adopted by some of the merchant publishers (most notably by Christopher Plantin) were complementary to their activities as capitalist entrepreneurs.

The formation of syndicates of heterodox businessmen and printers linked to far-flung distribution networks indicates how the new industry encouraged informal social groupings that cut across traditional frontiers and encompassed varied faiths. It also encouraged the adoption of a new ethos which was cosmopolitan, ecumenical, and tolerant without being secular, incredulous, or necessarily Protestant – an ethos that seems to anticipate the creed of some of the masonic lodges during the Enlightenment, not least because of its secretive and quasi-conspiratorial character.

One main center for advocates of the new ethos in the sixteenth century was the printing shop of Christopher Plantin in Antwerp, which retained its Catholic affiliations and won support from King Philip II of Spain even while serving Calvinists as well. Some members of the Plantin circle were also affiliated with the loosely organized, secret, heterodox sect called the "Family (or House) of Love." Familists were encouraged to conform outwardly to the religion of the region where they lived, while remaining true believers in the mystical tenets set down in familist tracts. Even while familist literature was being issued from his presses, Plantin managed to get Philip II to appoint him "Proto-Typographer," making him responsible for supervising the printing industry throughout the Low Countries and for checking on the competence and religious orthodoxy of every printer in the region.[56] He also won the friendship of Philip II's councillor and most distinguished court scholar, Benito Arias Montano, who was sent from Spain to supervise work on the Antwerp Polyglot and returned to win new honors from Philip II even while

[56] Kingdon, "Patronage, Piety and Printing," 24–5.

CHRISTOPHORVS PLANTINVS,   BENEDICTVS ARIAS MONTANVS.

Fig. 30. The largest printing firm in Western Europe in the second half of the sixteenth century was the Antwerp establishment of Christopher Plantin, portrayed here in an engraving by Philippe Galle. Galle, who belonged to a dynasty of engravers and print publishers, was affiliated with Plantin's circle. He also portrayed Benito Arias Montano, the scholarly court chaplain who was sent to Plantin by Philip II of Spain to supervise work on the Antwerp Polyglot. The two portraits come from a collection by Philippe Galle, *Virorum doctorum de disciplinis bene merentium effigies* (Antwerp, 1572, B1 recto and E4 recto). Reproduced by kind permission of the Folger Shakespeare Library.

maintaining a secret correspondence with his newfound circle of Netherlandish friends and altering the normal pattern of the book trade in Spain for a time. Part of the fascination exerted by the story of the Plantin circle and the "Family of Love" is its capacity to excite the paranoid imagination by revealing that an eminent Catholic official who was also a renowned Counter-Reformation scholar was actually engaged in organizing subversive "cells" in the very depths of the Escorial.

Plantin's vast publishing empire, which was the largest in sixteenth-century Europe, owed much to his capacity to hedge all bets by winning rich and powerful friends in different regions who belonged to diverse confessions. The permission granted to members of "Nicodemite" sects, such as the Family of Love, to obey whatever religious observances were common in the regions where they lived, also helped to smooth the way for the publishers' foreign agents and made it easier to hold potential persecutors at bay. The ecumenical and Nicodemite character of Plantin's secret faith may thus be seen, as Robert Kingdon says, as "yet another example of the ways in which religious conviction and economic self-interest can reinforce each other."[57] Businessmen, particularly printers, with antidogmatic views, were most fit to survive and even to prosper amid the shifting fortunes of religious warfare. If they adopted a tolerant creed that could be covertly sustained, they could avoid persecution by zealots even while attracting foreign financial support. The point is well taken. Still it leaves room for additional considerations.

Doubtless, the outlook of the successful merchant-publisher was related to his position as a capitalist entrepreneur in an era of shifting power centers and religious frontiers. But it was also related to the particular nature of the products he manufactured. Plantin's merchandise set him apart from other businessmen and tradesmen. It brought men of letters and learning into his shop. It encouraged him to feel more at ease with strange scholars, bibliophiles, and literati than with neighbors or relatives in his native town. The prospering merchant-publisher had to know as much about books and intellectual trends as a cloth merchant did about dry goods and dress fashions; he needed to develop a connoisseur's expertise about type styles, book catalogues, and library sales. He often found it useful to master many languages, to handle variant texts, to investigate antiquities and old inscriptions along with new maps and calendars. In short, the very nature of his business provided the merchant-publisher with a broadly based liberal education. It also led toward a widened circle of acquaintances and included close contacts with foreigners. If emigrés or aliens were welcome in his workshop, this was rarely because of previous ties of blood or friendship and not always because foreign financing, new market outlets, patrons, or

---

[57] Robert M. Kingdon, "Christopher Plantin and his Backers 1575–1590: A Study in the Problems of Financing Business during War," *Mélanges d'Histoire Economique et Sociale Homage à Anthony Babel* (Geneva, 1963), 315.

privileges were being sought. Foreign experts were also needed as editors, translators, correctors, and type designers. The demand for vernacular Scriptures, Psalters, and service books among enclaves of Protestants on foreign soil also encouraged an interchange between printers and "communities of strangers," based on the religious needs of alien enclaves. The provision of service books for an Italian community in London, an English community in Geneva, a French church in Holland led not only to affiliations with foreign merchants but also to more awareness of the varieties of Christian religious experience and of the different nuances associated with liturgy in diverse tongues.

Foreigners engaged in translation were welcomed into homes as well as shops. They were often provided with room and board by the local printer and sometimes taken into his family circle as well. The names of those who were admitted to the Basel workshop of Vesalius's publisher, Oporinus, were perhaps even more remarkable than the circle formed later around Plantin's Antwerp shop. Most of the leading lights of the "radical reformation" lodged at some point with Oporinus: Servetus, Lelio Sozzini, Ochino, Postel, Castellio, Oecolampadius, Schwenckfelt – not to mention the Marian exiles such as John Foxe. The Basel printer was also on good terms with Paracelsus. He provided a refuge for David Joris, one of the three heresiarchs who founded the Family of Love. Much later, among the Enlightenment *philosophes*, and still later among the followers of Saint-Simon, the use of the term "family" to mean a joint intellectual commitment became more symbolic and metaphorical. But the translators, correctors, and proofreaders who lodged with printers did become temporary members of real families. Polyglot households were not uncommon where major scholarly publishing ventures took place.

Once again, Bible printing should be brought into the picture. The peculiar polyglot character of the Christian Scriptures contributed to a rapid expansion of cultural contacts among scholar-printers who handled biblical editions and translations. Aldus Manutius's plans for a polyglot edition might be kept in mind when considering the circle around him. Plantin's later Antwerp program brought together sophisticated scholars representing diverse realms

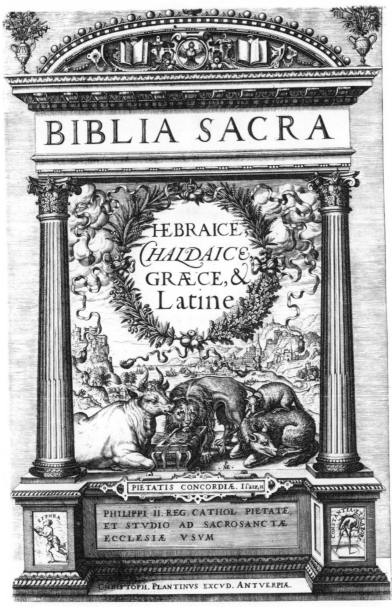

BIBLIA SACRA

HEBRAICE,
CHALDAICE,
GRÆCE, &
Latine

PIETATIS CONCORDIÆ. Iſaiæ,11

PHILIPPI II. REG. CATHOL. PIETATE,
ET STVDIO AD SACROSANCTÆ
ECCLESIÆ VSVM

CHRISTOPH. PLANTINVS EXCVD. ANTVERPIÆ.

Fig. 31 (above). The frontispiece to the Antwerp Polyglot with its "peaceable kingdom" imagery reflects the ecumenical conciliatory views of master printers, who needed both financial and scholarly aid from representatives of diverse creeds and countries and tried to avoid entanglement in religious and dynastic disputes. From *Biblia Sacra, Hebraice, Chaldaice, Graece, & Latine* (Antwerp: Christopher Plantin, 1571). The pages (overleaf), showing the beginning of Genesis, in Hebrew, Chaldaic, Greek, and Latin, like the frontispiece, come from the Antwerp Polyglot: *Biblia Sacra, Hebraice, Chaldaice, Graece, & Latine* (Antwerp: Christopher Plantin, 1571). Reproduced by kind permission of the Rare Book and Special Collections Division, Library of Congress.

Hebrew column

‫רֵאשִׁית בָּרָא אֱלֹהִים אֵת הַשָּׁמַיִם וְאֵת‬
‫הָאָרֶץ: וְהָאָרֶץ הָיְתָה תֹהוּ וָבֹהוּ וְחֹשֶׁךְ‬
‫עַל־פְּנֵי תְהוֹם וְרוּחַ אֱלֹהִים מְרַחֶפֶת עַל־‬
‫פְּנֵי הַמָּיִם: וַיֹּאמֶר אֱלֹהִים יְהִי־אוֹר‬
‫וַיְהִי־אוֹר: וַיַּרְא אֱלֹהִים אֶת־הָאוֹר כִּי־טוֹב וַיַּבְדֵּל‬
‫אֱלֹהִים בֵּין הָאוֹר וּבֵין הַחֹשֶׁךְ: וַיִּקְרָא אֱלֹהִים לָאוֹר‬
‫יוֹם וְלַחֹשֶׁךְ קָרָא לָיְלָה וַיְהִי־עֶרֶב וַיְהִי־בֹקֶר יוֹם אֶחָד:‬
‫וַיֹּאמֶר אֱלֹהִים יְהִי רָקִיעַ בְּתוֹךְ הַמָּיִם וִיהִי מַבְדִּיל‬
‫בֵּין מַיִם לָמָיִם: וַיַּעַשׂ אֱלֹהִים אֶת־הָרָקִיעַ וַיַּבְדֵּל בֵּין‬
‫הַמַּיִם אֲשֶׁר מִתַּחַת לָרָקִיעַ וּבֵין הַמַּיִם אֲשֶׁר מֵעַל לָרָקִיעַ‬
‫וַיְהִי־כֵן: וַיִּקְרָא אֱלֹהִים לָרָקִיעַ שָׁמָיִם וַיְהִי־עֶרֶב‬
‫וַיְהִי־בֹקֶר יוֹם שֵׁנִי: וַיֹּאמֶר אֱלֹהִים יִקָּווּ הַמַּיִם‬
‫מִתַּחַת הַשָּׁמַיִם אֶל־מָקוֹם אֶחָד וְתֵרָאֶה הַיַּבָּשָׁה וַיְהִי־‬
‫כֵן: וַיִּקְרָא אֱלֹהִים לַיַּבָּשָׁה אֶרֶץ וּלְמִקְוֵה הַמַּיִם קָרָא‬
‫יַמִּים וַיַּרְא אֱלֹהִים כִּי־טוֹב: וַיֹּאמֶר אֱלֹהִים תַּדְשֵׁא‬
‫הָאָרֶץ דֶּשֶׁא עֵשֶׂב מַזְרִיעַ זֶרַע עֵץ פְּרִי עֹשֶׂה פְּרִי לְמִינוֹ‬
‫אֲשֶׁר זַרְעוֹ־בוֹ עַל־הָאָרֶץ וַיְהִי־כֵן: וַתּוֹצֵא הָאָרֶץ דֶּשֶׁא‬
‫עֵשֶׂב מַזְרִיעַ זֶרַע לְמִינֵהוּ וְעֵץ עֹשֶׂה־פְּרִי אֲשֶׁר זַרְעוֹ־בוֹ‬
‫לְמִינֵהוּ וַיַּרְא אֱלֹהִים כִּי־טוֹב: וַיְהִי־עֶרֶב וַיְהִי־בֹקֶר‬
‫יוֹם שְׁלִישִׁי: וַיֹּאמֶר אֱלֹהִים יְהִי מְאֹרֹת בִּרְקִיעַ‬
‫הַשָּׁמַיִם לְהַבְדִּיל בֵּין הַיּוֹם וּבֵין הַלָּיְלָה וְהָיוּ לְאֹתֹת‬
‫וּלְמוֹעֲדִים וּלְיָמִים וְשָׁנִים: וְהָיוּ לִמְאוֹרֹת בִּרְקִיעַ‬
‫הַשָּׁמַיִם לְהָאִיר עַל־הָאָרֶץ וַיְהִי־כֵן: וַיַּעַשׂ אֱלֹהִים‬
‫אֶת־שְׁנֵי הַמְּאֹרֹת הַגְּדֹלִים אֶת־הַמָּאוֹר הַגָּדֹל לְמֶמְשֶׁלֶת‬
‫הַיּוֹם וְאֶת־הַמָּאוֹר הַקָּטֹן לְמֶמְשֶׁלֶת הַלַּיְלָה וְאֵת‬
‫הַכּוֹכָבִים: וַיִּתֵּן אֹתָם אֱלֹהִים בִּרְקִיעַ הַשָּׁמָיִם לְהָאִיר‬
‫עַל־הָאָרֶץ: וְלִמְשֹׁל בַּיּוֹם וּבַלַּיְלָה וּלְהַבְדִּיל בֵּין הָאוֹר‬
‫וּבֵין הַחֹשֶׁךְ וַיַּרְא אֱלֹהִים כִּי־טוֹב: וַיְהִי־עֶרֶב וַיְהִי־‬
‫בֹקֶר יוֹם רְבִיעִי: וַיֹּאמֶר אֱלֹהִים יִשְׁרְצוּ הַמַּיִם שֶׁרֶץ‬
‫נֶפֶשׁ חַיָּה וְעוֹף יְעוֹפֵף עַל־הָאָרֶץ עַל־פְּנֵי רְקִיעַ הַשָּׁמָיִם:‬

Latin column

CAPVT PRIMVM.

IN principio creauit Deus cœlum & terrã. [2] Terra autem erat inanis & vacua : & tenebræ erant super faciē abyſsi : & ſpiritus Dei ferebatur super aquas. [3] Dixitá; Deus, Fiat lux Et facta eſt lux. [4] Et vidit Deus lucem quòd eſſet bona: & diuiſit lucem à tenebris. [5] Appellauitá; lucem diem; & tenebras noĉte. Factumá; eſt veſpere & mane dies vnus. [6] Dixit quoque Deus, Fiat firmamentum in medio aquarum ; & diuidat a-quas ab aquis. [7] Et fecit Deus firmamentum, diuiſitá; aquas quæ erant sub firmamento, ab his quæ erant super firmamentū. Et factum eſt ita. [8] Vocauitá; Deus firmamentū, cœlum: & factum eſt veſpere, & mane dies ſecundus. [9] Dixit verò Deus , Congregentur aquæ quæ sub cœlo ſunt, in locum vnum: & appareat ari-da. Et factum eſt ita. [10] Et vocauit Deus aridã, terram: congregationeſá; aquarum appellauit maria. Et vidit Deus quòd eſſet bonum. [11] Et ait, Germinet terra herbã virentem & facien-tem ſemen; & lignum pomiferū faciens fructū iuxta genus ſuum, cuius ſemen in ſemetipſo sit super terram. Et factū eſt ita. [12] Et protulit terra herbam virentē, & faciente ſemen iuxta genus ſuū; lignumá; faciens fructū, & habens vnum-quodá; ſementem ſecundū ſpeciem ſuam. Et vidit Deus quòd eſſet bonum. [13] Et factū eſt veſpere & mane dies tertius. [14] Dixit autē Deus, Fiant luminaria in firmamento cæli ; & diui-dant diem ac noĉte ; & ſint in ſigna & tēpora & dies & annos: [15] Vt luceát in firmamēto cæli, & illuminent terrã. Et factum eſt ita. Fecitá; Deus duo luminaria magna: luminare maius, vt præeſſet diei: & luminare minus, vt præeſſet noĉti: & ſtellas. [16] Et poſuit eas Deus in firma-mēto cœli, vt lucerēt super terrã: [17] Et præeſſent diei ac noĉti; & diuiderent lucem ac tenebras. Et vidit Deus quòd eſſet bonū. [18] Et factū eſt veſpere, & mane dies quartus. [19] Dixit etiam Deus, Producant aquæ reptile animæ viuentis, & volatile super terram sub firmamento cæli.

תרגום אונקלוס

‫בְּקַדְמִין בְּרָא יְיָ יָת שְׁמַיָא וְיָת אַרְעָא: וְאַרְעָא הֲוָת צָדְיָא וְרֵקַנְיָא וַחֲשׁוֹכָא עַל אַפֵּי תְהוֹמָא וְרוּחָא דַיְיָ מְנַשְּׁבָא עַל‬
‫אַפֵּי מַיָא: וַאֲמַר יְיָ יְהֵא נְהוֹרָא וַהֲוָה נְהוֹרָא: וַחֲזָא יְיָ יָת נְהוֹרָא אֲרֵי טָב וְאַפְרֵישׁ יְיָ בֵּין נְהוֹרָא וּבֵין‬
‫חֲשׁוֹכָא: וּקְרָא יְיָ לִנְהוֹרָא יְמָמָא וְלַחֲשׁוֹכָא קְרָא לֵילְיָא וַהֲוָה רְמַשׁ וַהֲוָה צְפַר יוֹם חַד: וַאֲמַר יְיָ‬
‫יְהֵא רְקִיעָא בִּמְצִיעוּת מַיָא וִיהֵא מַפְרֵישׁ בֵּין מַיָא לְמַיָא: וַעֲבַד יְיָ יָת רְקִיעָא וְאַפְרֵישׁ בֵּין מַיָא דְמִלְּרַע לִרְקִיעָא וּבֵין מַיָא דְּמֵעֵיל לִרְקִיעָא וַהֲוָה כֵן: וּקְרָא יְיָ‬
‫לִרְקִיעָא שְׁמַיָא וַהֲוָה רְמַשׁ וַהֲוָה צְפַר יוֹם תִנְיָן: וַאֲמַר יְיָ יִתְכַּנְשׁוּן מַיָא מִתְּחוֹת שְׁמַיָא לַאֲתַר חַד וְתִתַחֲזֵי יַבֶּשְׁתָּא וַהֲוָה כֵן: וּקְרָא‬
‫יְיָ לְיַבֶּשְׁתָּא אַרְעָא וּלְבֵית כְּנִישׁוּת מַיָא קְרָא יַמְמֵי וַחֲזָא יְיָ אֲרֵי טָב: וַאֲמַר יְיָ תַּדְאֵת אַרְעָא דִּתְאָה עִשְׂבָּא דְּבַר זַרְעֵהּ מִזְדְּרַע אִילָן פֵּירִין עָבֵד פֵּירִין לִזְנוֹהִי דְּבַר זַרְעֵהּ‬
‫בֵּהּ עַל אַרְעָא וַהֲוָה כֵן: וְאַפֵּיקַת אַרְעָא דִּתְאָה עִשְׂבָּא דְּבַר זַרְעֵהּ מִזְדְּרַע לִזְנוֹהִי וְאִילָן עָבֵד פֵּירִין דְּבַר זַרְעֵהּ‬
‫בֵּהּ לִזְנוֹהִי וַחֲזָא יְיָ אֲרֵי טָב: וַהֲוָה רְמַשׁ וַהֲוָה צְפַר יוֹם תְלִיתָאי: וַאֲמַר יְיָ יְהוֹן נְהוֹרִין בִּרְקִיעָא דִשְׁמַיָא לְאַפְרָשָׁא בֵּין יְמָמָא‬
‫וּבֵין לֵילְיָא וִיהוֹן לְאָתִין וּלְזִמְנִין וּלְמִמְנֵי בְהוֹן יוֹמִין וּשְׁנִין: וִיהוֹן לִנְהוֹרִין בִּרְקִיעָא דִשְׁמַיָא לְאַנְהָרָא עַל אַרְעָא וַהֲוָה כֵן: וַעֲבַד יְיָ‬
‫יָת תְּרֵין נְהוֹרֵי רַבְרְבַיָּא יָת נְהוֹרָא רַבָּא לְמִשְׁלַט בִּימָמָא וְיָת נְהוֹרָא זְעֵירָא לְמִשְׁלַט בְּלֵילְיָא וְיָת כּוֹכְבַיָּא: וִיהַב יַתְהוֹן יְיָ בִּרְקִיעָא‬
‫דִּשְׁמַיָא לְאַנְהָרָא עַל אַרְעָא: וּלְמִשְׁלַט בִּימָמָא וּבְלֵילְיָא וּלְאַפְרָשָׁא בֵּין נְהוֹרָא וּבֵין חֲשׁוֹכָא וַחֲזָא יְיָ אֲרֵי טָב: וַהֲוָה רְמַשׁ וַהֲוָה‬
‫צְפַר יוֹם רְבִיעָאי: וַאֲמַר יְיָ יִרְחֲשׁוּן מַיָא רְחִישָׁא נַפְשָׁא חַיְתָא וְעוֹפָא דְּפָרַח עַל אַרְעָא עַל אַפֵּי רְקִיעַ שְׁמַיָא:‬

Fig. 31. (cont.)

Interp.ex Græc.lxx. GENESIS.   ΓΕΝΕΣΙΣ.   μεθερμήνευσις τῶν ο´   3

CAPVT PRIMVM.

N principio fecit Deus cælum & terrã. At terra erat inuisibilis et incõposita,et tenebræ super abys-sum: & spiritus Dei ferebatur su per aquam. Et dixit Deus,Fiat lux,& facta est lux. Et vidit Deus lucē,quòd bona: & diuisit Deus inter lucem,& inter tenebras. Et vocauit Deus lucē diē: & tenebras vocauit noctē: & factũ est vespere; & factũ est mane,dies vnus. Et dixit Deus,Fiat firmamentũ in medio aquæ: & sit diuidēs inter aquã,& aquã. Et fecit Deus firma mentũ,& diuisit Deus inter aquã;quæ erat sub firmamēto:& inter aquã,quæ super firmamentũ. Et vocauit Deus firmamentũ cæli: & vidit Deus,quòd bonũ.Et factũ est vespere,& factũ est mane,dies se cũdus. Et dixit Deus,Cõgregetur aqua quæ sub cælo, in cõgregatiõe vnã,& appareat arida. Et factũ est ita,et cõgregata est aqua quæ sub cælo,in cõgregatio nes suas:et apparuit arida. Et vocauit Deus aridã, terrã:et cõgregationes aquarũ,vocauit maria.Et vi dit Deus quòd bonũ. Et dixit Deus,Germinet terra herbã fæni seminante semē secundũ genus et secundũ similitudinẽ: & lignũ pomiferũ faciens fructũ,cuius semen ipsius in ipso secundũ genus super terrã.Et fa ctũ est ita. Et protulit terra herbã fæni seminantẽ semen secundũ genus & secundũ similitudinẽ: & lig nũ pomiferũ faciens fructũ, cuius semē eius in ipso, secundumgenus super terrã.Et vidit Deus quòd bo nũ. Et factũ est vespere,& factũ est mane,dies ter tius. Et dixit Deus: Fiant luminaria in firmamento cæli,vt luceant super terrã,ad dtuidendum inter diē, & inter noctē;& sint in signa,& in tēpora, & in dies,& in annos. Et sint in illuminatiõe in firma mento cæli,vt luceant super terram.Et factũ est ita. Et fecit Deus duo luminaria magna:luminare ma gnũ in principatus diei: & luminare minus in prin cipatu noctis:et stellas. Et posuit eas Deus in firma mēto cæli: vt lucerēt super terrã. Et præessent diei, & nocti, & diuiderēt inter lucē et inter tenebras:et vidit Deus quòd bonũ. Et factũ est vespere,& factũ est mane,dies quartus. Et dixit Deus,Producant a quæ reptilia animarũ viuentiũ, & volatilia volãtia super terrã,secundũ firmamentũ cæli:& factũ est ita.

CAPVT PRIMVM.

IN principio creauit Deus cælum & terram. ¹ Terra autem erat deserta & vacua; & tenebræ super faciem abyssi: & spiritus Dei insufflabat super faciem aquarum. ² Et dixit Deus, Sit lux: & fuit lux. ³ Et vidit Deus lucem quòd esset bona. Et diuisit Deus inter lucem & inter tenebras. ⁴ Appellauitque Deus lucem diem, & tenebras vocauit noctem. Et fuit vespere & fuit mane dies vnus. ⁵ Et dixit Deus, Sit firmamentum in medio aquarum & diuidat inter aquas & aquas. ⁶ Et fecit Deus firmamentum: & diuisit inter aquas quæ erant sub ter firmamentum: & inter aquas quæ erant super firmamentum : & fuit ita. ⁷ Et vocauit Deus firmamentum cælum. Et fuit vespere & fuit mane,dies secundus. ⁸ Et dixit Deus, Congregentur aquæ quæ sub cælo sunt, in locum vnum : & appareat arida. Et fuit ita. ⁹ Et vocauit Deus aridam terram: & locum congregationis aquarum appellauit maria. Et vidit Deus quòd esset bonum. ¹⁰ Et dixit Deus, Germinet terra ger minationem herbæ, cuius filius sementis seminatur: arboremque fructiferam facientem fructus secundum genus suum; cuius filius sementis in ipso sit super terram . Et fuit ita. ¹¹ Et produxit terra germen herbæ, cuius filius sementis seminator secundum genus suum; & arborem facientem fructus, cuius filius sementis in ipso secundum genus suum. Et vidit Deus quòd esset bonum. ¹² Et fuit vespere & fuit mane, dies tertius. ¹³ Et dixit Deus, Sint luminaria in firmamento cæli, vt diuidant inter diem & noctem : & sint in signa & in tempora : & vt numerentur per ea dies & anni. ¹⁴ Et sint in luminaria in firmamento cæli ad illuminandum super terram : & fuit ita. ¹⁵ Et fecit Deus duo luminaria magna : lu minare maius,vt dominaretur in die: & luminare minus,vt dominaretur in nocte:& stellas. ¹⁶ Et posuit eas Deus in firmamento cæli ad illuminan dum super terram. ¹⁷ Et vt dominarentur in die & in nocte: & vt diuiderent inter lucē & tenebras: & vidit Deus quòd esset bonũ. ¹⁸ Et fuit vespere & fuit mane, dies quartus. ¹⁹ Et dixit Deus, Serpant aquæ reptile animæ viuētis:& auem quæ volat super terrã super faciē aëris firmamenti cælorum.

A 2

Fig. 31. (cont.)

and faiths. In order to complete the eight-volume project, it was desirable to achieve smooth working relationships among heterogeneous editors. Domestic peace also hinged on encouraging toleration of varied views. The same consideration applies to the biblical editions turned out by Estienne. Representatives of ten different nationalities sat around the table of Robert Estienne and Perrette Badius. According to their son, Henri, even the Estiennes' servants picked up a smattering of Latin, the only tongue shared in common by all.[58] Similar heterodox and cosmopolitan circles were formed around the Amerbach-Froben shop in Basel and around many other printing firms in scattered cities throughout Europe. The notion of a single subversive cell in the depths of the grim Escorial may excite cloak-and-dagger fantasies. The idea of many print shops located in numerous towns, each serving as an intellectual crossroads, as a miniature "international house" – as a meeting place, message center, and sanctuary all in one – seems no less stimulating to the historical imagination. In the late sixteenth century, for the first time in the history of any civilization, the concept of a *Concordia Mundi* was being developed on a truly global scale and the "family of man" was being extended to encompass all the peoples of the world. To understand how this happened, there is no better place to begin than with the hospitality extended by merchant-publishers and scholar-printers who plied their trade during the religious wars. Plantin's correspondence shows him requesting advice about Syriac type fonts, obtaining a Hebrew *Talmud* for Arias Montano, responding to a request from Mercator concerning the map of France, advising a Bavarian official on which professor to appoint at Ingolstadt, asking for theological guidance on how to illustrate a religious book.[59] To look over the connections revealed in this correspondence is to see laid bare the central nervous system or chief switchboard of the Republic of Letters in its formative phase. Plantin's account books provide a fine opportunity for economic historians to examine the operations of one early modern entrepreneur. But his correspondence also points to the development of something other than early capitalism. All the

[58]   Elizabeth Armstrong, *Robert Estienne, Royal Printer* (Cambridge, 1954), 15.
[59]   Voët, *Golden Compasses*, I:383.

elements that will produce a later "crisis of the European conscience" are already drawn together there.

Here, again, as elsewhere, I think the suggestive discussion of "Erasmian" trends by Trevor-Roper would be strengthened by giving more attention to the role of printers and publishers. In order to explain the growth of attitudes encouraging theological reconciliation, it is insufficient to point to three intervals when religious warfare was at a low ebb. Even when the Spanish fury was at its height, an international peace movement was being quietly shaped. The problem of understanding the religious origins of the Enlightenment cannot be resolved by carving out an "age of Erasmus" or an "age of Bacon" to serve as a refuge for peace-loving philosophers. By taking into consideration the possibility that Bible reading could intensify dogmatism even while Bible printing might encourage toleration, the problem becomes somewhat easier to handle. The same approach may be helpful when dealing with other similar problems relating to crosscurrents and contradictory attitudes manifested during the Reformation.

It also seems worth giving more thought to the effects of printing when tackling the basic problems of causation which crop up repeatedly in Reformation studies:

> The basic question can be formulated as follows: Were the ecclesiastical conditions of the early sixteenth century such as to denote a precarious equilibrium that necessitated some kind of revolutionary or reformatory upheaval? Was Europe in the early sixteenth century "crying for the Reformation"?
>
> We know far too little...to offer more than tentative statements...Still the general conclusion at this point appears to be that European society was far more stable than has been traditionally assumed. In other words, if Luther and the other early reformers had died in their cradles, the Catholic church might well have survived the sixteenth century without a major upheaval.[60]

---

[60] Hans Hillerbrand, "The Spread of the Protestant Reformation in the Sixteenth Century," *The South Atlantic Quarterly* LXVII (Spring 1968): 270.

Granted that European society and ecclesiastical institutions seemed relatively stable around 1500, what about the state of the scriptural tradition fifty years after Gutenberg? As this chapter may suggest, it was in a highly volatile state. Conflict over new questions pertaining to priestly prerogatives and sacred studies could not have been postponed indefinitely. Even if Luther, Zwingli, and others had died in their cradles, it seems likely that some reformers would still have turned to the presses to implement long-lived pastoral concerns and evangelical aims. Perhaps civil war in Christendom was not inevitable, but the advent of printing did, at the very least, rule out the possibility of perpetuating the status quo.

On the whole, it seems safe to conclude that all the problems associated with the disruption of Western Christendom will become less baffling if we approach them by respecting the order of events and put the advent of printing ahead of the Protestant Revolt.

CHAPTER SEVEN

The Book of Nature Transformed

PRINTING AND THE RISE OF
MODERN SCIENCE

Introduction: "The Great Book of Nature" and the "Little Books of Men"

Problems associated with the rise of modern science lend themselves to a similar argument. In other words, I think the advent of printing ought to be featured more prominently by historians of science when they set the stage for the downfall of Ptolemaic astronomy, Galenic anatomy, or Aristotelian physics. This means asking for a somewhat more drastic revision of current guidelines than seems necessary in Reformation studies. In the latter field, the impact of printing may be postponed, but at least it is usually included among the agents that promoted Luther's cause. The outpouring of tracts and cartoons left too vivid and strong an impression for the new medium to be entirely discounted when investigating the Protestant Revolt. The contrary seems true in the case of the so-called scientific revolution. Exploitation of the mass medium was more common among pseudoscientists and quacks than among Latin-writing professional scientists, who often withheld their work from the press. When important treatises did appear in print, they rarely achieved the status of bestsellers. Given the limited circulation of works such as *De revolutionibus* and the small number of readers able to understand them, it appears plausible to play down the importance of printing. Given the wider circulation of antiquated materials, many authorities are inclined to go even further and assign to early printers a negative, retrogressive role. "There is no evidence that, except in religion, printing hastened the spread of new ideas... In fact the printing of medieval scientific texts may have delayed the acceptance of . . . Copernicus."[1]

As the previous chapter may suggest, however, even in religion, the "spread of new ideas" was only one of several new functions that deserve consideration. When seeking to understand scientific change, we also need to associate printers with functions other than popularization and propaganda. Textual traditions inherited from the Alexandrians were no more likely to continue unchanged after the shift from script to print than were scriptural traditions. For natural philosophers as for theologians, attempts at emendation and the pursuit of long-lived goals were likely to have a different outcome after printers replaced scribes.

At present, however, we are not only inclined to set the mass appeal of Lutheran tracts against the restricted appeal of Copernican treatises; we are also prone to discount textual traditions altogether when dealing with problems of scientific change. Conventional iconography encourages us to envisage Protestants with books in their hands (especially when we contrast them with Catholics holding rosaries). Early modern scientists, however, are more likely to be portrayed holding plants or astrolabes than studying texts. Insofar as natural philosophers may have studied early printed editions of Ptolemy, Pliny, Galen, or Aristotle, they are usually accused of looking in the wrong direction. "One would have thought that the breathtaking discoveries of the navigators would have turned attention from the little books of men to the great book of Nature but this happened much less often than one might expect."[2] Yet how could the "great book of Nature" be investigated, one is tempted to ask, without exchanging information by means of the "little books of men"? The question is worth posing if only to bring out our own tendency to look in the wrong direction when considering the rise of modern science and related trends. It is partly because we envisage the astronomer gazing away at unchanging heavens, and the anatomist taking human bodies as his only books, that the

---

[1]   Antonia McLean, *Humanism and the Rise of Science in Tudor England* (London, 1972), 22.

[2]   Sarton, *Six Wings*, 6.

conceptual revolutions of the sixteenth century – which came before methods of star gazing or dissection had been altered – seem particularly difficult to explain.

In this regard, the long-lived metaphorical image of bypassing other books in order to read in the book of nature, "that universal and publick manuscript that lies expans'd unto the Eyes of all," is a source of deception which needs further analysis. Conventional treatments of this metaphor by intellectual and cultural historians provide fascinating excursions into the history of ideas but rarely pause over the problem of making freshly recorded observations available "unto the Eyes of all."

> There are two Books from whence I collect my Divinity; besides that written one of God, another of His servant Nature, that universal and publick Manuscript, that lies expans'd unto the Eyes of all: those that never saw Him in the one, have discover'd Him in the other ... Surely the Heathens know better how to joyn and read these mystical Letters than we Christians, who cast a more careless Eye on these common Hieroglyphicks and disdain to suck Divinity from the flowers of Nature.[3]

When Sir Thomas Browne compared the Bible with the book of nature, he was not only reworking a theme favored by Francis Bacon, but he was also drawing on earlier sources. According to Ernst Curtius, the same two "books" were mentioned in medieval sermons and derive ultimately from very ancient Near Eastern texts. This lineage is viewed by Curtius as evidence of cultural continuity, and he uses it to argue against Burckhardt's thesis (or at least against vulgarized versions of it). "It is a favorite cliché ... that the Renaissance shook off the dust of yellowed parchments and began instead to read in the book of nature or the world. But this metaphor itself derives from the Latin Middle Ages."[4] The mere fact that references to a "book of nature" appear in medieval Latin texts, however,

---

3   Sir Thomas Browne, "Religio Medici" (1643), pt. 1, chap. 16. Cited by Ernst Curtius, *European Literature and the Latin Middle Ages*, tr. W. Trask (New York, 1963), 232.

4   Curtius, 319.

is not a valid objection to the otherwise objectionable cliché. The persistence of old metaphors often masks major changes. In this case, all the changes that were entailed by the shift from script to print have been concealed. A seventeenth-century author, who coupled Scripture with nature, might echo older texts. But both the real and metaphorical "books" he had in mind were necessarily different from any known to twelfth-century clerks.

Thus when Saint Bernard referred to a "book of nature," he was not thinking about plants and planets, as Sir Thomas Browne was. Instead, he had in mind monastic discipline and the ascetic advantages of hard work in the fields.[5] When his fellow monks celebrated natural fecundity, they also had pious ends in view. Many different vivid images were needed to serve as memory aids when learning moral lessons. "Mankind is blind," noted a fourteenth-century preacher's manual, containing excerpts drawn from works on natural history.

> The human soul is forgetful in divine matters; but examples from nature are excellent devices to seize the memory in inescapable fashion...to fix men's thoughts upon the Creator...natural *exempla* are indispensable for preachers. Not only do they serve to capture the attention, but such examples are more meaningful than exhortation.[6]

The preacher in search of meaningful *exempla* was well served by the abundance of variegated forms. In medieval sermons, where didactic purposes came first, Scripture and nature were not separate but were intertwined. The latter, swathed in allegory, played a subservient role.

> The remarks we find as to the behavior of animals...denote occasionally a certain sense of observation. Yet allegories from the *Bestiary* are often superimposed on the things seen. In Nature, everything is symbolic. The symbols come either from

---

[5]   Leclercq, *Love of Learning*, 135.
[6]   Richard and Mary Rouse, "The Texts Called Lumen Anime," *Archivum Fratrum Praedicatorum* LXI (1971): 28.

biblical...or...classical tradition but they all have moral overtones...works like the *Hortus deliciarum*...are used for teaching all the virtues through the imagery of the flowers that beautify a wholly spiritual garden. The meaning of the flowers and fruit lies...in their properties.[7]

When set against prefaces to medieval florilegia, Browne's reference to the "heathens" who did not "disdain" to "suck Divinity" from real "flowers of Nature" seems to indicate disenchantment with an earlier habit of mind. The seventeenth-century writer appears to be rejecting rather than echoing the literary allegorical conventions which had been cultivated by generations of monks.

By the seventeenth century, the circumstances which had given rise to such conventions had been changed. Plant forms were no longer needed for memorizing moral lessons in Stuart England. When flowers were associated with the virtues or vices, it was more for poetic than for pedagogic effect. The Bible itself was no longer conveyed by a variety of "mixed media" such as stained glass, altar pieces, stone portals, choral music, or mystery plays. Sacred stories could be more clearly separated from profane ones after the same authorized version had been placed in every parish church. To couple Bible reading and nature study, to link religious anthologies with botanical texts, no longer came naturally but required resorting to literary artifice, as is well demonstrated by Browne's baroque prose.

When he reworked the old theme, did Browne have in mind a contrast between gardens of verses and real flower gardens? Was he underscoring the difference between "Christian" florilegia and "heathen" nature study? When he wrote of joining and reading "mystical" letters or "common Hieroglyphicks," was he referring to the heliocentric hypothesis, set forth in a treatise such as Thomas Digges's "most auncient doctrine of Pythagoreans lately revived by Copernicus and by Geometricall Demonstrations approved"?[8] Did

---

[7] Leclercq, *Love of Learning*, 137.
[8] On Digges's treatise, see Alexandre Koyré, *From the Closed World to the Infinite Universe* (Baltimore, 1957), 35.

his paradoxical image of a "universal publick Manuscript" reflect an acquaintance with Galileo's reference to the "grand book the universe which stands continually open to our gaze . . . written in the language of mathematics . . . its characters are triangles, circles and other geometric figures"?[9]

Given the many levels of meaning that are compressed in his works, there is no easy way to answer such questions, and several digressions would be required to attempt to reply. For my purpose it is enough to note that, whatever else was on his mind, Browne was familiar with the medium of print and with printed visual aids. In this regard, his book metaphors were based on objects Saint Bernard had never seen.

Browne kept up with the publications of the Royal Society and with the work of Bible scholars. Bible reading and nature study were sufficiently distinguished in his mind that he could assign different functions and separate languages to each. Like his fellow virtuosi, he was well aware of the thorny problems associated with deciphering God's words from ancient Hebrew texts. Against the uncertain meanings and ambiguous allegories to be found in Scripture, he set the circles, triangles, and other "common hieroglyphicks" that "heathen" philosophers – such as Euclid or Archimedes – knew how to join and read. When "scriptural statements conflict with scientific truths," noted Basil Willey, "Browne will adhere unto Archimedes who speaketh exactly, rather than the sacred Text which speaketh largely."[10]

In opposing Archimedes's formula to that provided by Solomon in the book of Chronicles, Sir Thomas Browne was not shaking off "the dust of yellowed parchments" and taking a fresh look at the great outdoors. On the contrary, he remained in the library with his eyes trained on old texts. But he *was* looking at texts which

[9] From "The Assayer" (1623), in Drake, *Discoveries and Opinions of Galileo*, 237–8.
[10] Basil Willey, *The Seventeenth Century Background* (London, 1942), 68. The relevant passages are in Browne's "Pseudoxis Epidemica," chap. 9, *The Prose of Sir Thomas Browne*, ed. Norman Endicott (New York, 1967), 143.

enabled Euclid and Archimedes to speak more "exactly" (in Indo-Arabic numerals and by means of uniform diagrams) than had been the case before. Similar analysis can be applied to the varied activities of the virtuosi who lived in Browne's day. According to Robert Westman, for example:

> There is one very important feature of Kepler's actual procedure that I do not believe has ever come to light. It is, simply, that the hypotheses set forth were not developed inductively from an inspection of nature. Kepler was reading neither the Book of Nature nor the Book of Scripture but the books of ancient and contemporary writers.[11]

The notion that Renaissance men discarded "dusty parchments" in favor of the "book of Nature" is objectionable not merely because previous book metaphors have been overlooked but mainly because the investigation of natural phenomena has been misconstrued. The so-called cliché rests on a naive conception of scientific activity which is seen to consist of discarding old books or rejecting received opinion and making firsthand observations for oneself. "He who wishes to explore nature must tread her books with his feet," wrote Paracelsus. "Writing is learned from letters. Nature however by travelling from land to land: One land, one page. This is the Codex Naturae, thus must its leaves be turned."[12] This naive view of science takes Browne's tricky image of a "universal publick Manuscript" at face value – as if any one observer could actually don "seven-league boots" and see the whole world laid out before him, without recourse to maps and star catalogues, to atlases and travel guides; or as if observations made in varied regions at different times did not have to be collected, preserved, and correlated with each other before plants or animals or minerals could be classified and compared; or finally, as if experiments did not have to be recorded in more

---

[11] Robert S. Westman, "Kepler's Theory of Hypothesis and the 'Realist Dilemma'," *Studies in the History and Philosophy of Science* III (1972): 253–4.

[12] Cited from Paracelsus in W. Pagel and P. Rattansi, "Vesalius and Paracelsus," *Medical History* VIII (October 1964): 316.

EVCLID. ELEMENT.

ipsi BC æqualis. & quoniam est vt AC ad CD, ita DC ad CB; æqualis autem AC quidem ipsi KH, CD vero ipsi HE, & CB ipsi KL: erit vt K
17. sexti. H ad HE, ita EH ad HL. rectangulum igitur K HL est ęquale quadrato ex EH. atque est rectus vterque angulorum KHE EHL. ergo in KL descriptus semicirculus & per punctum E transibit. nam si coniungamus EL, angulus LEK fiet
8. sexti. rectus, cum triangulum ELK ęquiangulum sit vnicuiq; triangulorum ELH EKH. si igitur manente KL semicirculus cõuersus in eundem rursus locum restituatur, à quo cœpit moueri, etiã per puncta FG transibit, iunctis FL LG; & rectis similiter factis ad puncta FG angulis: atque erit pyramis comprehensa data sphæra; etenim KL sphæræ diameter est ęqualis diametro datæ sphærę AB, quoniam ipsi quidem AC ponitur æqualis KH; ipsi vero CB æqualis HL. Dico igitur sphæræ diametrum potentia sesquialteram esse lateris pyramidis. Quoniam enim AC dupla est ipsius CB, erit AB ipsius BC tripla. ergo per conuersionem rationis BA sesquialtera est ipsius AC. vt autem BA ad AC, ita est quadratum ex BA ad quadratum ex AD, quoniam iuncta BD, est vt BA ad AD, ita DA ad AC ob
Cor. 8 sexti. similitudinem triangulorum DAB DAC, &
Cor. 20. sexti. quòd vt prima ad tertiam, ita quadratum ex prima ad quadratum ex secunda. ergo quadratum ex BA sesquialterum est quadrati ex AD. atque est BA quidem datæ sphæræ diameter, AD vero æqualis lateri pyramidis. sphęræ igitur diameter sesquialtera est lateris pyramidis. quod demonstrare oportebat.

Itaque demonstrandum est vt AB ad BC, ita esse quadratum ex AD ad quadratum ex DC.

Exponatur enim semicirculi figura; iungaturq; DB: & ex AC describatur quadratum EC, & parallelogrammum FB compleatur. Quoniã
Cor. 8. sexti. igitur est vt BA ad AD, ita DA ad AC, propte-
17. sexti. rea quòd triãgulum DAB æquiangulum est triã-
1. sexti. gulo DAC; erit rectangulum contentum BAC quadrato ex AD æquale. & quoniam est vt AB ad BC, ita parallelogrammum EB ad parallelogrammum BF; atque est parallelogrammũ quidem EB, quod continetur BA AC; est enim EA æqualis AC; parallelogrammum uero BF æquale est ei, quod AC CB continetur: erit ut AB ad BC, ita rectangulum contentum BA AC ad cõtentum AC CB. est autem contentum BA AC
17. sexti. æquale quadrato ex AD: & contentum AC CB
Cor. 8. sexti quadrato ex DC. ęquale: perpendicularis enim DC media est proportionalis inter basis portio-

nes

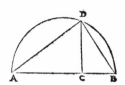

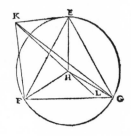

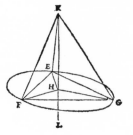

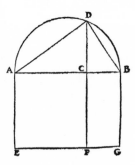

than one notebook to be checked out and be of any scientific value at all.

> Sell your lands . . . burn up your books . . . buy yourself stout shoes, travel to the mountains, search the valleys, the deserts, the shores of the sea, and the deepest depressions of the earth; note with care the distinctions between animals, the differences of plants, the various kinds of minerals . . . Be not ashamed to study the astronomy and terrestrial philosophy of the peasantry. Lastly, purchase coal, build furnaces, watch and operate the fire . . . In this way and no other you will arrive at a knowledge of things and their properties.[13]

Insofar as it entails rejection of secondhand accounts and insistence on using one's own eyes, this naive view owes much to the arguments of sixteenth-century empiricists who set fresh observation and folk wisdom against the Latin book learning that was transmitted in the schools. The movement championed by these empiricists has been diversely described. On the one hand, A. N. Whitehead views it as a "recoil against the inflexible rationality of medieval thought. . . . The world required centuries of contemplation of irreducible and stubborn facts . . . after the rationalistic orgy of the Middle Ages."[14] On the other hand, Hiram Haydn views it as a reaction to the bookish humanism of the Italian Renaissance.

[13] Cited in Peter Severinus, "Idea Medicinae Philosophicae" (1660), by Allen Debus, *The English Paracelsians* (New York, 1966), 20.

[14] A. N. Whitehead, *Science and the Modern World* (London, 1938), pp. 19, 28.

Fig. 32 (opposite). By Sir Thomas Browne's day, the multiform texts supplied by polyglot Bibles contrasted with the uniform diagrams, "the common hieroglyphs," contained in works by "heathen" philosophers such as Archimedes and Euclid. This page comes from a sixteenth-century Latin translation of Euclid's *Elements* made by the Italian scholar and mathematician Frederico Commandino, who had a press installed in his house in Urbino shortly after this work was printed in Pesaro. Euclid, *Elementorum*, libri XV . . . A Frederico Commandino . . . nuper in Latinum conversi (Pesaro: C. Franceschinum, 1572, folio 237 verso). Reproduced by kind permission of the Folger Shakespeare Library.

In my view, the movement Whitehead described as a "recoil" and Haydn calls a "counter-Renaissance" reflected disenchantment with those forms of teaching and book learning which had been inherited from the age of scribes. Insofar as memory training and "slavish copying" became less necessary, while inconsistencies and anomalies became more apparent after printed materials began to be produced, a distrust of received opinion and a fresh look at the evidence recommended itself to all manner of curious men. "The difference between my philosophising and that of Pico is this," wrote the Italian friar Campanella in 1607:

> I learn more from the anatomy of an ant or a blade of grass . . . than from all the books which have been written since the beginning of time. This is so, since I have begun . . . to read the book of God . . . the model according to which I correct the human books which have been copied badly and arbitrarily and without attention to the things that are written in the original book of the Universe.[15]

The idea of observing natural phenomena directly and carefully was, of course, as old as Aristotle. So too was a distrust of book learning. Ironically, the slogan of the empiricists – that one should use one's own eyes and trust nature, not books – derived from an experience which printing outmoded. Classical authors had warned against trusting hand-copied books and especially hand-copied pictures for the excellent reason that they degenerated over time. When Galen said that "the sick should be the doctor's books," he was justified by the circumstances of scribal culture. Sixteenth-century empiricists who repeated the phrase were actually being less responsive to changed circumstances than Latin-writing professors, such as Vesalius and Agricola, who had freshly rendered drawings transferred for duplication on durable woodblocks. Before printing, indeed, the detailed rendering of natural phenomena for readers had been a

---

[15] Tommaso Campanella, Letter of 1607, cited by Eugenio Garin, *Italian Humanism: Philosophy and Civil Life in the Renaissance*, tr. Peter Munz (New York, 1965), 215.

"marginal activity" in the most literal sense of the word. Given our present capacity to spot some "real" birds or plants on the margins of certain manuscripts or within the landscapes of certain paintings, we are prone to forget that earlier readers lacked plant guides and bird-watchers' manuals and could not discriminate between a fanciful and a factual rendering. This is not to deprecate the ability to render lifelike insects, plants, or birds, which was highly developed by certain masters in certain ateliers. It is merely to note that this ability was just as likely to be employed decorating the borders of Psalters or embroidered church vestments as to appear in books. It was rarely, if ever, used to demonstrate visually points made in technical texts.

In the age of scribes one might hire a particular illuminator to decorate a unique manuscript for a particular patron, but there would be little to gain by hiring illustrators, as Agricola did, to make detailed drawings of "veins, tools, vessels, sluices, machines, and furnaces" for embellishing a technical text. Agricola provided illustrations "lest descriptions which are conveyed by words should either not be understood by the men of our times or should cause difficulty to posterity."[16] In this approach he seems to prefigure the spirit of Diderot and the encyclopedists. He was also departing from scribal precedents by taking for granted that words and images would not be corrupted or drift apart over time.

> Historians have often been puzzled to account for the shocking difference between the crude and conventional woodcuts illustrating fifteenth-century herbals and the accuracy and artistic merit of the work of painters and miniaturists of the same period. It is reasonable to suppose that the fifteenth century saw no conflict; the woodcuts were copied from the illustrations of the manuscript whose text was also faithfully copied; the illustrations illustrated the text, not nature, a peculiar view, no doubt, but there was as yet no really independent botanical (or zoological) study.

[16] Cited by Paolo Rossi, *Philosophy, Technology and the Arts in the Early Modern Era*, tr. S. Attansio, ed. Benjamin Nelson (New York, 1970), 48.

That was to be the contribution of the sixteenth century . . . a revolution took place as authors, in despair at the inadequacies of purely verbal description, sought the aid of skilled draughtsmen and artists, trained to observe carefully and well.[17]

In duplicating crude woodcuts, publishers were simply carrying on where fifteenth-century copyists left off. Reversals, misplacements, the use of worn or broken blocks may have served to compound confusion, but the basic gap between master drawing and misshapen image was an inheritance from the age of scribes. It was not so much a new awareness of the "inadequacies of purely verbal description" as it was the new means of implementing this awareness that explains the "sixteenth-century revolution." For the first time the work of skilled draftsmen could be preserved intact in hundreds of copies of a given book.

In view of the output of corrupted data ("of human books copied badly") during the first century of printing and in view of the new possibility of duplicating fresh records, a reaction of some new kind against accepted texts, fixed lectures, and received opinion was almost inevitable. But it would be wrong to assume that a rejection of technical literature paved the way for the rise of modern science. It was not the burning of books but the printing of them that provided the indispensable step.

Given all the errors inherited from scribal records and the way habits of "slavish copying" persisted after they were no longer required, the empiricist reaction is understandable. It is easy to sympathize with those who placed more reliance on fresh observations than on rote learning. Nevertheless, insistence on going directly to the "book of Nature" soon took on the very attributes it was intended to repel. It became a ritualistic literary formula, devoid of real meaning. "As Olschki says of the natural philosophers: All of these thinkers who begin with the motto: 'Away from books!' . . . know natural phenomena only from books! What they offer as observational material is merely anecdotes based on their

---

[17] Boas, *Scientific Renaissance*, 52.

own experience or known from hearsay."[18] The unending stream of publications issued by exponents of the "new philosophy" suggests that the virtuosi were not entirely consistent in attacking the written word.

When the Royal Society published a volume of "Directions for Seamen, Bound for Far Voyages" in 1665, it defined its aim "to study Nature rather than Books," but it also noted its intention "from the Observations ... to compose such a History of Her [i.e., nature] as may hereafter serve to build a solid and useful Philosophy upon."[19] Presumably Royal Society publications were designed to be read. Did not the Society actually aim at getting more of nature *into* books? However much they valued knowledge acquired through direct experience, members of the new scientific academies were still engaged in processing data and purveying it at second hand. The notion of a "universal publick Manuscript" may tickle our fancy as a baroque conceit. But it is important to remember that there is no way of making fresh observations "universal" and "public" as long as they can be recorded only in manuscript form.

It is surprisingly easy to be absentminded on this point. Most authorities seem either to forget that all records had to remain in manuscript form until the fifteenth century or else to discount the importance of this fact. More often than not it seems sufficient to note that a "collective memory" was transmitted first by word of mouth and then by writing, without paying attention to the incapacity of scribal culture to make detailed records "public" and at the same time preserve them intact. When Kenneth Boulding describes the emergence of a "public image," for example, he mistakenly assigns to manuscript maps the capacity to convey a uniform spatial reference frame. Although world maps before print actually came in oddly assorted shapes and sizes, Boulding seems to imagine them as being

---

[18] Howard B. Adelmann, *Introduction to the Embryological Treatises of Hieronymus Fabricius of Aquapendente* (Ithaca, NY, 1942), 54.

[19] Notice appearing in "Philosophical Transactions," 8 January 1665/6, cited by Bernard Smith, "European Vision and the South Pacific," *Journal of the Warburg and Courtauld Institute* XIII (1950): 65.

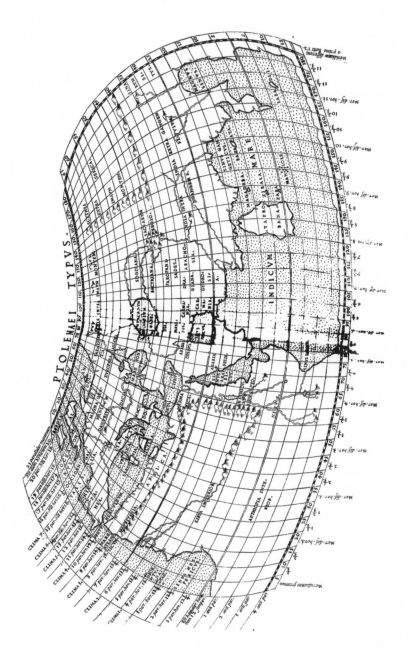

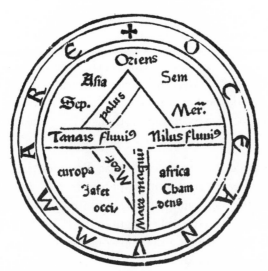

Fig. 33. The sixteenth-century reconstruction of a Ptolemaic world map on the opposite page is contained in a Venetian version of Ptolemy's *Geographia* (Venice: V. Valgrisius, 1562). The medieval pictogram, shown above, constitutes the first printed "world map." It is taken from an early edition of Isidore of Seville's *Etymologia* (Venice: Peter Löselein, 1483). Both plates are reproduced by kind permission of the Folger Shakespeare Library.

slightly fuzzier versions of our modern uniform outline maps. They were blurred around the edges, he suggests, until the voyages of discovery led to a "closure of geographic space ... looking over the long course of recorded history there is an orderly development in the ... spatial image ... early images can always be seen as partial unclear expressions of later more exact images."[20]

When one places a reconstruction of a Ptolemaic world map derived from the second century A.D. beside a *mappae mundi* designed later, it becomes clear that this statement needs qualification. Instead of demonstrating "orderly development," a sequence of hand-copied images will usually reveal degradation and decay. A survey of maps issued during a millennium or more shows how the "course of recorded history" produced spatial images that cannot be ordered

[20] Kenneth Boulding, *The Image* (Ann Arbor, MI, 1961), 77.

even by taking full advantage of hindsight and present techniques of placing and dating past records.

> More than 600 maps and sketches made between 300 and 1300 have survived the ravages of time . . . regardless of size and the quality of workmanship, it is impossible to trace in them a developmental process, a progression of thought . . . It is also impossible to grade them in terms of accuracy and utility.[21]

The "disassociated transcript" that Boulding describes could emerge only after the shift from script to print. To confuse our modern uniform reference frame with the multiform "world pictures" that hand copying produced is to lose sight of the obstacles to systematic data collection in the past and to misconstrue what happened when such obstacles were removed.

> We learn our geography mostly in school, not through our own personal experience. I have never been to Australia. In my image . . . however it exists with 100 percent certainty. If I sailed to the place where the map makers tell me it is and found nothing there but the ocean, I would be the most surprised man in the world. I hold to this part of my image . . . however purely on authority . . . what gives the map this extraordinary authority, an authority greater than that of the sacred books of all religions . . . is a process of feedback from the users of maps to the map maker. A map maker who puts out an inaccurate map will soon have this fact called to his attention by people . . . who find that it violates their . . . personal experience.[22]

The "process of feedback" described in this passage was one of the more important consequences of printed editions. This process has, indeed, never ceased; increments of information are still being added to geodetic surveys, and map makers (as Boulding notes) are still being "checked by the fact that it is possible to travel through

[21] Brown, *Story of Maps*, 94.
[22] Boulding, *The Image*, 66.

space." But this kind of checking could not occur until voyagers were provided with uniform maps and encouraged to exchange information with map publishers. Even then it took many centuries and cost many lives to achieve the absolute confidence a modern atlas conveys. The story of the prolonged impossible quest for a northwest passage indicates how difficult it was to achieve a final closure of geographic space and how important was the role played by communications in the process.

> In spite of one fruitless or fatal voyage after another the expeditions still sailed on their impossible missions. The difficulties were not only physical...but also sprang from the inability of one explorer to pass on his knowledge to another...The outlines traced on a chart might be clear enough, but when this information came to be incorporated in a map covering a larger area, it might as well be fitted into the wrong place in the jigsaw of straits, fjords and islands. Time after time the same mistakes were made, the same opportunities missed.[23]

The recurrence of mistakes and missed opportunities was much more prevalent before the advent of printing. That many surprises were encountered by mariners in the fifteenth and sixteenth centuries is something even American schoolchildren are taught. The maps consulted in the "age of discovery" entirely lacked the "extraordinary authority greater than that of the sacred books of all religions," which Boulding now consigns to his modern maps. This point is worth keeping in mind when considering changed attitudes toward divine revelation. Confidence in the sacred word was affected by the new authority assigned to literature which described the mundane.

> Some of the greatest obstacles holding back the exploration of the globe . . . are psychological not technical. It was not so much men's inability to overcome natural barriers which prevented them from

[23] J. R. Hale, *Renaissance Exploration* (New York, 1968), 75.

extending the range of their knowledge by new discoveries as the notions they had of the world around them.[24]

The statement goes on to note that Phoenicians and Vikings were not held back by the lack of technical equipment available to later mariners. Whatever landfalls were made, however, the goal of extending the range of knowledge by new discoveries was still technically as well as psychologically blocked throughout the age of scribes.

From 300 until 1300 there were many merchant adventurers, pious pilgrims, and fierce Norsemen who set out to sea or traveled overland. From evidence gathered after the thirteenth century, we know that trained cartographers took advantage of reports sent back to chart houses and merchant companies in the later Middle Ages. A special atlas once completed could not be "published," however. A fifteenth-century monastery near the University of Vienna served as a major center for the collection of geographic information and advanced cartography. Maps drawn in Klosterneuberg could be seen by visiting scholars and astronomers. But however such exceptional manuscript maps were handled, they were unavailable to scattered readers for guidance, for checking, and for feedback. The best maps, indeed, were often carefully hidden from view – like the map made for a fourteenth-century Florentine merchant which was placed in a warehouse "secretly and well wrapped so that no man could see it."[25] To make multiple copies would not lead to improvement, but to corruption of data; all fresh increments of information when copied were subject to distortion and decay.

This same point also applies to numbers and figures, words and names. Observational science throughout the age of scribes was perpetually enfeebled by the way words drifted apart from pictures, and labels became detached from things. Uncertainty as to which star, plant, or human organ was being designated by a given diagram or treatise – like the question of which coastline was being sighted

---

[24] Charles Issawi, "Arab Geography and the Circumnavigation of Africa," *Osiris* X (1952): 117.

[25] See reference in Datini's journal to a Florentine jewel merchant cited by Iris Origo, *The Merchant of Prato*, rev. ed. (London, 1963), 99.

from a vessel at sea – plagued investigators throughout the age of scribes. No wonder it was believed that one of the greatest secrets God entrusted to Adam was how to go about naming all things!

With regard to "the veins, tools, vessels, sluices, machines, furnaces," wrote Agricola, "I have not only described them, but have also hired illustrators to delineate their forms, lest descriptions which are conveyed by words should either not be understood by the men of our times, or should cause difficulty to posterity." The descriptions of the Alexandrians had often caused difficulty to Western scholars, partly because the texts of Ptolemy, Vitruvius, Pliny, and others had been transmitted without pictures to accompany the often copied and translated words. Vitruvius refers to diagrams and drawings, but after the tenth century they were detached from Vitruvian texts. Ptolemy's work on geography was retrieved, but any accompanying maps had been lost long before. Simple pictograms had a better survival value. In the sixteenth century, when the difficulties created by scribal transmission were not fully appreciated, it often seemed as though earlier authorities had been arbitrarily and deliberately obscure. In preparing his work on metallurgy, Agricola complained that "other books on this subject . . . are difficult to follow because the writers on these things use strange names which do not properly belong to the metals and because some of them employ now one name and now another although the thing itself changes not."[26]

Views of "animals, plants, metals and stones" which had been transmitted for centuries became unsatisfactory to Agricola and his contemporaries. They attributed the deficiencies and inconsistencies they found to the "linguistic barbarism" of the Gothic Dark Ages and to a prolonged "lack of interest" in natural phenomena. Present evidence suggests that medieval natural philosophers were not lacking in curiosity. They were, however, lacking some essential investigative tools. Agricola's concern with "communicable descriptive techniques" is certainly worth emphasizing, but it also ought to be related to the new communications system of his day. The "insistence that

---

[26] Rossi, *Philosophy, Technology*, 53.

all experiments and observations be reported in full and naturalistic detail preferably accompanied by the names and credentials of witnesses"[27] needs to be related to the new kind of reporting that became possible only after the shift from script to print.

> Writing of Conrad Gesner's *History of Animals* Professor Thorndike makes the simple but fundamental observation that even it is primarily concerned with names and words and with information and allusions for the use and enjoyment of the scholar and literary reader rather than with the collection and presentation of facts for scientific purposes.[28]

In my opinion, this observation is *too* simple. Gesner and his contemporaries lived in an era when science and scholarship were necessarily interdependent. To collect and present "facts" required mastery of records made by observers in the past. Sixteenth-century investigators had to be concerned with ancient languages and inscriptions, with "names and words," whether their interests were "literary" or not. To classify flora and fauna or place them on maps meant sorting out the records left by previous observers as well as observing freshly for oneself. "Historical" research and "scientific" data collection were close to being identical enterprises. Thus, geographers, such as Ortelius, had to engage in research on old place names and often inspired major studies in philology as well as topography.

Furthermore, the major achievements of the "golden age" of map publishing were predicated on thorough mastery of the Alexandrian heritage, which had to be assimilated before it could be surpassed. "In the history of human knowledge there are few stranger chapters than that which records the influence of the Ptolemaic revival in delaying the formation of an accurate world map in the 15th, 16th and 17th centuries."[29] This chapter seems strange because expectations

---

[27] Thomas Kuhn, "The Function of Measurement in Modern Physical Science," *Isis* 52 (1961): 192.

[28] Endicott, *Prose of Browne*, xv.

[29] C. R. Beazley, *The Dawn of Modern Geography* (Oxford, 1906), III:517.

formed by a print culture have been projected back into early modern times. Just as Copernicus began where the *Almagest* left off, so too did Ortelius and Mercator find in the ancient *Geographia* a point of departure for their mid-sixteenth-century work. Before an "accurate world map" could register new voyages, old rules governing the construction of world maps had to be studied and absorbed.

> The *Geographia* is a complete cartographer's handbook. It states clearly the fundamental distinction between chorography and geography; it specifies the need of precise astronomical measurement and correct mathematical contraction, describes the method of making terrestrial globes and of projecting maps on a plane surface.[30]

The duplication in print of extant scribal maps and ancient geographical treatises, even while seeming to provide evidence of "backsliding," also provided a basis for unprecedented advance. To found knowledge of the whole world on first-hand information is, literally speaking, quite impossible. Access to a wide variety of second-hand information furnished by reports, ships' logs, and charts over the course of many generations is required. Above all, a uniform grid is needed for assimilating all the assorted information that may be supplied. Before the outlines of a comprehensive and uniform world picture could emerge, incongruous images had to be duplicated in sufficient quantities to be brought into contact, compared, and contrasted.

The production of an atlas such as Ortelius's *Theatrum*, with its alphabetical index, list of authors consulted, and orderly progression of maps which expanded in number over time, entailed an enterprise whose novelty needs underscoring. Collaborative ventures in large-scale data collection, which had been intermittent and limited to the facilities provided by one chart house or manuscript library, became continuous and ever expanding. Here in particular it would be helpful to elaborate on comments made in passing about the way

---

[30] Dana B. Durand, *The Vienna-Klosterneuberg Map Corpus: A Study in the Transition from Medieval to Modern Science* (Leiden, 1952), 12–13.

A DESCRIPTION OF THE
WHOLE WORLD.

H is Map next enſuing containeth and repreſenteth the portraiture of the whole earth, and of the maine Ocean that enuirons & compaſſeth the ſame : all which earthly Globe the Ancients (who were not as then acquainted with the New world, not long ſince deſcried) diuided into three parts ; namely, *Africa*, *Europe*, and *Aſia*. But ſince that diſcouery of *America*, the learned of our age haue made that a fourth part, and the huge Continent vnder the South pole, a fifth. *Gerardus Mercator* the Prince of moderne Geographers in his neuer-ſufficiently-commended vniuerſall Table or Map of the whole world, diuides this Circumference of the earth into three Continents : the firſt he calles that, which the Ancients diuided into three parts, and from whence the holy Writ beares record, that mankinde had their firſt originall, & firſt was ſeated : the ſecond, is that which at this preſent is named *America* or the *VVeſt Indies* : for the third, he appoints the South maine, which ſome call *Magellanica*, as yet on very few coaſts thorowly diſcouered. That this orbe or maſſe of the earthly Globe containes in circuit, where it is largeſt, 5400 German or 21600, Italian miles, antiquity hath taught, & late Writers haue ſubſcribed to their opinion. *And theſe ſo manifold portions of earth* (ſayth *Plinie* in the 11. booke of his Naturall hiſtorie) *yea rather, as ſome haue termed them, the pricke or center of the world (for ſo ſmall is the earth in compariſon of the whole frame of the world) this is the matter, this is the ſeat of our glorie. Here we enioy honours, here we exerciſe authoritie, here we hunt after riches, here men turmoile and tire themſelues, here we moue and maintaine ciuill diſſenſions, and by mutuall ſlaughter make more roome vpon the earth. And to let paſſe the publike tumults of the world, this in which we force the borderers to giue place and remoue farther off, and where we incroch by ſtelth vpon our neighbors lands : as he that extends his lands & lordſhips fartheſt, and cannot abide that any ſhould ſeat themſelues too neere his noſe, How great, or rather how ſmall a portion of earth doth he enioy? Or when he hath glutted his auarice to the full, How little ſhall his dead carcaſe poſſeſſe?* Thus far *Plinie.*

The ſituation of this earth and ſea, the diſpoſition of the ſeuerall regions, with their inlets and gulfs, the maners and inclinations of the people, and other memorable and note-worthy matters are deſcribed by men of ancienter times, ſuch as follow :

PTOLEMY of ALEXANDRIA.
CAIVS PLINIVS 2, 3, 4, 5, and 6 books of his Natural hiſtory.
ARISTOTELES DE MVNDO written and dedicated to *Alexander* the Great.
STRABO in 17. books.
SOLINVS POLYHISTOR.
POMPONIVS MELA.
DIONYSIVS APHER and his Expoſitor.
EVSTATHIVS.
APVLEIVS in his booke of the World.
DIODORVS SICVLVS in his fiue former books.
MARTIANVS CAPELLA.
PAVLVS OROSIVS in the beginning of his Hiſtory.
ÆTHICVS and another of that name ſurnamed SOPHISTA, not yet printed.
IVLIVS the Oratour called by *Caſſiodore*, PRIMVS.
BEROSVS deſcribed the antiquitie of the World.
ANTONIVS AVGVSTVS (if the title be true) ſet downe the Iournals of the Romane empire.
SEXTVS AVIENVS, the ſea-coaſts.
STEPHANVS, the cities.
VIBIVS SEQVESTER, in an Alphabeticall order, the Riuers, Fountaines, Lakes, Woods, Hilles, and Nations thereof.

By new Writers, as

RAPHAEL VOLATERANVS.
ABILFEDEA ISMAEL, in the Arabian tongue.
IOANNES HONTERVS, and HIERONYMVS OLIVERIVS: both in verſe.
BARTHOLIMVS in the eighth booke of *Auſtria*.
SEBASTIAN MVNSTER, that learned Diuine, diligent Hiſtorian, painfull Hebrician and Linguiſt, well ſtudied in all maner of learning, and vnto whom the learned Student is ſo much beholding.
ANTONIVS the Archbiſhop of *Florence*, in his Hiſtorie, in the third chapter of the firſt Title.
DOMINICVS NIGER.
IOHN AVENTINE in his ſecond booke of his Annals.
IOHN CAMERS in his Commentaries vpon *Solinus*.
GEORGE RYTHAIMER.
IOACHIM VADIAN.
PETRVS IOANNES OLIVARIVS vpon *Mela*.
LAVRENTIVS CORVINVS NOVOF.
ANTONIVS VERONENSIS.

GVALTERVS LVDOVICVS in his Mirrour or Looking-glaſſe of the World.
S. ISIDORE of SIVILL in *Spaine*.
MICHAEL of VILLANOVA, in his Commentary vpon *Ptolemey*.
ZACHARIAS LILIVS VICENT.
HIERONYMVS GIRAVA in the Spaniſh tongue.
ALEXANDER CITOLINVS, in his *Typocoſmia* or Patern of the World written in the Italian tongue.
VINCENTIVS BELVACENSIS in the Mirrour of Hiſtories the ſecond booke.
GVILIELMVS POSTELLVS *Barentonius*.
S. IOHN MANDEVILL and his companion in his trauels.
ODERICVS of FRIVLY.
MICHAEL NEANDER of *Soraw*.
GAVDENTIVS MERVLA in his 5. booke of memorable things.
FRANCISCVS MONACHI, in his Epiſtle to the Archbiſhop of *Panormus*.
ANDREAS THEVETVS, FRANCISCVS BELLEFORESTIVS, and PETRVS HEYNSIVS, in French : but this latter alſo in Dutch rythmes or verſe.
LAVRENTIVS ANANIENSIS, in the Italian tongue.
ANTONIVS PINETVS, in French : and he hath withall ſet forth many Tables and Mappes (as the title ſheweth) of Countries, Cities and Townes, aſwell of *Europe*, as of *Affrike*, *Aſia* and *America*.
IVLIVS BALLINVS, hath put forth the Plots and drafts of the moſt famous Cities of the whole world, with a briefe hiſtorical diſcourſe, written in the Tuſcane tongue. The ſame is done by GEORGIVS BRVNO, in Latine, but much more beautifully and curiouſly.
BENEDICTVS BORDONIVS, hath deſcribed all the Ilands of the World. So alſo hath
THOMAS PORCACCIVS: both in the Italian tongue.
WOLFGANGVS LASIVS, and
IOANNES GOROPIVS BECANVS, the originall and ſhifting of the nations of the ſame.
PETRVS APPIANVS, and
BARTHOLOMAEVS AMANTIVS, haue gathered the ancient Inſcriptions : and ſo hath
MARTINVS SMETIVS, but with greater diligence and care than ordinary.
IOANNES BOHEMVS, and ALEXANDER SARDVS haue written of the maners, rites and cuſtomes of all nations and people of it. The ſame hath
FRANCISCVS BELLEFORESTIVS done in the French tongue.

new presses increased scholarly access to texts. "The tyranny of major authorities inherent in small libraries was broken. The scholar could indulge in an ease of computation and cross-referencing formerly unthinkable."[31]

Limits set by the very largest manuscript libraries were also broken. Even the exceptional resources available to ancient Alexandrians stopped short of those that were opened up after the shift from script to print. In a tribute to the Venetian printer Aldus Manutius, Erasmus underlined this very point. Whereas the Alexandrian Library was contained within the walls of a single structure, he wrote, the library being constructed by Aldus had no other limits than the world itself. The large library, George Sarton observed, is just as much a scientific instrument as is the telescope or cyclotron.[32] Laboratory facilities were lacking to sixteenth-century observers. Star gazers still had to rely only on their "naked" eyes. But the flow of information had been reoriented, and this had an effect on natural philosophy that should not go ignored.

RESETTING THE STAGE FOR THE COPERNICAN REVOLUTION

If the importance of archival research for astronomers were to receive more attention, the early phases of the Copernican revolution might be easier to understand. As a contemporary of Aldus Manutius, Copernicus had an opportunity to survey a wider range of records and to use more reference guides than had any astronomer before

---

[31] A. R. Hall, *The Scientific Revolution 1500–1800: The Formation of the Modern Scientific Attitude* (Boston, 1957), 10.

[32] George Sarton, "A Summing Up," *Sarton on the History of Science*, ed. D. Stimson (Cambridge, MA, 1962), 370.

Fig. 34 (opposite). An atlas publisher's bibliography. In his pioneering atlas, first published in 1570, Abraham Ortelius listed his sources in a manner that separated the ancients from the moderns. This page comes from an English translation of *Theatrum orbis terrarum: The Theatre of the Whole World* (London: John Norton, 1606, folio 7). Reproduced by kind permission of the Folger Shakespeare Library.

him. This obvious point is often obscured by heated debates over the role played by one textual tradition against another – over how much weight to assign continuous criticism of Aristotle against a new revival of Plato or the vogue for hermetic texts. Granted that such influences may be important to Copernicus's work and are worth investigating; it is also worth pausing over the interplay of many different texts upon his single mind. Given freedom from many hours of "slavish" copying, given an increased output of dictionaries and other reference guides, given title pages, book lists, and other rudimentary bibliographical aids, Copernicus was able to undertake a search of the literature on a vaster scale than had been possible before.

> Although his name has become more famous, Copernicus was in many ways less modern than Vesalius, in particular he had a far less acute sense of the reality of nature: like many medieval men he was far more concerned to devise a theory which should fit an uncritically collected series of observations than to examine the quality of observational material. Tycho Brahe half a century later was the Vesalius of astronomy.[33]

Yet Copernicus was by no means prepared to accept every "uncritically collected series of observations." In his *Letter against Werner*, for example, he was keenly critical of a colleague's procedures for dating and placing a particular observation made in the past, and elsewhere he seemed to be a keen-eyed observer of inconsistencies in prior reports.

As elsewhere, one must make some allowance for the disparity between scientific disciplines. Unlike anatomists and physicists, astronomers have to study observations made at different intervals over long periods of time. Data supplied by the Alexandrians and Arabs were indispensable for anyone concerned with the precession of the equinoxes, for example. The long-term cycle that had to be mastered to achieve successful calendar reform required lining up a series of observations made over the course of hundreds of years; and

---

[33] Hall, *Scientific Revolution*, 51–2.

this task in turn required mastering diverse languages and systems for describing locations in time and space. In this respect, Copernicus's failure to supply the kind of fresh findings that were later provided by Tycho Brahe needs to be balanced against his sustained and zealous efforts to unscramble dusty records made by observers in the past.

Increased access to a variety of records was not only useful when he decided "to read again the works of all the philosophers upon whom I could lay hand" in order to canvass possible alternatives to an "uncertain mathematical tradition."[34] Access to many records also enabled him to tackle certain technical problems relating to long-term cycles that had remained out of the reach of astronomers who were served by scribes. My teacher, wrote Copernicus's disciple, Rheticus, in 1540,

> made observations...at Bologna...at Rome...then here in Frauenberg when he had leisure for his studies. From his obser- vations of the fixed stars he selected the one which he made...in 1525... *Then comparing all the observations of previous writers with his own* he found that a revolution of the...circle of inequality had been completed...
>
> To reduce these calculations to a definite system in which they would agree with all the observations, my teacher computed that the unequal motion is completed in 1,717 Egyptian years...and the complete revolution of the mean motion will take 25,816 Egyptian years.[35]

To investigators concerned with celestial cycles that could take more than 25,000 years, it must have been helpful to gain increased access to written records and to be supplied with bibliographical guides.

Copernicus undoubtedly learned much from a neo-Platonist pro- fessor at Bologna and from the debates conducted by Aristotelians at Padua as well. But Copernicus later abandoned the role of wandering

---

[34] Prefatory letter to "De Revolutionibus," cited by Kuhn, *Copernican Revolution*, 141.

[35] Excerpts from the "Narration Prima" (1540) of Rheticus, in Edward Rosen, *Three Copernican Treatises*, 3rd ed. (New York, 1971), 111–14 (italics mine).

scholar for long years of study in Frombork. His work indicates that he was acquainted with a vast variety of texts – ranging from the Synoptic Gospels to tables of sines. He was an assiduous investigator of place names and calendars, of ancient chronologies and coins, as indeed he had to be in order to unravel scribal confusion between "Nebuchadnezzar" and "Nabornassar" or to ascertain the different points taken by past observers for the start of a new year. Neither the Platonic revival nor continued criticism of Aristotle enabled him to line up observations that went back to pre-Christian times, to compare observations made by Alexandrians and Arabs with his own, to establish the "names of Egyptian months" and the length of "Callippic cycles," or to point out that a colleague's dating of an autumnal equinox observed by Ptolemy was wrong by at least ten years.

> No fundamental astronomical discovery, no new sort of astronomical observation persuaded Copernicus of ancient astronomy's inadequacy or of the necessity for change. Until half a century after Copernicus' death no potentially revolutionary changes occurred in the data available to astronomers.[36]

Shortly before Copernicus was born, however, an actual revolution in book production had begun to affect the technical literature and mathematical tools available to astronomers. As a student at Cracow in the 1480s, the young Copernicus probably found it hard to get a look at a single copy of Ptolemy's *Almagest* – even in a corrupted medieval Latin form. Before he died, he had three different editions at hand. As a fourteen-year-old in Copenhagen in 1560, the young Tycho Brahe could purchase all of Ptolemy's work, including an improved translation of the full *Almagest* made from the Greek. Soon thereafter, while at Leipzig and still in his teens, Tycho picked up a copy of the *Prutenic Tables* that had recently been computed on the basis of Copernicus's major work. No "new sort of observation" had affected astronomy in this interval. Nevertheless, the transmission of old observations had undergone a major change. One need not wait until "half a century after Copernicus' death" to

---

[36] Kuhn, *Copernican Revolution*, 131.

observe the effect of this change, for it had begun to affect the study of astronomy shortly before Copernicus was born. Copernicus was not supplied, as Tycho's successors would be, with precisely recorded fresh data. But he was supplied, as Regiomontanus's successor and Aldus Manutius's contemporary, with guidance to technical literature carefully culled from the best Renaissance Greek manuscript collections and, for the first time, made available outside library walls.

To the jaded modern scholar looking back over five hundred years, early printed editions of the *Almagest* are disappointing – even retrogressive – works. But they opened up exciting new prospects to astronomers in Copernicus's day.

> Copernicus studied the *Almagest* very carefully indeed. For the *De Revolutionibus* is the *Almagest*, book by book, section by section rewritten to incorporate the new Copernican theory but otherwise altered as little as might be. Kepler was to remark later that Copernicus interpreted Ptolemy, not nature, and there is some truth in the remark.[37]

Actually, the alternative to interpreting Ptolemy that Kepler had in mind was not really "nature" but Tycho's data instead. By providing a fully worked-out parallel text containing an alternative theory, Copernicus furnished Tycho with a motive for collecting the data Kepler used.

> Already while Tycho was a youth of sixteen years of age his eyes were opened to the great fact which seems to us so simple to grasp but which escaped the attention of all European astronomers before him that only through a steadily pursued course of observations would it be possible to obtain a better insight into the motions of the planets.[38]

Tycho's "eyes were opened" to the need for fresh data partly because he had on hand more old data than young students in astronomy

[37] Boas, *Scientific Renaissance*, 74.
[38] J. L. E. Dreyer, *History of Astronomy, From Thales to Kepler*, rev. ed. (New York, 1953), 18–19.

had had before. Even as an untutored teenager he could compare Copernicus with Ptolemy and study tables derived from both. Contradictory predictions concerning the conjuction of planets encouraged him to reexamine the "writing in the skies." For the purpose of gathering fresh data, he was also supplied with newly forged mathematical tools which increased his speed and accuracy when ascertaining the position of a given star. In these and other respects, Tycho's case does not entirely fit that of "an astronomer who saw new things while looking at old objects with old instruments."[39] Printed sine tables, trigonometry texts, and star catalogues did represent new objects and instruments in Tycho's day. As a self-taught mathematician who mastered astronomy out of books, Tycho was himself a new kind of observer.

Because he lacked recourse to a telescope and yet saw a different writing in the skies than star gazers had seen before, the findings of the Danish astronomer pose a special problem for historians of science.

> Brahe's fine instruments were not required to discover the superlunary character of novas and comets... Maestlin needed only a piece of thread to decide that the nova of 1572 was beyond the moon... The observations... which speeded the downfall of traditional cosmology... could have been made at any time since remote antiquity. The phenomena and the requisite instruments had been available for two millenniums before Brahe's birth, but the observations were not made or, if made, were not widely interpreted. During the last half of the sixteenth century age-old phenomena rapidly changed their meaning and significance. Those changes seem incomprehensible without reference to the new climate of scientific opinion one of whose first outstanding representatives is Copernicus.[40]

One wonders how the "superlunary character of novas and comets" could, in fact, be established before scattered observations of

---

[39] Thomas Kuhn, *The Structure of Scientific Revolutions*, rev. ed. (Chicago, 1970), 116–17.

[40] Kuhn, *Copernican Revolution*, 209.

Hęc opera fient in oppido Nuremberga Germanię ductu Ioannis de Monteregio.

ALIENA.

Theoricę nouę planetarum Georgii Purbachii aftronomi ce /
lebratiffimi: cum figurationibus oportunis.

Marci Manlii aftronomica.   Hęc duo explicita funt.

Cofmographia Ptolemęi noua traductioé. Nā uetula ifta Iaco
bi Angeli florētini quę uulgo habetur uiciofa é: interpte ipfo
(bona ueia dictū fuerit) neqp ligus gręcę fatis neqp matheāticę
noticiam tenente. Qua i re fummis arbitris fidem haberi fas
erit: Theodoro Gazę clariffimo uiro ac gręcę latine qp do /
ctiffimo: & Paulo Florentino gręcarū quidem baud ignaro:
in mathematicis aūt plurimū excellenti.

Magna compofitio Ptolemęi: quā uulgo uocāt Almaieftū no/
ua traductione.

Euclidis elemēta cum anaphoricis Hypficlis editione Campani
euulfis tamen plerifqp mendis: quę pprio etiā idicabūtur cō /
mentariolo.

Theonis alexandrini clariffimi mathematici commentaria in
Almaieftum.

Procli fufformationes aftronomicę.

Quadriptitum Ptolemęi & Centum fructus eiufdē noua tra /
ductione.

Iulius Firmicus quantus reperitur.

Leopoldus de Auftria. & fi qui alii pdictores aftrologici illu/
ftratione digni uidebuntur. Nam Antonii quoqp de Montul
mo ȝuis fragmenta in ufum multiplicem exponentur.

Archimedis geometrę acutiffimi opa de fphęra & cylindro. De
circuli dimenfione. De conalibus & fphęralibus. De lineis fpi
ralibus. De ęquipōderātibus. De quadratura parabolę. De ba
reng numero. Cum cōmētariis Eutocai afcalonitę i tria opera
ex pędictis: fcilicet de fphęra & cylindro. de dimenfione cir/
culi. de ęquipōderātibus.   Traductio eft Iacobi cremonēfis:
fed nō nullȝ emendata.

Perfpectiua Vitelonis. opus ingens ac nobile.

Perfpectiua Ptolemęi.

Mufica Ptolemęi cum expofitione Porbyrii.

Menelai fphęrica noua editione.

Theodofii fphęrica. item de habitationibus. de diebus & nocti
bu. noua traductione.

Apollonii pergenfis conica. Item Sereni cylindrica.

Heronis inuenta fpiritualia. Opus mechanicā mirę uolptatis

Elementa arithmetica Iordani. Data eiufdem arithmetica.

Quadriptitū numerorū. Opus uariis fcatens argutiis

Problemata mechanica Ariftotelis.

Hygini Aftronomia cum deformatione imaginī cęleftium.

Facta pterea eft arbor rhetoricę tullianę fpeciofa imagine.
Et fiet defcriptio totius habitabilis notę quam uulgo appellant
Mappam mundi. Cęterū Germanię particularis tabula: itē
Italię: Hifpanię: Gallię uniuer'ę: Gręcięqp. Sed & fuas cuiqp
hiftorias ex auctoribus plurimis curfim colligere ftatutū eft :
quę uidelicet ad montes: quę ad maria: ad lacus amnes qp ac
alia particularia loca fpectare uidebuntur.

OPIFICIS tentata. quę effent ne
pdenda an non: pudor ingenuus & refpublica litteraria diu i
ter fe difceptauere. Ratio audendum cenfuit.

Kalendarium nouū quo promūf coniūctiones uerę atqp oppo/
fitiones lumiarium. item qp eclipfes eorūdē figuratę. loca lu
minarium uera quotidie. borarū tam equinoctialium ȝ tem/
poralium difcrimū duplici inftrumento ad quafuis habitati /
ones. ac alia pluria fcitu iucūdiffima.

Ephemerides quas uulgo uocāt Almanach ad trigintaduos an
nos futuros. ubi quotidie intueberis ueros motus oim plane/
tarū capitifqp draconis lunaris: una cū afpectibus lunę ad fo/
lem & planetas. boris etiam afpectuū eorundem baud friuole
adnotatis. neqp planetarū inter fe afpectibus pętermiffis. In
frontibus paginarum pofita funt indicia latitudinū. Eclipfes
denqp luminarium fi quę futurę funt locis fuis effigurantur.

Hęc duo opera iam prope abfoluta funt.

Commentaria magna in Cofmographiā Ptolemęi: ubi expo /
nitur fabrica ufuf qp inftrumēti Meteorofcopii: quo Ptolemę
us ip'e uniuerfos ferme numeros totī operis fui elicuit. Fal
fo enī quifpiā crediderit tot lōgitudinum latitudinum qp nu/
meros per fupernorum obferuationes inotuiffe. Pręterea de
fcripto fphęrę armillaris una cū tota habitabili i plano ita di/
lucidatur ut plerifqp omnes difcere ȝant. quam nemo antebac
latine intellexit uicio traductoris obftante.

Commentariolū fingulare contra traductionem Iacobi Angeli
Florentini. quod ad arbitros mittetur.

Theonis alexandrini defenfio i fex uoluminibȝ cōtra Georgiū
Trapezuntiū. ubi plane quis deprehendet friuola eius effe cō
mētaria i Almaieftū. traductione qp ipfam operis ptolemaici
uicio non carere.

Commentariolum quo cōmonftrantur placita Campani ex edi
tione elementorum geometricorum reiicienda.

De quinqp corporibus ęquilateris quę uulgo regularia nūcupā
tur: quę uidelicet eorum locii impleant corporalē & qs nō.
contra commentatorē Ariftotelis Auerroem.

Cōmētaria i libros Archimedis eos qui Eutocii expofitiōe carēt

De quadratura circuli. contra Nicolaum Cufenfem.

De directionibus. contra Archidiaconum parmenfem.

De diftinctione domiciliorū cęli. contra Campani & Ioannem
Gazulū ragufinū: cuius & alia de boris temporalibus decreta
ibidem retractantur

De motu octauę fphęrę. contra Tebith fuos qp fectatores.

De inftauratione kalendarii ecclefię.

Breuiarium Almaiefti.

De triangulis omnimodis quięqp uolumina.

Problemata aftronomica ad Almaieftum totum fpectantia.

De Cometę magnitudie remotiōe qp a fra. de loco eiȝ uero & cęt

Problemata geometrica oimoda. Opus fructuofę iucūditatis.

Ludus pānoniēfis. quę alias uocare libuit Tabulas directionū

Tabula magna pmi mobilis cū ufu multiplici ratōnibȝ qp certis
Radii uiforii multorum generum cū ufibus fuis.

De pōderibȝ et ęquęductibȝ cū figuratōnibȝ iftrumētoȝ ad eas
res neceffariorum.

De fpeculis uftoriis atqp aliis multorū generū ufufqp ftupendi.

In officina fabrili Aftrarium in continuo tractatu eft. Opus plane pro miraculo fpectandum.
Fiunt & alia inftrumenta aftronomicæad obferuationes cęleftium. item qp alia ad ufum uulga
rem quotidianum. quorum nomina longum eft recitare.
Poftremo omnium artem illam mirificam litterarum formatricem nouimentis ftabilibus mā
dare decretum eft. (deus bone fa ueas) qua re explicita fi mox obdormierit opifex mors acerba
non erit : quom tantum munus pofteris in bęreditate reliquerit : quo ipfi fe ab inopia librorum
ppetuo poterunt uindicare.

Fig. 35.   Copernicus was inadvertently supplied with a reader's guide to technical literature by the first astronomer-printer, Regiomontanus (Johann Müller of
Königsberg). The latter printed this advance book list in Nuremberg in 1474, listing the important works that were to come off his press. Although he died prematurely the same year, his list guided the publication programs of others and furnished
sixteenth-century astronomers with an important bibliographical tool. Reproduced
by kind permission of John Ehrman for the Roxburghe Club from Graham Pollard
and Albert Ehrman, *The Distribution of Books by Catalogue to A.D. 1800* (Cambridge:
The Roxburghe Club, 1965, fig. 12).

transitory stellar events could be made simultaneously, coordinated with other findings, checked, and confirmed. As long as accounts of separate stars and comets were transmitted by scribes; as long as separate observers lacked uniform methods for placing and record-ing what they saw; as long as the most careful observers lacked mas-tery of trigonometry; how could falling stars be permanently located beyond the moon's sphere? "The desire to find an orbit for a *purely transitory, ephemeral* phenomenon marked an important shift in the theoretical interpretation of comets."[41] Maybe Tycho's "fine instru-ments" were not needed, but certainly Maestlin's piece of thread was not enough to fix transitory, ephemeral stellar events so firmly that they could be seen to conflict with traditional cosmology. The nova of 1572 attracted more observers from all parts of Europe than had ever gazed at a single star before. When Tycho announced his find-ings, he had to struggle "to make his voice heard above the din." He succeeded so well in this unprecedented situation that long after the nova had faded, "Tycho's star" gleamed too brightly beyond the moon's sphere for cosmologists to ignore it or chroniclers to shift it around. "Almost every star chart and globe between 1572 and the end of the 17th century showed where [it] . . . had appeared, encour-aging astronomers to watch for its return."[42]

Stellar events that had been witnessed before the advent of print-ing could not be pinpointed so precisely and permanently that one man's name could be assigned to one such event. Nor could any one detailed account avoid getting blurred in the course of entering into the public domain. Much as was the case with mundane events when they were woven into tapestries or noted in monkish chronicles, diverse separate events merged into a single mythical category; con-ventional images and standard formulas smudged carefully observed detail. Jerusalem stayed at the center of the world, comets stayed

---

[41] Robert S. Westman, "The Comet and the Cosmos: Kepler, Mästlin and the Copernican Hypothesis," *The Reception of Copernicus' Heliocentric Theory* (Warsaw, 1972): 11 (italics mine).

[42] Deborah H. Warner, "The First Celestial Globe of Willem Janszoon Blaeu," *Imago Mundi* 25 (1971): 36.

Amongſt manie Pilots there is an opinion,that they had rather uſe the written Cardes, then ſuch as are printed, eſteeming the printed Cardes to be imperfect,and ſay that the writtenCardes are much better and perfecter, they meane the written Cardes that are daiely made with the penne,are everie daie corrected,and the printed never : but herein they are not a litle deceived, for the printed Cardes in each reſpect are as good, yea and better then the written, for that the printed Cardes are once in everie point with all care and diligence made perfect, in regarde that they ſerue for many , for that being once well made, all the reſt may with as litle labour be made good, as well as badde. But the Seacardes that are vvritten cannot be made ſo ſound, nor vvith ſuch ſpeed, becauſe ſo much coſt for once peece alone were to much, but are all one after the other, with the leaſt labour copied out,& many times , by ſuch perſons that haue little or no knowledge therein. Whatſoever there is yet reſting to be corrected or made better,is as eaſie to be corrected in the Cardes that are printed,as in them that are written, which we alſo are readie to doe at our charge,if any man can by good proofe ſhewe us any thing, that is to be corrected in the Cardes that are printed by us.

Fig. 36. W. J. Blaeu's challenge to pilots to find any errors on his printed "sea cards" (charts). From *The Light of Navigation* (Amsterdam: William Johnson, 1622, p. 38). Reproduced by kind permission of the Folger Shakespeare Library.

below the lunar sphere, and neither could be permanently dislodged from their appointed places until scribal transmission had come to an end.

"These stars marked out in gold are those of the Lord Tycho; the remaining ones correspond to those observed by the Ancients," runs an English translation of the Latin text placed on a celestial globe produced by the Dutch map publisher Willem Janszoon Blaeu between 1596 and 1599.[43] Blaeu had worked for Tycho before founding a celebrated Amsterdam firm which made and sold astronomical instruments as well as globes, sea charts, and books. His "exceedingly accurate globe" not only made clear what the great modern astronomer had added to skies studied by the greatest star gazers of antiquity, it also made clear that even more exciting news was

[43] Ibid., 37.

destined to be forthcoming from intrepid explorers who had ventured beyond the edge of the known world.

> Certain stars nearer to the Antarctic Pole, and avoiding our sight, are not less remarkable for their magnitude than those lying in the northern region, whether by report of the extent of their brilliances or by the annals of writers, nevertheless having delineation as uncertain, we have here omitted the measuring of them.[44]

What Blaeu cautiously omitted in the late 1590s a competitor was able to fill in by 1600, suggesting how competition between profit-driving printers – no less than collaboration among scattered observers – helped to accelerate data collection and push it along new paths. Just as Blaeu was finishing supervision of his plates, an expedition was returning which entailed "the first systematic attempt to organize and catalogue the southern stars." Two Dutchmen, who had embarked on the 1595–7 voyage of the *Hollandia*, kept records of the observations of the southern skies they made while voyaging in the East Indies. One, the chief pilot, died at sea; but his data, carried back to Amsterdam, were exploited by Blaeu's chief competitor, Jocondus Hondius, for his celestial globe of 1600. No less than fourteen new constellations were displayed on the Hondius globe.

> So Blaue who doubtless expected his first celestial globe to be widely acclaimed and distributed, instead saw it become obsolete just a short time after publication. There was nothing to do but to withdraw it from the market and begin again.[45]

To begin again in the age of print had a different meaning from what had been the case in the age of scribes. By 1602, Blaeu turned out an updated smaller globe which contained all the fresh data brought back from the Dutch expedition and, in addition, registered a brand-new observation that was uniquely his own. In August 1600, he had noted a new star of the third magnitude in the constellation

[44] Ibid., 36.
[45] Ibid., 37.

Cygnus, and this also he placed upon his globe – where it remained to be duplicated repeatedly, long after the star faded from everyone's view. Moreover, he never really did begin all over again. In 1603 the large plates for his first globe, which had been too valuable to discard, were reused after corrections had been made on them and resulted in the "now justly famous 34 centimeter globe of 1603" with his own name prominently displayed alongside that of his former master, "Lord Tycho," on the revised title text.[46]

According to Wightman, Tycho Brahe was the first Western astronomer to pursue the kind of program that was later articulated by the Royal Society.[47] He was the forerunner of a new breed of astronomers who "studied to make it not onely an enterprise of one season or of some lucky opportunity; but a business of time; a steddy, a lasting, a popular, an uninterrupted work."[48] It does not detract from Tycho's justly distinguished position in the history of astronomy to suggest that he was favored by a "lucky opportunity" by being born at the right time. No one man, however gifted, could put so vast a collaborative enterprise as astronomy on a new footing or live long enough to assure that it would be a steady, lasting, popular, uninterrupted enterprise. The "business of time" lies outside the control of any one generation, let alone that of a single mortal creature. Geoffrey of Meaux's nightly observations of the comet of 1315 suggest that Tycho's program of steady observation to obtain fresh data was not unprecedented. Much as Viking landfalls preceded Columbus, careful star gazers had been at work before Tycho. What was unprecedented (with new stars and new worlds alike) was the way observed phenomena could be recorded and confirmed.

As the foregoing may suggest, when we try to explain the new sixteenth-century view of "age-old phenomena" such as novas and comets, the changes wrought by printing need to be taken into account. General references to a turbulent age or even more specific

---

[46] Ibid., 38.

[47] W. P. D. Wightman, *Science and the Renaissance* (Edinburgh, 1962), I:120.

[48] Thomas Sprat, *History of the Royal Society* (1667), ed. J. I. Cope and H. W. Jones (St. Louis, 1958), pt. 2, sect. 5, p. 62.

QVADRANS MVRALIS
SIVE TICHONICVS.

EFFIGIES TYCHONIS BRAHE O.F.
ÆDIFICII ET INSTRVMENTORVM
ASTRONOMICORVM STRVCTORIS
Aº DOMINI 1587 ÆTATIS SVÆ 40

Fig. 37. Tycho Brahe's most celebrated self-portrait (above) shows him directing operations at Uraniborg, framed by his great mural quadrant. The middle tier contains rooms where his assistants are engaged in printing and correcting works such as the *Astronomiae instauratae mechanica* (Hamburg, 1598) for which this engraving was designed. The book also contains on the title page (opposite) the portrait of

Fig. 37. (cont.) the astronomer-author which stresses his noble ancestry and exemplifies the tendency to self-advertisement which printing encouraged. Both plates are reproduced by kind permission of the Department of Special Collections, Stanford University Libraries.

evocation of the "new climate of scientific thought" represented
by Copernicus do not help very much to explain phenomena such
as Tycho's star. The neo-Platonic and Aristotelian currents that
entered into Copernicus's studies with Italian masters had no counterpart in the young Danish nobleman's case. Indeed, Tycho set out
to become an astronomer by defying his tutor and teaching himself.
He bypassed the traditional master–apprentice relationship by taking
advantage of printed materials. It seems likely that his freedom from
prevailing cosmological assumptions owed something to his unusual
position as a largely self-made astronomer. Symmetry and sun worship seem to have been subordinated to other concerns in Tychonic
astronomy. Its architect did not share Copernicus's esthetic or meta-
physical concerns. The two astronomers were not linked by mutual
admiration for a particular classical or Christian textual tradition.
As sixteenth-century astronomers, they may be distinguished from
their predecessors not so much because they were influenced by one
or another Renaissance current of thought but rather because they
were freed from copying and memorizing and could make use of new
paper tools and printed texts.

It was not because he gazed at night skies instead of at old books
that Tycho Brahe differed from star gazers of the past. Nor do I think
it was because he cared more for "stubborn facts" or precise measurement than had the Alexandrians or the Arabs. But he did have
at his disposal, as few had before him, two separate sets of computations based on two different theories, compiled several centuries
apart, which he could compare with each other. The study of records
was no less important for Tycho than it had been for the astronomers
of the past. Like his predecessors, he had no telescope to aid him. But
his observatory, unlike theirs, included a library well stocked with
printed materials as well as assistants trained in the new arts of printing and engraving. For he took care (and went to much trouble and
expense) to install printing presses and a paper mill on the island of
Hveen.

Given the more than fifty assistants at work on the island, and
the stream of publications that issued forth, Tycho's "Uraniborg" has
been suggested as a possible prototype for Bacon's "Salomon's House"

and for the later Royal Society.[49] Uraniborg did see collaboration and publication applied to astronomical observation on a scale the Western world had not seen before. Insofar as Tycho's observations were made with the aid of instruments, he could tap the talents of engravers who "knew the meaning of 'within a hair's breadth.'" He also exploited the arts of engraving to display astronomical instruments for readers of his books. His own printing press is displayed in his most celebrated self-portrait. Ever since he started to sneak books past his tutor, he profited greatly from the product of other presses. In these respects, he differed from his predecessors in ways that need to be underlined. The Danish astronomer was not only the last of the great naked-eye observers; he was also the first careful observer who took full advantage of the new powers of the press – powers which enabled astronomers to detect anomalies in old records, to pinpoint more precisely and register in catalogues the location of each star, to enlist collaborators in many regions, fix each fresh observation in permanent form, and make necessary corrections in successive editions.

The unusual fate of Tycho's star has already been noted. The expansion of his star catalogue by Kepler is equally worthy of note.

> The *Tabulae Rudolphinae* remained for more than a century an indispensable tool for the study of the skies . . . The bulk of the work consists of . . . rules for predicting the positions of the planets and of Tycho's catalogue of 777 star places enlarged by Kepler to 1,005. There are also refraction-tables and logarithms put for the first time to astronomic uses; and a gazetteer of the towns of the world, their longitudes referred to Tycho's Greenwich – the meridian of Uraniborg on Hveen.[50]

Kepler struggled heroically from 1623 to 1627 to get these useful tables in print during the turmoil of the Thirty Years' War. As an overseer of a technical publication program, who saw a manuscript of 568 pages through the press, he coped successfully with political

---

[49] John Christianson, "Astronomy and Printing," paper presented at the Sixteenth Century Studies Conference, Concordia Seminary, St. Louis, Oct. 26, 1972.
[50] Koestler, *Sleepwalkers*, 410–11.

emergencies and personnel problems, procured adequate supplies of paper, supervised the punch cutting of symbols and the setting of type, and finally – in the guise of a traveling salesman – set out in the company of tradesmen to peddle his finished products at the Frankfurt book fair of 1627. While he was at Ulm during the final stages of the four-year ordeal, Kepler found time to help local officials solve problems pertaining to weights and measures. As an ingenious gadgeteer, he provided Ulm with a new standard measuring device. That he was capable of using his hands as well as his head is also shown by the fact that he himself designed the frontispiece to his massive work.

The House of Astronomy as envisaged by Kepler is modeled on baroque lines that may seem somewhat dreamlike – even surreal – to modern eyes. Like the memory theaters described by Frances Yates, it presents oddly assorted motifs closely juxtaposed. Ancient sages and modern masters are displayed in a temple of eclectic design. Muses representing the mathematical sciences stand around the dome, while the German imperial eagle hovering above (hopefully) furnishes patronage and gold. Not only the reference to financial sponsorship from on high, but also the instruments hanging on pillars and the printing press engraved on a wall at the base, suggest that the "sleepwalker" had his practical side.

It seems significant that Koestler's romantic portrait of Kepler as a dreamy, mystical astronomer contains a description of this same frontispiece which omits the press and the other instruments. Despite his praise of the *Tabulae Rudolphinae* as an "indispensable tool" and as Kepler's "crowning achievement in practical astronomy," Koestler seems almost contemptuous of the tedious "herculean donkey work" such tables entailed. One can understand why he might sympathize with Kepler's weary reaction to the "treadmill of mathematical computation,"[51] but it seems unfair to withhold sympathy from Kepler's predecessors, who deserved it perhaps even more. The compiling of hand-copied tables had much more of a "treadmill" character than was the case after print. The herculean analogy also seems

[51] Ibid., 407.

to be better suited to labors performed in the age of scribes, when astronomers knew that their tables would be refilled with errors almost as soon as they had been cleansed.

In using Napier's logarithms for the *Rudolphine Tables* Kepler was doing something his master could not do. Although Tycho had hoped to put such tables to use, they were not published until the Danish astronomer had died. Tycho had, however, been able to compare the *Prutenic Tables* with the *Alphonsine Tables* as Copernicus could not do, for the latter were compiled from the older man's posthumous work. In reworking all of Ptolemy's computations, in charting every planet's course as from a moving earth, did Copernicus also achieve something that could not have been accomplished in the age of scribes? The answer is necessarily speculative, yet it seems likely that a complete recasting of the *Almagest* – like a thoroughgoing calendar reform – required freedom from hours of copying and access to reference works that were rarely available to astronomers after Alexandrian resources had been dispersed.

Perhaps the most significant contribution made by Copernicus was not so much in hitting on the "right" theory as in producing a fully worked-out *alternative* theory and thus confronting the next generation with a problem to be solved rather than a solution to be learned. In the frontispiece to Riccioli's *Almagestum novum* of 1651, the Copernican and Tychonic schemes are diagrammed on either side of a scale held by a muse, while the Ptolemaic scheme is displayed on the ground with the notation: "I will rise only if I am corrected." The fact that the balance is tilted in favor of Tycho or that the notion of "restoring" Ptolemy is retained, should not distract attention from the novelty of presenting three clearly diagrammed alternative planetary models within a single frame. Much as contradictory scriptural commentaries encouraged recourse to the text of the Good Book itself, so too did conflicting verdicts rendered by the "little books of men" encourage a persistent checking against the "great book of Nature."

By the time Kepler was a student at Tübingen, astronomers had to choose from among three different theories. A century earlier, when

Fig. 38. The House of Astronomy as envisaged by Kepler (opposite). Taken from Johannes Kepler, *Tabulae Rudolphinae*...(Ulm, 1627, frontispiece). Close-up of printing operations at base of Kepler's frontispiece (above). Both plates reproduced by kind permission of the Rare Book and Special Collections Division, Library of Congress.

STELLÆ
MARTIS
SVPERIORVM INFIMI

Anni côpleti.	Motus Medii. Sig.Gr. ' "	Aphelii. Sig.Gr. ' "	Nodi Ascend. Sig.Gr. ' "
4000	3. 3.45.38	14.51.35 ♉	14.55. 0 ♓
3000	11.20.27.16	3.27.21 ♊	25.57.25 ♓
2000	8. 7. 8.54	22. 2. 7 ♊	6.59.50 ♈
1000	4.23.50.32	10.38.53 ♋	18. 2.15
900	6.25.30.42	12.30.28	19. 8.29
800	8.27.10.51	14.22. 3	20.14.44
700	10.28.51. 1	16.13.37	21.20.58
600	1. 0.31.11	18. 5.12	22.27.13
500	3. 2.11.21	19.56.47	23.33.27
400	5. 3.51.31	21.48.21	24.39.42
300	7. 5.31.41	23.39.56	25.45.56
200	9. 7.11.50	25.31.31	26.52.11
100	11. 8.52. 0	27.23. 5 ♋	27.58.25 ♈
Christi	1.10.32.10	29.14.40 ♋	29. 4.40 ♈
100	3.12.12.20	1. 6.14 ♌	0.10.54 ♉
200	5.13.52.30	2.57.49	1.17. 9
300	7.15.32.40	4.49.24	2.23.23
400	9.17.12.49	6.40.58	3.29.38
500	11.18.52.59	8.32.33	4.35.52
600	1.20.33. 9	10.24. 8	5.42. 7
700	3.22.13.19	12.15.42	6.48.21
800	5.23.53.29	14. 7.17	7.54.36
900	7.25.33.39	15.58.51	9. 0.50
1000	9.27.13.48	17.50.26	10. 7. 5
1100	11.28.53.58	19.42. 1	11.13.19
1200	2. 0.34. 8	21.33.35	12.19.34
1300	4. 2.14.18	23.25.10	13.25.48
1400	6. 3.54.28	25.16.45	14.32. 3
1500	8. 5.34.37	27. 8.19	15.38.17
1600	10. 7.14.47	28.59.54 ♌	16.44.32 ♉
1700	0. 8.54.57	0.51.28 ♍	17.50.46
1800	2.10.35. 7	2.43. 3	18.57. 1
1900	4.12.15.17	4.34.38	20. 3.15
2000	6.13.55.27	6.26.12	21. 9.30
2100	8.15.35.36	8.17.46 ♍	22.15.45 ♉

EPOCHÆ SEV RADICES.

MOTVS MEDII. MARTIS ab Æquinoctio.

In Diebus. Gr. ' "	In hor. ' " "
1 0.31.27	1.19
2 1. 2.53	2.37
3 1.34.20	3.56
4 2. 5.46	5.15
5 2.37.16	6.33
6 3. 8.40	7.52
7 3.40. 6	9.10
8 4.11.23	10.29
9 4.43. 0	11.48
10 5.14.27	13. 6
11 5.45.53	14.25
12 6.17.20	15.43
13 6.48.46	17. 2
14 7.20.13	18.21
15 7.51.40	19.39
16 8.23. 6	20.58
17 8.54.33	22.16
18 9.26. 0	23.35
19 9.57.27	24.54
20 10.28.53	26.12
21 11. 0.20	27.31
22 11.31.46	28.49
23 12. 3.13	30. 8
24 12.34.40	31.27
25 13. 6. 6	32.45
26 13.37.33	34. 4
27 14. 9. 0	35.22
28 14.40.27	36.41
29 15.11.53	38. 0
30 15.43.20	39.18
31 16.14.46	40.37

In minutis

Ad Meridiem æquabilem diei primi Ianuarii Iuliani, qui annum in margine, ante Christum, inchoat; post Christum, proxime sequitur, jam finitum.

Sub Meridiano, qui transit per fretum Maris Balthici, eiusque insulam HVEN-NAM, et arcem VRANIBVRGVM.

Ante Christum Anno 3993. die 24. Iulii, Vraniburgi
H. 0. 33'. 26".
Medius ♂   Aphelium ♂   Nodus asc.
10.43'.52" ♋   15. 0'. 0" ♋   15. 0'. 0" ♓
Quidsi 0. 0'. 0"   0. 0. 0 ♈ vel ♋   0.0.0 ♈

In Mensibus anni simplicis.

Completi.	♂ ab Æquin. Sig.Gr. ' "	Aph. ' " "	Nodi ' " "
Ianuarius	0.16.14.46	0. 6	0. 3
Februarius	1. 0.55.13	0.10	0. 6
Martius	1.17. 9.59	0.16	0.10
Aprilis	2. 2.53.18	0.21	0.13
Maius	2.19. 8. 5	0.27	0.17
Iunius	3. 4.51.24	0.33	0.20
Iulius	3.21. 6.11	0.38	0.23
Augustus	4. 7.20.57	0.43	0.27
September	4.23. 4.16	0.49	0.30
October	5. 9.19. 3	0.55	0.34
November	5.25. 2.23	1. 1	0.37
December	6.11.17. 8	1. 7	0.40

Copernicus was at Cracow, students were fortunate to gain access to one. The fact that Kepler's teacher, Maestlin, gave instruction in all three schemes has been cited to show that university instruction was backward and resistant to innovating currents from outside.[52] That a given student at one university was being instructed in three different ways of positioning the sun and earth when computing planetary orbits seems to me to indicate a remarkable change. All three authorities fell short of correctly describing planetary orbits. Tycho's brand-new scheme, no less than Ptolemy's very old one, was destined to be discredited later. But after 1543 (the year when Copernicus's *De revolutionibus* was published in Nuremberg by Johannes Petreius), commentaries, epitomes, or addenda devoted to one master's work had been superseded by a confrontation with alternatives that forced some sort of choice. Given the hundreds of years that had been spent compiling, retrieving, and preserving the *Almagest*, the appearance of two alternative full-fledged planetary theories in the course of a single century does not point toward cultural lag or the presence of an inertial force. On the contrary, it points toward a cognitive breakthrough of an unprecedented kind.

Furthermore, it should be noted that alternative theories were accompanied by alternative sets of tables which also forced astronomers to make choices and focused special attention on key astronomical events. Exclusive reliance on the *Alphonsine Tables* until the 1540s might be contrasted with the array of six different sets of tables confronting astronomers in the 1640s. Detailed instructions in the use of six different sets were actually provided by Galileo's friend Rienieri in a single work: the *Tabulae medicae* of

---

[52] Stillman Drake, "Early Science and the Printed Book: The Spread of Science Beyond the University," *Renaissance and Reformation* 6 (1970): 49.

Fig. 39 (opposite). A page from Kepler's *Rudolphine Tables* (Ulm, 1627, p. 60). These tables, based on Tycho's data and compiled with the aid of Napier's logarithms, proved so accurate in their predictions that they encouraged favorable reception of their author's laws of planetary motion. Reproduced by kind permission of the Department of Special Collections, Stanford University Libraries.

Jam poſtquam ſemel hujus rei periculum fecimus,audacia ſubvecti porro liberiores eſſe in hoc campo incipiemus. Nam conquiram tria vel quotcunque loca viſa Martis, Planeta ſemper eodem eccentrici loco verſante: & ex iis lege triangulorum inquiram totidem punctorum epicycli vel orbis annui diſtantias a puncto æqualitatis motus. Ac cum ex tribus punctis circulus deſcribatur, ex trinis igitur hujusmodi obſervationibus ſitum circuli, ejusque augium, quod prius ex præſuppoſito uſurpaveram, & eccentricitatem a puncto æqualitatis inquiram. Quod ſi quarta obſervatio accedet, ea erit loco probationis.

C A P.
XXIV.

Primvm tempus eſto anno mdxcx D. v Martii veſperi H. vii M. x eo quod tunc & latitudine pene caruit,ne quis impertinenti ſuſpicione ob hujus implicationem in percipienda demonſtratione impediatur. Reſpondent momenta hæc, quibus & ad idem fixarum punctum redit: A. mdxcii D. xxi Jan. H. vi M.xli: A.mdxciii D. viii Dec. H.vi. M. xii: A. mdxcv D. xxvi Octob. H.v M.xliv. Eſtq; longitudo

Martis primo tempore ex Tychonis reſtitutione ĩ. 4.38. 50: ſequentibus temporib. toties per ĩ. 36 auctior. Hic enim eſt motus præceſſionis congruens tempori periodico unius reſtitutionis Martis Cumq; Tycho apogæum ponat in 23½♌, æquatio ejus erit 11.14.55: propterea lógitudo coæquata anno mdxc ĩ.15.53.45.

Eodem vero tempore & commutatio ſeu differentia medii motus Solis a medio Martis colligitur 10.18.19.56 :coæquata ſeu differentia inter medium Solis & Martis coæquatum eccentricum 10.7.5.1.

Primvm hæc in forma Copernicana ut ſimpliciori ad ſenſum proponemus.

Sit a punctum æqualitatis circuitus terræ , qui putetur eſſe circulus ♂γ ex a deſcriptus : & ſit Sol in partes β,ut aβ linea apogæi

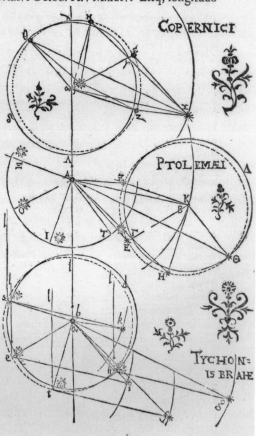

1639. By then, the idiosyncratic experience of the young Tycho, who checked two conflicting tables against the writing in the skies, was becoming commonplace. The accuracy of competing tables was tested by simultaneous observations made from different places and by many eyes.

An open letter alerting astronomers to a forthcoming transit of Mercury (to occur on November 7, 1631) was published by Kepler in Leipzig in 1629 and in Frankfurt in 1630. Kepler urged readers to observe the event so that they could check the accuracy of his tables against those of his competitors. Although Kepler died before the transit occurred as predicted, his "admonition to astronomers" had the desired effect. A German astronomer, Wilhelm Schickard, made the requisite observations and concluded that the *Rudolphine Tables* gave the most accurate prediction.[53] He published a pamphlet in 1632 which informed the reading public of his findings, outlined Kepler's theory, and referred interested readers to Kepler's publications for further details. This pamphlet, in turn, alerted some of the publishers and editors of almanacs and ephemerides, who were spurred by competitive conditions to investigate rival claims made by different astronomers and who were eager to hit on the most foolproof schemes. Resistance to strange logarithms and seemingly cumbersome procedures, as well as reluctance to struggle with Kepler's difficult prose, were overcome once a given publisher became persuaded that better tables could be printed only by mastering Kepler's

---

[53] I have corrected my original version (in the two-volume work as well as in the first edition of this one), which was based on a misleading reference by J. L. Russell, "Kepler's Laws of Planetary Motion, 1609–1666," *British Journal for the History of Science* II (June 1964): 10–11, who made Gassendi rather than Kepler responsible for alerting astronomers to the transit. Thanks are due to Michael John Gorman for spotting this error.

←———

Fig. 40 (opposite). By the time Kepler was a student at Tübingen, astronomers had to choose among three different theories of planetary motion. All three are presented by Kepler in his study of Mars, *Astronomia nova . . . commentariis de motibus stellae martis . . .* (Prague, 1609, p. 131). Reproduced by kind permission of the Department of Special Collections, Stanford University Libraries.

techniques. One English almanac publisher who entered flourishing popular markets during the English civil war concluded that Kepler was the "most subtle mathematician that ever was" and described his work as "the most admirable and best restauration of astronomy of any that did precede him."[54] This publisher was Vincent Wing, author of the *Astronomia Britannica* that was later read and annotated by Newton. By the time Newton had come of age, the *Rudolphine Tables* and the *Epitome Astronomiae Copernicae* had begun to drive out competitors – at least in regions where there was a free trade in ideas.

ANOTHER LOOK AT GALILEO'S TRIAL

While Kepler was busy with the publication of his presentation of the Copernican theoretical structure . . . Copernicus' work was banned. In the summer of 1619 . . . he received . . . news that the first part of his *Epitome* which appeared in 1617 likewise had been placed on the Index of prohibited books. The news alarmed Kepler . . . He feared that should censorship be granted in Austria also, he could no longer find a printer there . . . He pictured the situation so black that he supposed he would be given to understand he should renounce the calling of astronomer.[55]

Kepler was reassured by his friends that his worst fears were exaggerated. They wrote to tell him that his book could be read, even in Italy, by learned men who secured special permits. One Venetian correspondent suggested, shrewdly, that authors often benefited from having their books banned. In Italy, he wrote, "books by distinguished German scholars even if prohibited would be secretly bought and read so much the more attentively."[56]

Similar reassurances are still being issued by historians who discount the significance of the Catholic condemnation of pro-Copernican works. Once publication has been assured, it may well be advantageous to have one's book banned in certain regions. But

[54] Russell, "Kepler's Laws," 18–19.
[55] Max Caspar, *Kepler*, tr. C. Doris Hellman, rev. ed. (London, 1959), 298.
[56] Ibid., 299.

when one is having trouble getting technical printing completed, official proclamations aimed at frightening printers are not advantageous at all. As these remarks suggest, to understand the circumstances confronting seventeenth-century scientists we need to assign more significance to the act of publication and to the role of intermediaries who got the printing done. If this were done, moreover, one might be able to draw significant connections between the rise of modern science and seemingly extraneous political events. For the outcome of dynastic and religious wars obviously affected the kind of publication programs that could be undertaken in a given realm. It determined the degree of risk that printing a given work entailed. Forms of piety and patronage, licensing and censorship, literacy and book-reading habits varied from region to region in accordance with this outcome. Since the distribution of printing industries can be determined with a fair degree of accuracy, the "geography of the book" can be mapped out, and the movement of printing centers can be correlated with the fixing of religious and dynastic frontiers.

What about the movement of scientific centers? Obviously it is more difficult to trace. Indeed, it is open to question whether there were any real centers of scientific activity when printing shops began to cluster in towns. The printer can be readily identified before the role of the scientist had clearly emerged. The latter is still a problematic creature, as current definitions suggest. In the early modern era, it may be a mistake to use the label at all. The distribution of talents contributing to "scientific" advances in the early modern era hinges on a wide variety of activities. The question of where and how to apply the term "scientist" to men who did not regard themselves as such is open to dispute. Furthermore, from the 1500s to the 1640s, investigations now regarded as "scientific" were still largely uncoordinated. Scattered regions containing varied clusters of talents – an observatory on a Danish island, groups of instrument makers in Nuremberg, lens grinders in Amsterdam, or Jesuit astronomers in Rome – dot the map somewhat randomly. Some highly energetic "centers," such as Tycho's Uraniborg or Mersenne's "Letterbox" or Rudolph II's court at Prague, were so short-lived and so dependent on the movements of a particular individual that their location cannot be taken as proving any rule.

Ne extra hanc Bibliothecam efferatur. Ex obedientiâ.

Given inevitable uncertainty over the location of the "main centers" of scientific activity, there is bound to be disagreement over the factors that encouraged their formation and early growth. There are those who argue that a prime role during the strategic take-off phase was played in Catholic regions, especially in Italy, where the Platonic revival flourished, the study of natural philosophy was propelled by lay university faculties, and the first scientific societies appeared. There are those who look instead to regions that broke away from Rome. They believe Protestant teachings spurred a new systematic investigation of God's open book. Some single out Wittenberg, rather than Padua, as *the* university which served as the seed bed for modern science; others play variations on Max Weber's theme by emphasizing Calvinist centers such as Leiden and Puritan academies established elsewhere. Yet another school regards all universities and confessions as too conservative and tradition-bound and looks to heterodox circles and nonacademic groups, represented by "invisible colleges" and "schools of the night." "The presence or absence of Protestantism" is thus regarded by Frances Yates as less significant than the "Hermetic-Cabalist" tradition. Virtuosi such as Newton owed less to Anglican bishops and Puritan divines than to the Renaissance magus who sought to play the "pipes of Pan." Yet others argue that Newton's mathematical physics ought not to be confused with his alchemy or theology and agree with Edward Rosen that "out of Renaissance magic ... came not modern science, but modern magic."[57] They stress the demystifying aspects of the new philosophy, its open and public character, and the predictive powers

[57] Edward Rosen, "Was Copernicus a Hermetist?" *Historical and Philosophical Perspectives of Science*, ed. R. H. Stuewer (Minneapolis, 1970), 171.

←————————————————————————————

Fig. 41 (opposite). This frontispiece to the work of a Jesuit astronomer who championed the Tychonic over the Copernican system shows the balance tilted in favor of the Danish astronomer. But it also alerts viewers to the need for a theory choice by presenting three contradictory schemes within a single frame. From Riccioli, *Almagestum novum* (1651). Reproduced by kind permission of the Department of Special Collections, Stanford University Libraries.

that made it useful to practical men. For the most part, they identify science with materialism and regard it as incompatible with belief in a spirit world. Anticlerical circles and libertine groups are thus singled out, along with the revival of pre-Christian pagan views associated with atomism and hedonism.

Finally, there are the eclectics who find some truth in all views even while holding to a multivariable approach. No one region or institution, tradition, creed, or class played a strategic role in the great collaborative venture, which was itself composed of diverse methods and pursuits. Competing claims for the primacy of diverse "external" forces when taken all together tend to cancel each other out. The way is paved for detaching the "internal" life of science from "external" social events by stressing the autonomy of activities which owed something to all groups but nothing special to any one. The "sublime quest for truth" is envisaged as a neutral and nonpartisan cerebral activity unaffected by the clash of warring creeds and conducted *au-dessus de la mêlée*.

Although all these arguments have some merit, none, in my opinion, goes far enough. Discussion of research activities ought to be accompanied by consideration of publication of results. In the search for seed beds or nurseries, moreover, early printers' workshops deserve a closer look. So too does the problem of how scattered circles were linked and how they began to cooperate on many different fronts. However they differ, the various interpretations now offered share in common a tendency to assume that coordination was inevitable and that the flow of information would not be disrupted or cut off. As we have seen, modern authorities take more for granted than a seventeenth-century printer or virtuoso could.

When the new presses are left out of account, it may seem plausible to argue: "It is only by ignoring the enormous Catholic scientific activity" between the 1540s and 1640s that "major claims can be made for the importance of Protestantism."[58] Once technical publication is brought into the picture, one may fully acknowledge

---

[58] T. K. Rabb, "Religion and the Rise of Modern Science," *Past and Present* 31 (July 1965): 117.

Catholic activity and still make "major claims" for the way Protestants encouraged and Catholics discouraged its development and expansion. "The lack of noticeable difference between protestant and Catholic resistance to change...must be explained away if the reformed religion is considered inherently more conducive to science or in any way responsible for the rise of the new form of inquiry."[59] When resistance to changes wrought by printing is brought into the picture, the difference between the two confessions is not merely noticeable; it is striking. The common practice of treating anti-Copernican *statements* made by sixteenth-century Protestants as if they were equivalent to anti-Copernican *measures* taken by seventeenth-century Catholics is, in this regard, misleading. A popular undergraduate text, for example, gives readers the mistaken impression that Luther's contempt for Copernicus "strangled" the scientific revolution in Germany (the achievements of Rheticus, Reinhold, Maestlin, Kepler notwithstanding!).[60] Theological statements do not represent the same kind of resistance to change as do measures taken to prevent publication. The latter threatened the life of science as the former did not.

Protestant printers often ran afoul of authorities by producing political or theological tracts, but when serving mathematicians and astronomers they were left in relative peace. This was true not merely in late seventeenth-century England when (it is often said) religious zeal had begun to lose its force. It was also true in the age of Luther and Melanchthon when zeal was at its height. The evangelical drive which powered the presses of Wittenberg and other centers of the reformed religion encouraged the expansion of book markets from the first. At the same time, the theology of the reformers, drawing on older Christian traditions, also promoted scientific research. The positive impulse given both to the establishment of printers' workshops and to scientific publication programs was, to my knowledge, never checked or reversed. Although Protestant and Catholic

---

[59] Ibid., 113.
[60] Jacob Bronowski and Bruce Mazlish, *The Western Intellectual Tradition: From Leonardo to Hegel* (New York, 1960), 124.

theologians did adopt very much the same position – both assigning a provisional hypothetical status to geokinetic theories; both denying that the earth's motion could be anything other than a useful fiction – Protestant publicists and astronomers were not deterred from rejecting this position, in marked contrast to Catholics after the papal condemnation of Copernican theory in 1616.

Even before the 1616 condemnation and after Luther and Melanchthon's pronouncements, Catholic publishers still did less than did Protestants to promote the Copernican cause. In this regard, too much emphasis on Copernicus's position as a Catholic canon who relied on church patronage most of his life can be misleading: "While Copernicus was aided by a Protestant mathematician," says Sarton, "he received his greatest encouragement from prelates.... His book was published under the highest Catholic auspices."[61] It is true that as a churchman Copernicus was aided by several Catholic prelates and he had his major treatise dedicated to a Catholic pope. Nevertheless the actual work of publishing De revolutionibus was done under Protestant auspices. Beginning with Rheticus's First Narration, works describing or promoting Copernican theories, whether under the guise of a new astronomy or as "the ancient doctrine of the Pythagoreans lately revived," never ceased to come from Protestant presses. It is worth noting that this point applies just as well to the mystical Copernicanism of Catholic friars such as Giordano Bruno and Tommaso Campanella as to such English virtuosi as Thomas Digges and William Gilbert. The imprints of Venice and Paris on the first editions of Bruno's works were fictitious. It was during Bruno's stay in London between 1583 and 1585 that the English printer, John Charlewood, printed his six major treatises. Charlewood belonged to a group of London publishers who obtained both profits and patronage by taking advantage of free publicity provided by the Index. He engaged in "surreptitious" operations, turning out works in foreign vernaculars, bearing foreign imprints, and aimed at Continental markets.

[61] Sarton, Six Wings, 61.

In contrast to the active role played by Protestant firms in propelling early Copernicanism, Catholic presses seem to have been relatively inactive – until Galileo's *Sidereus nuncius* was published in the spring of 1610. An overnight sensation, *The Starry Messenger* not only catapulted its author into the position of an international celebrity, it also did for astronomy what had been done for theology by Luther's early tracts – stimulated literary excitement and generated publicity of a new kind. "The extent and rapidity of the spread of Galileo's telescopic discoveries can scarcely be exaggerated. Only five years after *The Starry Messenger* appeared, the principal facts announced by Galileo were published by a Jesuit missionary in Peking."[62] Not only were Jesuit presses in China activated, but so too were Italian printers in Venice and Rome. The Republic of Letters, which had previously looked to Wittenberg and other northern centers for the most sensational fast-breaking stories, began to turn back toward Italy once more. Even in England the accomplishments of earlier English virtuosi were overshadowed by literary excitement generated by reports of what could be seen through "Galileo's tube." "It is 'the Italian's moon' and the 'Florentine's new world' we find in English poetry, not the same moon as it had appeared to Hariot in London and to Lower in Wales."[63] For the first time in many decades, Italian publishers were able to take advantage of the excitement generated by a new bestselling author who appealed to a vernacular-reading public. A flurry of pamphlets brought profits to local firms and probably helped to spur fresh observations along with sales of instruments and books. But this promising windfall for Italian publishers lasted only five or six years. The stimulus supplied by Galileo ricocheted to the benefit of foreigners in the end. The "dangerous consequences" of "spreading" Copernican views "among the people by writing in the vernacular"[64] were arrested by the

---

[62] Drake, *Discoveries and Opinions*, p. 59, n. 1.

[63] Marjorie Hope Nicolson, *Science and Imagination* (Ithaca, NY, 1956), 34.

[64] Citation from the letter sent to Kepler, Aug. 13, 1619, which described the "practical effect of the prohibition" aimed at Foscarini's vernacular work in Jerome Langford, *Galileo, Science and the Church*, rev. ed. (Ann Arbor, MI, 1971), 104.

decree of the Congregation of the Index in 1616. Open promotion of Copernican theories and indeed any vernacular treatise dealing with astronomy or physics became risky for Catholic printers and thus all the more profitable for Protestant ones.

One may agree that Galileo's *Letter to the Grand Duchess Christina* reflected a "long-standing continental tradition" and expressed views that were by no means peculiar to Protestants like Francis Bacon, but were common among many Catholic virtuosi as well.[65] But it should also be noted that had Galileo not been aided by Protestant intermediaries such as the Swiss diplomat Elias Diodati and the Dutch printer Louis Elsevier, this very same *Letter* would have never seen the light of day.

Many Protestant professors and churchmen objected to the new astronomy. Several Catholic virtuosi presided at its birth. The fact remains that Protestant authorities interposed few obstacles in the way of scientific publication and actively encouraged (however inadvertently) expanding lay book markets, which attracted printers to Protestant realms. The Counter-Reformation church pursued a contrary course. Beginning with the banning of vernacular Bibles and the prohibitions issued against other secular bestselling works, Catholic printers were subject to pressures that worked against diversification and that led to greater and greater reliance on turning out "safe" devotional literature and on serving a clerical clientele.

Here a word of warning may be needed. Serving a clerical clientele did not invariably render a disservice to science. Seventeenth-century Jesuits furnished much useful data for serious astronomers. Profit-driving lay printers who served vast markets by churning out prognostications were not invariably helpful to scientific advance. Parallels often drawn between the "Protestant who interpreted God's word for himself and the scientist who interpreted nature for himself" need to be handled with caution. "Everyman his own scientist" is a slogan that Puritan pamphleteers often seemed to push too far. "Culpeper translated into English the sacred text of the

---

[65] Rabb, "Religion and the Rise of Modern Science," 117.

College ... He hoped it would make everyman his own physician as the Bible made everyman his own theologian."[66] Culpeper was neither the first nor the last to question the usefulness of Latin prescriptions and medical degrees or to encourage more self-help among long-suffering patients. In the early modern era, doctors rarely did more good than harm, and there was every reason to be critical about the way physicians were trained. Yet even in that benighted era, the advancement of medical science still owed much to Latin treatises on anatomy, physiology, and embryology.

Insofar as they encouraged literacy among surgeons and apothecaries and pressed for more mathematics as against Greek and Latin in the schools, the campaigns led by the more radical Protestant pamphleteers were not unhelpful to science. But they could also take an excessively anti-intellectual form. As discussion of naive empiricism suggests, there is a difference between surpassing the ancients after mastering their technical literature and simply attacking the ancients while imitating Paracelsus and burning old books.

> The Protestant doctrine ... proclaimed the duty of everybody to read the book of Scripture for himself. As a consequence ... the duty to read the book of nature without regard to the authority of ... Aristotle, Pliny, Ptolemy, Galen was put forward ... everybody ... might be a priest to the book of creation in defiance ... of the ancient authorities. When Palissy was derided because of his ignorance of the classical languages ... he proudly answered ... I have no book but heaven and earth and it is given to everyman to know and read this beautiful book.[67]

As an artisan-author, the French potter Bernard Palissy both contributed to public knowledge and produced a new ceramic glaze. In his public lectures he spelled out a program that was taken up by Francis Bacon and proved highly significant later. Nevertheless, the attack on learned authorities and the defense of everyone's right

---

[66] Christopher Hill, *The World Turned Upside Down* (London, 1972), 240.
[67] Reijer Hooykaas, *Humanisme, Science et Réforme: Pierre de la Ramée 1515–1572* (Leiden, 1958), 215–16.

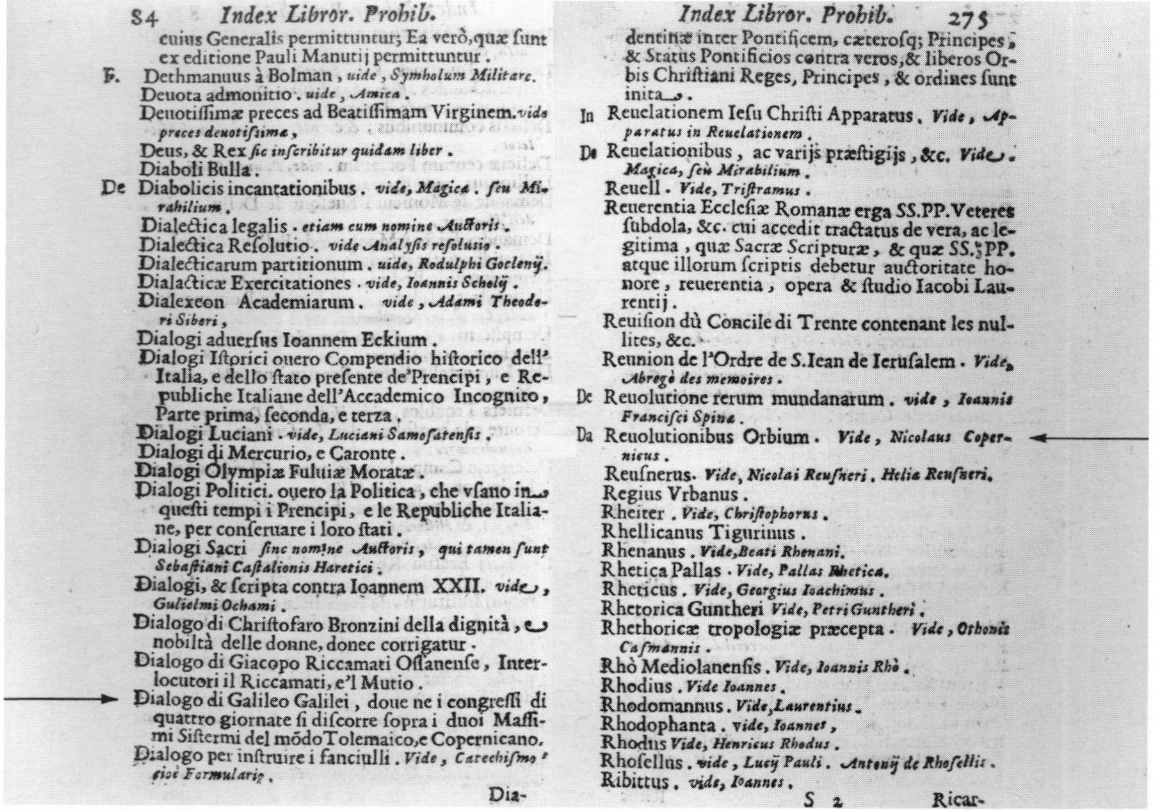

84 *Index Libror. Prohib.*

cuius Generalis permittuntur; Ea verò,quæ ſunt ex editione Pauli Manutij permittuntur.

F. Dethmanuus à Bolman, *uide, Symbolum Militare.*

Deuota admonitio. *uide, Amica.*

Deuotiſſimæ preces ad Beatiſſimam Virginem. *vide preces deuotiſsimæ,*

Deus, & Rex *ſic inſcribitur quidam liber.*

Diaboli Bulla.

De Diabolicis incantationibus. *vide, Magica. ſeu Mirabilium.*

Dialectica legalis. *etiam cum nomine Auctoris.*

Dialectica Reſolutio. *vide Analyſis reſolutio.*

Dialecticarum partitionum. *uide, Rodulphi Goclenij.*

Dialacticæ Exercitationes. *vide, Ioannis Scholij.*

Dialexeon Academiarum. *vide, Adami Theodori Siberi,*

Dialogi aduerſus Ioannem Eckium.

Dialogi Iſtorici ouero Compendio hiſtorico dell' Italia, e dello ſtato preſente de'Prencipi, e Republiche Italiane dell'Accademico Incognito, Parte prima, ſeconda, e terza.

Dialogi Luciani. *vide, Luciani Samoſatenſis.*

Dialogi di Mercurio, e Caronte.

Dialogi Olympiæ Fuluiæ Moratæ.

Dialogi Politici. ouero la Politica, che vſano in queſti tempi i Prencipi, e le Republiche Italiane, per conſeruare i loro ſtati.

Dialogi Sacri *ſine nomine Auctoris, qui tamen ſunt Sebaſtiani Caſtalionis Hæretici.*

Dialogi, & ſcripta contra Ioannem XXII. *vide, Gulielmi Ochami.*

Dialogo di Chriſtofaro Bronzini della dignità, e nobiltà delle donne, donec corrigatur.

Dialogo di Giacopo Riccamati Oſſanenſe, Interlocutori il Riccamati, e'l Mutio.

Dialogo di Galileo Galilei, doue ne i congreſſi di quattro giornate ſi diſcorre ſopra i duoi Maſſimi Siſtemi del mõdo Tolemaico, e Copernicano.

Dialogo per inſtruire i fanciulli. *Vide, Catechiſmo cioè Formulario.*

Dia-

Index Libror. Prohib. 275

dentinæ inter Pontificem, cæteroſq; Principes, & Status Pontificios contra veros, & liberos Orbis Chriſtiani Reges, Principes, & ordines ſunt inita.

In Reuelationem Ieſu Chriſti Apparatus. *Vide, Apparatus in Reuelationem.*

De Reuelationibus, ac varijs præſtigijs, &c. *Vide, Magica, ſeù Mirabilium.*

Reuell. *Vide, Triſtramus.*

Reuerentia Eccleſiæ Romanæ erga SS.PP.Veteres ſubdola, &c. cui accedit tractatus de vera, ac legitima, quæ Sacræ Scripturæ, & quæ SS. PP. atque illorum ſcriptis debetur auctoritate honore, reuerentia, opera & ſtudio Iacobi Laurentij.

Reuiſion dù Concile di Trente contenant les nullites, &c.

Reunion de l'Ordre de S.Iean de Ieruſalem. *Vide, Abregè des memoires.*

De Reuolutione rerum mundanarum. *vide, Ioannis Franciſci Spinæ.*

Da Reuolutionibus Orbium. *Vide, Nicolaus Copernicus.*

Reuſnerus. *Vide, Nicolai Reuſneri, Heliæ Reuſneri.*

Regius Vrbanus.

Rheiter. *Vide, Chriſtophorus.*

Rhellicanus Tigurinus.

Rhenanus. *Vide, Beati Rhenani.*

Rhetica Pallas. *Vide, Pallas Rhetica.*

Rheticus. *Vide, Georgius Ioachimus.*

Rhetorica Guntheri *Vide, Petri Guntheri.*

Rhethoricæ tropologiæ præcepta. *Vide, Othonis Caſmannis.*

Rhò Mediolanenſis. *Vide, Ioannis Rhò.*

Rhodius. *Vide Ioannes.*

Rhodomannus. *Vide, Laurentius.*

Rhodophanta. *vide, Ioannes,*

Rhodus *Vide, Henricus Rhodus.*

Rhoſellus. *vide, Lucij Pauli. Antonij de Rhoſellis.*

Ribittus. *vide, Ioannes.*

S 2 Ricar-

Fig. 42. Galileo's *Dialogue* ("Dialogo di Galileo Galilei") (left) and Copernicus's *De revolutionibus* ("De Revolutionibus Orbium") (right) on the *Index librorum prohibitorum* (Rome, 1670, pp. 84 and 275). Reproduced by kind permission of the Rare Book and Special Collections Division, Library of Congress.

to read the "book of Nature" for himself was not always helpful to the advancement of science. Did not later fundamentalists stand on much the same ground when they claimed the right to judge Darwin's teachings for themselves? Even Galileo, who appealed on occasion over the heads of Latin-reading professors to the ordinary "horse sense" of intelligent compatriots, pointed out that understanding the organs of the human body or the movement of the stars called for special training and required much more than merely looking with untutored eyes.

> The eyes of an idiot perceive little by beholding the external appearance of a human body, as compared with the wonderful contrivances which a careful and practiced anatomist or philosopher discovers . . . Likewise that which presents itself to mere sight is as nothing in comparison with the . . . marvels that the ingenuity of learned men discovers in the heavens by long and accurate observation.[68]

In another celebrated passage, Galileo again underlined his conviction that the "book of Nature," although always open to public inspection, was not really "given to everyman to know and read."

> Philosophy is written in this grand book, the universe which stands continually open to our gaze. But the book cannot be understood unless one first learns to comprehend the language and read the letters in which it is composed. It is written in the language of mathematics.[69]

The language of mathematics certainly differed from Latin or Greek, but not because it was as easy to learn as one's mother tongue. On the contrary, it became increasingly sophisticated in the course of the seventeenth century and was subject to incremental change.

> Newton was as incomprehensible to the average mechanic as Thomas Aquinas. Knowledge was no longer shut up in the Latin Bibles which priestly scholars had to interpret; it was increasingly

---

[68] "Letter to the Grand Duchess Christina," in Drake, *Discoveries and Opinions*, 196.
[69] "The Assayer," in Drake, *Discoveries and Opinions*, 237–8.

shut up in the technical vocabulary of the sciences which the new specialists had to interpret.[70]

There are not only affinities but there are also contradictions that have to be considered when applying a "priesthood of all believers" doctrine to the study of nature. As Rabb suggests, the parallels and analogies that are frequently drawn between early Protestant and early scientific thought "do not prove the existence of any significant connection between the two movements."[71]

I agree that mere analogies prove nothing and believe they are sometimes pushed too far. Yet here again, by assigning more significance to publication programs, one may find some valid connections that still remain to be drawn. For example, the larger the vernacular-reading public, the larger the pool of potential scientific talent that could be tapped, and the more craftsmen would be encouraged to disclose trade secrets by printing treatises and attracting purchasers to their shops. New and useful interchanges between publishers and readers were also encouraged by the social penetration of literacy. When authors of atlases and herbals called on their readers to send in notes about coastlines or dried plants and seeds, a form of data collection was launched in which "everyman" *could* play a supporting role. Even the output of prognostications probably stimulated sales of almanacs and ephemerides and may have encouraged some readers to buy telescopes, thereby stimulating instrument makers to turn out more pamphlets designed to bring purchasers to their shops.

The expansion of a large heterogeneous public for their products was especially important for booksellers, map publishers, instrument makers, mathematical practitioners, and other contributors to applied sciences, whose prefaces are often cited when the new scientific ethos is described. Reijer Hooykaas has described how

> the defenders of the "new" science called upon the unlearned
> to contribute to the knowledge of natural history, geography
> and physics by communicating their observations on birds and

[70] Hill, *World Turned Upside Down*, 239.
[71] Rabb, "Religion and the Rise of Modern Science," 120.

flowers, on ebb and flood tide, on celestial phenomena and the . . . magnetic needle. Travellers and mariners especially were invited to do so.[72]

Hooykaas plausibly links such invitations to Protestant notions pertaining to a priesthood of believers and to the belief that "everyone should read the book of nature according to his capacities." Yet the men who solicited responses from readers were not all of them devout Protestants or conscious defenders of a "new science." In many instances they were acting rather as conscientious manufacturers of globes, maps, and almanacs or of other guidebooks or instruments, who hoped to attract purchasers, outdo competitors, and ensure steady sales by building up their reputation as makers of reliable and useful products.

In repudiating vulgar Marxism, Hooykaas writes somewhat indignantly that Protestant insistence "on the benefit that may come to mankind from useful inventions . . . is not a manifestation of the capitalistic mentality of a rising merchant class hiding mammonistic intentions behind a pious pretence. Genuine love for God and one's fellow beings is the main driving force."[73]

Yet it seems mistaken to set one motive against another when "having it both ways" is what most human beings seek. Whatever artisan-authors wrote about the glory of God and the good of humanity in their prefaces to treatises describing some new instrument or reckoning device, the fact remained that they were not only better able to serve others by contributing to the new stream of technical literature, they were also better able to serve themselves. As noted in Chapter 4, high-minded prefaces were often coupled with appeals to the reader to visit the author's shop and with the inclusion of addresses where new instruments and globes were on sale. Insofar as technical publication was spurred, the driving force was fueled not by love of God *or* Mammon but by love of God *and* Mammon – and of one's compatriots and of oneself – in short, by the very same powerful

---

[72] Reijer Hooykaas, "Science and the Reformation," *The Protestant Ethic and Modernization*, ed. S. N. Eisenstadt (New York, 1968), 216.

[73] Ibid.

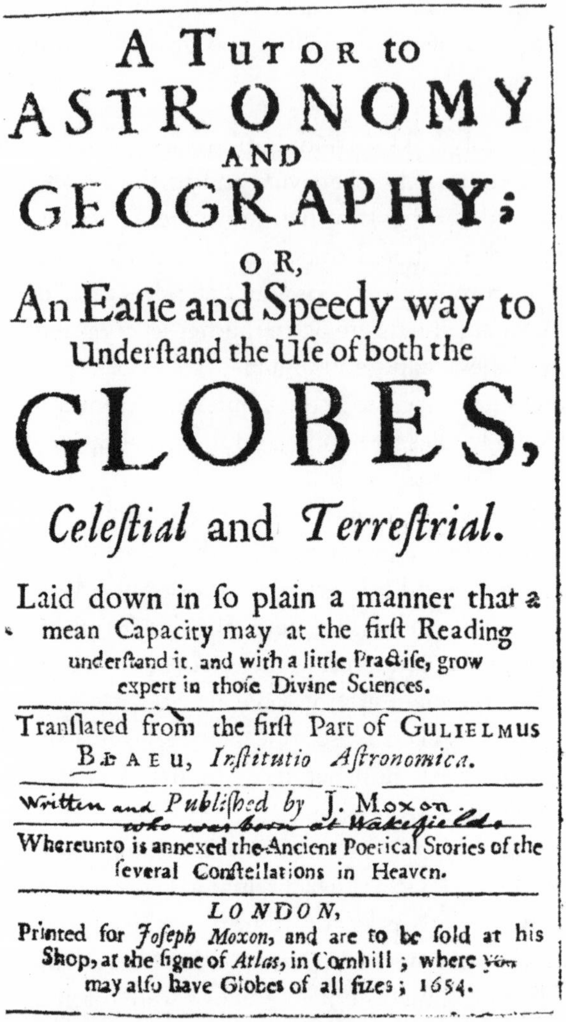

A TUTOR to
ASTRONOMY
AND
GEOGRAPHY;
OR,
An Easie and Speedy way to
Underſtand the Uſe of both the
GLOBES,
Celeſtial and *Terreſtrial*.

Laid down in ſo plain a manner that a
mean Capacity may at the firſt Reading
underſtand it, and with a little Practiſe, grow
expert in thoſe Divine Sciences.

Tranſlated from the firſt Part of GULIELMUS
BLAEU, *Inſtitutio Aſtronomica.*

Written and *Publiſhed by* J. Moxon
who was born at Wakefield.
Whereunto is annexed the Ancient Poetical Stories of the
ſeveral Conſtellations in Heaven.

LONDON,
Printed for *Joſeph Moxon,* and are to be ſold at his
Shop, at the ſigne of *Atlas,* in Cornhill ; where you
may alſo have Globes of all ſizes ; 1654.

Fig. 43. On this title page, Joseph Moxon (whose *Mechanick Exercises* are noted above) promotes his English translation of the first part of W. J. Blaeu's Latin *Institutio astronomica* as a quick and easy way to master the "divine sciences." He also advertises that he has globes on sale at his shop at the sign of the Atlas in Cornhill, thus characteristically combining pedagogic and pecuniary motives. This title page of Moxon's first publication is reproduced by kind permission of The Huntington Library, San Marino, California.

mixture of altruistic and self-serving motives which propelled early Bible printing along with map publishing and instrument making.

I would imagine that the chance to serve God and help mankind, even while making money and establishing one's name, was just as attractive to instrument makers, reckon masters, and map publishers in Catholic realms as in Protestant ones. But official church policies diverged significantly. Catholic enterprise was braked in a manner that encouraged Protestants to move into high gear. Thus the same censorship policies that discouraged Catholic Bible printers and curtailed their markets later closed up scientific publication outlets in Catholic lands. The same forces that encouraged expanding markets for vernacular Bibles also favored interchanges between readers and publishers of useful vernacular works.

Of course, some authorities question whether vernacular treatises by craftsmen should be linked to true scientific advance. They dismiss "Baconian" arguments, noting that Bacon contributed nothing to seventeenth-century science, and instead point to the series of creative acts by a small group of virtuosi who gave the century of genius its name. Collecting facts or promoting "useful knowledge" are set aside by this school as irrelevant to the investigations of Pascal, Harvey, Kepler, Galileo, Malpighi, and other great men.

> The Scientific Revolution was surely utilitarian only to a limited degree. The classical experiments were anything but useful in their application ... The improvement of man's lot on earth was an irrelevant consideration ...
>
> What has been said about Pascal applies equally to Kepler's planetary investigations, Galileo's mechanics, Mersenne's study of music, the Cartesian theory of the universe, Harvey's discovery of the circulation of the blood and Newton's *Principia*. Intellectual curiosity is relevant here, not crude utilitarianism ... Investigation ... must concentrate attention not upon technology and economic need but upon the social and intellectual conditions which favored the development of originality.[74]

---

[74] Hugh F. Kearney, "Puritanism and Science: Problems of Definition," *Past and Present* 29 (July 1965): 108.

Once again it seems possible to avoid an either-or approach. Intellectual curiosity *and* useful trigonometry texts entered into "Kepler's planetary investigations." In laboring over the *Rudolphine Tables* during the Thirty Years' War, Kepler himself produced a work that was designed to do more than satisfy "intellectual curiosity," a work that proved useful to editors of ephemerides and publishers of sky maps. Activities such as compiling tables of functions or developing logarithms and slide rules also involved the production of useful tools and at the same time spurred new creative acts.

In this connection it is worth recalling Laplace's dictum that logarithm tables doubled the life of the astronomer. Consideration of the intellectual labor saved by printed materials points to aspects of early modern scientific activities which are neglected by those sociologists of science who emphasize the Puritan work ethic. Present guidelines, derived from Max Weber, focus attention on the appearance of a set of values that discouraged unrelieved idleness on the part of a leisure class.[75] Something more should be said about the new *leisure* that printing gave to a *learned* class. Within the Commonwealth of Learning, systematic work habits were coupled with released time *from* grinding labor such as compiling long tables of numbers by hand. Less reliance on memory work and rote repetition in lecture halls also brought new mental talents into play. Printing enabled natural philosophers to spend more time solving brain teasers, designing ingenious experiments and new instruments, or even chasing butterflies and collecting bugs if they wished. The pleasure principle should not be ruled out when considering the rapid development of new puzzle-solving techniques by men who were aptly described as *dilettanti* and *amateurs*. "Homo Ludens" as well as "Homo Faber" was encouraged after printing to use his mental energies in new ways – as the modern chess player or bird watcher may suggest. Early modern science owed something to playfulness and "idle" curiosity as well as to piety and profit-seeking drives.

[75]   Robert K. Merton, *Science, Technology and Society in Seventeenth Century England*, rev. ed. offset reprint (New York, 1970), 96.

Even black-robed Latin-writing professional lawyers, physicians, and astronomers took advantage of new leisure by browsing at book fairs and indulging in mathematical fun and games. The use of print to mobilize European talents by issuing open letters and challenges was not confined to sponsoring inventions deemed useful by bureaucrats and capitalists, such as methods of finding longitude at sea. Newton's image of himself as a child playing on the seashore diverting himself "by finding a smoother pebble or prettier shell than ordinary" seems to be singularly at odds with a work ethic and even somewhat pagan in its implications. The satisfaction of pure intellectual curiosity, as Hugh Kearney says, needs to be given due weight.

Nevertheless, even the most seemingly impractical cerebral feats required repeated recourse to various printed materials. Tables and charts were not turned out in idle moments by members of a leisured class. The output of better maps and globes, the new ventures in data collection which led to improved estimates of the dimensions of the earth were helpful to pure science as well as to applied science. When publishers competed to get news from an expedition the minute it docked or instrument makers took time off to advertise their wares, such actions contributed to *all* kinds of scientific experiments – whether they were aimed at bearing fruit or intended only to shed light.

Even when we consider only the light-shedding experiments performed by a very small number of highly gifted men, the many practical problems posed by publication still have to be taken into account. Where publication outlets were imperiled, speculative freedom was also endangered. Official censorship could affect even the hidden life of the mind. One wonders, for example, whether the "Cartesian Theory of the Universe" was ever fully disclosed, even to Descartes himself. When hearing of Galileo's fate in 1633, he stopped working on his grand cosmological treatise and perhaps clipped the wings of his own imagination by this negative act. Newton's creative energies could be given freer rein. Conditions that guarantee speculative freedom are probably related to the "development of originality." They are also related to mundane matters involving economics, technology, and affairs of church and state.

By 1640, we are told, "it is safe to say that modern science had risen." By then, "the work of Descartes, Galileo and Harvey was virtually complete." But Descartes's work was surely incomplete. The complete *Monde* was never issued, even in a posthumous form. By 1640, moreover, Kepler's laws had not won acceptance. Three alternative planetary models and six sets of conflicting tables were in circulation. During the same interval, the fate of the Continental publishing firms that were used by Kepler, Galileo, and Harvey also hung in the balance and hinged on the shifting fortunes of war. Perhaps it is *un*safe to say that science had risen – especially in those regions where printers were being subjected to new controls. In Italy, for example, a clandestine book trade had taken hold, and scientific publication programs were winding down. One might be better advised to think less of science as "rising" among Galileo's compatriots than of its going underground. At least it was able to go abroad, thanks to the help provided by the Royal Society, whose efforts at underwriting foreign work deserve to be better known.

For example, all the major treatises of Marcello Malpighi, indeed every work that he published after 1669, were published by the Royal Society. Much as Copernicus was served by Rheticus, Galileo by Diodati, or Newton by Halley, so too was Malpighi served, not by Italian colleagues, but by Henry Oldenburg and Robert Hooke. These secretaries of the Royal Society furnished the great embryologist with the most recently published technical literature. (It was easier to wait for books from England than to turn to local booksellers by that time.) They solicited contributions and assured him repeatedly of the fine reception accorded his papers by the "company of philosophers abroad."[76] In general, they provided the Italian virtuoso with the encouragement and group support he lacked at home. That the atmosphere in Italy was less receptive is shown by Malpighi's many letters. Even while expressing some concern about possible reprisals for engaging in the "commerce with Protestants," Malpighi commented that a friend had mentioned there were advantages in

---

[76] Howard B. Adelmann, *Marcello Malpighi and the Evolution of Embryology* (Ithaca, NY, 1967), I:670.

having works "condemned by Italian censors sail to England to be printed."[77]

This opportunity was advantageous not only to Malpighi but to the Commonwealth of Learning at large, as Oldenburg recognized at the time. His correspondence with the Italian embryologist shows that the secretary of the Royal Society was fully aware of the special service the press was rendering to scientific advance. Having assured the anxious author that his history of the silkworm was to be published "in splendid style," Oldenburg noted that publication would "bring out the opinion of all the learned, and perhaps where you have not yet seen clearly, they will shed fuller light."[78] With these words, Oldenburg underscored a theme which has been running through this book; namely, that printing rendered a special service to the learned Latin-reading community. Publication would not serve to acquaint "everyman" with Malpighi's highly technical treatise on the silkworm. But it would "bring out the opinion of all the learned," that is, it would elicit contributions from other qualified investigators who could check observations, repeat experiments, or devise new tests and present fresh data. Given Oldenburg's clear understanding of the value of scientific publication and the vigorous efforts he made on its behalf, it seems odd that this aspect of his activities is not acknowledged more often.

Along with the special services rendered by Royal Society publications, the special threats posed by press censorship also are likely to be discounted. It has become increasingly fashionable to muffle the repercussions of Galileo's trial and to view the stir it caused as a consequence of clever Protestant propaganda.

> It is very doubtful whether the dramatic events of the condemnation of Galileo were in themselves of far-reaching significance. The indignation aroused... probably increased the popularity of science. There is no sign of cessation of scientific activity following the condemnation... It is true that the activities of the

<hr>

[77] Ibid., I:347.
[78] Ibid., I:674 (Letter of March 25, 1669).

Lincei were curtailed...but some of its members...continued
to be active...and participated in the foundation...of the
Cimento.[79]

Although scientific activity did not cease in Italy after 1632, studies
of the Lincei, the Cimento, the Investiganti, and of individual members of these early scientific societies show how it was being crippled.
The Lincei had to discontinue the study of physics and astronomy;
its short-lived successor, the Cimento, which relied entirely on the
personal patronage of a Medici duke, was disbanded ten years after its
formation. Two of its members were imprisoned by the Inquisition.
Its collective papers, the *Saggi* (*Examples* or *Samples*), were published
in 1667 but could not be purchased in Italian bookshops. Indeed,
it required action once again by the Royal Society for the *Saggi* to
become known abroad.

A brief comparison of the policy of the Royal Society with that of
its Italian counterpart, the Cimento, in the 1660s seems worth making if only to suggest how divergent publication policies might serve
to stimulate or to stifle scientific advance. With the *Transactions*, the
Royal Society launched a continuous series that attracted an expanding list of subscribers and readers all over the world. The Cimento
issued only one single compendium, whose first edition could not
be locally bought or sold. The *Transactions* encouraged signed contributions and attracted authors even from abroad with the lure of
fame. Its editors took measures to ensure the protection of intellectual property rights by dating contributions and adjudicating priority
disputes. The *Saggi* tried to protect contributors from persecution by
leaving them anonymous. It thereby deprived them of the incentive
to make a public contribution while achieving personal fame.

As an institution which failed to survive...[the Cimento]
shows us something interesting about...the "reward structure"
of science. Within the social system of modern science, one
of the primary incentives for...original research is the desire

---

[79] Joseph Ben-David, "The Scientific Role: The Conditions of Its Establishment
in Europe," *Western Civilization: Recent Interpretations*, ed. C. D. Hamilton
(Chicago, 1973), 571. Originally published in *Minerva* IV (1965): 15–20.

for recognition and status . . . The Academy failed . . . because the enthusiasm of its most talented researchers was dampened by the anonymity of its only publication.[80]

Adverse publication policies also hurt the chief scientific society of Naples, as Max Fisch's article on the Academy of the Investigators suggests.[81] Its members were often on the verge of publication but almost never ventured over the brink. One of them, Tommaso Cornelio, postponed publication to the point where he "lost credit" for significant work in anatomy and physiology. English virtuosi, although slower in their research, were quicker to win eponymous fame. It has been suggested that Naples should have a place alongside Padua, Florence, Copenhagen, Paris, and London as a center of seventeenth-century scientific activity. Seventeenth-century Naples contained many distinguished virtuosi. But it was not a good location for any scientist who hoped to get his major works into print before he himself expired.

For Italian virtuosi, the "book of Nature" was not open to public inspection but was subject to expurgation, and large tracts were declared out of bounds. Libraries were ransacked and printers were imprisoned. Fear of persecution led to a different kind of self-censorship than that enjoined upon members of the Royal Society, who had to stay clear of politics and theology but could wander freely within nature's realm.

It is true that many Italians kept in touch with innovative literature from abroad. In Venice, especially, literati contributed much to republican and antipapist propaganda and also to the prolonged struggle for a free press. But what about the access of virtuosi and literati to funds for publication programs and to printers and patrons willing to risk carrying them out? Because this question is rarely posed, the most telling blows to early modern science dealt by clerical censorship are often overlooked. Instead of pointing to the clear and present threats posed by the decree of 1616 and the trial of

---

[80] Robert S. Westman, book review, *Renaissance Quarterly* XXVIII (Summer 1974): 223.

[81] "The Academy of the Investigators," *Science, Medicine and History. Essays . . . in Honor of Charles Singer.* ed. E. A. Underwood. 2 vols. (Oxford, 1953), I: 521–63.

A *T a Council of the* Royal Society *for Improving* Natural Knowledge, 27°· *Novembris* 1683. *Ordered, That a Book Entituled,* Essays of Natural Experiments, made in the Academie del Cimento, &c. *Tranſlated by Mr.* Richard Waller, *Fellow of this Society, be Printed.*

John Hoskyns *P. R. S.*

Fig. 44. The *Saggi*, or collected papers, of the Accademia del Cimento of Florence were translated and published in England before being issued in Italy, thanks to the Royal Society. Opposite, an engraved frontispiece showing a figure representing the Royal Society sitting on the right being handed the *Saggi*. Above, an order that the book be printed. Reproduced by kind permission of the Folger Shakespeare Library.

1633, careful distinctions are drawn between different theological positions taken by churchmen on the two occasions. These theological subtleties, however intrinsically interesting, still strike me as being somewhat beside the point.

The decree of 1616 described the doctrine of Copernicus as contrary to Scripture and therefore not to be defended or held. Nevertheless, we are told, the Copernican theory could still be presented as a hypothesis (albeit as an indefensible and absurd one). Moreover, "if there were any Catholic astronomers who had no doubt that the Copernican system was true," they did not have to violate their inner conviction of certitude. The decree requiring "interior assent" came from a fallible authority, and those who had no doubt "were excused."[82] Interior assent could be withheld. But what

[82] Langford, *Galileo, Science*, p. 103, n. 50.

about external dissent? On the strategic issue of publication, recent Catholic apologists have singularly little to say.

Whatever interpretation is placed on the edicts of 1616 and 1633, it can scarcely be doubted that they had an inhibiting effect on scientific publication programs in Catholic lands. When it asserted that the old world system had to be maintained as long as the new one was inadequately proved, and when it forbade further "attempts to demonstrate" that the new system was "true in fact,"[83] the church was not encouraging suspension of judgment or urging further investigation of the matter. The condemnations not only curtailed scientific publication programs, they also did much to block "thought experiments" based on envisaging the Copernican scheme as physically real.

> Poor Borelli! He was truly on the road to the great discovery . . . He renounced all theory beyond the brute, experimental fact and by this very means barred the road to progress. Hooke and Newton had more courage. It is the intellectual audacity of Newton just as much as his genius which permitted him to overcome the obstacles that stopped Borelli.[84]

When comparing Hooke and Newton with Borelli, one cannot afford to confine the terms of discussion to "internal" factors alone. Of course, the state of the art and the special talents of the gifted puzzle solvers have to be considered. But one must also give due weight to unevenly distributed "external" forces. Otherwise an unfair comparison will result. Borelli may or may not have been less courageous and less audacious than Newton. Surely he had fewer incentives to spur him on and more formidable obstacles to surmount. It is difficult to envisage a member of an Italian scientific society acting as Halley did, urging Newton to overcome his hesitations and to bring his grand design to completion, and then supervising its publication and assuring it favorable publicity. Friends of Catholic virtuosi were

---

[83] Ibid., 98–9.
[84] Alexandre Koyré, *La Revolution Astronomique: Copernic, Kepler, Borelli* (Paris, 1961), 506 (translation mine).

more likely to dissuade them from taking the condemned theory too seriously. Even without friends to dissuade them, devout Catholics would feel qualms about moving ahead on their own.

In this regard, the stage is set just as awkwardly for Galileo's trial as for other major historical events. The placing of *De revolutionibus* on the Index by the decree of 1616 and the prohibition of the *Lettera* by Paolo Antonio Foscarini (a sixty-four-page treatise published in 1615 by a Carmelite friar, which argued that the Copernican theory was physically plausible and theologically sound) are discussed in many studies. The hard lesson learned by Foscarini's printer, Lazaro Scoriggio, however, is rarely taken into account. "By the beginning of February 1616 Galileo . . . felt . . . victory was in sight. He wrote to secure permission . . . for a visit to Naples, probably to see Foscarini and if possible Campanella and to organize the campaign in favor of Copernicus."[85]

On March 5 the decree pertaining to Copernican doctrines was officially published. Foscarini's *Lettera*, which sought to reconcile Copernican views with Scripture, was "altogether prohibited and condemned." *De revolutionibus*, however, was merely "suspended until it be corrected." The distinction between the prohibition of the theological argument and the suspension of the astronomical treatise is frequently stressed by Catholic apologists and by others who try to soften the effect of the blow. Thus Langford suggests that it was "not really a serious setback to progress in astronomy" and Koestler argues that, despite the mistaken impression of "the man in the street," the "effect of the decree on scientific discussion and research was to leave things almost exactly where they had been."[86] Neither notes that in 1617, one year after the decree, the Amsterdam globe maker and map publisher, Willem Janszoon Blaeu, brought out a third edition of *De revolutionibus*. Perhaps Blaeu, like many of his competitors, was hoping to trade on the advantages of being listed on the Index. Perhaps he had laid plans for a 1617 publication date long before. Whatever the case, Blaeu's edition appeared at a time when

---

[85] Drake, *Discoveries and Opinions*, 218–20.
[86] Langford, *Galileo, Science*, 58–9; Koestler, *Sleepwalkers*, 458.

scientific publication programs bearing on physics and astronomy were being caught up in a familiar pattern – one that had already affected Erasmus, Boccaccio, Rabelais, Luther, and Machiavelli. New opportunities to profit from banned titles were extended to Protestant firms. At the same time, new risks and uncertainties were posed for scientific publishers in Catholic lands. Virtuosi engaged in scientific research were not unaffected by this turn of events. A member of the Lincei resigned, accusing Galileo of upholding forbidden views. Galileo withdrew his plan to visit Naples, ostensibly because of "bad roads." As Drake suggests, after March 5, 1616, the "road to Naples was . . . bad . . . in more than one sense . . . The printer who had published Foscarini's book there was soon to be imprisoned and the author died that same year under obscure circumstances."[87] The road to Naples never did improve so far as scientific publication programs were concerned.

Very much like Luther during the decade after 1517, Galileo during the decade after 1633 could count on the support of numerous publishers, printers, and booksellers to render papal actions ineffective even while they made profits on the side. The fate of the banned *Dialogue* demonstrated once again the advantage that accrued to Protestant publishers from purveying titles listed on the Index and the attraction exerted even by fairly recondite scientific treatises that were designated as forbidden fruit. According to de Santillana's colorful account, the black market profits made by the *Dialogue* were high:

> Priests, monks, prelates even, vie with each other in buying up copies of the *Dialogue* on the black market . . . the black market price of the book rises from the original half-scudo to four and six scudi [almost a hundred dollars in American money] all over Italy.[88]

Galileo's *Dialogue on Two World Systems* was such a provocative and polemical treatise, however, it almost seemed to court censorship

---

[87] Drake, *Discoveries and Opinions*, 219–20.
[88] Giorgio de Santillana, *The Crime of Galileo* (Chicago, 1955), 325.

in a way that is quite atypical of most serious scientific work. The same thing cannot be said of his later treatise which helped to found classical physics: the *Discourses on Two New Sciences*.

> No great cosmic or philosophical questions intrude into this unimpassioned treatise ... it is about as controversial and stirring as some freshman lecture on mechanics, of which indeed, it is the ultimate source.
>
> The crowning irony of Galileo's career is that the failure of the great *Dialogues* should be so much more interesting than the success of the unobjectionable *Discourses*.[89]

It is hard to think of a better example of the kind of "pure science" that is naturally placed *au-dessus de la mêlée* than the "ultimate source" of a "freshman lecture on mechanics." Yet the dull "unobjectionable" *Discourses* were also caught up in the fray. They were not deemed unobjectionable by those who kept Galileo under house arrest; their success was not uninteresting when one considers the means by which the book was brought out. Given an aging but resolute political prisoner whose captors had forbidden him to publish or even write anything ever again, a Dutch printer's visit to Italy, and the smuggling of a manuscript in a diplomat's pouch, the ingredients do not lack interest. They could even be woven into a narrative involving considerable suspense. "The book was completed in 1636 when Galileo was seventy-two," writes Arthur Koestler. "As he could not hope for an imprimatur in Italy, the manuscript was smuggled out to Leiden and published by the Elseviers. But it could also have been printed in Vienna where it was licensed, probably with imperial consent, by the Jesuit Father Paulus."[90]

One wonders what grounds there are for Koestler's optimism concerning possible Viennese publication, in view of the risk of reprisals Viennese printers would have to run. There were, after all, many powerful officials in Vienna who disapproved of the licensing and viewed any support of Galileo as a subversive act. Koestler's account,

---

[89] Charles C. Gillispie, *The Edge of Objectivity* (Princeton, NJ, 1960), 52.
[90] Koestler, *Sleepwalkers*, 494.

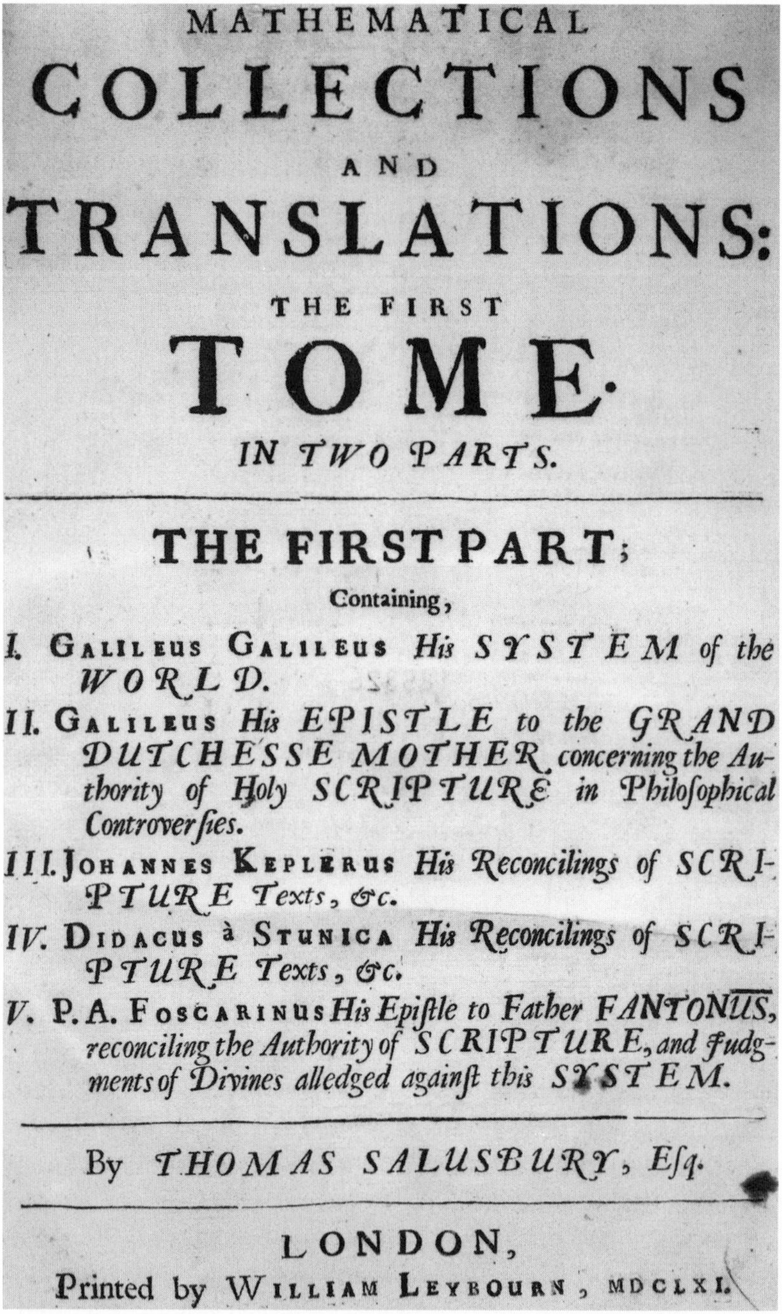

MATHEMATICAL
COLLECTIONS
AND
TRANSLATIONS:
THE FIRST
TOME.
IN TWO PARTS.

THE FIRST PART;

Containing,

I. GALILEUS GALILEUS *His* SYSTEM *of the* WORLD.

II. GALILEUS *His* EPISTLE *to the* GRAND DUTCHESSE MOTHER *concerning the Authority of Holy* SCRIPTURE *in Philosophical Controversies.*

III. JOHANNES KEPLERUS *His Reconcilings of* SCRIPTURE *Texts,* &c.

IV. DIDACUS à STUNICA *His Reconcilings of* SCRIPTURE *Texts,* &c.

V. P. A. FOSCARINUS *His Epistle to Father* FANTONUS, *reconciling the Authority of* SCRIPTURE, *and Judgments of Divines alledged against this* SYSTEM.

By THOMAS SALUSBURY, *Esq.*

LONDON,
Printed by WILLIAM LEYBOURN, MDCLXI.

Fig. 45. A key figure in the English exploitation of the publicity value of church action against Galileo was Thomas Salusbury, who translated all the censored treatises and published them by popular subscription after the Restoration. This title page shows how banned works by Kepler and Foscarini as well as Galileo were publicized for Protestant readers. Reproduced by kind permission of the Department of Special Collections, Stanford University Libraries.

DISCORSI
E
DIMOSTRAZIONI
MATEMATICHE,
intorno à due nuoue scienze

Attenenti alla

MECANICA & i MOVIMENTI LOCALI,

del Signor

GALILEO GALILEI LINCEO,

Filosofo e Matematico primario del Serenissimo
Grand Duca di Toscana.

Con vna Appendice del centro di grauità d'alcuni Solidi.

IN LEIDA,
Appresso gli Elsevirii. M. D. C. XXXVIII.

Fig. 46. Although Galileo's final treatise was devoid of polemics and consisted of a dry exposition of mechanics, it had to be smuggled out of his house. A member of the Dutch printing dynasty, Louis Elsevier, made a trip to Italy to secure the manuscript, and, as this title page shows, it was printed by the Elsevier firm in Leiden in 1638. Reproduced by kind permission of the Department of Special Collections, Stanford University Libraries.

here as elsewhere, seems to underrate the forces of reaction and needs to be balanced against evidence supplied by other accounts.

> As soon as the *Discourses on Two New Sciences* is licensed in Olmutz by the bishop and then in Vienna, obviously under direct imperial orders by the Jesuit Father Paulus, the other Jesuits start in hot pursuit after the book. "I have not been able" writes Galileo . . . in 1639, "to obtain a single copy of my new dialogue . . . Yet I know that they circulated through all the northern countries. The copies lost must be those which, as soon as they arrived in Prague were immediately bought by the Jesuit fathers so that not even the Emperor was able to get one." The charitable explanation would be that they knew what they were doing. Someone at least may have understood that Galileo's work in dynamics went on quietly establishing the foundations of the system that he had been forbidden to defend. But they were like that gallant man of whom Milton speaks who thought to pound in the crows by shutting the park gate.[91]

When considering the factors that affected the establishment of the foundations of modern science, the difference between getting published by the Elseviers in Holland and being licensed by Father Paulus in Vienna is worth keeping in mind.

On this one issue the currently unfashionable and undeniably old-fashioned "Whig interpretation of history" may still have a useful message to convey. Milton's plea for the "liberty of Unlicenc'd Printing" and his comments in *Areopagitica* about visiting Galileo "grown old as a prisoner of the Inquisition for thinking in Astronomy otherwise than the Dominican licensers thought"[92] ought not to be lightly dismissed as *nothing* but antipapist propaganda – although it certainly was that. Granted that the case of Galileo was exploited to the hilt by Protestant publicists and pamphleteers such as Milton himself, it

---

[91] de Santillana, *Crime of Galileo*, 326.

[92] John Milton, "Areopagitica," reprinted in *The Complete Prose Works of John Milton*, ed. Don M. Wolfe (New Haven, 1959), II:538.

was not merely used to link science with Protestantism. It disclosed a link that had been forged ever since printing industries had begun to flourish in Wittenberg and Geneva and had begun to decline in Venice and Lyons. The continuous operation of printing firms beyond the reach of Rome was of vital concern to Western European scientists. The case of Galileo simply drove this lesson further home.

CHAPTER EIGHT

CONCLUSION

SCRIPTURE AND NATURE
TRANSFORMED

The elements which go into the making of "modernity" may be seen ... first ... in the sixteenth and seventeenth centuries. Some historians attributed the change to the liberation of men's minds during the Renaissance and the Reformation. Today many historians would be more likely to stress the conservatism of these two movements ... Their emphasis tends instead to fall on ... "the Scientific Revolution."

By this is meant above all the imaginative achievements associated with the names of Copernicus, Galileo and Newton ... Within the space of a century and a half a revolution had occurred in the way in which men regarded the universe. Most of this was made possible by the application of mathematics to the problems of the natural world ...

All this is by now well known ... though many of the details are still to be worked out ... What is not clear is how it all came about.[1]

This book has been aimed at developing a new strategy for handling the issues posed by the opening citation. It seems futile to argue over "the elements which go into the making of modernity," for "modernity" itself is always in flux, always subject to definitions which have to be changed in order to keep up with changing times. As the age of Planck and Einstein recedes into the past, "achievements associated with Copernicus, Galileo and Newton"

---

[1] Hugh F. Kearney, introduction, *Origins of the Scientific Revolution* (London, 1966), xi.

will probably come to share the fate of the achievements of earlier Renaissance humanists and Protestant reformers. Indeed, recent interpretations of Copernicus show that his work is already coming to seem more and more conservative, less and less associated with emancipation from traditional modes of thought. Pointing early modern science toward an elusive modernity leads to invidious comparisons between "liberating" later movements and earlier "conservative" ones and brings us no closer to understanding "how it all came about."

To ask historians to search for elements which entered into the making of an indefinite "modernity" seems somewhat futile. To consider the effects of a definite communications shift which entered into each of the movements under discussion seems more promising. Among other advantages, this approach offers a chance to uncover relationships which debates over modernity serve only to conceal. Thus one may avoid entanglement in arguments over whether the first-born sons of modern Europe were to be found among the humanists of Renaissance Italy, or whether we must wait for the pope to be defied by Luther, or for the Calvinists to turn Geneva into a Protestant Rome; whether genuine modernity came with the scientific revolution or should be postponed even further until industrialization. Energies can be directed toward the more constructive task of discerning, in each of the contested movements, features which were not present in earlier epochs and which altered the textual traditions upon which each movement relied.

By setting aside the quest for theoretical "modernizing" processes and focusing attention on the paradoxical consequences of a real duplicating process, it should be possible to handle periodization problems more deftly. We can see how movements aimed at returning to a golden past (whether classical or early Christian) were reoriented in a manner that pointed away from their initial goal and how the very process of recovering long-lost texts carried successive generations ever further away from the experience of the church fathers and of the poets and orators of antiquity. We can also see how lay humanists, priests, and natural philosophers alike shared the common experience of acquiring new means to achieve old ends and that this experience led, in turn, to a division of opinion and ultimately to a reassessment of inherited views.

To adopt this strategy does not make it possible to provide a complete answer to questions of "how it all came about," but it does open the way to supplying more adequate answers than have been offered up to now. Thus we would be in a better position to explain why long-lived scientific theories were deemed less acceptable even before new observations, new experiments, or new instruments had been made.

> It is one of the paradoxes of the whole story with which we have to deal that the most sensational step leading to the scientific revolution in astronomy was taken long before the discovery of the telescope – even before ... improvement ... in observations made with the naked eye ... William Harvey ... carried out his revolutionary work before any serviceable kind of microscope had become available ... even Galileo discusses the ordinary phenomena of everyday life [and] ... plays with pellets on inclined planes in a manner that had long been customary.[2]

Current efforts to account for this seeming paradox do not take us very far. We are asked to guess about a transformation that took "place inside the minds of the scientists themselves" when they "put on new thinking caps" to gaze at the unchanging heavens. Yet the technical literature upon which astronomers relied had undergone change even before the "new thinking caps" were put on. More careful consideration of the shift that altered the output and intake of this literature would help to explain the timing of the "sensational step" and also help us analyze its relationship to other "modernizing" trends.

When considering Copernicus's intellectual environment, changes wrought by printing deserve a more central place. Present tactics either encourage us to wander too far afield compiling lists of everything that happened and marveling at the general turbulence

[2]   Herbert Butterfield, *The Origins of Modern Science 1300–1800*, rev. ed. (New York, 1951), 1.

of the times, or else trap us into prolonging old debates – between Platonists and Aristotelians, scholastics and humanists; Catholics and Protestants, Anglicans and Puritans; even, on occasion, among Italians, Germans, Danes, and Poles. By placing more emphasis on the shift from script to print, many diverse trends may be accommodated without resort to an indiscriminate mélange and in a way that avoids prolongation of intellectual feuds. The sixteenth-century astronomer may be seen to owe something to the neo-Platonists and to the Renaissance Aristotelians; to his masters in Catholic Poland and Italy and to a disciple from Protestant Wittenberg later; to calculations made by ancient Alexandrians, observations made by medieval Arabs, and a trigonometry text compiled in Nuremberg around the time he was born.

We are less likely to set Plato against Aristotle or any one textual tradition against another when we appreciate the significance of setting many disparate texts side by side. The character of Copernicus's studies and of the currents of thought which influenced him are certainly worth studying. But this investigation should not divert us from recognizing the novelty of being able to assemble diverse records and reference guides and of being able to study them without having to transcribe them at the same time. If we want to explain heightened awareness of anomalies or discontent with inherited schemes, then it seems especially important to emphasize the wider range of reading matter that was being surveyed at one time by a single pair of eyes.

Similarly, in seeking to explain why naked-eye observation produced unprecedented results, it is worth paying more attention to the increased output of materials relating to comets and conjunctions and the increased number of simultaneous observations made of single celestial events. Nor should we neglect to note how stars which faded from the heavens (and brief landfalls made on distant shores) could be fixed permanently in precise locations after printed maps began to replace hand-copied ones. Although inferior maps continued to be duplicated and many map publishers perpetuated errors for a century or more, a process of transmission had been fundamentally reoriented when this replacement occurred. Analogies with inertial

motion do not apply to this sort of reversal. When considering a
shift in direction, it is misleading to draw analogies with uniform
motion in a straight line. Since corrupt data were duplicated and thus
perpetuated by print, one may say that scribal corruption was prolonged for some time. But one must also take into account that an
age-old process of corruption was being decisively arrested and was
eventually reversed.

Even while we acknowledge the appeal of the slogan "from books
to nature," we need to recognize the importance of putting more of
nature into books. Here as elsewhere, claims made for the significance of particular developments in special fields such as Renaissance
art or Renaissance Aristotelianism need to be coupled with more
consideration of how separate developments (the separate talents
of painters and physicians, for example) could be coordinated and
combined. When Agricola and Vesalius hired illustrators to render
"veins" or "vessels" for their texts, they were launching an unprecedented enterprise and not simply continuing trends that manuscript
illuminators had begun.

The advantages of issuing identical images bearing identical labels
to scattered observers who could feed back information to publishers enabled astronomers, geographers, botanists, and zoologists to
expand data pools far beyond all previous limits – even those set by
the exceptional resources of the long-lasting Alexandrian Museum.
Old limits set by the pillars of Hercules and the outermost sphere
of the Grecian heavens were incapable of containing findings registered in ever-expanding editions of atlases and sky maps. The closed
world of the ancients was opened; vast expanses of space (and later
of time) previously associated with divine mysteries became subject
to human calculation and exploration. The same cumulative cognitive advance which excited cosmological speculation also led to
new concepts of knowledge. The notion of a closed sphere or single
corpus, passed down from generation to generation, was replaced by
the new idea of an open-ended investigatory process pressing against
ever-advancing frontiers.

In the attempt to explain "how it all came about," finally, new
elements involving coordination and cooperation deserve not only
more attention but also a more central place. When searching for

the nurseries of a new philosophy, it seems unprofitable to linger too long in any one region, university, court, or town – or to focus too much attention on any one special skill or special scientific field. Certain universities, ateliers, or lay academies may be singled out for special contributions. But the chief new feature that needs further attention is the simultaneous tapping of many varied talents at the same time. As the chief sponsors of field trips, open letters, advertisements for instruments, and technical handbooks of all kinds, early printers ought to receive as much attention as is currently given to special occupational groups such as Paduan professors, Wittenberg botanists, or quattrocento artist-engineers. Publication programs launched from urban workshops in many regions made it possible to coordinate scattered efforts and to expand the scope of investigations until (like the *Grand Atlas* produced by the son of W. J. Blaeu) they became truly worldwide.

Attempts to account for the rapid growth and expansion of scientific enterprise during the century of genius may be handled in much the same manner as treatments of nurseries, seed beds, and births. In explaining the "acceleration of scientific advance," there is much disagreement over whether to stress the role played by individual genius, the internal evolution of a speculative tradition, a new alliance between intellectuals and artisans, or a host of concurrent socioeconomic or religious changes affecting the "environment against which these discoveries took place."[3] To say that argument over such issues is pointless, because *all* these "factors" were at work, still leaves open the question of how and why they became operative when they did. Unless some new strategy is devised to handle this question, the old argument will break out once again. Since it perpetually revolves about the same issues, diminishing returns soon set in. One advantage of bringing printing into the discussion is that it enables us to tackle the open question directly without prolonging the same controversy ad infinitum.

As previous remarks suggest, the effects produced by printing may be plausibly related to an increased incidence of creative acts, to

---

[3]   Hugh F. Kearney, "Puritanism, Capitalism and the Scientific Revolution," *Past and Present* 28 (July 1964): 81.

FRANCISCI
DE VERULAMIO/
Summi Angliæ
CANCELARII/
Instauratio
magna.

Multi pertransibunt & augebitur scientia.

LONDINI
Apud Joannem Billium
Typographum
Regium.

Anno

1620.

Fig. 47. This engraved title page of Francis Bacon, *Instauratio magna* (London, 1620), shows how the image of "sailing beyond the pillars of Hercules" was associated with the advancement of learning in the early seventeenth century. Overseas voyages were linked to an expansion of data pools, which enabled modern investigators to outstrip ancient ones. Reproduced by kind permission of the Folger Shakespeare Library.

internally transformed speculative traditions, to exchanges between intellectuals and artisans, and indeed to each of the contested factors in current disputes. Thus we need not invoke some sort of "mutation in the human gene pool" to explain an entire "century of genius"; nor do we need to deny that random motives (both personal and playful) entered into the successful puzzle solving of the age. Without detracting from the strong personal flavor of each separate creative act, we may also make room for the new print technology which made food for thought much more abundant and allowed mental energies to be more efficiently used.

A similar approach would also take us further toward bridging the false dichotomy between the life of science and that of society at large. Changes wrought by printing had a more immediate effect on cerebral activities and on the learned professions than did many other kinds of "external" events. Previous relations between masters and disciples were altered. Students who took advantage of technical texts which served as silent instructors were less likely to defer to traditional authority and more receptive to innovating trends. Young minds provided with updated editions, especially of mathematical texts, began to surpass not only their own elders but the wisdom of ancients as well. Methods of measurement, records of observations, and all forms of data collection were affected by printing. So too were the careers that could be pursued by teachers and preachers, physicians and surgeons, reckon masters and artist-engineers. "It is easy to agree with . . . contentions that a neat separation of internal and external factors is out of the question . . . but, as G. R. Elton wrote several years ago, there is work to be done rather than called for."[4]

Before work can be done, however, some promising avenues of inquiry have to be opened up and more attention given to the presence of new workshops alongside older lecture halls. Printed materials should be allowed to affect thought patterns, facilitate problem solving, and, in general, penetrate the "life of the mind." Printers themselves must be allowed to work with Latin-writing professors

[4] "Toward a New History of the New Science," *Times Literary Supplement* (15 September 1972): 1058.

as well as with vernacular-writing publicists and pamphleteers. In other words, the divisions that are often assumed to separate scholars from craftsmen, universities from urban workshops, need to be reappraised.

This point applies to theories which internalize scientific problem solving to the extent of ignoring the communications revolution and neglecting its possible relevance to the lectures and studies of learned men. It also applies to theories which deny that churchmen and schoolmen are capable of launching innovating trends. In this respect, Marxist theories of class struggle seem to be more of a hindrance than a help. To set an avant garde of early capitalists against a rear guard of Latin-reading clerks does little to clarify medieval developments and much to conceal the new interchanges that came after print shops spread. There are perfectly good reasons for associating printers with merchants and capitalists. There are none for detaching them from association with professors and friars – especially in the age of scholar-printers, when close collaboration was the rule. Indeed, preachers and teachers often turned to new forms of publicity with less conflict than did artisans accustomed to preserving trade secrets. Early printers were invited to set up presses in monasteries and colleges, while schoolmasters and tutors were much in demand as editors and translators. The formation of lay cultural centers outside universities and of the vernacular-translation movement was of major significance. But no less significant were changes that affected university faculties and students seeking professional degrees. When Latin-writing professional elites are insulated from the effects of the new technology, internal divisions within the scholarly community become more puzzling than they need to be, and a rare opportunity to watch "external" forces enter into the "internal" life of science is lost.

These points carry beyond the special field of the history of science to the more general problem of relating socioeconomic and political developments to intellectual and cultural ones. Attention focused on a communications shift encourages us to relate mind to society and at the same time avoid forcing connections between economic class and intellectual superstructure in order to fit a prefabricated scheme.

Plausible relationships can be traced by taking into account the connecting links provided by a new communications network which coordinated diverse intellectual activities while producing tangible commodities to be marketed for profit. Since their commodities were sponsored and censored by officials as well as consumed by literate groups, the activities of early printers provide a natural way of linking the movement of ideas to economic developments and to affairs of church and state.

The policies pursued by some of the more successful sixteenth-century merchant-publishers offer a useful corrective to the conventional wisdom, which opposes "forward-looking" centralizing rulers and nation-building statesmen to "backward" petty principalities and late medieval walled city-states. The printing industries represented a "forward-looking," large-scale enterprise which flourished better in small loosely federated realms than in well-consolidated larger ones. Printers also injected into diverse Protestant literary cultures foreign secular ingredients which will appear anomalous unless the peculiar workings of a censored book trade are taken into account. When tracing the movement of ideas from Catholic South to Protestant North, factors which led to the prior movement of printing industries ought to be given due weight. How the center of gravity of the Republic of Letters shifted from sixteenth-century Venice to late seventeenth-century Amsterdam warrants special consideration in any social history of ideas.

When searching for the "seedplots of Enlightenment thought," the modus operandi of the more celebrated master printers (such as Aldus Manutius, Robert Estienne, Oporinus, Plantin) deserves a closer look and so too does the relatively aristocratic nature of their clientele. As Martin Lowry's biography of Aldus points out, when the Venetian printer discarded the large folio in favor of a smaller octavo format, he was aiming at serving the convenience of scholar-diplomats and patrician councillors of state. He was not thinking, somewhat absurdly, of tapping popular markets with texts devoted to classical Greek works. From the Aldine octavo of the 1500s to the Elsevier duodecimo of the 1630s, the circulation of convenient pocket-sized editions altered circumstances within the Commonwealth of Learning first of all. Before we assume that an altered worldview implies the rise of a new class, it seems worth devoting more thought to intellectual regrouping among Latin-reading elites. By this means we may also rectify an imbalance created by current emphasis on popularizing trends and mass movements.

The evangelical impulse which powered early presses had the most rapid, spectacular consequences and provoked mass participation of new kinds. But this should not divert attention from more subtle, yet equally irreversible, transformations which altered the worldview of Latin-reading elites. Several new features other than dissemination which were introduced by printing entered into the scientific revolution and played an essential part in the religious reformation as well. In relating the two movements, we need to consider the way old attitudes were being implemented within learned communities before expecting new attitudes to be created, let alone knowledge to be disseminated to whole new classes. Even when dealing with evangelical trends, this approach has merit. Earlier attitudes exhibited by Lollards, Waldensians, Hussites, and the Brethren of the Common Life were being newly implemented by printing before full-fledged Protestant doctrines were born. In setting the stage for the Reformation, moreover, some attention must be given to those many pre-Reformation controversies which had less to do with vernacular translation than with trilingual studies and learned exegesis of Latin texts. In the scholar-printer's workshop, editors of patristic and of Alexandrian texts had a common point of encounter. More attention to changes affecting textual transmission among learned elites should bring us closer to understanding how different strands of early modern intellectual history may be related to each other. In particular, it may help to clarify the relationship between religious and scientific change.

Thus we may see that the fate of texts inherited from Aristotle, Galen, and Ptolemy had much in common with that of texts inherited from church fathers, such as Saint Jerome. Just as scribal scholars had all they could do to emend Saint Jerome's translation of the Bible and to protect it from further corruption, so too did medieval astronomers labor to preserve and emend Ptolemy's *Great Composition*. Much as trilingual studies, repeatedly called for, did not get launched until after the advent of printing, so too was reform of the Julian calendar frequently requested and never obtained. After the advent of printing, Jerome's version was protected from further corruption only to be threatened by the annotations of scholars who had acquired mastery of Hebrew and Greek. Similarly, Ptolemy's work was no sooner emended and purified than it too came under attack. As the "second Ptolemy," Copernicus (despite his personal distance from printing shops) was cast in much the same role as was Erasmus, who had set out to redo the work of Saint Jerome. Both men set out to fulfill traditional programs: to emend the Bible and reform the church; to emend the *Almagest* and help with calendar reform; but both used means that were untraditional, and this propelled their work in an unconventional direction, so that they broke new paths in the very act of seeking to achieve old goals.

The new issues posed by sixteenth-century path-breaking works also led natural philosophers and theologians to divide along similar lines. Conservatives within both groups were placed in the awkward position of departing from precedents even while defending the status quo. Defenders of Aristotle and Galen who sought to fine professors for departing from fixed texts resembled those defenders of Jerome's translation who censored scholars for annotating scriptural editions. At the same time many churchmen and lay professors were attracted by new opportunities extended by printers to reach a wide audience, win new patrons, and achieve celebrity. Members of both groups contributed their services as editors, translators, and authors to popular as well as to scholarly trends. Theologians who argued for a priesthood of all believers and translated Bibles were in much the same position as the friars, physicians, and schoolmasters who compiled craft manuals and translated mathematical and medical texts. The vernacular-translation movement not only enabled evangelists to bring the Gospel to everyman but also tapped a vast reservoir of latent scientific talent by eliciting contributions from reckon masters, instrument makers, and artist-engineers. Protestant encouragement of lay reading and self-help was especially favorable for interchanges between readers and publishers – which led to the quiet displacement of ancient authorities, such as Pliny, and to expansive data collection of a new kind. Finally, the same censorship policies and elitist tendencies that discouraged Catholic Bible printers eventually closed down scientific publication outlets in Catholic lands.

But although Protestant exploitation of printing linked the Reformation to early modern science in diverse ways, and although scientific publication was increasingly taken over by Protestant printing firms, evangelists and virtuosi were still using the new powers of print for fundamentally different ends. The latter aimed not at spreading God's words, but at deciphering His handiwork. The only way to "open" the book of nature to public inspection required (paradoxically) a preliminary encoding of data into ever more sophisticated equations, diagrams, models, and charts. For virtuosi the uses of publicity were much more problematic than for evangelists. The case of Galileo may be misleading in this regard. Exploiting his flair for publicity and gifts as a polemicist, he *did* act as a proselytizer for the Copernican cause. Catholic friars such as Bruno, Campanella, and Foscarini also exhibited a kind of evangelical zeal in the same cause. So, too, did Rheticus, in his master's behalf. Nevertheless, the downfall of Ptolemy, Galen, and Aristotle did not come about as a result of cartoons and pamphleteering. Scientific change follows a different pattern from religious revivals. Publication was indispensable for anyone seeking to make a scientific contribution, but the kind of publicity which made for bestsellerdom was often undesirable. Even now, reputable scientists fear the sensational coverage which comes from premature exposure of their views. Early modern virtuosi had even better reasons for such fears. Many Copernicans (including Copernicus himself) took advantage of printed materials while shrinking from publicity. Many Puritan publicists and disciples of Francis Bacon proselytized on behalf of a "new science" without favoring or even comprehending the technical Latin treatises which marked significant advance.

Visionary schemes for promoting useful knowledge, belief in science for the citizen and mathematics for the millions, did, to be sure, enter into the views of the group responsible for the

Transactions of the Royal Society. Nevertheless, contributions to this pioneering scientific journal were of significance insofar as they accomplished the purpose Oldenburg conveyed in his letter to Malpighi: to "bring out the opinion of all the learned." To make possible consensual validation by trained observers, experimenters, and mathematicians entailed a different use of the press from efforts to spread glad tidings to all men. Eventually, access to scientific journals and societies was shut to all save a professionally trained elite. The rise of modern science entailed the discrediting, not only of Aristotelians, Galenists, or Ptolemaists, but also of self-proclaimed healers, "empirics," and miracle workers who attacked book learning while publicizing themselves. From Paracelsus through Mesmer and on to the present, the press has lent itself to the purposes of pseudo-scientists as well as those of real scientists, and it is not always easy to tell the two groups apart. Distinguishing between scientific journals and sensational journalism is relatively simple at present. But during the early years of the Royal Society, when sightings of monsters and marvels were still being credited and recorded, the two genres were easily confused. Confusion was further compounded by the workings of the Index, which lumped dull treatises on physics with more sensational forbidden tracts and transformed advocacy of Copernicanism into a patriotic Protestant cause.

Thus a sixteenth-century English writer did not find it incongruous to place the secretive Latin-writing Catholic Copernicus in the company of Lutheran reformers for having "brought Ptolemeus' Rules Astronomicall and Tables of Motions" to "their former puritie." His argument suggests that Protestants linked the fate of the Vulgate with that of the *Almagest* – along lines which are by now familiar to the readers of this book. Much as the Protestants had purified Scripture, he said, "by expelling the clowdes of Romish religion which had darkened the trueth of the worde of God," so too Copernicus had purified tables which had become corrupted "by a long excess of time."[5] Copernicus was thus cast in much the

---

[5]   Cited by Debus, *English Paracelsians*, p. 59, from a treatise by "R. Bostocke Esq.," London, 1585.

same role as the editor of the London "Polyglotte" who claimed in his prospectus to have freed the Scriptures "from error, from the negligence of scribes, the injury of times, the wilful corruption of sectaries and heretics."[6] This relatively conservative theme, with its emphasis on emendation and purification, also lent itself to the purposes of those who sought to legitimize the Royal Society, as is suggested by the often-cited comment from Bishop Sprat's *History of the Royal Society*. The Royal Society and the Anglican church, the bishop said, both may lay equal claim to the word Reformation,

> the one having compassed it in Religion, the other purposing it in Philosophy . . . They both have taken a like course to bring this about each of them passing by the corrupt copies and referring themselves to the perfect originals for their instruction; the one to Scripture the other to the huge Volume of Creatures.[7]

It seems significant that when such remarks are cited by historians they are not seen to relate to the shift from script to print (despite the reference to the passing by of "corrupt copies"), but are used instead to reiterate the bishop's three-hundred-year-old claim that the Reformation and the scientific revolution are somehow connected. As long as printing is left out of the account, this thesis seems destined to engender an inconclusive debate. To leave printing out of the picture is not only to conceal significant links but also to overlook important disjunctions.

Scriptural and scientific traditions had taken a "like course" in the age of scribes. By the time of the Reformation, however, they had come to a parting of the ways. Even while providing both biblical scholars and natural philosophers with new means of achieving long-lived goals, the new technology had driven a wedge between the two groups and was propelling them in different directions.

---

[6]   Brian Walton's prospectus for the London "Polyglotte" of 1657 is cited by Donald Hendricks, "Profitless Printing: Publication of the Polyglots," *The Journal of Library History* II (April 1967).

[7]   Sprat, *History of the Royal Society*, pt. 3, sec. 23, p. 371.

Until the advent of printing, scientific inquiries about "how the heavens go" were linked with religious concerns about "how to go to heaven." Erasmus and Copernicus had shared a common interest in deciphering ancient place names and dating old records. Insofar as the movable holy festival of Easter posed problems, astronomers were needed to help the church commemorate Gospel truths. After the advent of printing, however, the study of celestial mechanics was propelled in new directions and soon reached levels of sophistication that left calendrical problems and ancient schemes of reckoning far behind.

The need to master philology or learn Greek became ever more important for Bible study and less so for nature study. Indeed, difficulties engendered by diverse Greek and Arabic expressions, by medieval Latin abbreviations, by confusion between Roman letters and numbers, by neologisms, copyists' errors, and the like were so successfully overcome that modern scholars are frequently absent-minded about the limitations on progress in the mathematical sciences which scribal procedures imposed. From Roger Bacon's day to that of Francis Bacon, mastery of geometry, astronomy, or optics had gone together with the retrieval of ancient texts and the pursuit of Greek studies. But by the seventeenth century, nature's language was being emancipated from the old confusion of tongues. Diverse names for flora and fauna became less confusing when placed beneath identical pictures. Constellations and landmasses could be located without recourse to uncertain etymologies, once they were placed on uniform maps and globes. Logarithm tables and slide rules provided common measures for surveyors in different lands. Whereas the Vulgate was followed by a succession of polyglot editions and multiplying variants, the downfall of the *Almagest* paved the way for the formulation by Newton of a few elegant, simple universal laws. The development of neutral pictorial and mathematical vocabularies made possible a large-scale pooling of talents for analyzing data and led to the eventual achievement of a consensus that cut across all the old frontiers.

Vesalius's recourse to pictorial statements, like Galileo's preference for circles and triangles, suggests why it is unwise to dwell too long on whether treatises were written in the vernacular or in Latin and why parallels between evangelical reformers and early modern scientists should not be pressed too far. Many proponents of the new philosophy favored plain speaking and opposed mystification just as did evangelical reformers. Nevertheless, the language employed by new astronomers and anatomists was still incomprehensible to the untutored layman and did not resemble anything spoken by the man in the street. For the most part, it was an *unspoken* language quite unlike that favored by Protestants, who preserved links between pulpit and press in seeking to spread the Word. Recourse to "silent instructors" conveying precisely detailed nonphonetic messages helped to free technical literature from semantic snares. "The reign of words" had ended, noted Fontenelle in 1733. "Things" were now in demand. Two hundred years earlier, verbal dispute was already being abandoned in favor of visual demonstration. "I dare affirm a man shall more profit in one week by figures and charts well and perfectly made than he shall by the only reading or hearing the rules of that science by the space of half a year at the least." So wrote Thomas Elyot in 1531, in the course of recommending courses in drawing to educators.

Publication before printing had often entailed giving dictation or reading aloud. In contrast to scribal culture, which had fostered "hearing the rules of a given science," print culture made possible the simultaneous distribution of well-made figures and charts. In this way, it not only transformed communications within the Commonwealth of Learning, but it laid the basis for new confidence in human capacity to arrive at certain knowledge of the "laws of Nature and of Nature's God."

What threatened the very foundations of the Church was the new concept of truth proclaimed by Galileo. Alongside the truth of revelation comes now an independent and original truth of nature. This truth is revealed not in God's words but in his work; it is not based on the testimony of Scripture or tradition but is visible to us at all times. But it is understandable only to those who know nature's handwriting and can decipher her text. The truth of nature cannot be expressed in mere words . . . [but] . . . in mathematical constructions, figures and numbers. And in these symbols nature presents itself in perfect form and clarity. Revelation by means of the sacred word can never achieve . . . such precision, for words are always . . . ambiguous . . . Their meaning must always be given them by man . . . In nature . . . the whole plan of the universe lies before us.[8]

This famous passage from Ernst Cassirer's *The Philosophy of the Enlightenment* brilliantly describes a major intellectual transformation but stops short of explaining why it happened when it did. Cassirer's description needs to be supplemented by noting that "mathematical constructions, figures and numbers" had not always presented themselves "in perfect form and clarity." "To discover the truth of propositions in Euclid," wrote John Locke, "there is little need or use of revelation, God having furnished us with a natural and surer means to arrive at knowledge of them."[9] In the eleventh century, however, God had not furnished Western scholars with a natural or sure means of grasping a Euclidean theorem. Instead, the most learned men in Christendom engaged in a fruitless search to discover what Euclid meant when he referred to interior angles.

A new confidence in the accuracy of mathematical constructions, figures, and numbers was predicated on a method of duplication that transcended older limits imposed by time and space and that presented identical data in identical form to men who were otherwise divided by cultural and geographical frontiers. The same confidence was generated by pictorial statements which, as Sir Joseph Banks observed in connection with engravings of plants and rocks observed on Captain Cook's expedition, provided a common measure which spoke "universally to all mankind."[10] It was conveyed by the maps to which Kenneth Boulding assigns an "extraordinary authority greater

---

[8] Cassirer, *The Philosophy of the Enlightenment*, tr. F. Koellen and J. Pettegrove (Princeton, 1951), 43.

[9] John Locke, *An Essay on Human Understanding*, book IV, chap. XVIII.

[10] Bernard Smith, "European Vision and the South Pacific," 67.

than that of all sacred books."[11] But it was not generated by the scholarly controversies which accompanied the expanding editions of the sacred book of Western Christendom.

Even while the study of nature was increasingly freed from translation problems, the study of Scripture was becoming more ensnared. Not only did vernacular translations fragment the religious experience of the peoples of Latin Christendom and help to precipitate prolonged civil wars, but successive polyglot versions brought the erudite scholars of the Commonwealth of Learning no closer to finding the pure original words of God. Tycho Brahe, confronted by conflicting astronomical tables based on corrupted data, could carry out his vow to check both versions against a "pure original" – against fresh observation of uncorrupted "writing in the sky." But dissatisfaction with corrupted copies of Saint Jerome's Latin translation could not be overcome in the same way. Instead, it led to multilingual confusion and a thickening special literature devoted to variants and alternative theories of composition. The mystical illumination which had presided over creation flickered ever more dimly as pedants argued about how to date the event and how to authenticate versions of Genesis. Baroque monuments of erudition, which had been designed to obtain a clear view of the divine will, not only fell short of their objective; in the end, they made it seem more elusive than before.

It is surely one of the ironies of the history of Western civilization that Bible studies aimed at penetrating Gothic darkness in order to recover pure Christian truth – aimed, that is, at removing glosses and commentaries in order to lay bare the pure "plain" text – ended by interposing an impenetrable thicket of recondite annotation between Bible reader and Holy Book. In his inaugural lecture at Wittenberg, the young Philip Melanchthon scornfully referred to the neglect of Greek studies by angelic doctors, to the superficial glosses of ignorant scribes, and to the soiling of sacred Scriptures with foreign matter. He called for a return to the "pure" Greek and Hebrew sources.[12] But the more trilingual studies progressed,

[11]   Boulding, The Image, 67.
[12]   Melanchthon's lecture is cited in The Reformation, ed. Hillerbrand, 59–60.

the more scholars wrangled over the meaning of words and phrases and even over the placement of vowel points. The very waters from which the Latinists drank became roiled and muddy as debates among scholars were prolonged. Hobbes and Spinoza both plunged into Bible study and found in the sharp clarity of Euclidean proofs a refreshing contrast to the murky ambiguities of scriptural texts. Sir William Petty protested against teaching boys "hard Hebrew words in the Bible" and contrasted the profitable "study of things to a Rabble of Words."[13] We have already encountered Sir Thomas Browne's preference for "Archimedes who speaketh exactly" as against "the sacred text which speaketh largely." Robert Boyle might endow a lecture series to reconcile scriptural revelation with the mathematical principles of natural philosophy; Isaac Newton might struggle to prove Old Testament tales conformed to a chronology that meshed with celestial clockwork. God's "two books," nevertheless, had come to a parting of the ways.

> One day in the eighteenth century, some Swedish scientists dis-
> covered a certain alteration in the shores of the Baltic ... the the-
> ologians of Stockholm made representations to the Government
> that "this remark of the ... scientists, not being consistent with
> Genesis must be condemned." To whom reply was made that God
> had made both the Baltic and the Genesis ... if there was any con-
> tradiction between the two works, the error must lie in the copies
> we have of the book rather than in the Baltic Sea of which we
> have the original.[14]

Thus the effect of printing on Bible study was in marked con-trast with its effect on nature study. This contrast is concealed when one places an exclusive emphasis on popularizing themes and cou-ples the spread of vernacular Bibles with that of technical texts. It is also obscured by the antipapist propaganda which linked the emendation of the *Almagest* with that of the Vulgate. Corruption by copyists had provided churchmen and astronomers with a common

[13] Petty's comments are cited by Jones, *Ancients and Moderns*, 91.
[14] Wilson, *Diderot*, 143.

enemy; but once this enemy was vanquished, former collaborators took divergent paths. To observe this divergence requires studying internal transformations within a Commonwealth of Learning where Latin Bibles had long been studied although full polyglot editions had not been seen. In addition to new problems posed for this community by polyglot versions of sacred words, old limits set on data collection and new advantages provided by printed tables, charts, and maps also need to be taken into account. One may then set the stage for Enlightenment thought without resorting to vague concepts such as "modernity" or becoming entangled in debates over bourgeois ideology. At least, in my view, the changes wrought by printing provide the most plausible point of departure for explaining how confidence shifted from divine revelation to mathematical reasoning and man-made maps.

The fact that religious and scientific traditions were affected by printing in markedly different ways points to the complex and contradictory nature of the communications shift and suggests the futility of trying to encapsulate its consequences in any one formula. When we consider Protestant iconoclasm or increased Bible reading, it may seem useful to envisage a movement going from "image to word"; but one must be prepared to use the reverse formula "word to image" when setting the stage for the rise of modern science. In the latter case, printing reduced translation problems, transcended linguistic divisions, and helped to bridge earlier divisions between university lectures and artisan crafts. In religious affairs, however, the communications shift had a divisive effect, permanently fragmenting Western Christendom along both geographic and sociological lines. Not only were Catholic regions set off from Protestant ones, but within different regions religious experience was also internally bifurcated. Loss of confidence in God's words among cosmopolitan elites was coupled with enhanced opportunities for evangelists and priests to spread glad tidings and rekindle faith. Enlightened deists who adhered to the "Laws of Nature and Nature's God" were thus placed at a distance from enthusiasts who were caught up in successive waves of religious revivals.

In all regions the ebb and flow of religious devotion affected diverse social strata at different times. But the Bible became "the treasure of the humble," with unpredictable consequences only in Protestant realms. Among Protestants, the universalistic impulse to spread the Gospel far and wide had special paradoxical results. Vernacular Bibles authorized by Protestant rulers helped to balkanize Christendom and to nationalize what had previously been a more cosmopolitan sacred book. Bible-reading householders acquired an enhanced sense of spiritual dignity and individual worth. An "inner light" kindled by the printed word became the basis for the shared mystical experiences of separate sects. Yet even while spiritual life was being enriched, it was also being tarnished by commercial drives. Where indulgence sellers were discredited, Bible salesmen multiplied.

In printing shops especially, old missionary impulses were combined with the demands imposed by an expanding capitalist enterprise. But there, also, several other impulses converged. Was the driving power of capitalism stronger than the long-lived drive for fame? Both together surely were stronger than either one alone. Did not the presses also offer rulers a way of extending their charisma and furnish significant help to impersonal bureaucrats? Among map publishers, reckon masters, and artisans, as we have seen, printing acted by a kind of marvelous alchemy to transmute private interest into public good. It also catered to the vanity of pedants, artists, and literati. When dealing with the new powers of the press, one can make a sound case for a multivariable explanation even while stressing the significance of the single innovation. The mixture of many motives provided a more powerful impetus than any single motive (whether that of profit-seeking capitalist or Christian evangelist) could have provided by itself. In this sense the use of early presses by Western Europeans was "overdetermined." The convergence of different impulses proved irresistible, producing a massive irreversible cultural "change of phase."

The early presses, which were established between 1460 and 1480, were powered by many different forces which had been incubating in the age of scribes. In a different cultural context, the same technology might have been used for different ends (as was the case in China and Korea) or it might have been unwelcome and not been used at all (as was the case in many regions outside Europe where Western missionary presses were the first to be installed). In this light one may agree with authorities who hold that the duplicating process which was developed in fifteenth-century Mainz, was *in itself* of no more consequence than any other inanimate tool. Unless it had been deemed useful to human agents, it would never have been put into operation in fifteenth-century European towns. Under different circumstances, moreover, it might have been welcomed and put to entirely different uses – monopolized by priests and rulers, for example, and withheld from free-wheeling urban entrepreneurs.

Such counterfactual speculation is useful for suggesting the importance of institutional context when considering technological innovation. Yet the fact remains that once presses were established in numerous European towns, the transforming powers of print did begin to take effect. However much one may wish to stress reciprocal interaction and avoid a simplistic "impact" model, one must leave room for the special features which distinguish the advent of printing from other innovations.

One cannot treat printing as just one among many elements in a complex causal nexus, for the communications shift transformed the nature of the causal nexus itself. It is of special historical significance because it produced fundamental alterations in prevailing patterns of continuity and change. On this point one must take strong exception to the views expressed by humanists who carry their hostility to technology so far as to deprecate the very tool which is most indispensable to the practice of their own crafts.

> The powers which shape men's lives may be expressed in books and type, but by and of itself printing . . . is only a tool, an instrument, and the multiplication of tools and instruments does not of itself affect intellectual and spiritual life.[15]

---

[15] Archer Taylor, "The Influence of Printing 1450–1650," *Printing and Progress: Two Lectures* (Berkeley, 1941), 13.

Intellectual and spiritual life, far from remaining unaffected, were profoundly transformed by the multiplication of new tools for duplicating books in fifteenth-century Europe. The communications shift altered the way Western Christians viewed their sacred book and the natural world. It made the words of God appear more multiform and His handiwork more uniform. The printing press laid the basis both for literal fundamentalism and for modern science. It remains indispensable for humanistic scholarship. It is still responsible for our museum without walls.

Some Final Remarks

This book has stopped short in the age of the wooden handpress. It has barely touched on the industrialization of paper making and the harnessing of iron presses to steam. Nothing has been said about the railway tracks and telegraph wires that linked European capitals in the mid-nineteenth century, or about the Linotype and Monotype machines that went together with mass literacy and tabloid journalism. The typewriter, the telephone, and a vast variety of more recent media have been entirely ignored. Too much territory has been traversed too rapidly as it is. Because contrary views have been expressed, however, it seems necessary to point out that there are irreversible aspects to the early modern printing revolution. Cumulative processes were set in motion in the mid-fifteenth century, and they have not ceased to gather momentum in the age of the computer printout and the television guide.

Of course, it would be foolish to ignore the fact that communication technologies are undergoing transformations even now. Movable metal type has already gone the way of the handpress; nineteenth-century institutions associated with publishing are being rapidly undermined. Commercial copy centers, for example, have begun to appear within the precincts of modern universities, much as stationers' stalls did near medieval universities. In preparing assignments for students, teachers now have to weigh the advantages of making up special course packs against the disadvantages of infringing on copyright. Even while university libraries are also taking on the function of copy centers, professors are beginning to acquire their own word processors, which will enable them to bypass university presses and turn out justified copy in their homes.

But although extant presses and publishing firms may be rendered obsolete eventually, it still seems likely that the modern knowledge industry will continue to expand. Surely there are no signs at present to indicate that pressure on library facilities is diminishing or that problems posed by overload are being eased. Since the advent of movable type, an enhanced capacity to store and retrieve, preserve and transmit, has kept pace with an enhanced capacity to create and destroy, innovate and outmode. The somewhat chaotic appearance of modern Western culture owes as much, if not more, to the duplicative powers of print as it does to the harnessing of new powers in the present age. It may yet be possible to view recent developments in historical perspective provided one takes into account neglected aspects of a massive and decisive cultural "change of phase" that occurred five centuries ago.

Some of the unanticipated consequences that came in the wake of Gutenberg's invention are now available for retrospective analysis – certainly more than could be seen in Bacon's day. Others are still unfolding, however, and *these* unanticipated consequences are, by definition, impossible to gauge at present. Few, if any, of the changes we have outlined could have been predicted. Even with hindsight they are difficult to describe. Clearly, more study is needed, if only to counteract premature leaps in the dark. A continuous accumulation of printed materials has certain disadvantages. (The voracious appetite of Chronos was feared in the past. A monstrous capacity to disgorge poses more of a threat at present.) But the capacity to scan accumulated records also confers certain modest advantages. We may examine how our predecessors read various portents and auguries and compare their prophecies with what actually occurred. We may thus discern over the past century or so a tendency to write off by premature obituaries the very problems that successive generations have had to confront.

This impulse to end tales that are still unfolding owes much to the prolongation of nineteenth-century historical schemes, especially those of Hegel and Marx, which point logical dialectical conflicts toward logical dialectical ends. The possibility of an indefinite prolongation of fundamentally contradictory trends is not allowed for in these grand designs. Yet we still seem to be experiencing the contradictory effects of a process which fanned the flames of religious zeal and bigotry while fostering a new concern for ecumenical concord and toleration, which fixed linguistic and national divisions more permanently while creating a cosmopolitan Commonwealth of Learning and extending communications networks which encompassed the entire world. At the very least, this book may have indicated the premature character of prevailing grand designs and of the fashionable trend spotting that extrapolates from them. For the full dimensions of the gulf that separates the age of scribes from that of printers have yet to be fully probed. The unevenly phased continuous process of recovery and innovation that began in the second half of the fifteenth century remains to be described.

AFTERWORD

REVISITING THE PRINTING
REVOLUTION

The writing of history, it is said, entails a dialogue between past and present. Such a dialogue helps to account for the prolonged interest in the topic of this book. The introduction of new communications technologies in recent years has stimulated curiosity about possible historical precedents and has given *The Printing Revolution* an unexpectedly long lease on life.[1]

But the coming of a new "information age" was still in the future during the decade (the mid-1960s to 70s) that saw publication of my preliminary articles.[2] When I added "some final remarks" to my book, the chief innovation I had in mind was the photocopier. My final version was duplicated not as "hard" copy but on carbon paper. It reflected years of study under the guidance of historians who were influenced by a different set of "present-day" concerns.

Although elementary school teachers had pointed to the introduction of printing as a significant event, the history courses I attended during my years of college and graduate study left the topic out. Advanced courses in medieval and early modern French history provided large bibliographies on a variety of subjects; few of the works on the long lists even mentioned the advent of printing. We were assigned several volumes of a multivolume, collaborative,

---

[1] See, e.g., James A. Dewar, "The Information Age and the Printing Press: Looking Backward to See Ahead," RAND Paper no. 8014 (Santa Monica, CA, 1998).

[2] The earliest articles were: "Clio and Chronos," *History and Theory* (Special Issue: *History and the Concept of Time*, 1966): 36–65; "Some Conjectures about the Impact of Printing on Western Society and Thought," *Journal of Modern History* 40 (1968): 1–56.

French series devoted to the "evolution of humanity." Henri Berr, its
original editor, had planned separate books on the development of
language, the invention of printing, and the advent of the newspaper. But the projected volume on printing, which was intended to
close the Middle Ages and introduce the modern world, remained
unwritten during the years when I was in graduate school.[3]

During those years, a quasi-Marxist "social history" was in vogue.
Topics associated with warfare, diplomacy, and politics had fallen
out of favor while intellectual and cultural trends were relegated
to the "back of the book." Demographic and economic developments loomed large. Significant changes were generally attributed (as
J. H. Hexter observed) to a seemingly omnipotent, ever-rising middle
class.[4] Students of European history were introduced first to a commercial revolution and then to agricultural and industrial ones. Concerning a possible communications revolution, nothing was heard.

It was in this (now-forgotten) context that I sought to draw attention to the introduction of a new communications technology in
mid-fifteenth-century Europe. This context has been so completely
forgotten that one young scholar is under the mistaken impression
that historians have "always tried to track down changes wrought
by printing on all parts of early modern life."[5] My 1970 survey of
the position of printing in historical literature persuaded me that the
opposite was true.[6]

---

[3] Lucien Febvre and Henri-Jean Martin, L'Apparition du Livre, L'Evolution de
L'Humanitè Series, no. 49 (Paris, 1958). When it did appear, it was reviewed
in library journals but few historians took note. It was only eighteen years later,
after the publication of the English translation, The Coming of the Book, tr. David
Gerard (London, 1976), that Febvre and Martin began to attract the attention it
deserves. Even now, however, the work is likely to be mischaracterized as a product of the so-called Annales school. Jared Jenisch, "The History of the Book,"
Portal: Librarians and the Academy 3, no. 2 (April 2003), attributes the work to
Lucien Febvre, who helped found the school. But the entire book was actually
written by Henri-Jean Martin, who was not an annaliste.

[4] J. H. Hexter, Reappraisals in History (Evanston, IL, 1961), chap. 5.

[5] Adrian Johns, "Science and the Book in Modern Cultural Historiography,"
Studies in History and Philosophy of Science 29, no. 2 (1998): 175.

[6] "The Advent of Printing in Current Historical Literature," American Historical
Review 75 (Feb. 1970): 727–43. Sections of this article are repeated in my big

Now, of course, the situation is different. The field of book history has been established as a new site of inquiry where historians, literary scholars, and bibliographers are fully engaged in collaborative teaching and research.[7] Following the lead of the pioneering history of the book in France,[8] numerous other multivolume national histories are well under way. Given scholarly involvement in book history and public concern over the Internet, the once-neglected topic is attracting so much attention that the title of my first chapter seems to be somewhat out of date. As I recently observed: perhaps the printing revolution should no longer be described as unacknowledged.[9]

It is now featured in works dealing with varied topics ranging from art history to nationalism.[10] Especially in literary studies, numerous variations have been played on pertinent themes.[11] It has also become subject to vigorous dispute. In some instances, objections have been aimed at exaggerated claims that are not of my making,[12] and positions taken by others (especially by media analysts) are wrongly assumed to be mine.[13] In one instance my "McLuhanesque

book: *The Printing Press as an Agent of Change*, 2 vols. in 1 (Cambridge, 1979), 30–1 [hereafter, *Agent of Change*].

[7] For a succinct account of the emergence of the field of book history see Anthony Grafton's introduction to "Forum," *The American Historical Review* 107 (Feb. 2002): 85 [hereafter *AHR Forum*].

[8] *Histoire de l'Edition Française*, ed. Henri-Jean Martin and Roger Chartier, 4 vols. (Paris, 1984).

[9] "An Unacknowledged Revolution Revisited," *AHR Forum*, 89.

[10] Benedict Anderson, *Imagined Communities* (London, 1983); Anthony Wells-Cole, *Art and Decoration in Elizabethan England* (New Haven, CT, 1997).

[11] A few titles that come to mind: Adrian Armstrong, *Technique and Technology: Script, Print and Poetics in France 1470–1550* (Oxford, 2000); Martin Elsky, *Authorizing Words* (Ithaca, NY, 1989); Joseph Loewenstein, "The Script in the Marketplace," *Representations* 12 (Fall 1985): 10–14; Arthur Marotti, *Manuscript, Print and the English Renaissance Lyric* (Ithaca, NY, 1995); Michael McKeon, *The Origins of the English Novel* (Baltimore, 1987); Walter L. Reed, *An Exemplary History of the Novel* (Chicago, 1981); Evelyn Tribble, *Margins and Marginality* (Charlottesville, VA, 1993).

[12] See, e.g., interview with Robert Darnton and my response, *Sharp News* (Summer 1994): 3 and (Winter 1994–5): 5. See also *Books and the Sciences in History*, ed. M. Frasca-Spada and N. Jardine (Cambridge, 2000), 3, 13.

[13] Michael Warner, *Letters of the Republic* (Cambridge, MA, 1990), 5, in an odd coupling discerns a "Whig-McLuhanite" school. For my disagreement with

view of history" is found objectionable, along with my failure to consult certain special studies on printing and bookbinding.[14] I am accused of dismissing such studies by commenting that "we need to think less abstractly, more historically and concretely." The quotation is accurate[15] but has been given the wrong antecedent. My comment refers not to bibliographical studies but to McLuhan's "typographical man."

In other instances, however, legitimate questions have been raised that need to be addressed and new approaches have developed that ought to be taken into account. In what follows, I will discuss some of the issues at stake.

From the first, my approach has been criticized for exaggerating revolutionary aspects and failing to do justice to evolutionary ones. Several recent studies tend to reinforce this criticism.[16] In one case, even evolutionary changes are called into question. It is suggested that we ought to "reinscribe the emergence of the printing press" in a long-term history that starts with the shift from scroll to codex and concludes with the recent presentation of texts on screens.[17] The advent of the printed codex alongside the hand-copied one would appear as a very minor episode (a blip or hiccup) when set within

McLuhan's views, see *Agent of Change*, pp. 40ff. My approach has also been likened to that of Walter Ong, Alvin Gouldner, and Alvin Kernan, none of whom share my concern with historiography. See, e.g., introduction by M. Bristol and Arthur Marotti, eds., *Print, Manuscript and Performance* (Columbus, OH, 2000), 1–2; David McKitterick, *Print, Manuscript and the Search for Order 1450–1830* (Cambridge, 2003), 224.

[14] Joseph Dane, *The Myth of Print Culture* (Toronto, 2003), 14.

[15] Ibid., 13. The wrong page reference is given. See *Agent of Change*, I, 129 (not I, 91).

[16] "The Slow Revolution" is a typical characterization. It is used as the title of a review of McKitterick's work by John Barnard, *Times Literary Supplement*, 19 March 2004, 27. See also: Asa Briggs and Peter Burke, *A Social History of the Media* (Cambridge, 2002), 22 [hereafter Briggs and Burke]; introduction by Julia Crick and Alexandra Walsham, eds., *The Uses of Script and Print, 1300–1700* (Cambridge, 2004) [hereafter Crick and Walsham].

[17] Roger Chartier, "Texts, Printing, Readings," *The New Cultural History*, ed. Lynn Hunt (Berkeley, CA, 1989), chap. 6, pp. 154–71. See also Bristol and Marotti, *Print, Manuscript and Performance*, 8.

this *longue durée*. The ramifications of the adoption of the codex form are certainly worth more study.[18] But so too are several later innovations that left basic format unchanged.

Moreover, the heightened significance assigned to book format tends to deflect attention from the effects of rapidly duplicating diverse, "nonbook" materials (proclamations, edicts, broadsides, calendars, and the like) that were especially well suited for mass production. The fate of indulgences (as discussed in my book) offers a case in point. So too does the fate of maps, charts, diagrams, and drawings. It may be partly because nonbooks are of secondary interest to most book historians that they are prone to underestimate the significance for technical literature of the introduction of woodcuts and engravings.

My work was not intended to serve as a contribution to book history. (The field had not been formed when my first articles were written.) Instead, I had in mind a broader, currently unfashionable, unit of study: Western Civilization (or "Western Christendom" – as it was known in the fifteenth century). I was dissatisfied with conventional periodization schemes, especially with semantic confusion over characterizations of the Renaissance. I also found problems with prevailing explanations for the disruption of Western Christendom and for the discrediting of those ancient "scientific" theories (Ptolemaic, Galenic, and Aristotelian) that had long been regarded as authoritative.

As noted in my original preface, it was the publication in 1962 of Marshall McLuhan's *Gutenberg Galaxy* that alerted me to a dimension of change I had not considered previously.[19] Its author did not

---

[18] G. Cavallo, "Between Volumen and Codex," *A History of Reading in the West*, ed. G. Cavallo and R. Chartier, tr. Lydia Cochrane (1999), chap. 2 [hereafter Cavallo and Chartier]; Peter Stallybrass, "Books and Scrolls: Navigating the Bible," *Books and Readers in Early Modern England*, ed. J. Andersen and E. Sauer (Philadelphia, 2002); and references given by Stuart Hall, "In the Beginning Was the Codex: The Early Church and Its Revolutionary Books," *The Church and the Book* (papers given at Ecclesiastical History Society Meetings 2000 and 2001) ed. R. N. Swanson (Rochester, NY, 2004), 1–11.

[19] See discussion in *Agent of Change*, 40–1.

share my concern (and that of other historians) for solid evidence, chronological order, or appropriate context. But he did stimulate my curiosity about a topic that seemed relevant to some of the unresolved issues I had in mind. I began to think about the possible effects of printing on the flow of information, the retrieval of records, and the duplication of fresh findings. I was especially interested in how changes affecting the transmission of records over the course of many generations might have impinged on historical consciousness.[20] Thus, I became concerned with diachronic as well as with synchronic aspects; not only with the rapid installation of printing shops throughout Europe but also with the way the loss and erosion of texts and images copied by hand were superseded by an ever-growing accumulation of written materials duplicated in print.

From my perspective, the adoption of a new way to duplicate writing in fifteenth-century Europe was not a "slow revolution" but a remarkably rapid one. Given the state of communications at the time, it was also remarkably widespread. Book historians, however, are more likely to be impressed by how little the book itself was changed. One recent study on "the evolution of the book" omits printing when listing the four major changes that are deemed to be of consequence.[21] Many other studies argue that the most significant changes that ensued after the introduction of the codex were initiated by medieval scribes. They are fond of citing M. B. Parkes's thought-provoking comment, "the late medieval book differs more from its early medieval predecessors than it does from the printed book of our own day."[22] Whereas the medieval scribe had pioneered by separating words and inventing new letter forms (such as Carolingian minuscule), the early printer, who

---

[20] This was the theme of my early essay, "Clio and Chronos."

[21] Frederick G. Kilgour, *The Evolution of the Book* (Oxford, 1998), applies the biologists' theory of "punctuated equilibrium" to book history and comes up with four transformations during the last five thousand years: clay tablet, papyrus roll, codex, electronic book. He supplies a chart that contains three additions: printing, steam power, and offset printing, but they are not integrated into his main scheme.

[22] M. B. Parkes cited by McKitterick, *Print, Manuscript*, 11.

simply aimed at duplicating extant texts, appears to have been less innovative.[23]

On such issues, the frame provided by book history strikes me as being too restrictive.[24] Economic and social historians are more likely to share my concern with the innovative aspects of early printing.[25] From their perspective, the early printer belongs in the company of other early capitalists and urban entrepreneurs who were engaged in wholesale production. The scribe who became a printer did not undergo a gradual change but experienced a veritable metamorphosis.

Just how many scribes turned to printing is uncertain because of the "unsettled character" of terms used in fifteenth-century tax rolls. During the fifteenth century, the meaning of such labels as "scriptor" or "schreiber" (scribe) and "impressor" or "trucker" (printer) was much more ambiguous than is often acknowledged.[26] Some printers called themselves "scribes."[27] (Even today there's a certain ambiguity in the way we use the term "printing." The phrase "I was taught to print" may mean merely that I was not taught to use cursive style when forming my letters.)

Nevertheless, there are at least a few well-documented cases of this particular transformation. Peter Schoeffer, who founded a printing dynasty, is the most celebrated example. Schoeffer offers an intriguing contrast with Vespasiano da Bisticci, the most noteworthy of all manuscript bookdealers. Schoeffer, the former scribe,

---

[23] Armando Petrucci, *Writers and Readers in Medieval Italy*, tr. and ed. Charles M. Radding (New Haven, CT, 1995), 200.

[24] I agree that it is misguided to place "the book at the center of a cultural web," Nicholas Hudson, "Challenging Eisenstein: Recent Studies on Print Culture," *Eighteenth Century Life* 26 (2002): 85.

[25] See discussion in *Agent of Change*, 22.

[26] Sheila Edmunds, "From Schoeffer to Vérard: Concerning the Scribes who Became Printers," *Printing the Written Word*, ed. Sandra Hindman (Ithaca, NY, 1991), 24–7. Edmunds questions statements by Curt Bühler *The Fifteenth-Century Book* (Philadelphia, 1960), 48, that "countless scribes" took up printing, and by Rudolf Hirsch, *Printing, Selling and Reading 1450–1550* (Wiesbaden, 1974), 18, that this was the "usual" route to the new occupation.

[27] Hirsch, 18n.

took up printing; Vespasiano, the former manuscript bookdealer, closed shop.

But Vespasiano was atypical according to recent work on publishing history. Advocates of gradualism tend to set aside the metamorphosis of scribe into printer and emphasize instead the continued activities of manuscript bookdealers, especially the *cartolai* of Renaissance Italy. According to the most authoritative account, in Italy at least, manuscript bookdealers not only set the pattern for a later printed book trade; they accommodated themselves fairly easily to its requirements.

> Cartolai were involved at all levels in book production for the first twenty or twenty-five years of printing in Italy. They supplied the raw materials – the paper, the ink, the colours. They arranged for printed sheets to be decorated and bound . . . And they sold the finished product, locally or even at long distances. In some instances [they] put up the capital . . . housed the press and the printer on his premises and collected . . . the major portion of the finished edition . . .[28]

The description applies largely to deluxe, hand-illuminated volumes that served as transitional "hybrid" products. It omits mention of the supplies of type, special inks, and pads, together with the larger more diversified workforce that differentiated the shops run by printers from those run by manuscript dealers. This particular account, however, does not deny that there were revolutionary as well as evolutionary aspects: the abrupt change from producing books one at a time to turning out hundreds of copies at once, we are told, "struck contemporaries" as a "stunning novelty," "almost literally overwhelming."[29]

Other studies either pass over this "stunning" novelty or deny its validity: "Of course printing made books cheaper and more easily available but the difference in scale of output should not be

---

[28] Mary A. Rouse and Richard H. Rouse, *Cartolai, Illuminators and Printers in Fifteenth-Century Italy* (UCLA Occasional Paper no. 1, 1988), 66–7.
[29] Ibid., 21.

exaggerated ... some medieval texts had circulated in hundreds of copies."[30] The difference between turning out hundreds of copies at once and issuing them seriatim goes unremarked. Moreover, mention of "hundreds of copies" does not specify whether the books in question were large or small. The reference is based on a much-cited passage taken from Febvre and Martin. It refers to one order made by a fifteenth-century Flemish bookdealer for three very brief texts that were to be combined into a "little manual."[31] Whether the order was ever filled in part or in toto is not known. When this example is set beside the large texts that printers issued on a single date, it appears that difference in scale is too often *under*estimated. A similar tendency to exaggerate the capacity of copyists to achieve the effects produced by printers is evident in allusions to the "pecia system" that was employed at certain thirteenth-century universities. This piecemeal copying system is often assumed to be more efficient, widespread, and long-lived than was the case.[32]

It has been said that, with the exception of book fairs, Italian manuscript bookdealers laid down the path that early printers would follow.[33] Yet the earliest printers set up shop in locales that were

---

[30] Keith Thomas, "The Meaning of Literacy in Early Modern England," *The Written Word: Literacy in Transition*, ed. Gerd Baumann (Oxford, 1986), 119. Citing Febvre and Martin, *Coming of the Book*, 28.

[31] The desired texts consisted of the Seven Penitential Psalms, Cato's *Disticha* in Flemish, and a "small prayer book." The same passage from Febvre and Martin, *Coming of the Book*, 28, is cited by Warner, *Letters of the Republic*, 8, in support of an unwarranted claim that medieval scriptoria sustained "uniform mass production."

[32] Although McKitterick refers to "the *widespread use* of the pecia system from the mid-thirteenth century *onwards*," p. 100 (italics mine), it appears that the system was always limited to certain universities and was no longer in use by the end of the fourteenth century. Warner also gives a misleading impression of the efficacy of this so-called system, p. 8. David d'Avray, "Printing, Mass Communication and Religious Reformation," in Crick and Walsham, 52–4, agrees that "pecia" is often overrated.

[33] That Italian *cartolai* produced a "large quantity" of books and, except for not holding book fairs, anticipated early printers is asserted by Anthony Grafton, who cites the Rouses on this point. "The Humanist as Reader," in Cavallo and Chartier, 190.

at some distance from the bookshops of Renaissance Italy. Indeed, the first craftsmen to introduce printing in Italy (and in France and Spain) came from Germany. These pioneers were followed by their compatriots to the point where the German presence among printers on the peninsula (especially in Venice) provoked complaints about "German interlopers driving honest Italian scribes out of work."[34] Moreover, stationers and scribes were by no means the only groups to take up printing. The "bewildering variety"[35] of occupations that were represented among practitioners of the new craft argues against assuming any one previous occupation was prototypical.

The entrepreneurial activities of the master printer differed from those undertaken by any of his supposed precursors. In addition to holding book fairs, other departures from earlier practices included: obtaining presses and sets of type (or casting type on the spot), organizing shop routines, hiring compositors and correctors, meeting deadlines, and avoiding work stoppages.

Useful data on the difficulties experienced by one early master printer in the 1470s are offered by Giovanni Mardersteig. The master printer Petrus Maufer managed to surmount all obstacles, including strikes, in order to complete the printing of an edition of a large (1000-page, double-column) folio volume containing a commentary on Avicenna. Between May 1477, when the first reams of paper were obtained, and December 1477, when the last sheet came off the press, 6,800,000 pieces of type had been procured and used, four presses had been put in operation, and, according to the printer's boast, "not a working day had been wasted."[36]

Almost exactly three hundred years later, from June to November 1778, a similar story was unfolded as told in Robert Darnton's study of the wage book of the *Société Typographique de Neufchâtel*.[37]

34 Martin Lowry, *The World of Aldus Manutius* (Ithaca, NY, 1979), 26.
35 Ibid., 9. Previous occupations constituted a "strange conglomeration" according to Hirsch, 20.
36 *The Remarkable Story of a Book Published in Padua in 1477*, tr. H. Schmoller (London, 1967), 16–7.
37 Robert Darnton, *The Business of Enlightenment. A Publishing History of the Encyclopedie 1775–1800* (Cambridge, MA, 1979), chap. 5.

Because of the fine detail which this eighteenth-century wage book provides, we are able to learn much more than Mardersteig tells us about the disorderly behavior of individual journeymen and the extent to which problems of labor management were compounded by absenteeism and erratic habits of work. The two accounts are nevertheless remarkably similar considering that three hundred years had intervened. When it came to problems of financing, labor management, and marketing, the master printers of 1477 were closer to the men of 1788 than they were to their contemporaries who provided hand-illuminated, hand-copied books to an elite clientele.

It seems that evidence has to be strained in order to sustain a thesis of continuity with regard to changes in book production. Gradualism appears to be less problematic with regard to book consumption. Whereas silent reading was at one time attributed to the advent of printing, medievalists have shown that it was practiced by laymen as well as by churchmen in the age of the scribe. The carryover of format and layout reinforced an impression of continuity.

Whereas manuscripts and printed products are now assigned to separate categories by cataloguers, curators, and dealers, fifteenth-century readers found both kinds of books for sale in the same locales, often in the same shops. Purchasers placed them together in the same cabinets or on the same shelves and sometimes had them bound together as single volumes. The contrast with twentieth-century practices is striking and helps to explain why authorities insist that "the fifteenth century ... made little distinction between hand written and press printed books."[38]

Indeed, at first, no distinctive neo-Latin terminology was employed to distinguish printed from hand-copied products.[39] (One is reminded of present-day encounters with computer printouts

---

[38] Bühler, *Fifteenth-Century Book*, 40. Bühler goes on to mention the interest expressed by Francesco Filelfo in July 1470 in acquiring printed books which Filelfo described as being equivalent to "the work of a skilled and exact scribe" (p. 41).

[39] David Shaw, "Ars formularia: NeoLatin Synonyms For Printing," *The Library* 6th Series XI, no. 3 (Sept. 1989): 220–30.

that are often mistakenly described as "typescripts" – not to mention encounters with typescripts that are mistakenly described as manuscripts.[40]) Because "liber, volumen, codex were used indiscriminately" for both kinds of books, Silvia Rizzo holds that the humanists drew no clear line of demarcation between the products of the pen and those of the press.[41]

But philology is not always an adequate guide in such matters. Calling a computer printout a "typescript" does not indicate failure to distinguish word processor from typewriter. Similarly, using the same terminology was compatible with recognizing the "stunning novelty" of presswork. Distinctions between manuscript and printed text were clearly drawn by the humanists. They not only debated the merits and defects of the new medium;[42] they were sufficiently impressed by its advantages that they sought out printers when it came time to duplicate their own work. (It was in this way that the first Paris press was set up within the precinct of the Sorbonne.)

As readers, rather than as potential authors, however, Renaissance scholars did not always make clear whether the text they were perusing was in hand-copied or printed form. Historians concerned with reading practices tend to follow suit. The approach developed by Roger Chartier (the preeminent scholar in this field) is primarily concerned with how a given text was appropriated by different communities and individual readers. Whether a text is presented in hand-copied or in printed form is of less significance than how its meaning is construed.[43] Indeed, pen marks are likely to be valued more highly than printed passages because they offer clues to a given reader's thought processes.

Accordingly, attention is focused on marginalia, on handwritten insertions and additions in printed books, and on hand-copied

---

[40] A "typewritten manuscript" was on sale at Sotheby's according to Felicia R. Lee, "In Brief," *New York Times*, Saturday, 19 June 2004, sec. A, p. 9.

[41] Silvia Rizzo, *Il Lessico Filologica degli Umanisti*, Sussidi Eruditi Series, no. 26 (Rome, 1973), 7, 69.

[42] Brian Richardson, "The Debates on Printing in Renaissance Italy," *La Bibliofilia* 100 (1998): 133–55.

[43] See Chartier, "Texts, Printing, Readings," 154–75.

passages in printed commonplace books.[44] Given abundant evidence of this sort, researchers are inclined to agree with Crick and Walsham that it was not the printed word alone but "intermixture and hybridity" that characterized communication in the early modern era.[45]

But the intermingling of pen work with presswork and the occasional failure of readers to differentiate between the two do not mean that the introduction of print had no effect on reading practices. The reorganization of texts was not as obvious an innovation as the introduction of the codex or the separation of words. Nevertheless, repeated encounters with title pages, arabic numerals, running heads, alphabetical arrangements, and the like probably affected the mental habits of readers. Whereas book historians are likely to point out that almost all these elements were derived from scribal practices, my emphasis is on the repeated encounters that became common after printing. Title pages had figured in some hand-copied books, but they really only came into their own with printed bibliographies and booksellers' catalogues. David McKitterick complains that "titles are misleading and give only partial access to the individual copies."[46] But surely the lists of titles that were compiled by booksellers, librarians, and bibliographers provided better guidance to readers than had been the case when books were best known by their *incipits*.

The enrichment of literary diets that went together with increased output is also relevant to any history of reading. A so-called "*lesen* revolution" in the eighteenth century, when "intensive" reading purportedly gave way to "extensive" reading among some German burghers and American colonists (New Englanders), has attracted

---

44 The fact that handwritten marginalia is the only kind discussed here, should not be taken as overlooking the importance of printed marginalia. On the latter, see William W. E. Slights, *Managing Readers: Printed Marginalia in Englsh Renaissance Books* (Ann Arbor, MI, 2002), and Tribble, *Margins and Marginality.*

45 Introduction, Crick and Walsham, 12. See also the "bi-directional . . . script-print interface" in William Sherman, *John Dee* (Amherst, MA, 1995), 117. The title of Anthony Grafton's essay on the reading practices of Guillaume Budé is suggestive: "Is the history of reading a marginal enterprise?" *Papers of the Bibliographical Society of America* 191 (June 1997): 139–59.

46 McKitterick, *Print, Manuscript*, 136.

much attention.[47] That Latin-reading scholars had previously been concerned about an "early modern information overload" is just now beginning to be explored. As Ann Blair points out, whereas early medieval scholars are depicted reading a single text, early modern ones are shown with many books and manuscripts spread out on desk, shelves, and floor in considerable disarray.[48] The latter were also supplied with books of advice on the right way to read, to take notes, to keep commonplace books, and even to cut out pages and wield scissors and paste.[49] At the same time, a special kind of intensive reading was required of "correctors" (or proofreaders) who worked in printing houses. Gabriel Harvey's selective reading of a classical text which was designed to provide his superiors with political guidance has been described in a seminal article.[50] Gabriel Harvey also served the printer John Wolfe as a proofreader. In that capacity, he probably had to adopt a different reading style.[51]

With a few notable exceptions, however, the practices of the learned readers who worked in printing shops and compiled reference guides tend to attract less attention than do the practices of a reading public at large.[52] "The social power of print can only be felt when large numbers of people know how to read and write," write two editors who point to the presumably less limited "social power" exerted by theatrical productions in early modern London.[53]

---

[47] Carvallo and Chartier, introduction, 24, and Reinhard Wittman, "Was There a Reading Revolution?" chap. 11. Robert Darnton, "First Steps toward a History of Reading," *The Kiss of Lamourette* (New York, 1990), 166, notes that both David Hall and Rolf Engelsing have found a similar pattern in two different locales. Darnton's notes on pages 358–62 offer useful bibliographical guidance.

[48] Ann Blair, "Reading Strategies for Coping with Information Overload," *Journal of the History of Ideas* 64 (Jan. 2003): 15–16.

[49] Ibid., 16.

[50] Lisa Jardine and Anthony Grafton, "Studied for Action: How Gabriel Harvey Read his Livy," *Past and Present* 129 (1990): 30–78.

[51] Clifford C. Huffman, *Elizabethan Impressions: John Wolfe and His Press* (AMS Press, 1998).

[52] See discussion of anti-intellectual tendencies inherent in recent book history studies in my *Grub Street Abroad* (Oxford, 1992), 33–5.

[53] Bristol and Marotti, *Print, Manuscript and Performance*, 3–4.

But what about the smaller numbers of people who were already fully literate? Wasn't the effect of increased output likely to be especially powerful when markets were very small?

Historians are likely to be more interested in the typical early modern reader, who tended to be neither fully literate nor completely illiterate. Accordingly, they tend to subordinate the printed (or written) word to the spoken one:

> It only needs one or two members of . . . illiterate groups who have acquired an ability to read to read aloud to their friends and neighbors for a bridge to be thrown across any supposed divide between exclusively literate and illiterate groups . . . [54]

True enough. Yet the difference between hearing a report read by others and reading it oneself strikes me as something more than a "supposed" divide.

A renewed interest in speech (perhaps influenced by twentieth century re-oralization, via phone, radio, TV, tape) also tends to deflect attention from the historical significance of print.

> too great a preoccupation with writing and printing as technologies of literacy may lead us to forget the superior virtues of speech. After all we did not stop speaking when we learned to write nor writing when we learned to print nor reading writing and printing when we entered the electronic age. For those who market texts in those forms some of them may seem mutually exclusive . . . but for the speaker, auditor, reader or viewer the texts tend to work in complementary not competitive ways . . . [55]

These comments by the late Donald McKenzie have been followed up by Harold Love, who discusses "print, voice and script" as intertwined parts of a "communicative spectrum" and questions the

---

[54] Thomas, "The Meaning of Literacy," 107, citing a comment by Roger Schofield.

[55] D. F. McKenzie, "Speech-Manuscript-Print," *Making Meaning: Printers of the Mind and Other Essays*, ed. P. MacDonald and M. Suarez S. J. (Amherst, MA, 2002), 238.

usefulness of monistic models (such as mine) that artificially isolate print.[56]

No doubt, if one wished to describe fully the "communicative spectrum" in any society, it would be foolish to ignore the primacy of speech or the "mutuality of exchange between the spoken, handwritten and printed":

> Speaking, and singing, reading, writing and reciting, looking at texts on walls and in books, half hearing, half understanding, rereading and rewriting, set the scripts and books of the seventeenth century, like those of the fourteenth, in multilayered communications of eyes and ears.[57]

But I am not trying to describe the entire communicative spectrum in early modern Europe. Rather, I am concerned with how this spectrum was affected by the introduction of printing. From this perspective, I would distinguish the "scripts and books of the seventeenth century" from those of the fourteenth. It is incautious to assume that the habit of silent scanning reduced recourse to the spoken word. But it may be useful to consider how speech itself (a parliamentary debate, for example) was affected by printed publicity. Reading out loud to hearing publics not only persisted after printing but was, indeed, facilitated by the new abundance of texts. The same point applies to the singing of psalms and the mass distribution of printed psalters.[58] It seems likely that vernacular repertoires were enriched in the early modern era by the circulation of printed ballads and broadsheets.[59]

---

[56] Harold Love, "Oral and Scribal Texts in Early Modern England," *Cambridge History of the Book in Britain IV 1557–1695*, ed. John Barnard and D. F. McKenzie with the assistance of Maureen Bell (Cambridge, 2002), chap. 3 (pp. 119–21) [hereafter *CHB IV*].

[57] Margaret Aston, "Epilogue," Crick and Walsham, 289.

[58] For references to the "mass distribution" of psalters in France in 1561–2, see *Agent of Change*, 352, n. 170.

[59] Adam Fox, *Oral and Literate Culture in England* (Oxford, 2000), 8–10, 410–11. Christopher Marsh, "The Sound of Print . . . The Broadside Ballad as Song," in Crick and Walsham, chap. 9. On sixteenth-century France, see Kate Van Orden,

Recent work stresses the primacy of orality among Protestants no less than Catholics.[60] Despite Protestant reliance on scripture and Catholic repudiation of the "inky divinity," both confessions valued the living presence of the preacher more highly than the inanimate word in print. "Almost every printed sermon in the first half of the [seventeenth] century has something to say by way of apology for the loss of the preacher's presence."[61] Moreover, word of mouth (together with pen work) played a significant part in the spread of Protestantism just as it had in the spread of earlier heresies, whether Hussite, Waldensian, or Lollard.

> Orality was as important as the printed word in the formation of opinion . . . Scribal culture was no less important . . . The handwritten pasquillade could . . . work as effectively as the printed broadside to focus views and precipitate political action.[62]

When these diverse views are presented, it is often assumed that they are in contradiction to the views expressed in my book. No doubt there are differences in emphasis and in matters of degree. As noted earlier with regard to the "communicative spectrum," I am less concerned with the prolonged coexistence of speech and writing than with the ways in which printing may have altered the balance between these interactive modes. Thus I would argue that a "handwritten pasquillade" could *not* work as effectively as a printed one to mobilize scattered groups and produce a relatively simultaneous response – to get "the thirteen clocks to strike as one," as was said about the mobilization of the thirteen colonies. Similarly, it seems misguided to place an "imagined" society such as "Mr. Spectator's Club" under the rubric of "oral communication."[63] All such "virtual" communities owed their existence entirely to print.

"Cheap Print and Street Song," *Music and the Cultures of Print*, ed. K. Van Orden (New York and London, 2000), 312.

[60] Jean François Gilmont, "Protestant Reformations and Reading," in Carvallo and Chartier, 236. See also essays in Crick and Walsham.

[61] McKenzie, "Speech-Manuscript-Print," 241.

[62] Crick and Walsham, 68 (citing from article by Bob Scribner).

[63] Briggs and Burke, 30–1.

With regard to the Reformation, I warn against setting press against pulpit and agree that diverse media contributed to the spread of the Lutheran heresy.[64] But the "spread" of heresy is by no means the only issue explored in the relevant chapter of this book. How orthodox beliefs and institutions were also affected, how priestly authority was subverted by lay scholars and editors, how vernacular translations and polyglot bibles led to dissension among churchmen – such issues tend to be neglected when the persistence of old media is assigned too much weight.

The continued importance of oral teaching and preaching for preserving the vitality of a given church is undeniable.[65] But recent work has also pointed to new opportunities extended by printing to preachers who were deprived of their pulpits by unfriendly regimes. The two essay titles given by Alexandra Walsham for her discussion of recusant preachers are suggestive: "Domme Preachers" and "Preaching without Speaking."[66] Under Mary Tudor's reign, the same titles could be applied to some of the Marian exiles. When traveling on the Continent, they were never far from printing shops and made full use of them; personal experience underlies John Foxe's celebrated tributes to printing.[67] The same point holds for those Huguenot exiles and emigrés in the Netherlands who ran widely read cosmopolitan periodical journals after the revocation of the Edict of Nantes.[68]

As was true of preaching, so too of teaching. "Dumb preachers" went together with "silent instructors." "By the early sixteenth century some of the most innovative teachers were . . . creating an

---

[64] *Agent of Change*, 374.

[65] McKenzie, "Speech-Manuscript-Print," 133. Fox, *Oral Literature and Culture*, x.

[66] Alexandra Walsham, "Domme Preachers?" *Past and Present* 168 (August 2000): 73–123; "Preaching without Speaking," in Crick and Walsham, chap. 11.

[67] J. F. Mozley, *John Foxe and His Book* (London, 1940). The Foxe industry has recently generated a huge literature, including a new biography of Foxe's English printer, John Day. See Elizabeth Evenden and Thomas Freeman, "John Foxe, John Day and the Printing of the 'Book of Martyrs,'" *Lives in Print*, ed. R. Myers, M. Harris, and G. Mandelbrote (London, 2002).

[68] Eisenstein, *Grub Street Abroad*, passim.

imaginary classroom far larger than an individual classroom could be."[69] And so too with political oratory. To the dumb preacher and the silent instructor I would add a third paradoxical figure: the "mute orator." New forms of political influence were exerted by would-be tribunes, who lacked oratorical skills but knew how to attract attention when harnessing their pens to presses.[70] "What the orators of Rome and Athens were in the midst of a people assembled, our men of letters are to a people dispersed."[71]

To be sure, dumb preachers and mute orators represent exceptions to the general rule. A gift for eloquent speech has never ceased to be advantageous for most evangelists and politicians. Among natural philosophers, however, skill at handling nonverbal forms of interchange, printed equations, tables, diagrams, charts, and maps would be increasingly prized. Eloquence was not helpful for producing logarithm tables. The silent, colorless, odorless world of the new physics did not lend itself to vocalization. Sustained by print, it was designed to appeal, rather, to "reason's inner ear."

This nonverbal aspect of printed communications also had political implications. They were made explicit during the French Revolution by activists such as Condorcet. A mathematician turned politician who lacked oratorical skills and disdained appeals to passion and sentiment, Condorcet assigned a special historical significance to the advent of printing. It had reduced the power of eloquence, he believed, and had increased the opportunity to shape a new polity in the "light of cold reason."[72] Ironically enough, the French Revolutionary press, itself, proved Condorcet wrong. As previous

---

[69] Grafton, "Humanist as Reader," 199.

[70] The phrase "mute orator" was actually used by a deputy about Volney. Tom Paine, John Wilkes, Camille Desmoulins, and Jacques Pierre Brissot are among other examples cited in my essays: "The Tribune of the People: A New Species of Demagogue," *Studies on Voltaire and the 18th century* 288 (1991): 145–59; "Le Publiciste comme Démagogue: *La Sentinelle du Peuple* de Volney," *La Révolution du Journal*, ed. Pierre Rétat (Paris 1989), 189–97.

[71] See *Agent of Change*, 132. Malesherbes's theme is echoed by Benjamin Franklin in a letter to Richard Price (13 June 1782) as cited by Michael Warner, "Franklin and the Letters of the Republic," *Representations* 16 (Fall 1986): 128, n. 11.

[72] Keith Baker, *Condorcet* (Chicago, 1975), 298.

generations who had witnessed pamphlet warfare could have told him, printing was just as compatible with fear mongering and dema-goguery as any other medium. Nor was it incompatible with religious fanaticism. As I have noted elsewhere, in conjunction with Bible reading, open books sometimes go together with closed minds.

As these comments indicate, my chief concern is with change rather than with continuity. Or rather I am interested in the ways in which "continuity" itself was altered when texts became more fixed and less likely to drift over time. Without denying the persistence of previous forms of communication, I am especially curious as to how speech and writing were themselves altered by the printed word. Despite this difference in emphasis, most of the new studies seem to me to be more complementary than contradictory.

When taken all together, they serve to confirm my assertion that efforts to summarize changes wrought by printing in any simple or single formula are likely to lead us astray. Insofar as they stress reci-procity and interchange among speech, pen, and press, the new stud-ies also reinforce my conviction that an "impact" model is unsatis-factory and should be discarded. Even before the English translator of Febvre and Martin used the "Impact of Print" as a subtitle, I regret-ted using that phrase in a preliminary article[73] and had begun to look for more satisfactory models. When titling my big book, I discarded the metaphor of billiard balls colliding and sought instead to evoke the process that physicists describe as a "cooperative transition" or chemists term a "change of phase"; a process where the mixture of elements remains more or less the same even while the whole is trans-formed into a different state.

"The printing press was not, on its own, an agent of change," writes John Barnard. He goes on to explain that "print, politics and religion were inextricably linked to one another."[74] This strikes me as a non sequitur. In medieval Europe, the hand copying of texts had also been "inextricably linked" to politics and religion. After

[73] Eisenstein, "Conjectures about the Impact of Print" (see n. 2). Perhaps I picked up the phrase from *Printing and the Mind of Man: A Descriptive Catalogue Illustrating the Impact of Print . . .* ed. J. Carter, P. H. Muir, et al. (London, 1967).
[74] John Barnard, introduction, *CHB* IV, 2.

the advent of printing, however, the character of the linkage itself underwent change – as any history of censorship will show.

When referring to printing as "an agent of change," I had in mind that historical change, in and of itself, is indeterminate, always contingent on numerous factors and usually compatible with movement in diverse directions. Thus the increased availability of vernacular Bibles to readers at large, the provision of polyglot versions to a scholarly elite, and the reactions of Roman churchmen to both developments did not point Western religion in any one direction. But however contradictory these three developments were, they shared in common the fact that they represented change.

****

The title of this abridged version also calls for comment.[75] The term "revolution," which used to refer to the circular movement of the planets, is now most often used to indicate two different processes. When titling this book, I had both processes in mind. First, there is the conventional use of the term to cover any relatively abrupt and decisive change. The replacement of hand copying by printing as the *chief* mode of book production in the West (I emphasize "*chief*" to make room for the persistence of hand copying, as noted earlier), this replacement occurred in so many locations in such a short time that it has to be designated by the term "revolution" – even though some semantic confusion may be generated thereby.

For the same term may also be used to designate a long-range irreversible process; a process whose effects become more pronounced the longer it goes on. This is the sense that governs references to an "industrial revolution" or to a "demographic revolution." This is the sense that led Raymond Williams to entitle his study of the growth of literacy *The Long Revolution*,[76] and this sense also seems applicable to changes wrought by printing. When we consider the

[75] What follows recapitulates passages in Eisenstein, "On Revolution and the Printed Word," *Revolution in History*, ed. R. Porter and M. Teich (Cambridge, 1986), 186–206.

[76] Raymond Williams, *The Long Revolution* (New York, 1966). Briggs and Burke, 22, cite the same title while questioning its relevance to print. But they ignore all diachronic aspects along with the cumulative effects of ever-increased output.

way written materials have been accumulating since the fifteenth
century, it seems evident that a long-range irreversible process has
been at work. Five hundred years of printing have given rise to an
ever-expanding knowledge industry that is unlike anything that was
sustained by hand copying over the course of millennia. In view of
current distaste for triumphant narratives, let me hasten to point out
that abundance can be no less dispiriting than scarcity. At present,
problems of overload have become more acute than they were a century ago, and it seems likely they will weigh even more heavily on
future generations than they do on our own.

In this regard, the typographical revolution that started in the fifteenth century bears some resemblance to the later agricultural revolution. In both cases old problems of scarcity were solved only to be
replaced by new problems of glut. The ten farmers required to feed
one townsman in the Middle Ages may be likened to the ten scribes
required to furnish Chaucer's clerk of Oxford with the twenty books
he wanted to fill his shelves.[77]

During the millennia that intervened between the invention of
writing and the introduction of printing in the West, it never took
fewer than ten scribes to feed one clerk. The production, collection,
and circulation of books were subject to an economy of scarcity.
Recovery and preservation were naturally of paramount concern.
Within a century after the installation of printing shops in Western Europe, however, even while old texts reflecting problems of
scarcity were becoming more available, a new economy of abundance
began to make its presence felt. A landmark in this process, which
reversed earlier trends, is the bibliography compiled by Conrad
Gesner and published by Christopher Froschauer in Zurich in 1545.
Gesner's *Biblioteca Universalis* – his "universal library" – excluded
all vernacular publication but attempted to list all Latin, Greek,

---

[77] The scarcity of books at Oxford in the fourteenth century was noted by the
bishop of Armagh, who complained that the mendicant orders had grabbed
everything for their priories and left not a single book of philosophy or theology
and very few in medicine or law. Jacqueline Harnesse, "The Scholastic Model of
Reading," in Carvallo and Chartier, 119.

and Hebrew printed works. Making use of new printed materials –
including booksellers' lists and publishers' catalogues – the author
managed to track down roughly a third of actual output. Gesner's
bibliography (which went through several editions and expanded
with each one) was not only the first; it was also the last attempt
to encompass the entire output of the Commonwealth of Learning
within the confines of one work. New bibliographies issued thereafter
became increasingly specialized. Eventually they multiplied at such a
rate that bibliographies of bibliographies had to be compiled. When
I was a student, we were introduced to a list of bibliographies of bibliographies of bibliographies. The end of this somewhat regressive
sequence is surely not yet in sight. The introduction of new media
has done nothing to slow down, let alone arrest, this process – as any
librarian can testify.

The end of this "long revolution" is still undetermined. But its
beginnings can be ascertained. They lie in the interval between
the 1450s and 1470s when European printing shops first appeared.
Why take fifteenth-century Western Europe as a point of departure
instead of beginning much earlier with China, where the very first
printed products were turned out?[78] It is instructive to look outside
the boundaries of Western Christendom if only in order to learn that
the mere introduction of a new technology tells us little about the
uses to which it will be put. No doubt the difference between uneven
development in Asia and rapid exploitation in the West has something to do with the difference between ideographic and alphabetic
systems of writing.

But other considerations are also pertinent. All the diverse
"factors" that have to be considered in any causal analysis – political,
economic, intellectual, etc. – can be seen to have played a role. Religion in particular should not be overlooked. There are some non-
Asian societies where alphabets were used but where printers were
forbidden to apply their craft to sacred texts. In the vast empire

---

[78] A recent study of woodblock printing in one province of China is instructive:
Lucille Chia, *Printing for Profit: The Commercial Publishers of Jianyand, Fujian*
(*11th–17th Centuries*) (Cambridge, MA, 2003).

governed by the Ottoman Turks, prohibitions against printing not only the *Koran* but any text in Arabic script remained in effect for hundreds of years.[79] Of course, other variables are also significant. In Eastern Christendom, religious printing was sanctioned and, indeed, sponsored by the church. Yet in contrast to Western developments, Russian printers started almost a century after Gutenberg and there-after maintained a very sluggish pace.[80] Only within Western Chris-tendom was the wooden handpress so energetically exploited by so many free-wheeling entrepreneurs that some forty thousand editions of books (not to mention indulgences, broadsides, and the like) had been issued in the first forty years.

This brief venture in comparative study may help to drive home the point that the most remarkable aspect of the story is *not* what did or did not happen in Gutenberg's shop in Mainz; it is, rather, the way that so many presses went into operation in so many places in so short a time. As noted by Denys Hay, printing spread "at a phenomenal speed . . . by the 1490s each of the major states had one important publishing centre and some had several."[81] One might add that printing spread in this manner nowhere else in the world. To explain why this happened, moreover, the role of a few major states seems less significant than the role played by many minor ones.

Most histories of printing follow the convention of organizing developments around the rise of the major nation-states. This pro-cedure works well enough for nineteenth-century developments, but it is likely to skew patterns when applied to the earlier, more cosmopolitan age of the handpress. The major centers of book production down through the eighteenth century were *not* congruent

---

[79] Halil Inalcik, *The Ottoman Empire: The Classical Age 1300–1600*, tr. N. Itzkowitz and C. Imber (London, 1973), 174; Juan R. I. Cole, "Printing and Urban Islam in the Mediterranean World 1890–1920," *Modernity and Culture from the Mediter-ranean to the Indian Ocean*, ed. L. Tarazi Fawaz, C. A. Bayley, and R. Ilbert (New York, 2001), 1–28; Francis Robinson, "Technology and Religious Change: Islam and the Impact of Print," *Modern Asian Studies* 27, no. 1 (1993): 229–51.

[80] Gary Marker, *Publishing, Printing and the Origins of Intellectual Life in Russia 1700–1800* (Princeton, NJ, 1985).

[81] Denys Hay, introduction, *Printing and the Mind of Man*, xxii.

with the major political capitals such as Paris, Berlin, Vienna, Rome, Madrid, and London. They were, rather, great commercial centers such as Venice, Antwerp, and Amsterdam. This pattern persisted until the Napoleonic era. The central city for the French-language press of the eighteenth century was not Paris; it was Amsterdam.[82]

Indeed, nation building worked at cross purposes with the rapid expansion of early modern printing industries. The rise of a few large, well-consolidated, dynastic states was less helpful than the presence in late medieval Europe of numerous small political units: bishoprics, communes, free cities, and other assorted quasi-independent states. Through the eighteenth century, rulers of small principalities continued to invite printers to set up shop within their realms and thus provide revenues and publicity – fill town coffers and satisfy civic pride.[83] The numerous place names which illustrate the spread of printing across fifteenth-century Europe indicate the eagerness of petty rulers and town councils to get their town's name in print at least once. Many printing offices in small Italian city-states issued only one or two editions before dropping out of the picture. The cluster of printing houses in Venice is reminiscent of what happened to "Silicon Valley" – not least because so many "startups" (like recent "dot-coms") rapidly went bankrupt and closed down.[84] The absence of any powerful central authority, whether provided by emperor or pope (in contrast once again to China or the Ottoman empire or Muscovy); the prolonged rivalry between the Pope and other rulers; quarrels among diverse rulers themselves; the fragmentation of political authority, in short, provided opportunities for printers,

---

[82] Febvre and Martin, *Coming of the Book*, 298. J. H. de la Fontaine Verwey, "The Netherlands Book," *Copy and Print in the Netherlands*, ed. W. G. Hellinga (Amsterdam, 1962), 29, asserts that more books were printed in the United Provinces during the seventeenth century than in all other countries taken together. [That this assertion is based on guesswork is noted by K. W. D. Haley, *The Dutch in the Seventeenth Century* (London, 1972), 123.]

[83] This point is elaborated in *Grub Street Abroad*. See also the case history by Raymond Birn, "Pierre Rousseau et les Philosophes of Bouillon," *Studies on Voltaire and the Eighteenth Century* XXIX, ed. T. Besterman (Geneva, 1964).

[84] Lowry, *Aldus Manutius*, 13–18.

as it did for other merchants and early capitalists, to play one power against another while extending far-flung trade networks from the shelter provided by small walled towns.

As mention of trade networks suggests, economic developments ought to be coupled with political ones. Late medieval particularism had to be combined with early modern capitalism in order to produce favorable conditions for rapid expansion.[85] Among cultural and intellectual factors that contributed to the rapid growth of Western printing industries, Italian humanism is often singled out. The important role played by book-hunting literati in stimulating elite patronage is undeniable. But so too was the impetus supplied by the Roman Church, which had long commanded the largest supply of scribal labor and played a dominant role in selecting texts for duplication. The initial welcome given by the Church to a technology that promised to help with standardizing liturgies and educating young priests is suggested by the location of the first presses in Italy: a monastery in Subiaco and the papal city of Rome.

Clearly, one must consider the varied ingredients which were incubating in the fourteenth and early fifteenth centuries in order to understand the spread and rapid development of early printing. In this sense, I would agree with those who adopt an evolutionary model of change and stress how ripe conditions were in late medieval Europe. The absence of any powerful central authority was, after all, a heritage from the pre-Gutenberg age. So too were the far-flung networks and sophisticated systems of financing developed by the late medieval merchants who were engaged in a wholesale cloth trade. Textile manufacture, moreover, was linked to rag paper production. Buying and selling paper went together with a retail trade in manuscript books. As already discussed, some of the practices of manuscript bookdealers would be carried over into the publishing of printed books.

[85] Anderson, *Imagined Communities*, uses the hyphenated phrase "print-capitalism" to suggest that print alone was not responsible for the phenomena he discusses. One wonders why he singles out capitalism from so many other significant variables (political structures, for example). See p. 47, n. 21, where the absence of capitalism in China and not the presence of a particular governmental structure is singled out as the sole determinant.

But, of course, all revolutions have preconditions as well as precipitants. The expansion of a regular manuscript book trade and of a literate laity together with the prior introduction of paper and oil-based ink, of credit and the requisite metallurgical technique may be plausibly regarded as preconditions. As my conclusion suggests, one may make a sound case for a multivariable explanation when dealing with the printing revolution. A convergence of many different impulses and motives helps to explain why printing shops were installed in fewer than five decades across all of Europe from the Atlantic coasts to the mountains of Montenegro, from Mt. Etna to regions north of Stockholm.

****

Because the term "revolution" implies acknowledgment of prerequisites and preconditions, I am comfortable about using it for the title of this book. But I failed to anticipate the problems that would ensue when I suggested possible ways of labeling the revolution and mentioned "a shift from script to print." It turns out that this phrase is too easily misconstrued. Thus it has been taken to mean that the hand-written text was "an early casualty" of the introduction of printing.[86] The contents of my own files belie such a notion. Writing letters, producing autograph manuscripts, keeping ledgers, and numerous other practices that entail pen work not only coexisted and persisted with the output of printers; printers, who circulated model letters and manuals on bookkeeping, did more to encourage such practices than had been the case with scribes.

The same point applies to hand copying (as distinguished from handwriting). Just as touch typists thrived when word processors appeared, so too were the skills of copyists in greater demand after printers set to work. As Curt Bühler noted many years ago, the employment of copyists continued for centuries until typewriters came into play. The need for secretaries to take dictation has proved even longer lived – from the days of Caesar and Charlemagne to today's CEO. The hand copying of passages from printed books also persisted through the twentieth century. When DeWitt Wallace

---

[86] Crick and Walsham, introduction, 3.

sought material for the first issues of the *Reader's Digest*, he sat in the New York Public Library copying out passages by hand. I myself engaged in similar practices until the photocopier appeared. "Scholars remained scribes for a long time. Some of us still are," writes Anthony Grafton.[87]

But although scholars continued to remain scribes, they ceased to rely *solely* on hand-copied texts and images as soon as it became possible for them to do so. In this respect, I believe earlier generations were clearly disadvantaged in a way that affected their intellectual activities. It has been said that I "demeaningly" refer to Petrarch and others as "scribal scholars."[88] I do so to distinguish them from later humanists, such as Poliziano, who had a more "sophisticated historical understanding"[89] and access to printed materials. The appellation serves to remind readers that the early humanists were entirely reliant on hand-copied materials. Far from being demeaning, it makes their achievements (and those of their medieval predecessors) appear to be all the more impressive. To recognize the disadvantages under which they labored enhances appreciation of their abilities and rescues them from "the enormous condescension" exhibited by later generations.

When I use terms such as "scribal culture" and "print culture," I do so to draw attention to two distinctly different literary ecologies – only one of which favored the sustained and systematic development of diverse fields of learning. The terms seem helpful for describing the large concatenation of activites entailed in duplicating, distributing, and collecting written materials before and after the use of the wooden handpress.[90]

---

[87] Anthony Grafton, "The Importance of Being Printed," *Journal of Interdisciplinary History* XI, no. 2 (Autumn 1980): 281.

[88] Ibid., 284.

[89] Ibid.

[90] Adrian Johns's definition of print culture comes close to agreeing with mine: "a vast array of representations, practices and skills which extended from the printing shop through the bookshop and marketplace to the . . . study . . . and home – and thence back to the printing house again." Johns, *Nature of the Book*, 58.

This large concatenation of activities was fundamentally changed once print culture became dominant. An eminent authority on punctuation in manuscripts makes it clear how hand-copying practices themselves came to be dominated by printed ones:

New conventions became established and were disseminated more quickly through printed books than through manuscripts because of the number of identical copies produced through the new process . . . Practices established by printers soon began to appear in manuscripts . . . the written word had become associated in the minds of readers with the printed word and the conventions of written language had become dominated by those employed in printed texts.[91]

In this sense, it seems fair enough to say that scribal culture had come to an end. It is in this sense that I refer to a shift from script to print. But this does not mean that manuscripts were no longer being produced or that copyists had stopped plying their trade. The prolonged coexistence of printers with copyists is not ignored in my book. There it is noted how early printers copied the work of scribes and how scribes returned the compliment. But there, too, notice is taken of how printers departed from scribal procedures by marking up "copy" before duplicating it. In addition, there is mention of how printed specimen books affected the forming of letters so that even hand copying itself was influenced by mechanical duplication.

There was "no sudden break in the production of manuscript books," writes an admiring reviewer of David McKitterick's book.[92] But no one has ever claimed that there was such a break. According to McKitterick, the persistence of copying makes it "misleading to speak of any transition from manuscript to print as if it were a finite

---

[91] Malcolm Beckwith Parkes, *Pause and Effect: An Introduction to the History of Punctuation in the West* (Berkeley, CA, 1993), 56.

[92] Barnard, "Slow Revolution" (see n. 15).

process . . . or indeed that the process was all in one direction."[93] I argue, to the contrary, that there was such a "transition" and that it was irreversible. Although manuscript production persisted, it did so in a changed form. As Harold Love asserts, it assumed more "specialized functions"[94] and never again resumed its central role. No doubt having a printed text serve as the "original" of a manuscript is something of an oddity. Perhaps the most celebrated instance of such an inversion is our own Declaration of Independence.[95] But whether scribes copied from printed books or vice versa seems to me to be beside the point. The point is that all parties were still contributing to a historic process that *was* "all in one direction," leading toward accumulation and growing abundance in contrast to earlier scarcity and repeated loss.

Since my first edition was published, the fallacy of doctrines of "supersession" has been brilliantly illuminated by Paul Duguid and Geoffrey Nunberg.[96] Elsewhere I've made clear my agreement with their position while questioning recent doomsday pronouncements about the supersession of print.[97] Here, let me simply reiterate: printed texts did not supersede manuscripts any more than engraving and woodcuts superseded drawing and painting. Nevertheless, the introduction of printing did arrest and then reverse the process of loss, corruption, and erosion that had accompanied the hand copying of texts and images.

In his discussion of library catalogues, David McKitterick laments the "great divorce" that saw manuscripts, which were for a long time filed together with printed books, placed in a separate category.

---

[93] McKitterick, *Print, Manuscript*, 47. Julia Crick "The Art of the Unprinted," in Crick and Walsham, 119, similarly argues that copying from a printed exemplar reverses the flow of information.

[94] Love, "Oral and Scribal Texts," 105.

[95] Thomas Starr, "Separated at Birth: Text and Context of the Declaration of Independence," *Proceedings of the American Antiquarian Society* 110, pt. 1 (Worcester, MA; 2002): 152–99.

[96] Geoffrey Nunberg ed., *The Future of the Book* (Berkeley, CA; 1996), intro.; and Paul Duguid, "Material Matters," 66–73.

[97] Eisenstein, "From the Printed Word to the Moving Image," *Social Research* 64, no. 3 (Fall 1987): 1049–65.

Wherever manuscripts were placed and however they were classified, however, the main problem confronting successive generations
of cataloguers was of a different order. Over the course of the last
five centuries, librarians have had to cope with a cumulative process unlike anything produced by hand copying for two millennia or
more.[98] "Surely there are no signs at present that pressure on library
facilities is diminishing or that problems posed by overload are being
eased." These "final remarks" were written in the first edition of this
book.[99] Some thirty years later, after the introduction of new equipment and new "information sciences" into modern libraries, they still
seem relevant.

The theme of there being too many books in the world is an
ancient one. Nevertheless, early modern scholars confronted what
seemed to them to be an unprecedented "information overload."[100]
The continued output of hand-copied books, far from reversing
or even slowing down the accumulation of written materials, only
added to the growing supply. This diachronic aspect of print culture,
stemming from its preservative capacity, tends to be overlooked by
numerous critics. Perhaps it should have been given more emphasis
in my book.

Recent studies have greatly enriched our knowledge of manuscript
production, in England at least,[101] during the age of the handpress.
The advantages of hand copying for avoiding government seizure

---

[98] Seventeenth-century libraries "threatened to become huge and potentially
unmangeable," Mark McDayter, "The Hunting of St. James Library . . . ," *Huntington Library Quarterly* 66 (2003): 24.

[99] See "Some Final Remarks."

[100] See earlier on Conrad Gesner and the proliferation of bibliographies. See also
essays by Ann Blair and others on "early modern information overload" in *Journal
of the History of Ideas* 64 (Jan. 2003): 1–73; essays by Blair and Richard Yeo
in *Books and the Sciences* (n. 12), 69–90, 207–25; and Blair, "The Practices of
Erudition according to Morhof," *Mapping the World of Learning*, ed. Françoise
Waquet (Wiesbaden, 2000); 59–74. I owe thanks to Ann Blair for alerting me
to recent literature on this topic and for her several contributions.

[101] As noted in the editors' introduction by Crick and Walsham, 6–7, the inferior
condition of English printing may have encouraged more manuscript production
than was the case on the Continent.

(rather like the Russian "samizdhat") has long been well established.[102] But hand-copied texts were not only produced for clandestine purposes. They also served certain authors (especially certain
poets and women writers) who evaded the "stigma of print"[103] (today
we might say the glare of publicity) by circulating their compositions
in hand-copied form among a restricted group of friends.[104] Margaret
Ezell, among others, objects to the marginalization of this coterie literature, which is treated by many authorities as archaic or frivolous
or aristocratic and dismissed prematurely long before it had actually
passed from the scene. Even after 1710, she points out, hand copying was still "a competitive if not a dominant mode" of transmitting
written materials.[105] Similarly, Harold Love notes that the medieval
tradition of transmitting texts through handwritten copies was not
extinguished by print and should not be regarded as a symptom of a
dying political order.[106] This point is well taken. (Circulating poems
among friends out of the public eye persisted after the disappearance
of court culture; even now, the same function is fulfilled by "privately
printed" slim volumes.) Yet none of the literati who "published" their
works in manuscript form failed to consult the printed materials that
were circulating in their day. They benefited, along with all other
writers and scholars, from access to printed editions of reference

---

[102] See, e.g., Ira Wade, *The Clandestine Organization and the Diffusion of . . . Ideas in France from 1700 to 1750* (Princeton, NJ, 1938); François Moureau, ed., *De Bonne Main: La Communication Manuscrite au XVIIIe siècle* (Paris, 1993).

[103] The thesis put forth by J. W. Saunders, "The Stigma of Print," *Essays in Criticism* I (1951): 137–64, which was echoed for many decades, has been modified and qualified by (among others) Nita Krevans, "Print and the Tudor Poets," *Reconsidering the Renaissance*, ed. M. A. DiCesare (Binghamton, NY, 1992); A. F. Marotti, *Manuscript, Print and the English Renaissance Lyric* (Ithaca, NY, 1995); Steven May, "Tudor aristocrats and the Stigma of Print," *Renaissance Papers* X (1980): 11–18; Wendy Wall, *The Imprint of Gender* (New York, 1993).

[104] Harold Love, *Scribal Publication in Seventeenth Century England* (Oxford, 1993); Marotti, *Manuscript, Print*; H. R. Woudhuysen, *Sir Philip Sidney and the Circulation of Manuscripts 1558–1640* (Oxford, 1996); Margaret Ezell, *Social Authorship and the Advent of Print* (Baltimore, 1999).

[105] Ezell, *Social Authorship*, 12.

[106] Love, "Oral and Scribal Texts," *CHB* IV, 97–121.

books[107] and classical authors. Robert Cotton, the antiquary, offers a telling example. He devoted much time to copying out old charters and has been described by Harold Love as an "exceptionally pure example of the continuity of an intellectual culture grounded on the handwritten word."[108] Yet he owned printed books, many obtained from abroad. Writing about Cotton and the Society of Antiquaries, Julia Crick observes that "print recurs as the destination, source and contaminant of scribally transmitted texts."[109] Deep involvement in the circulation of hand-copied texts did not preclude living in a literary environment marked by the new features that were characteristic of early modern print culture.

****

These new features ought to be regarded as relative, not absolute, phenomena. Recent studies show that this point is worth more emphasis. More abundantly stocked bookshelves and enriched literary diets resulted from increased output. But this does not mean that all books in print were made immediately available to Renaissance readers.[110] Of course, this was far from the case. Sixteenth-century bookhunters were frequently disappointed. Nevertheless, they were in a better position to get what they sought than were those who lived in the age of the scribe.[111]

The relative, not absolute, character of features associated with print culture is especially pertinent to questions raised by Adrian

---

[107] According to Blair, "Reading Strategies," 12, n. 4, "reference book" is a nineteenth-century term but fits a category that was recognized in the early modern era.

[108] Cited by Julia Crick, "The Art of the Unprinted," Crick and Walsham, chap. 6, 116.

[109] Crick, ibid., 134.

[110] Joseph Loewenstein, "Martial, Johnson and the Assertion of Plagiarism," *Reading, Society and Politics in Early Modern England*, ed. Kevin Sharpe and Steven Zwicker (Cambridge, 2003), 277.

[111] As early as 1481, a scholar rejoiced at the good fortune that provided him and his contemporaries with a huge supply of books unknown to any previous generation. Julia H. Gaisser, *Catullus and His Renaissance Readers* (Oxford, 1993), 35.

Johns with regard to standardization. To say that early printed products were more standardized than were late medieval manuscripts is not to deny that they were also more multiform than were the later products of mechanical presses, or of lithography or photography. Far from denying this point, I warn against ignoring it. Yet Johns seems to believe he is refuting my arguments when he devotes much of his massive study of scientific publication in early modern England to documenting the multiformity of early printed output. That so-called exactly repeatable pictorial images were often reproduced inexactly is evident from my own reference to "reversals, misplacements, and the use of worn and broken blocks." Many more examples are cited by Johns. They all confirm the fact that the output of the handpress fell short of meeting modern standards. But they do not contradict the point that early printed products were more standardized than were hand-copied ones.[112]

Some multiformity resulted from mishandling by careless and inadequately supervised printers, but some was also built into early printing methods. Insofar as the latter was the case, the resultant variations that now trouble bibliographers tended to be taken for granted by earlier readers. "Few appreciated the importance of differences between copies...it was generally accepted that the process of printing involved variation – not just standardization."[113] This acceptance of some variation is ignored by Johns. In his view, the one concern that possessed early readers and provided a key to all others was whether one could trust any printed report. To show that distrust was endemic, he cites numerous complaints about piracy and plagiarism. "Piracy and plagiarism occupied readers' minds just as prominently as fixity...Unauthorized translations, epitomes, imitations...were, they believed, routine hazards."[114] Piracy,

---

[112] McKitterick acknowledges that there was a "greater measure of standardization in the printed book" but at the same time seems to object to my asserting that this was the case. *Print, Manuscript*, 99–100.

[113] Ibid., 111.

[114] Johns, *Nature of the Book*, 30. Of course, "piracy and plagiarism" also posed definitional problems before laws pertaining to literary property rights had been enacted.

plagiarism, and the other "hazards" may have been vexing. But they have no o'bvious connection with the issue of standardization.

Whether duly authorized or not, all editions were subject to the relative multiformity that was engendered by early printing methods. In this respect, Johns's detailed account of the English Stationers' Company, however intrinsically fascinating and well researched, is of questionable relevance. Rules and regulations (whether observed or not) were incapable of remedying the defects that were intrinsic to handpress production. The actual working routines of pressmen, compositors, and correctors, as demonstrated by the late D. F. McKenzie in his classic essay, usually included the concurrent printing of more than one book and always resulted in a degree of multiformity.[115] This was true whether or not a work was published by London Stationers in good standing.

To dwell on the incapacity of the handpress to meet modern standards, moreover, is to assume an anachronistic posture. Johns is so intent on contrasting early printed products with modern ones that he often forgets this contrast was unavailable to early modern Europeans. A Milanese humanist, Bonus Accursius, in a prefatory letter to a 1475 edition of Ovid's *Metamorphoses*, described why printed books were superior to manuscripts: "when the impression . . . is correct . . . it runs through all the copies always in the same order, with scarcely the possibility of error – a thing which in a manuscript is apt to result very differently."[116] Modern critics who are aware of the incapacity of the handpress to produce truly standard editions may regard this opinion as naive and misleading. Yet there is ample evidence that it was widely held. It was not just put forth

---

[115] McKenzie, "Printers of the Mind," *Making Meaning*, 13–86.

[116] Victor Schölderer, "Printers and Readers in Italy in the Fifteenth Century," Annual Italian Lecture of the British Academy (1949) Brochure (*The Proceedings of the British Academy* XXXV): 15, n. 1. See also editor's preface to Augustine's *De Arte Praedicandi* (Strassburg: J. Mentelin, ca. 1467–8) cited by M. B. Parkes, *Scribes, Scripts and Readers* (London, 1991), xxi. The editor regarded printing primarily as a means of producing identical copies of a text he had corrected, "thereby eliminating the accumulation of errors inherent in manuscript transmission."

by printers who stood to gain from it[117] but was also assumed to be true by churchmen who were anxious about irregular liturgies and lay officials who sought to instill more uniformity throughout their realms. It became a significant element in religious disputes concerning veracity in printed Bibles. Early Protestants regarded print as a "providential medium because it seemed to guarantee the unity of the text in copy after copy."[118]

The idea that irregularities in early printing methods led readers to distrust all their books – ranging from lowly almanacs to costly folios – is not backed up by evidence [119] and has an anachronistic air. "Contemporaries had good reason to be wary," Johns writes. "Their editions of Shakespeare, Donne, Sir Thomas Browne were liable to be dubious." The first folio of Shakespeare contained "non uniform spelling and punctuation . . . No two copies were identical . . . In such a world, questions of credit took the place of assumptions of fixity."[120] In what world were readers concerned about nonuniform spelling or about variants in the first folio of Shakespeare? In a seventeenth-century world? Or is a late modern author projecting such concerns back into a milieu where they do not belong? "It is a commonplace that the spelling of English authors in the sixteenth and early seventeenth centuries was varied."[121] The virtuosi with whom Johns is concerned were surely not troubled by "variants in the first folio of Shakespeare" since the device used to uncover and count them was not developed until the twentieth century.

These same virtuosi were also less likely to be studying a collection of playscripts published by English stationers than corresponding about technical texts that were for the most part in Latin and published abroad. To confine scientific interchange to the English scene is to lose sight of its fundamentally cosmopolitan character. Johns's detailed account of the orders and bylaws governing English

---

[117] Johns, *Nature of the Book*, 5.

[118] Scott Mandelbrote, "The Authority of the Word," in Crick and Walsham, 136.

[119] The dates printed in almanacs were considered so trustworthy that they were accepted as evidence in English law courts. Bernard Capp, *English Almanacs 1500–1800* (Ithaca, NY, 1979), 284.

[120] Johns, *Nature of the Book*, 30.

[121] Philip Gaskell, *A New Introduction to Bibliography* (Oxford, 1972), 344.

Stationers is also of doubtful relevance to the Latin texts (by Vesalius, Copernicus, Kepler, Harvey, et al.) that constituted landmarks in early modern science.[122] These works were published outside England by Continental printers who worked at some distance from Stationers' Hall. As Johns himself notes: "domestic printing was generally worse and more expensive than Continental" so that "many learned writers took their texts abroad to be printed."[123] Those who didn't take their own texts abroad read works that were published under foreign auspices and corresponded with foreign authors. A survey of this correspondence shows no evidence that the reliability of printed editions was distrusted in the manner that Johns suggests.[124]

However relative was the degree of standardization obtained by the handpress, the fact remains that early modern Europeans were much better able than their forebears had been to consult more or less the same text, chart, or table at more or less the same time and to correspond with each other about the same items on the same page.[125] Even polemical pamphlet controversies showed a capacity on the part of participants to refer to identical passages when carrying on an argument. Readers were also alerted to the location of certain errors that had been caught too late to be corrected before publication by means of the (standardized) errata slips that were inserted in many printed books.[126]

Johns's treatment also suggests the need for further clarification concerning the duplication of error. Far from holding to the implausible notion that merely printing a text might make it more

---

[122] That Latin books formed a single European-wide market with England on its periphery is noted by Andrew Pettegree, "Printing and the Reformation: The English Exception," *The Beginnings of English Protestantism*, ed. Alex Ryrie and Peter Marshall (Cambridge, 2002); 157–8.

[123] Johns, *Nature of the Book*, 170.

[124] See review essay by John Henry, "Trusting Print/Making Natural Philosophy," *Metascience* (2001): 6–14.

[125] See, e.g., exchanges concerning Copernicus' *De Revolutionibus* in ed. Robert Westman, "Three Responses to the Copernican Theory," *The Copernican Achievement* (Berkeley, CA, 1975), chap. 9.

[126] Seth Lerer, "Errata: Print, Politics and Poetry in Early Modern England," in Sharpe and Zwicker, *Reading, Society and Politics*, 41–72.

accurate,[127] I simply point out that the duplication of a given error
made it more visible to many eyes and thus more susceptible to being
corrected. Unlike a single blunder made by a scribe, the omission of
the word "not" in the Seventh Commandment was "fixed" in print,
giving rise to fining the printer and to labeling the entire edition as
the "wicked" Bible. Other single words were similarly standardized
throughout other biblical editions, giving rise to a "britches" Bible,
etc. How single inscriptions were precisely duplicated in hundreds
of copies is shown by references to the dates of 4004 and 1694; the
first assigned to Creation (by Bishop Ussher) the latter to the end of
the world (by Alsted). Pierre Bayle exhibited scepticism about many
issues, but when he published his *Dictionnaire* in 1697 he could assert
"with absolute confidence" that Alsted was in error.[128] Such confidence on the part of an otherwise sceptical reader does not indicate
that distrust of print was endemic. On the contrary!

Printers initially contributed to cognitive advance not by producing texts that were free of error but rather by reproducing more copies
of the error-ridden texts that had been circulating in manuscript
form. New errors of commission and omission were also introduced
by editors as well as by printers. But the first printed edition of a
classical text, however riddled with errors it might be, performed
a function no manuscript copy had fulfilled. It served as a "textus
receptus" – a text that provided a common base for later disputes
among scholars.

> The average classical text first saw print in a state that represented
> what one might call a more or less random dip into the stream of
> tradition, at a point as far from the source as could be; and in that
> state it was, as it were, "frozen" by the new medium.[129]

However many variants the *editio princeps* contained, the "textus
receptus" was sufficiently standardized to serve as a common basis
for scholarly disputation.

---

[127] I reattribute the "intelligence and skill" of readers "to the printed page," according to Johns, *Nature of the Book*, 19.

[128] Bayle, "Alstedius," *Dictionnaire* (1820 edn.), 1:460.

[129] E. J. Kenney, "The Character of Humanist Philology," *Classical Influences on
European Culture*, ed. R. R. Bolgar (Cambridge, 1971), 127.

A sequence of defective early editions of Pliny's *Natural History* offers a useful example of the sort of collaborative (and competitive) enterprise that was entailed. A Florentine scholar, Niccoló Perotti, was so upset by errors in an early printed edition that he wrote to the Pope asking him to set up a board of learned correctors who would scrutinize every text before it could be printed.[130] Although this letter has been described as a "call for censorship," it would be more accurate (as Martin Davies notes) to describe it as "a demand for institutionalized press correction."[131]

Ironically enough, when Perotti published his own version of the same work, he was accused by another scholar of making some 275 dreadful errors himself.[132] It seems likely that any board of learned correctors would soon be at loggerheads if, indeed, an agreement could be obtained over who was fit to serve. As is often the case with academic infighting, scholarly squabbles had unanticipated benefits.

> Constant claims to have uncovered flaws in the work of their predecessors led inevitably to bitter personal rivalries as Pliny scholars competed for reputation, patronage and academic appointments. But these disputes also led to explicit and fruitful discussions of the proper canons of editorial practice.[133]

The persistence of learned quarrels over each edition had the additional benefit of stimulating continuous investigatory activity, leading to an accumulation of fresh findings bearing on classical studies and natural history.

The reference to fresh findings brings up the need to distinguish between duplicating ancient texts such as Pliny's *Natural History* that had long been transmitted (and corrupted) by hand and

---

[130] John Monfasani, "The First Call for Press Censorship; Niccoló Perotti, Giovanni Andrea Bussi . . . and the Editing of Pliny's *Natural History*," *Renaissance Quarterly* 41 (Spring 1988): 1–31.

[131] Martin Davies, "Making Sense of Pliny in the Quattrocento," *Renaissance Studies* 9 (June 1995): 248, n. 31.

[132] Ibid., 250.

[133] Charles G. Nauert, Jr., "Humanists, Scientists and Pliny: Changing Approaches to a Classical Author," *American Historical Review* 84 (Feb. 1979): 78.

duplicating freshly recorded observations and newly drawn images. That new reports, charts, tables, maps, and drawings were made more secure when replicated in one thousand printed copies than when copied out one thousand times by hand seems to me to be unassailable. To be sure, accurate reproduction of new data by means of engravings, woodcuts, or letterpress printing required careful supervision. In case my warnings on this point are missed by readers in the future, as is true among some critics in the past, let me repeat that in the hands of ignorant printers driving to make quick profits, data tended to get garbled at an ever more rapid pace. But under the guidance of technically proficient masters, printing provided a way of transcending the limits that scribal procedures had imposed.

This mention of "guidance" by "technically proficient masters" needs additional emphasis. By taking the wooden handpress as an "agent of change," several critics complain, I have assigned more importance to the tool than to the humans who put it to use.[134] They ignore my comment about necessary guidance and seem to think that I hold printing in and of itself capable of transcending earlier limits. That "print itself did not guarantee the value of what it produced and reproduced"[135] seems to me to be too obvious to need saying. That the use of print by learned authors and skillful artisans enabled them to achieve goals that had been out of reach in the age of scribes is, I think, worth spelling out.

To ignore a single comment in a big book is understandable. It is more puzzling that my critics also ignore numerous references to specific scholars, natural philosophers, map makers, artisan-authors, and the like who worked together with master printers (or set up presses themselves) in order to supervise the reproduction of significant texts and illustrations. Johns ignores this cast of characters partly because he stays across the Channel, where he attributes

---

[134] Warner, *Letters of the Republic*, 6, objects that human agency disappears from my narrative. John Feather, "Revolutions Revisited," *Sharp News* (Autumn 1999): 10–11, contrasts my unfortunate preoccupation with "impersonal influences" with the "real world" and "real people" described by Johns. See similar criticism from Briggs and Burke, 58.

[135] Johns, *Nature of the Book*, 174.

"the reliability of every published page" to "a well ordered stationers' community and government licensing system" – a doubtful attribution in my view. Despite a passing reference to the well-known "autonomy and creativity of Continental printers" he also seems persuaded that authors and printers were incapable of supervising operations on their own and that institutional constraints were required to "discipline the domains of print."[136] In his view, an institution such as the Royal Society was required to insulate printing from the "hugger mugger of the coffee house and the tumult of Amsterdam bookshops."[137] Lacking such an institution, Tycho Brahe had achieved temporary success only by maintaining a "sterilized way of printing," that is, by setting up a private press on an island.[138] After Tycho's death, his work "descended into the hands of the book trade," presumably to be forever contaminated. In fact, Kepler managed to put Tycho's data to good use amid the "hugger mugger" of the Thirty Years' War, and numerous Dutch printers and publishers managed to produce celebrated atlases and other paper tools amid the "tumult of Amsterdam bookshops."[139] One might add that the output of the "well ordered" London stationers' commmunity during the sixteenth and early seventeenth centuries was inferior to that produced by the less restrained, more freewheeling entrepreneurs on the Continent.

To suggest, as Johns does, that I attribute intelligence and skill to the printed page is to ignore my discussion of the *modus operandi* of these entrepreneurs, of the patronage they secured, and of the authors who collaborated with them. After all, most of the authors mentioned in my book had a stake in having their work properly produced. Some authors (such as the astronomer Regiomontanus or the anatomist Charles Estienne) acted as their own

---

[136] Ibid., 624, 37, 188.

[137] Johns, "Reading and Experiment in the Early Royal Society," in Sharpe and Zwicker, *Reading, Society and Politics*, 253.

[138] Johns, *Nature of the Book*, 52. A more detailed criticism of this view and of Johns's one-sided depiction of Galileo is in *AHR Forum*, 99–100.

[139] For more details concerning the fate of Tycho's work and the Dutch master printer Willem Janszoon Blaeu see *AHR Forum*, 100–1.

printers[140] but, for the most part, collaboration (not always amicable, to be sure) prevailed. Vesalius and Oporinus, Conrad Gesner and Christopher Froschauer, Erasmus and Froben, John Foxe and John Day were among the more celebrated collaborators, but there were many others.[141] In addition to collaboration between author and printer, there were authors, such as Vesalius and Agricola, who hired and supervised the work of illustrators so that "descriptions which are conveyed by words" would not "cause difficulty to posterity."[142] And then there were numerous other intermediaries – editors, correctors, translators, and the like – who were needed to supervise large projects and had to be given room and board for weeks, even months on end. There is nothing impersonal about the extended households described in my work or about the remarkable range of talents over which the most celebrated master printers presided.[143]

One of the unexpected rewards of working on this topic was encountering these previously unfamiliar entrepreneurs who found financing and patronage from diverse sources, played one power against another, and presided over shops that served as a focal point for all manner of interchange. Indeed, I have also been criticized for making too much (not too little) of the role played by certain exceptional master printers while ignoring the more numerous artisans who worked in cramped, dirty, noisy shops and rapidly turned out whatever came to hand. (The number of shops that sprang up in Venice and then disappeared, rather like our modern "startups" and "dot-coms," was noted earlier.)

It is true that my account "conveys little of the variety, fragility and tiny scale of the majority of printing shops,"[144] not to mention

---

[140] See references in Eisenstein, "The Early Printer as a Renaissance Man," *Printing History* (American Printing History Association Journal) (Nov. 1981): 6–17.

[141] See names cited by Hirsch, 47, who notes that a full list "could easily be extended to fill many pages."

[142] Cited in *Agent of Change*, 469.

[143] Since my book was published, a close-up view of the world of a justly celebrated master printer has been offered by Barbara C. Halporn, *The Correspondence of Johann Amerbach: Early Printing in Its Social Context* (Ann Arbor, MI, 2000).

[144] Grafton, "Importance of Being Printed," 277. This point is echoed by Sandra Hindman, who complains that I focus on a few "highbrow" printers and authors

the often disruptive behavior of journeymen and masters alike.[145] But my work was never intended to provide an in-depth description of the average early modern printing shop. My emphasis on a few exceptional master printers, like my concern with Latin-reading elites, is deliberately selective. It is aimed at demonstrating what could be accomplished by means of print that had been desired but remained out of reach (the reach of the most talented and gifted professsionals) during the age of scribes. But I also think that it is a mistake to underestimate the role played by the exceptional master printers. The diversely located printing shops that served as cultural centers are worth more extended treatment than they have been accorded up to now.

The same point applies to the activities of the many opportunistic printers who served as independent agents of change. These activities are discussed, all too briefly, in connection with the way printers flocked to Wittenberg and Geneva and later "voted with their feet" after the Council of Trent. Reactions to the Index of Prohibited Books are also relevant. By using the Catholic Index as a guide, printers inadvertently deflected publication policies in Protestant regions in favor of heterodox and libertine trends that were at odds with Lutheran and Calvinist views.

But even though I regard the more exceptional master printers as the true protagonists of my book, impersonal processes must also be given due attention. Surely one may fully acknowledge the role played by human agents without denying that impersonal processes also came into play after the widespread adoption of printing and engraving. "Print spread texts in a different way from manuscripts; it multiplied them not consecutively but simultaneously."[146] Note that this unexceptional statement refers to print and not to the printer as an agent of change. Incidentally, the issue of simultaneity deserves more attention that it has hitherto received. As is true

and neglect the many "second or third string" ones. Hindman, *Printing the Written Word*, introduction, 3.

[145] Gaskell, *New Introduction to Bibliography*, 47–8, discusses the disruptive behavior of workmen, a long-lived theme that receives its most memorable form in Robert Darnton's title essay in *The Great Cat Massacre* (New York, 1984), 74–107.

[146] Crick and Walsham, introduction, 20.

of simultaneity, an economy of scale is, by its very nature, impersonal. But that is no reason to regard either of these phenomena as insignificant or to ignore their possible ramifications.

Closely related to the question of impersonal agency is the issue of technological determinism. "To describe the printing press as an agent of change," writes Michael Warner in an influential critique, "is to make the mistake of privileging a particular technology over culture and worse, to assume that technology is prior to culture."[147] I'm not sure what Warner means by "prior" to culture since I discuss all manner of diverse phenomena (the complexity of a polyglot bible compared to the *Koran*, the calendrical problems posed by celebrating Easter, etc.)[148] that were embedded in Western culture and were prior to printing. Nor can I imagine why he thinks my work "presupposes printing and culture" to be "discrete entities."[149] My repeated use of the terms "scribal culture" and "print culture" may be questionable on many counts, but it does, at least, indicate that the two "entities" are fused. Supervising presswork, pouring metal in moulds, sorting out pieces of type, and the like called for a different set of skills from hand copying. In this restricted sense, the character of the tool(s) determined the character of the new labor force; in this restricted sense, the new technology *was* "prior" to a new occupational culture.

But the fifteenth-century printing shop is not the locale that Warner has in mind when he objects to my view about "technology's presumed effects." In his view, fifteenth-century presses have been wrongly endowed with powers that form part of a much later construct. "Everything that has been ascribed to the agency of printing has been retrodetermined."[150] To support this opinion he asserts that "early printers in no way distinguished their work from hand produced documents."[151] But this is simply wrong, as is shown by

---

[147] Warner, *Letters of the Republic*, 8.
[148] *Agent of Change*, 335, 609.
[149] Warner, *Letters of the Republic*, 6.
[150] Ibid., 9.
[151] Ibid., 6.

numerous self-congratulatory colophons, editorial prefaces, and the like. "Who dares glorify the pen made book/when so much better brass-stamped letters look."[152]

The colophon, like the codex, was a scribal innovation. After printers set to work, however, new wine was poured into old bottles. Whereas the scribe often complained about frozen or cramped fingers, the early printer boasted about the superiority of his new tools. Recognition of the "stunning novelty" of printing was not confined to early printers, who engaged in self-congratulation even while advertising their wares. Cardinals, patricians, and Sorbonne professors hailed printing as a "divine art" almost as soon as the first Bibles had come off the Mainz press.[153] Of course, there were competing narratives.[154] Nevertheless, by the sixteenth century, the wooden handpress was being assigned a priveleged position among other inventions and discoveries (new stars and new colonies) that signified the dawning of a new age.[155] Given such a well-documented early modern context for the construct, it is puzzling why anyone wants to relegate it to a later age. To argue, as Warner does, that eighteenth-century Anglo-American belief in the "emancipatory character" of printing has been retrospectively injected into functions performed by the fifteenth-century handpress is to ignore early Protestant rhetoric celebrating emancipation from papal rule and also to ignore how printing figured in seventeenth-century radical attacks on bishops and kings.

In his *History of the Royal Society* (1667), Bishop Sprat singled out contributors to the new astronomy: "They sought to make it not only an enterprise of one season or of some lucky opportunity: but

---

[152] This colophon, translated from Latin by Pollard and taken from Wendelin of Spira's 1470 edition of Sallust, is one of many examples in Alfred Pollard, *An Essay on Colophons with Specimens and Translations* (Chicago, 1905), 37.

[153] Paul Needham, "Haec sancta ars," *Gazette of the Grolier Club* 42 (New York, 1991): 101–21.

[154] Richardson, "The Debates on Printing," passim.

[155] See the discussion of the series of prints entitled "Nova Reperta" designed by Vasari's pupil Jan van der Straet (Stradanus) and engraved and published repeatedly by the Antwerp firm of Galleus in *Agent of Change*, 20.

a business of time: a steddy, a lasting, a popular, an uninterrupted work."[156] No human being, however well protected from outside interference; no single generation of humans, however gifted it might be, could put so vast a collaborative enterprise as the study of astronomy (or any other branch of learning) on a new footing. None could live long enough to ensure that it would be a steady, lasting, popular, uninterrupted enterprise.

The "business of time" lies outside the control of any mortal creature. But it is amenable to investigation. It is, indeed, a topic that the study of history is well designed to explore. In my view, a good starting point for undertaking such an exploration is the printing revolution in early modern Europe. Bon voyage!

[156] Thomas Sprat, *History of the Royal Society* (1667), ed. J. I. Cope and H. W. Jones (St. Louis, MO, 1958), part 2, sect. 5, p. 62.

Selected Reading

A full bibliographical index listing every work consulted is in my unabridged book *The Printing Press as an Agent of Change*. These short reading lists were compiled for the first edition of the abridged version to enable readers, without special expertise, to sample various treatments and begin to explore diverse topics. Some of the pertinent works that have appeared since then are cited in the footnotes to the afterword to this second edition.

General and Preliminary

Berry, W. T., and Poole, H. W. *Annals of Printing: A Chronological Encyclopaedia from Earliest Times to 1950* (London, 1966). Useful reference work.

Binns, Norman E. *An Introduction to Historical Bibliography* (London, 1962). Contains some useful data on early printing not duplicated by Gaskell.

Bühler, Curt. *The Fifteenth-Century Book, the Scribes, the Printers, the Decorators* (Philadelphia, 1960). Good coverage of essential aspects. By a distinguished curator of rare books.

Butler, Pierce. *The Origin of Printing in Europe* (Chicago, 1940). Elementary. Written for undergraduates by a professor of library science. Contains useful selection of translated records pertaining to invention of printing.

Carter, Harry. *A View of Early Typography Up to About 1600* (Oxford, 1969). More up-to-date and more succinct than Updike's two-volume work on types.

Clapham, Michael. "Printing." In *A History of Technology*. Vol. 2, *From the Renaissance to the Industrial Revolution*, ed. Charles Singer et al. (Oxford, 1957), 377–411. Competent, brief account of technological innovations associated with Gutenberg's "invention."

Darnton, Robert. "What Is the History of Books?" *Daedalus* (Summer 1982): 65–85. Review article surveying European and American work. By influential American historian of eighteenth-century French book trade.

Febvre, Lucien, and Martin, H.-J. *The Coming of the Book*, tr. David Gerard (London, 1976). First ed.: *L'Apparition du livre* (Paris, 1958). Readers competent in French should get the original 1958 French version, which is superior in every way (including its bibliography and index) to this English translation. The book (which was written almost entirely by Martin) is a masterful survey and has more comprehensive coverage than any other title on this list.

Gaskell, Philip. *A New Introduction to Bibliography* (Oxford, 1972). The best introductory guide to all aspects of the book as an object.

Goldschmidt, E. P. *Medieval Texts and Their First Appearance in Print* (London, 1943). Brings out differences between hand-copied and printed books. By a knowledgeable dealer in rare books.

Hay, Denys. "Literature: The Printed Book." In *The New Cambridge Modern History*. Vol. 2. *The Reformation 1520–1599*, ed. G. R. Elton (Cambridge, 1958), 356–86. Brief but sound introduction to topic by distinguished British authority on Italian Renaissance history.

Hirsch, Rudolf. *Printing, Selling, and Reading 1450–1550* (Wiesbaden, 1967; rev. ed. 1974). Crammed with facts; emphasis on German developments. By a rare-book librarian who is especially knowledgeable about European bookselling and printing.

Ivins, William M. Jr. *Prints and Visual Communication* (Cambridge, MA, 1953). Idiosyncratic work, by a former curator of prints, who overstates the case for his specialty but also brings out more clearly than others the significance of printed visual aids.

McLuhan, Marshall. *The Gutenberg Galaxy: The Making of Typographical Man* (Toronto, 1962). Deliberately departs from conventional book format. Bizarre "mosaic" of citations drawn from diverse texts designed to stimulate thought about effects of printing. By a Canadian literary scholar turned media analyst. Careless handling of historical data may mislead uninformed readers. Surprisingly useful bibliography.

McMurtrie, Douglas. *The Book* (Oxford, 1943). Holds up well after six decades as a useful reference work.

Steinberg, S. H. *Five Hundred Years of Printing*, rev. ed. (Bristol, 1961). Remarkably succinct survey. Better coverage of first century of printing than of later ones.

Stillwell, Margaret Bingham. *The Beginning of the World of Books 1450 to 1470: A Chronological Survey of the Texts Chosen for Printing . . . With a Synopsis of the Gutenberg Documents* (New York, 1972). Despite a misleading title (the "world of books" began long before printing), this is a useful checklist for introductory purposes.

Woodward, David (ed.). *Five Centuries of Map Printing* (Chicago, 1975). Chapter I by Arthur Robinson on map making and map printing provides a good introduction. Other chapters contain excellent illustrations of relevant tools and techniques.

Orality, Literacy, and Scribal Culture:
Hearing and Reading Publics

Altick, R. *The English Common Reader: A Social History of the Mass Reading Public 1800–1900* (Chicago, 1963). The first chapter covers material before 1800 and deals with many pertinent issues.

Aston, Margaret. "Lollardy and Literacy." *History* 62 (1967): 347–71. Discussion of literacy among English Bible readers before printing.

Auerbach, Erich. *Literary Language and Its Public in Late Latin Antiquity and in the Middle Ages*, tr. R. Manheim (New York, 1965). Intriguing speculations by distinguished literary critic. Pioneering work somewhat outdated by more recent research.

Chaytor, H. J. *From Script to Print: An Introduction to Medieval Vernacular Literature* (Cambridge, 1955). Deals with difference between hearing and reading publics addressed by vernacular-writing literati before and after printing. Has come under attack for overstating changes wrought by printing. See Saenger entry later in this section.

Cipolla, Carlo M. *Literacy and Development in the West* (London, 1969). Brief introductory survey.

Clanchy, Michael. *From Memory to Written Record: England 1066–1307* (Cambridge, MA, 1979). Focus is on legal records, but questions pertaining to literacy before printing are also addressed.

Davis, Natalie Z. "Printing and the People." In *Society and Culture in Early Modern France: Eight Essays* (Palo Alto, CA, 1975), 189–227. Influential article that explores some of the effects of printing on popular culture in sixteenth-century France.

Foley, John Miles. "Oral Literature: Premises and Problems." *Choice* 18 (Dec. 1980): 187–96. Useful review article covering works dealing with the composition of epics, sagas, and so forth.

Gerhardsson, Birger. *Memory and Manuscript: Oral Tradition and Written Transmission in Rabbinic Judaism and Early Christianity* (Uppsala, 1961). Fascinating, detailed examination of regulations governing scribal procedures among rabbis and early Christians.

Goody, J., and Watt, I. "The Consequences of Literacy." *Comparative Studies in Society and History* 5 (1963): 304–45. A seminal article by an anthropologist and a professor of English which has set off a prolonged debate. Goody's later books, notably *The Domestication of the Savage Mind* (Cambridge, 1977), are also pertinent.

Graff, Harvey J. *Literacy and Social Development in the West: A Reader* (Cambridge, 1982). Contains pertinent articles by M. Clanchy, N. Z. Davis, Margaret Spufford, and others.

Havelock, Eric. *The Literate Revolution in Greece and Its Cultural Consequences* (Princeton, NJ, 1982). In this collection of essays, as in his *Preface to Plato* (1961), Havelock explores the effect of the shift from orality to literacy on Greek thought in a controversial, idiosyncratic, and stimulating manner.

Humphreys, K. W. *The Book Provisions of the Medieval Friars 1215–1400* (Amsterdam, 1964). Scholarly monograph describing new arrangements with lay copyists designed to provide books for Dominicans, Franciscans, and others.

Knox, Bernard M. W. "Silent Reading in Antiquity." *Greek, Roman, and Byzantine Studies* 9 (1968): 421–35. Important analysis questioning thesis that silent reading was an exceptional practice in antiquity. Overlooked by Saenger in article cited here.

Lord, Albert B. *The Singer of Tales* (Cambridge, MA, 1962). Problems associated with oral composition and with the transcription of the Homeric epics are discussed along lines laid out by the pioneering work of the late Milman Parry.

Ong, Walter J. *Interfaces of the Word* (Ithaca, NY, 1977).

Ong, Walter J. *Orality and Literacy* (London, 1982). Collections of essays by a Jesuit scholar concerned with literary and intellectual history who has long been investigating the effects of printing on the Western mind.

Parkes, Malcolm B. "The Influence of the Concepts of Ordinatio and Compilatio on the Development of the Book." In *Medieval Learning and Literature: Essays Presented to R. W. Hunt*, ed. J. J. G. Alexander and M. T. Gibson (Oxford, 1976), 115–45.

Parkes, Malcolm B. "The Literacy of the Laity." In *Literature and Western Civilization*. Vol. 2, *The Medieval World*, ed. D. Daiches and A. Thorlby (London, 1972–6), 555–76. Two essays by a medievalist who is knowledgeable about codicology and paleography and who downplays the differences between script and print.

Reynolds, L. D., and Wilson, N. G. *Scribes and Scholars* (Oxford, 1968). By far the best introduction to issues associated with the transmission of hand-copied texts in Western Europe.

Root, Robert K. "Publication before Printing." *Publications of the Modern Language Association* 28 (1913): 417–31. Despite being published long ago, still a useful article.

Saenger, Paul. "Silent Reading: Its Impact on Late Medieval Script and Society." *Viator* 13 (1982), 367–414. Presents evidence showing that silent reading occurred before the advent of printing. Overstates novelty of practice in late Middle Ages and ignores the extent to which silent reading was reinforced and institutionalized after printing.

Suleiman, Susan R., and Crosman, Inge. *The Reader in the Text: Essays on Audience and Interpretation* (Princeton, NJ, 1980). Collection of essays, primarily by literary critics, bearing on the problematic figure of the reader.

Vansina, Jan. *Oral Tradition: A Study in Historical Methodology*, tr. H. M. Wright (London, 1973). First ed., in French, 1961. By Africanist who pioneered in developing study of oral history.

Williams, Raymond. *The Long Revolution* (New York, 1966). Survey of gradual spread of literacy. By English literary critic who espouses Marxist view of culture.

Yates, Frances. *The Art of Memory* (London, 1966). Remarkable reconstruction of lost arts of memory as set forth in ancient treatises, used by medieval preachers, and elaborated upon in early modern era.

Advent of Printing: Some Early Printers and Their Output

Armstrong, Elizabeth. *Robert Estienne, Royal Printer: An Historical Study of the Elder Stephanus* (Cambridge, 1954). First-rate portrait of a distinguished member of a great printing dynasty. Persecution by Sorbonne censors, which led the printer to leave Paris for Geneva, arouses the author's indignation.

Clair, Colin. *Christopher Plantin* (London, 1960). Designed to introduce uninformed students to the activities of the most important printer of second half of sixteenth century.

Davies, David W. *The World of the Elseviers, 1580–1712* (The Hague, 1954). Self-explanatory title. View of important printing dynasty during Dutch "golden age."

Ehrman, Albert, and Pollard, Graham. *The Distribution of Books by Catalogue from the Invention of Printing to A.D. 1800* (Roxburghe Club, Cambridge, 1965). Includes a valuable account of early booksellers' catalogues and of book fairs.

Evans, Robert. "The Wechel Presses: Humanism and Calvinism in Central Europe 1572–1627." *Past and Present*, Supplement 2 (1975). Detailed monograph on output of Frankfurt firm which turned out heterodox works during religious wars. Takes for granted readers' familiarity with prevailing cultural and intellectual trends.

Kingdon, Robert M. "The Business Activities of Printers Henri and François Estienne." In *Aspects de la propagande religieuse*, ed. H. Meylan (Geneva, 1957), 258–75.

Kingdon, Robert M. "Christopher Plantin and His Backers 1575–1590: A Study in the Problems of Financing Business During War." In *Mélanges d'histoire économique et social en hommage au Professeur Antony Babel* (Geneva, 1963), 303–16.

Kingdon, Robert M. "Patronage, Piety and Printing in Sixteenth-Century Europe." In *A Festschrift for Frederick Artz*, ed. D. Pinkney and T. Ropp

(Durham, NC, 1964), 19–36. Kingdon's three articles are helpful in bringing out the way printers interacted with religious and political developments. This last listed essay is especially useful.

Lehmann-Haupt, Hellmut. *Peter Schoeffer of Gernsheim and Mainz* (Rochester, NY, 1950). Excellent introduction to the life and work of the son-in-law of Gutenberg's financial backer.

Lowry, Martin. *The World of Aldus Manutius: Business and Scholarship in Renaissance Venice* (Ithaca, NY, 1979). First full-length study of Aldus and the Aldine Press to appear in English. Based on solid research; well written.

Mardersteig, Giovanni. *The Remarkable Story of a Book Made in Padua in 1477*, tr. H. Schmoller (London, 1967). A reconstruction of the operations of an early printer, who turned out a large folio edition of Avicenna in a single year, despite strikes and financing problems. By the late owner and operator of the famed Bodoni press.

McKenzie, D. F. "Printer of the Mind: Some Notes on Bibliographical Theories and Printing House Activities." *Studies in Bibliography 22* (1969): 1–75. The actual (often slapdash) practices of real flesh-and-blood compositors and typesetters are shown to be quite different from those imagined by analytical bibliographers. Thoroughly researched, influential critique.

Oastler, C. L. *John Day, The Elizabethan Printer*. Oxford Bibliographic Society Occasional Publication 10 (Oxford, 1975). Densely detailed monograph on a privileged, prosperous, pious English printer.

Painter, George D. *William Caxton: A Quincentenary Biography* (London, 1976). The best of the biographies celebrating the quincentenary.

Schoeck, Richard J. (ed.). *Editing Sixteenth Century Texts* (Toronto, 1966). Collection of relevant essays. See especially N. Z. Davis on Gilbert Rouillé.

Thompson, James Westfall (ed.). *The Francofordiense Emporium of Henri Estienne* (Chicago, 1911). An edited, translated account of the Frankfurt book fair by Henry II Estienne, who is, of course, eager to promote the institution.

Uhlendorf, B. A. "The Invention and Spread of Printing till 1470 with Special Reference to Social and Economic Factors." *The Library Quarterly 2* (1932): 179–231. Although it was published more than half a century ago and is an old-fashioned, heavy-handed treatment, this article is still one of the few that does not take for granted the rapid spread of printing in Western Europe and attempts to account for it.

Updike, D. B. *Printing Types, Their History, Forms, and Use: A Study in Survivals.* 2 vols. (Cambridge, MA, 1937). A lavishly illustrated, detailed description by an American printer and publisher who died in 1941. Old-fashioned, anecdotal approach.

Voët, Leon. *The Golden Compasses: A History and Evaluation of the Printing and Publishing Activities of the Officina Plantiniana at Antwerp.* 2 vols. (Amsterdam,

1969). The curator of the Plantin–Moretus Museum in Antwerp provides a wealth of data – too much for the average reader. The chapter on the printing office "as a humanist center" is worth consulting, however.

Wilson, Adrian. *The Making of the Nuremberg Chronicle*, introduction by Peter Zahn (Amsterdam, 1976). A marvelous reconstruction based on careful research. Describes just how this massive collaborative work was produced. Chapter 6 on Anton Koberger and his printing house is of special interest. By a leading American typographer.

Printing and Related Developments: Scholar-Printers and Renaissance Humanists

Allen, P. S. *The Age of Erasmus* (Oxford, 1914).

Allen, P. S. *Erasmus: Lectures and Wayfaring Sketches* (London, 1934). These old studies bring out more clearly than do many later accounts the importance of printing in shaping Erasmus's career.

Bietenholz, P. G. *Basle and France in the Sixteenth Century: The Basle Humanists and Printers in Their Contacts with Francophone Culture* (Toronto, 1971). Dense and detailed account of French-language writers and printers in Basel.

Bloch, Eileen. "Erasmus and the Froben Press: The Making of an Editor." *Library Quarterly* 41 (1965): 109–20. Self-expanatory title.

Bolgar, R. R. *The Classical Heritage and Its Beneficiaries: From the Carolingian Age to the End of the Renaissance* (New York, 1964). A useful survey.

Dorsten, Jan van. *The Radical Arts* (London, 1973). Treatment of cross-channel currents between Netherlands and Elizabethan England in which printers and booksellers loom large.

Ebel, J. G. "Translation and Cultural Nationalism in the Reign of Elizabeth." *Journal of the History of Ideas* 30 (1969): 593–602. Brings out importance of translation movement.

Geanokoplos, Deno J. *Greek Scholars in Venice: Studies in the Dissemination of Greek Learning from Byzantium to Western Europe* (Cambridge, MA, 1962). Study of Cretan and Greek refugees who worked in Venice mainly for Aldus's firm.

Geisendorf, Paul F. "Lyons and Geneva in the Sixteenth Century: The Fairs and Printing." In *French Humanism 1470–1600*, ed. W. Gundesheimer (New York, 1969), 146–63.

Gilmore, Myron P. *Humanists and Jurists* (Cambridge, MA, 1963). See especially chapter on Boniface Amerbach.

Goldschmidt, E. P. *The Printed Book of the Renaissance: Three Lectures on Type, Illustration, Ornament* (Cambridge, 1950). Full of useful data.

Harbison, E. Harris. *The Christian Scholar in the Age of the Reformation* (New York, 1956). Essays on Luther, Calvin, and others viewed as scholars rather than as charismatic leaders.

Keller, A. "A Renaissance Humanist Looks at 'New' Inventions: The Article 'Horlogium' in Giovanni Tortelli's *De Orthographia*." *Technology and Culture* 2 (1970): 345–65. Provides background for understanding Renaissance schemes linking printing with gunpowder and the compass.

Kline, Michael B. "Rabelais and the Age of Printing." In *Etudes rabelaisiennes IV: Travaux d'humanisme et renaissance* (Geneva, 1963), vol. 60, 1–59. Self-explanatory title.

Lievsay, J. L. *The Englishman's Italian Books 1550–1700* (Philadelphia, 1969). Suggests influence of importations from Italy on Tudor and Stuart literary culture.

Nauert, Charles. "The Clash of Humanists and Scholastics: An Approach to Pre-Reformation Controversies." *Sixteenth Century Journal* 4 (April 1973): 1–18. Suggestive essay. Shows importance of printing in extending debates beyond academic circles.

Ong, Walter J. *Ramus: Method and the Decay of Dialogue. From the Art of Discourse to the Art of Reason* (Cambridge, MA, 1958). An influential study of Ramus's method. Stresses importance of print.

Panofsky, Erwin. *Renaissance and Renascences in Western Art* (Uppsala, 1960).

Strauss, Gerald. "A Sixteenth-Century Encyclopedia: Sebastian Münster's *Cosmography* and Its Editions." In *From the Renaissance to the Counter-Reformation*, ed. C. H. Carter (New York, 1965), 145–63. Useful examination of successive printed editions of a sixteenth-century reference work.

Yates, Frances. *Giordano Bruno and the Hermetic Tradition* (London, 1964). Pioneering study of the authority exerted upon Renaissance scholars by writings attributed to the Egyptian scribal god, Hermes Trismegistus – writings that were translated into Latin by Marsilio Ficino and printed in the late fifteenth century.

Printing and Related Developments: Bible Printing, Protestantism, Religious Propaganda

Black, Michael H. "The Printed Bible." In *Cambridge History of the Bible*. Vol. 3, *The West from the Reformation to the Present Day*, ed. S. L. Greenslade (Cambridge, 1963), 408–75. A mine of information on early Bible printing by a former editor of the Cambridge University Press.

Bossy, John. "The Counter Reformation and the People of Catholic Europe." *Past and Present* 47 (May 1970): 51–70. Stresses comparative perspectives and deals with questions pertaining to "household religion."

Box, G. H. "Hebrew Studies in the Reformation Period and After." In *The Legacy of Israel*, ed. E. R. Bevan and Charles Singer (Oxford, 1927), 315–75. Self-explanatory title.

Chrisman, Miriam Usher. *Lay Culture, Learned Culture, Books and Social Change in Strasbourg, 1480–1599* (New Haven, CT, 1982). Comprehensive study of Strasbourg books and printers during age of Reformation.

Davis, Natalie Z. "The Protestant Printing Workers of Lyons in 1551." In *Aspects de la propagande religieuse*, ed. H. Meylan (Geneva, 1957), 247–57.

Davis, Natalie Z. "Strikes and Salvation in Lyons." *Archiv für Reformationsgeschichte* 56 (1965): 48–64. Two articles that offer close-up views of journeyman typographers' activities during era of religious wars.

Elton, Geoffrey R. *Policy and Police: The Enforcement of the Reformation in the Age of Thomas Cromwell* (Cambridge, 1972). See especially chapter 4. Brings out measures taken by Thomas Cromwell to control public opinion by exploiting print.

Grendler, Paul F. *The Roman Inquisition and the Venetian Press 1540–1605* (Princeton, NJ, 1977). Self-explanatory title. Careful study based on archival research.

Grossmann, Maria. "Wittenberg Printing, Early Sixteenth Century." *Sixteenth Century Essays and Studies* 1 (1970): 53–74. Helps to set stage for Lutheran printing.

Hall, Basil. "Biblical Scholarship: Editions and Commentaries." In *Cambridge History of the Bible*. Vol. 3, *The West from the Reformation to the Present Day*, ed. S. L. Greenslade (Cambridge, 1963), 38–93. Contains useful material on trilingual studies.

Haller, William. *The Elect Nation: The Meaning and Relevance of Foxe's Book of Martyrs* (New York, 1963). Places more emphasis on importance of printing than do most studies of Foxe's work. Exaggerates nationalistic themes according to critics.

Hillerbrand, Hans. "The Spread of the Protestant Reformation of the Sixteenth Century." *The South Atlantic Quarterly* 67 (Spring 1968): 265–86. Elementary. Brief survey.

Holborn, Louise. "Printing and the Growth of a Protestant Movement in Germany from 1517–1524." *Church History* II (June 1942): 1–15. Useful brief account.

Loades, D. M. "The Theory and Practice of Censorship in Sixteenth Century England." *Transactions of the Royal Historical Society*, ser. 5 (1974): 141–57. Excellent brief account.

Monter, E. William. *Calvin's Geneva* (New York, 1967). Contains useful data on rise of printing industry after Calvin's arrival.

Ong, Walter J. *The Presence of the Word* (New Haven, CT, 1967). Provocative essays relating orality, chirography, and typography to religious experiences within Western Christendom.

Rekers, B. *Benito Arias Montano, 1527–1598*. Studies of the Warburg Institute 3 (London, 1972). Close-up study of chaplain of Philip II of Spain, who was sent to Antwerp to supervise the printing by Christopher Plantin of a polyglot Bible and who was converted to Plantin's heterodox "familist" faith.

Schwartz, W. *Principles and Problems of Biblical Translations: Some Reformation Controversies and Their Background* (Cambridge, 1955). Helpful guidance to diverse schools of Bible translation.

Schweibert, Ernest C. "New Groups and Ideas at the University of Wittenberg." *Archiv für Reformationsgeschichte* 49 (1958): 60–78. Brings out connections between Wittenberg librarian and Aldine press in Venice.

Scribner, R. W. *For the Sake of Simple Folk: Popular Propaganda for the German Reformation* (Cambridge, 1981). Emphasizes importance of nonverbal images, cartoons, caricatures, and so forth in conveying Lutheran message to masses.

Smalley, Beryl. *The Study of the Bible in the Middle Ages* (South Bend, IN, 1964). Authoritative work. Provides data on how scribal scholars tried repeatedly to emend Jerome's version and protect it from corruption.

Spitz, Lewis. *The Religious Renaissance of the German Humanists* (Cambridge, MA, 1963). Biographical sketches of Northern humanists who took advantage of printing.

Trevor-Roper, Hugh R. *The Crisis of the Seventeenth Century: Religion, the Reformation, and Social Change* (New York, 1968). Stimulating essays on the religious origins of the Enlightenment.

Verwey, H. de la Fontaine. "The Family of Love." *Quaerendo* 6 (1976): 219–71. Introduction to the heterodox sect which attracted circles of printers and engravers in the Netherlands.

Williams, George H. *The Radical Reformation* (Philadelphia, 1962). Useful background on heterodox sects which attracted many Continental printers, booksellers, and engravers during the age of religious wars.

Woodfield, Dennis. *Surreptitious Printing in England 1550–1690* (New York, 1973). Provides close-up view of clandestine operations in Tudor and Stuart England.

Yates, Frances. "Paolo Sarpi's History of the Council of Trent." *Journal of the Warburg and Courtauld Institutes* 7 (1944): 123–44. Study of influential antipapist treatise written by Venetian churchman and popularized in England.

Printing and Early Modern Science:
The Copernican Revolution

Ben-David, Joseph. "The Scientific Role: The Conditions of Its Establishment in Europe." *Minerva* 4 (1965): 15–20. Typical sociological treatment of problem.

Boas, Marie. *The Scientific Renaissance* (New York, 1962). Standard survey. Downplays role of printing.

Butterfield, Herbert. *The Origins of Modern Science 1300–1800*, rev. ed. (New York, 1951). Best introductory account.

Butterfield, Herbert. *Dictionary of Scientific Biography*, ed. C. C. Gillispie, 14 vols. (New York, 1970). Should be consulted for biographies of individuals associated with rise of modern science. Excellent brief essays by acknowledged authorities.

Drake, Stillman (ed. and tr.). *Discoveries and Opinions of Galileo* (New York, 1957). Selections from Galileo's writings combined with historical commentary by editor make this a most useful little book for undergraduates.

Drake, Stillman. "Early Science and the Printed Book: The Spread of Science Beyond the University." *Renaissance and Reformation* 6 (1970): 38–52. One of few discussions of relationship between printing and sixteenth-century science by specialist in Galileo studies. As subtitle suggests, popularization and vernacular translation are stressed. Effects of printing on Latin-writing professors are discounted. Nonverbal (pictorial and mathematical) printing is ignored.

Gingerich, Owen. "Copernicus and the Impact of Printing." *Vistas in Astronomy* 17 (1975): 201–9. By Harvard professor of astronomy who has drawn up an inventory of extant copies of *De revolutionibus*.

Hall, A. Rupert. "The Scholar and the Craftsman in the Scientific Revolution." In *Critical Problems in the History of Science*, ed. M. Clagett (Madison, WI, 1969), 3–24. Important essay (in an important collection) concerning role of both Latin learning and craft experience in scientific developments.

Haydn, Hiram. *The Counter Renaissance* (New York, 1950). Sixteenth-century empirical reaction to "bookish" classicizing trends is documented and discussed.

Hellmann, C. Doris. *The Comet of 1577: Its Place in the History of Astronomy* (New York, 1944). Detailed and dry monograph, but useful in that it provides an appropriate context for Tycho's "discoveries."

Hooykaas, Reijer. *Religion and the Rise of Modern Science* (Edinburgh, 1972). Sets forth thesis that Protestant theology was a necessary prerequisite for rise of modern science.

Ivins, William. *Three Vesalian Essays* (New York, 1952). Brings out importance of prints and engravings for anatomical study.

Keller, Alex (ed.). *A Theatre of Machines* (New York, 1965). An edited, translated edition of Jacques Besson's 1579 work, with a useful introduction and notes.

Koestler, Arthur, *The Sleepwalkers* (London, 1959).

Koyré, Alexandre. *From the Closed World to the Infinite Universe* (Baltimore, 1957). English translation of French work by an important historian of astronomy who discusses the cosmological implications of Copernicanism.

Kuhn, Thomas S. *The Copernican Revolution: Planetary Astronomy in the Development of Western Thought* (Cambridge, MA, 1957). A well-received, now-standard account. Role of printing not noted.

Kuhn, Thomas S. *The Structure of Scientific Revolutions*, rev. ed. (Chicago, 1970). An enormously influential reinterpretation of scientific innovations relevant to the downfall of Ptolemy, Aristotle, Galen, and others. Ignores the printing "revolution."

McGuire, J. E., and Rattansi, P. M. "Newton and the 'Pipes of Pan.'" *Notes and Records of the Royal Society* 21 (Dec. 1966): 108–43. Documents Newton's concern with the "hermetic" tradition.

Merton, Robert K. *Science, Technology, and Society in Seventeenth Century England*, rev. ed. (New York, 1970). Influential attempt to apply the "Weber thesis" to seventeenth-century English science. Work is now outdated, but updated bibliography is useful.

Middleton, W. E. K. *The Experimenters: A Study of the "Accademia del Cimento"* (Baltimore, 1971). Monograph on the chief Italian scientific society.

Rosen, Edward. "Renaissance Science as Seen by Burckhardt and His Successors." In *The Renaissance: A Reconsideration*, ed. T. Helton (Madison, WI, 1964), 77–103. Defense of the Burckhardt thesis against attacks by medievalists.

Rosen, Edward. (ed. and tr.). *Three Copernican Treatises*, 3rd ed. (New York, 1971). A very useful collection of Copernican writings, translated and edited by an acknowledged authority. A brief biography of Copernicus is included.

Rossi, Paolo. *Philosophy, Technology, and the Arts in the Early Modern Era*, tr. S. Attanasio, ed. Benjamin Nelson (New York, 1970). First Italian ed., 1962. Useful brief essays by Italian biographer of Francis Bacon. Deals with many of the same issues that are raised in this book.

Sarton, George. *Six Wings* (Bloomington, IN, 1957).

Sarton, George. *Appreciation of Ancient and Medieval Science During the Renaissance 1450–1600*, 2d ed. (New York, 1958).

Sarton, George. "The Quest for Truth: Scientific Progress During the Renaissance." In *The Renaissance: Six Essays*. Metropolitan Museum Symposium (New York, 1962), chap. 3. By the late Harvard professor who helped to introduce the history of science as an academic discipline in the

United States. Unlike later scholars, Sarton stresses the importance of "the double invention of printing and engraving."

Shipman, Joseph. "Johannes Petreius, Nuremberg Publisher of Scientific Works, 1524–1550." In *Homage to a Bookman, Essays . . . for Hans P. Kraus*, ed. Hellmut Lehmann-Haupt (Berlin, 1967), 154–62. Brief essay on publisher of Copernicus, Cardano, and other sixteenth-century natural philosophers.

Stillwell, Margaret Bingham. *The Awakening Interest in Science During the First Century of Printing, 1450–1550: An Annotated Checklist of First Editions* (New York, 1970). Helpful reference guide.

Thorndike, Lynn Jr. *A History of Magic and Experimental Science: The Sixteenth Century*, Vols. 5 and 6 in single volume (New York, 1941). Part of a massive work emphasizing the amount of pseudoscientific trash printed in the sixteenth century.

Warner, Deborah H. "The First Celestial Globe of Willem Janszoon Blaeu." *Imago Mundi* 25 (1971): 29–38. Contains much pertinent data.

Webster, Charles (ed.). *The Intellectual Revolution of the Seventeenth Century*. Past and Present series (London, 1975). Collection of essays (by Christopher Hill, Hugh Kearney, Theodore Rabb, and others) that first appeared in *Past and Present* debating issues pertaining to religion and the rise of modern science in England.

Westman, Robert. "The Melanchthon Circle, Rheticus, and the Wittenberg Interpretation of the Copernican Theory." *Isis* 66 (June 1975): 285–345. By leading authority on the reception of the Copernican theory.

Westman, Robert. (ed.). *The Copernican Achievement* (Los Angeles, 1975). Contains articles by Gingerich, Swerdlow, and other historians of astronomy including the editor.

Whiteside, D. T. "Newton's Marvellous Year: 1666 and All That." *Notes and Records of the Royal Society of London* 21 (June 1966): 32–42.

Whiteside, D. T. "Before the Principia: The Maturing of Newton's Thought . . . 1664–1684." *Journal for the History of Astronomy* 1 (1970): 5–20. By a leading authority on Newton's mathematical papers. Useful data on young Newton's reading materials.

Wightman, W. P. D. *Science and the Renaissance*. 2 vols. (Edinburgh, 1962). Considerable space devoted to role of printing.

INDEX

Academy of the Investigators, 275
accountancy books, 37
Accursius, Bonus, 347
Actes and Monuments . . .
    Touching . . . Great Persecutions
    (Foxe, 1563), 197. *see also*
    Book of Martyrs, 193
Address to the Estates of the Empire
    (Sleidan), 167
Age of Reason, 51
Agricola (Georg Bauer), 218, 219,
    227, 290, 354
Alciato, Andrea, 79
Alcuin, 56, 71
Aldus Manutius, 20, 112, 140, 202,
    231, 235, 295
Alexandrian Library and Museum,
    xviii, 8, 71, 84, 231, 290
Almagest (Ptolemy), 234, 235, 245,
    251, 297, 299, 301
Almagestum novum astronomiam
    veteran (Riccioli, 1651), 245,
    257
alphabet systems, 71–2
Alphonsine Tables, 245, 251
Alsted, Johann Heinrich (Alstedius),
    350
Altick, R., 38
Amerbach, 79, 112
Amerbach-Froben shop, 203

anthology, literary, 118
antiqua types, 137, 138
Antwerp Polyglot, 199, 200, 205
"apostolate of the pen," 175–6
Aquinas, Thomas, 174, 265
Arabic, 48, 76, 140, 215, 301, 336
    arabic numbers, for pagination, 81
archeology, 141
Archimedes, 214, 217
architecture, 42, 58–9
Areopagitica (Milton), 284
Aretino, Pietro, 145, 195
Arias Montano, Benito, 199, 200,
    203
Aristotle, 95, 174, 218, 232, 234,
    289, 298
art history, 40, 59, 147, 315
Astronomia Britannica (Wing), 254
Astronomia nova . . . commentariis de
    motibus stellae martis (Kepler,
    1609), 253
Astronomiae instauratae mechanica
    (Tycho Brahe, 1598), 246
astronomy, 209, 232, 242, 244, 262,
    288, 357. *see also* Copernican
    revolution
atlases and maps, 17, 24, 48, 59, 70,
    76, 81, 83, 87, 89, 97, 98, 215,
    266, 290
Augustine, 143, 180

authors, 5, 22, 28, 33, 37, 85, 86, 95–6, 194, 344, 345, 348, 349, 352, 353, 354
authorship, 36, 96, 112, 118
autobiographies, 146

Bacon, Francis, 158, 211, 262, 263, 292, 298, 301
Bacon, Roger, 301
Badia library, 15
Badius, Perrette, 203
Balbus of Genoa, Friar Johannes, 68
Baldung-Grien, Hans, 149
Banks, Sir Joseph, 303
Barker, R., 57
Barnard, John, 332
Baronius, Cardinal, 53
Bauer, Georg. see Agricola
Bayle, Pierre, 110, 350
Beatus Rhenanus, 170
Bellarmine, Robert, Cardinal, 56
Bernard, Saint, 143, 212, 214
Berr, Henri, 314
Berthelet, Thomas, 80
Bible, 17, 21, 22, 25, 36, 56, 73, 76, 348, 357. see also polyglot Bibles; vernacular translation movement; Vulgate
    authorized version, 181
    Biblia pauperum praedicatorum ("poor man's"), 36
    English, 181–3
    Geneva, 182, 185, 186
    King James, 183, 185
    Latin, 81
    Lutheran, 137
    Matthew, 179
    "wicked," 56
Bible Belts, 186, 189
Biblia Sacra, Hebraice, Chaldaice, Graece, & Latine (1571), 205. see also polyglot Bibles

bibliography, bibliographies, 84, 86, 231, 334, 335
Bibliotheca universalis (Gesner, 1545), 84, 334
biography, 147, 295
Blaeu, Willem Janszoon, 239–41, 279
Blair, Ann, 326
Boccaccio, Giovanni, 280
Boissard, Jean Jacques, 149
Bomberg, Daniel, 112, 140
Bonaventura, Saint, 95
book fairs, 127, 269, 321, 322
Book of Martyrs (Foxe), 167, 196
"Book of Nature," 159, 209–31, 245, 265, 275, 298
bookbinders, 22
bookdealers, 9, 10, 21, 28, 29
bookhands, xviii, 58, 59, 77, 134, 137
booksellers, 72, 129, 148, 158, 190, 192, 280, 325
Borelli, Giovanni Alfonso, 278
botany, 82–3
Boulding, Kenneth, 221, 223, 224, 303
Boyd, Julian, 90
Brahe. see Tycho Brahe
Brethren of the Common Life, 29, 296
Breydenbach, Bernhard von, 69
Brief Narration (Cartier, 1545), 98
broadsides, 29, 33, 165, 317, 336
Browne, Sir Thomas, 211, 212, 214
Bruno, Giordano, 195, 260
Budé, Guillaume, 79
Bühler, Curt, 23, 339
Burckhardt, Jacob, 21, 124–5, 131, 142–3, 211
Bussi, Gianandrea de (Bishop of Aleria), 176
Butler, Pierce, 123, 124, 130

calendars, 33, 53, 57, 79, 89, 201, 234, 245, 297, 317
calligraphy, 58
Calvin, John, 39, 177, 185, 192
Campanella, Tommaso, 218, 260, 279, 298
carbon paper, 313
caricatures, 40, 165, 166
Carolingian minuscule, 134, 135, 137
Carolingian revival, 131
Cartier, Jacques, 98
cartolai, 10, 20, 320
cartoons, 40, 165, 166, 209, 298
Casaubon, Isaac, 51
Cassirer, Ernst, 303
Castellio, Sebastian, 195
catalogues, 24, 36, 37, 71, 72, 73, 77, 124, 129, 148, 158, 201, 215, 236, 243, 325, 335, 342
cataloguing of data, 70–81
censorship, 194, 195, 255, 268, 271, 273, 275, 280, 298, 333, 351. see also Index librorum prohibitorum
Charlewood, John, 260
Chartier, Roger, 324
Chaucer, Geoffrey, 334
Cimento, Academia del, 274, 277
Cipolla, Carlo, 34
classical revival, 90, 99, 123, 124, 126, 130, 136, 139, 163
codex, 79, 215, 316, 318, 325, 357
collective unconscious, 41
College of Physicians, 183
colophons, 357
Comenius, Johann Amos, 41, 43
Commandino, Frederico, 217
Commonwealth of Learning, xvii, 28, 42, 50, 86, 110, 112, 182, 273, 296, 302, 304, 306, 311, 335
communicative spectrum, 327, 328, 329

Complutensian Polyglot Bible (Alcalá, 1517–1522), 76
compositors, 24, 56, 127, 141
Compostella, 68
concordances, 73
Concordia Mundi, 203
Condorcet, Marie, Marquis de, 161, 331
confession, sacrament of, 174
Confrérie des Libraires, Relieurs, Enlumineurs, Ecrivains et Parcheminiers, 21
Congregation of the Index, 262
Congregation of the Propaganda, 191
Cook, Captain James, 303
cookbooks, 37
Copernican revolution, 231–54
Copernicus, Nicholas, 86, 158, 161, 210, 213, 229, 231–6, 237, 242, 245, 251, 254, 260, 277, 279, 287, 288, 289, 299, 301, 349
copy centers, university, 310
copy editing, 77, 79, 177
copyists. see scribes and copyists
copyright, 94, 309
Cornelio, Tommaso, 275
Corpus Juris, 78, 79
correctors. see proofreaders
Corvinus, Matthias, 84
Cosmographical Glasse (Cunningham, 1559), The, 55
costume books, 59, 63, 65
Cotton, Robert, 345
Council of Trent, 174, 194, 355
Cranach, Lucas, 40, 149
Crick, Julia, 325, 345
Cromwell, Thomas, 108, 172, 179
Cujas, Jacques, 79
Culpeper, Nicholas, 183, 263
Cunningham, William, 55
Curtius, Ernst, 211

Darnton, Robert, 109, 322
Darwin, Charles, 265
Das Wolffgesang (Watt, 1520), 166
data collection, xviii, 81, 84, 86, 144,
    153, 224, 228, 229, 240, 266,
    271, 293, 298, 306
Davies, Martin, 351
Day, John, 354
De captivitate babylonica (Luther,
    1520), 149
De historia stirpium (Fuchs, 1542), 151
De humani corporis fabrica libri septem
    (Vesalius, 1555), 30
De laude scriptorum (Trithemius), 11
De revolutionibus (Copernicus, 1543),
    209, 235, 251, 260, 264, 279
Dee. John, 325
Defoe, Daniel, 175
Degli habiti antichi et moderni di diverse
    parti del mondo (Vecellio,
    1590), 63
Del modo tenuto nel trasportare
    l'obelisco Vaticano (Fontana,
    1589), 154
Delineatio pompae triumphalis qua
    Robertus Dudlaeus comes
    Leicestrensis Hagae Comitis fuit
    exceptus (Savery, 1586), 107
Descartes, René, 78, 98, 271
devotional works, 36, 174, 178
Dialogue on Two World Systems
    (Galileo, 1632), 280
Dialogues (Plato), 15
Dialogus (William of Ockham, 1494),
    9
Dickens, A. G., 164
dictionaries, 53, 76, 141, 184, 232
Digges, Thomas, 213, 260
Diodati, Elias, 262
Dioscorides, 83
"Directions for Seamen, Bound for
    Far Voyages," 221

Discourses on Two New Sciences
    (Galileo, 1638), 281–4
Doctrinal des Filles, 37
Drake, Stillman, 280
dressmakers, pattern books for, 62
Duguid, Paul, 342
dumb preachers, 330, 331
Dürer, Albrecht, 40

Eastern Christendom, 336. *see also*
    Western Christendom
Ehrman, Albert, 9, 237
Ehrman, John, 9, 237
Elementorum (Euclid, 1572), 217
Elsevier firm, 283, 295
Elsevier, Louis, 262, 283
Elton, G. R., 293
Elyot, Thomas, 42, 302
emblem books, 41
embryology, 263
emendation, 56, 57, 79
empiricists, 217, 218
engravings, 24, 54, 59, 64, 108, 148,
    152, 317, 352
Enlightenment, 51, 53, 86, 90, 109,
    161, 184, 199, 202, 204, 295
Epitome Astronomiae Copernicae
    (Kepler), 254
Erasmus, 56, 113, 132, 148, 149, 175,
    180, 194, 204, 231, 301, 354
errata, 56, 65, 349
Essays (Montaigne), 62
Estienne, Charles, 353
Estienne firm, 49
Estienne, Henry (son of Robert),
    203
Estienne, Robert, 73, 77, 81, 179,
    203, 295
etiquette books, 37
Etymologia (Isidore of Seville, 1483),
    223
Euclid, 133, 214, 215, 217, 303

excommunication, 93
Ezell, Margaret, 344

Family of Love, 200, 202
family of man, 203
fashion books, 59
Febvre, Lucien, 4, 17, 112, 321, 332
feedback, 84, 100, 224
Ferguson, Wallace K., 126
Ficino, Marsilio, 15, 50
First Narration (Rheticus), 260
Fisch, Max, 275
Florentine Codex, 79
Florio, John, 184
Fludd, Robert, 41
Fontana, Domenico, 152, 154
Fontenelle, Bernard, 302
Foscarini, Paolo Antonio, 279–80
Foxe, John, 167, 196, 202, 330, 354
Franklin, Benjamin, 113, 114
Freemasons, 51, 98
Freyle, Diego de, 62
Froben, Johannes, 203, 354
Froschauer, Christopher, 334, 354
Fuchs, Leonhart, 151
Fust, Johan, 22

Galen, 42, 210, 218, 263, 296, 297
Galileo, 53, 94, 110, 158, 214, 254,
    261, 262, 264, 265, 273, 279,
    280, 282, 284
Galle, Philippe, 200
Gart der Gesundheit (Schoeffer,
    1485), 65
Gaskell, Philip, 33
Geoffrey of Meaux, 241
Geographia (Ptolemy, 1562), 223, 229
geography, 42, 144, 224, 227, 229,
    255, 266
*Geometria y traca para el oficio de los
    sastres* (Freyle, 1588), 62
geometry, 42, 301

Germania (Tacitus), 100, 136
Gerson, Jean, 68
Gesner, Conrad, 84, 228, 334, 335,
    354
Giant Bible of Mainz, 25
Gilbert, Neal, 78
Gilbert, William, 260
globes, 229, 239, 267, 271
Goldschmidt, E. P., 22
Gothic script, 136, 137
Gothic type, 59, 137
Grafton, Anthony, 340
Grafton, Richard, 179
Graña, César, 116
Grand Atlas (Joan Blaeu), 291
Gravier, Maurice, 171
Great Boke of Statutes 1530–1533, 80
Great Composition. see *Almagest*
Greek studies, 139, 180, 301
Greek type, 90
Gregory I (the Great), Pope, 39
Grimm, Heinrich, 169
Grosseteste, Robert, 73
Guidobaldo da Montefeltro, 21
Gutenberg, Johann, 45, 93, 99, 103,
    119, 165, 176, 317, 336

Habsburg kings, 62, 92
Halley, Edmund, 278
Hariot, Thomas, 261
Harvey, Gabriel, 326
Harvey, William, 268, 272, 288
Hay, Denys, 336
Haydn, Hiram, 217
Hebrew studies, 179, 182
Hegel, Georg Wilhelm Friedrich, 311
Henry VIII of England, 108, 172, 180
herbal, 65, 82, 151, 155, 219, 266
heresy, 93, 172, 177, 330
Hermes Trismegistus, 50, 157, 366
Herodotus, 100, 144
Hexter, J. H., 185, 314

hieroglyphs, 51, 53, 217
Hirsch, Rudolph, 4
Historical Collections (Hazard), 90
History of Animals (Gesner), 228
History of the Royal Society (Sprat, 1667), 300, 357
Hobbes, Thomas, 305
Holbein, Hans, 40
Hollandia, voyage of (1595–7), 240
Homer, 140
Hondius, Jocondus, 240
Hooke, Robert, 272, 278
Hooykaas, Reijer, 266
Hornschuch, Jerome, 33, 138
Hortus deliciarum, 213
House of Astronomy, as envisaged by Kepler, 244, 248–9
House of Love. *see* Family of Love
Hugo, Victor, 39
Huizinga, Johan, 125, 126
humanists, 21, 28, 77, 78, 96, 113, 131, 132, 134, 135, 140, 162, 165, 175, 287, 289, 308, 324, 340
Hume, David, 86

Icones quinquaginta virorum illustrium (Boissard, 1597–9), 149
illuminators, 22, 25, 27, 148, 151, 290
illustration, 24, 26, 40, 41, 42, 80, 82, 95, 161, 179, 193, 219, 352
images, 24–7, 39, 40, 41, 42, 57, 64, 98, 108, 112, 118, 135, 212, 219, 223, 229, 238, 290, 318, 340, 342, 352
impressor, 319
Imprimatur, 178, 191, 281
incunabula, 8, 14, 17, 127
Index librorum prohibitorum, 99, 178, 191, 194, 198, 254, 264, 279, 355

index(es), xv, 29, 70, 71, 72, 73, 75, 77, 81, 229
indulgences, 29, 33, 170, 189, 317
Inquisition, 274, 284
Instauratio magna (Bacon, 1620), 292
Institutes (Calvin), 39
Institutio astronomica (W. J. Blaeu), 270
inventions, 3, 13, 75, 94, 146, 153
Investiganti, 274
Isidore of Seville, 223
Ivins, William, 24

James I of England, 181
Jefferson, Thomas, 89, 90
Jerome, Saint, 296, 304
Jesuits, 191, 262, 284
Johns, Adrian, 346, 347, 348, 349, 352, 353
Joris, David, 202
Journal of Modern History, 124
Joyeuse & Magnifique Entrée de Monseigneur Francoys, fils de France, 106

Kearney, Hugh, 271
Kepler, Johann, 215, 235, 243, 244–54, 269, 272, 353
Keysersberg, Geiler von, 174
Kingdon, Robert, 201
Kircher, Athanasius, 53
Klaits, Joseph, 108
Koestler, Arthur, 49, 244, 279, 281
Kohn, Hans, 181
Koran, 336, 356
Kuhn, Thomas, 86

Langford, Jerome, 279
Laplace, Pierre Simon, Marquis de, 269
law printing and legal studies, 80, 183
Leers, Reiner, 110

Lefèvre d'Etaples, Jacques, 179
Lehmann-Haupt, Hellmut, 29
Leo X, Pope, 168
"*lesen* revolution," 325
Letter against Werner (Copernicus), 232
Letter to the Grand Duchess Christina (Galileo), 262
Lettera (Foscarini, 1615), 279
Leupold, Jacob, 44
Lewis, C. S., 75
lexicography, 73, 77
Liber chronicorum (Schedel, 1493). see Nuremberg Chronicle
libraries, 48, 49, 51, 76, 119, 231, 275, 309, 343
library catalogues. see catalogues
library sciences, 84
life sciences, 42
Light of Navigation, The (W. J. Blaeu, 1622), 239
Lilburne, John, 183
Lincei, 274, 280
Linotype machines, 309
literacy, xvii, 34, 35, 36, 38, 47, 101, 104, 128, 327, 333
literary properties, 94, 96
literati, 20, 28, 85, 119, 134, 139, 145, 153, 162, 201, 275, 307, 338
Lives of Illustrious Men (Vespasiano), 21
Lives of the artists (Vasari, 1550), 147
Livy, 134
Locke, John, 303
Louis XIII of France, 108
Louis XIV of France, 108
Louis XVI of France, 64
Love, Harold, 327, 342, 344, 355
Lower, Sir William, 261
Lowry, Martin, 28, 295
Loyola, Ignatius, 148, 178

Luther, Martin, 17, 40, 41, 148, 149, 164, 165, 168, 169, 170, 171, 174, 177, 180, 190, 260

Machiavelli, Niccolò, 161, 195, 198, 280
Machlinia, William de, 80
Maestlin, Michael, 236, 238, 251
magic, 157, 171, 257
Magna Carta, 93
Magnum Abbreviamentum (Rastell), 80
Maitland, Frederic William, 136
Malesherbes, Chrétien, 105
Malpighi, Marcello, 268, 272, 273
Mannheim, Karl, 113, 114
manuals, 53, 58, 66, 186, 219, 297, 339
manuscript books, 15, 21, 22, 134, 338, 341
maps. see atlases and maps
Mardersteig, Giovanni, 322, 323
Marlowe, Christopher, 48
Martin, H.-J., 17, 112, 321, 332
Marx, Karl, 311
Mary Tudor of England, 181, 187, 330, 383
mathematics, 131, 214, 263, 265, 286
Mattioli, Pierre, 83
Maufer, Petrus, 322
McKenzie, D. F., 327, 347
McKitterick, David, 325, 341, 342
McLuhan, Marshall, xiv, xv, 70, 102, 103, 316, 317
McLuhanesque view of history, 315
Mechanick Exercises . . . Applied to the Art of Printing (Moxon), 113, 115, 270
Medici, Cosimo de, 15, 50
medicine, 27, 50, 78, 183

Melanchthon, Philip, 259, 304
memory arts, 38, 39, 41, 98
men of letters, 20, 105, 109, 110,
    113, 114, 145, 201, 331
Mercator, Gerardus, 203, 229
merchant-publishers, 201, 203, 295
Mersenne, Marin, Friar, 255, 268
Merton, Robert K., 99
Mesmer, Franz, 299
Mesnard, Pierre, 145
Milton, John, 284
mnemonics. see memory arts
Moeller, Bernd, 189
Monde (Descartes), 272
Monotype machine, 309
Montaigne, Michel de, 48, 62, 64
Montano. see Arias Montano, Benito
More, Thomas, 80, 180
Moxon, Joseph, 115, 158, 270
Müller, Johann. see Regiomontanus
Murner, Thomas, 166
museum culture, 118
mute orator, 331
mysticism, 174

natural sciences, 84, 86, 131
naturalists, 84, 85
New Cambridge Modern History, 4
newspapers, 89, 105, 110
Newton, Isaac, 53, 98, 158, 254, 257,
    265, 268, 271, 272, 278, 286,
    301
Nicholas V, Pope, 140
Nicholas of Cusa, Cardinal, 176
Nicodemite sects, 200
Ninety-five Theses, of Luther,
    168–71
Notre Dame de Paris (Hugo), 39
numbers, Arabic, for pagination, 81
Nunberg, Geoffrey, 342
Nuremberg Chronicle, 65, 66, 68,
    69

Obelisci aegyptiaci (Kircher, 1666), 53
occult, 41, 50, 51, 99, 157
Ochino, Bernardino, 202
Oecolampadius, 202
Oldenburg, Henry, 272
Olschki, Leonardo, 220
Ong, Walter, 105
Oporinus, Johannes, 112, 202, 295,
    354
Orbis sensualium pictus (Comenius,
    1658), 43
Ortelius, Abraham, 70, 81, 82, 85,
    144, 229–31
Orthotypographia (Hornschuch,
    1608), 33, 138

pagination, 81
Palissy, Bernard, 263
Panofsky, Erwin, 130, 132, 133, 136,
    137, 153, 155
paper, 8, 11, 20, 29, 59, 64, 72, 73,
    88, 89, 139, 193, 242, 244,
    309, 313, 338, 339
Paracelsus, 159, 202, 215, 263, 299
Parkes, M. B., 318
Pascal, Blaise, 268
patents, 94, 146
patrons, 20, 21, 112, 113, 180
pattern books, 25, 58
Paulus, Father, 281, 284
pecia system, 10, 321
Peregrinatio in Terram Sanctam
    (Breydenbach, 1486), 65, 69
Perotti, Niccoló, 351
Peter the Venerable, 175
Petrarch, 94, 124, 128, 132, 139
Petreius, Johannes, 251
pharmacopeia, 38
Pharmacopeia Londinensus, 183
Philip II of Spain, 92, 180, 199, 200
Philip IV (the Fair) of France, 172
philology, 134, 179, 301, 324

philosophers' stones, 158
philosophes, 167, 184, 202
Philosophy of the Enlightenment,
    (Cassirer), 303
Physica (Aristotle), 74
Piccolomini, Aeneas Sylvius, 140
Pico della Mirandola, 218
Pilgrim's Progress (Bunyan), 184
plagiarism, 94, 346
Plantin, Christopher, 49, 76, 77, 92,
    295
Plato, 15, 51, 232
pleasure principle, 269
Pliny the Elder, 210, 227, 263, 298,
    351
Pole, Reginald, 187
Poliziano, Angelo, 340
Pollard, Graham, 9, 237
polyglot Bibles, 141, 180, 182, 217,
    330. *see also* Bible
    Antwerp, 200
    Complutensian (Alcalà), 76
    London, 76, 141, 300
    Paris, 76
popular culture, xvii
pornography, 6, 104
Postel, Guillaume, 202
Praise of Scribes (Trithemius), 11
Praz, Mario, 117
preservative powers of print, xvi, 87,
    89, 90, 118, 146, 155, 163
Principia (Newton), 53, 268
printers, 8, 12, 14, 15, 22, 23, 24,
    27, 28, 33, 37, 47, 48, 49, 65,
    66, 82, 91, 92, 93, 96, 104,
    110, 113, 127, 129, 137, 146,
    155, 163, 164, 169, 170, 178,
    180, 189, 190, 319, 322, 339,
    350
printing, xv
    advent of, xv, 10
    and literary vernaculars, 91
    and regrouping of skilled workers,
        27, 322
    as divine art, 35, 153, 357
    data collection process, xviii,
        81–7, 153, 224
    dissemination, 47, 53, 178
    innovations, xix, 14
    preservative powers, xvi, 87, 90,
        155
    rationalizing, codifying, and
        cataloguing data, 70
    spread (maps), 17
    standardization, 56–70
    stereotypes and sociolinguistic
        divisions persist in, 99–101
printing office, picture of, 337
printing shops, 10, 14, 22, 49, 75,
    113, 127, 195, 199, 255, 258,
    259, 318, 326, 330, 334, 356
proclamations, royal, 80
proofreaders, 326
propaganda, 40, 108, 109, 156, 165,
    166, 178, 184, 191, 210, 273,
    284
Prutenic Tables, 234, 245
Ptolemy (Claudius Ptolomaeus), 42,
    210, 227, 234, 235, 236, 245,
    263, 296, 298
public domain, 94, 157, 238
publicity, 33, 94, 103, 116, 146, 158,
    168, 171, 194
putting-out system, 10–11
Pynson, Richard, 80

Rabb, T. K., 266
Rabelais, Francois, 48, 195, 280
Raleigh, Sir Walter, 158
Ramist doctrine, 78
Ramus, Peter, 78
Rastell, John, 80, 183
rationalizing of data, 70–81
Redman, John, 80

Regiomontanus (Johann Müller of Königsberg), 129, 237, 353

Regola de cinque ordini d'architettura (Vignola, 1642), 61

Reinhold, Erasmus, 259

Renaissance, 21, 46, 48, 94, 123–63

Republic of Letters, 102–9, 110, 111, 113, 145, 203, 295

Reuwich, Erhard, 65, 69

Reynolds, L. D., 71

Rheticus, 233, 259, 260, 272, 298

Richelieu, Cardinal, 108

Rienieri, Vincento, 251

rinascita (Petrarchan revival), 124, 161, 168

Ripoli Press, 15

Rizzo, Silvia, 324

roman type, 59, 134, 136, 138, 301

Rosen, Edward, 257

Rosicrucians, 41, 51, 98

Royal Society, The (of London for Improving Natural Knowledge), 76, 214, 221, 241, 272, 273, 274, 275, 299, 300, 353, 357

Rudolph II of Prague, Emperor, 255

Rudolphine Tables (Kepler, 1627), 244, 245, 249, 251, 253, 254, 269

Saggi, 274–5, 276

Saint Barbara's Charterhouse, 12

Saint-Simon, Henri, 202

Salusbury, Thomas, 282

Santillana, Giorgio de, 280

Sarpi, Paolo, 195

Sarton, George, 27, 42, 97, 231

Savonarola, Girolamo, 174

Schedel, Hartmann, 66

Schickard, Wilhelm, 253

schism, 172

Schoeffer, Peter, 23, 28, 29, 66, 72, 319

scholar-printers, 177, 179, 182, 202, 203, 294

Schwenckfelt, Kaspar, 202

scientific centers, 255, 257

Scoriggio, Lazaro, 279

Scott, Sir Walter, 114

scribal innovation, 357

scribes and copyists, xvii, 8–9, 10, 11, 15–17, 23, 27, 29, 56, 87, 113, 301, 305, 319, 321, 341

scriptoria, 8, 10–12, 27, 175

secrecy, 156, 159

secularization, 105

self-awareness, 144

sermon literature, 174

Servetus, Michael, 195

Shepherd's Almanacks, 37

Sidereus nuncius. see *Starry Messenger*

Sixtus V, Pope, 152, 154

Sleidan, Johann, 167

Sozzini, Lelio, 202

specimen books, calligraphy, 58

Speculum, 124

speech arts, 134

Spinoza, Benedict de, 305

Sprat, Thomas, Bishop, 76, 159, 300, 357

standardization (as an effect of printing), 56–70, 346–50

star maps, 98, 215

Starry Messenger (*Sidereus nuncius*) (Galileo, 1610), 261

stationers, xviii, 10, 11, 20, 27, 29, 309, 322, 348

Statutes of Virginia (Hening), 90

Steinberg, S. H., 4, 91, 192

stereotypes, 99–101

Strong, E. W., 152

Studies in the Renaissance, 124

style books, typography, 58

succès d'estime, 118

succès de scandale, 117

Syllabus of Errors, 131, 178
Syriac type, 203

Tabulae medicae (Rienieri, 1639), 251
Tabulae Rudolphinae. see *Rudolphine Tables*
Tacitus, 100, 136
tailors, pattern books for, 62
Talmud, 203
textbooks, 78
Theatrum arithmetica-geometricum ... (Leupold), 44
Theatrum orbis terrarum:
    The Theatre of the Whole World (Ortelius, 1606), 70, 82–3, 144, 231
Thesaurus theutonicae linguae, 77
Thirty Years' War, 243, 269, 353
Thomas Aquinas. see Aquinas, Thomas
Thomism, 174
Thoth. see Hermes Trismegistus
title page, 24, 33, 58, 80, 81, 129, 148, 193, 232, 325
Tournes, Jean II de, 193
Transactions (of the Royal Society), 274, 298
translation. see vernacular translation movement
Trevor-Roper, Hugh, 204
Trithemius, Johannes, 11
Tudor, Mary. see Mary Tudor of England
Twain, Mark, 114
Tycho Brahe, 38, 232, 233, 234, 236, 241, 242, 246, 353
Tyndale, William, 180
typefounders, 49, 127
typescripts, 324
typography, 26, 58, 91, 103, 129, 137, 176

Urbino library, 21
Urbino, Duke of, 21, 217
Ussher, James, Bishop, 350
Utriusque cosmi maioris (Fludd, 1621), 41

Valla, Lorenzo, 68, 134
Valois kings, 92
Vasari, Georgio, 147
Vatican II, 178
Vecellio, Cesare, 63
vernacular translation movement, xvii, 36, 92, 101, 163, 172, 179, 180, 182, 296, 304, 330
Vesalius, Andreas, 30, 158, 202, 218, 232, 290, 301, 354
Vespasiano da Bisticci, 15, 20, 28, 319, 320
Vignola, Giacomo Barozzio, 61
Virorum doctorum de disciplinis bene merentium effigies (Galle, 1572), 200
Vitruvius, 42, 59, 61, 227
Voltaire, 109
Vulgate, 76, 177–82, 189, 299, 301, 305

Wallace, DeWitt, 339
Walsham, Alexandra, 325, 330
Warner, Michael, 356, 357
Watt, Joachim von (Vadianus), 166
Weber, Max, 114, 188, 193, 257, 269
Wechel family firm, 112
Weiss, Roberto, 141
Werke for Householders, A, 187
Western Christendom, 164, 317, 335, 336. see also Eastern Christendom
Westman, Robert, 215
Whitehead, Alfred North, 217
Wightman, W. P. D., 241
Willey, Basil, 214

William of Ockham, 9
Williams, Raymond, 333
Wilson, N. G., 71
Wing, Vincent, 254
Wolfe, John, 326
women, books on behavior of, 37
woodcuts, 24, 25, 54, 58, 65, 148,
    219, 220, 317, 352
Wythe, George, 89

xylography, 26

Yates, Frances, 39, 41, 157, 244,
    257
York library, 71

Zanobi di Mariano, 21
Zilsel, Edgar, 152
Zwingli, Ulrich, 170, 177, 208